Teaching Problem Students

TEACHING PROBLEM STUDENTS

JERE BROPHY

THE GUILFORD PRESS
New York London

For Arlene

©1996 The Guilford Press
A Division of Guilford Publications, Inc.
72 Spring Street, New York, NY 10012
www.guilford.com

Paperback edition 2003

Printed in the United States of America

This book is printed on acid-free paper.

Last digit is print number: 9   8   7   6   5   4

Library of Congress Cataloging-in-Publication Data

Brophy, Jere E.
    Teaching problem students / Jere Brophy.
      p. cm.
    Includes bibliographical references and index.
    ISBN   1-57230-144-9 (hard)   ISBN   1-57230-956-3 (paper)
    1. Problem children–Education–United States.   2. Classroom
management–United States.   I. Title.
LC4802.B76   1996
371.93'0973–dc20
                                    96-19772
                                       CIP

Preface

Teachers have always had to contend with students who require special management and motivational handling that go beyond what is needed for the class as a whole. In recent years, however, mainstreaming and inclusion policies have increased the range and severity of the chronic personality, behavioral, and school adjustment problems facing regular classroom teachers. This book is written to help such teachers, especially elementary and middle school teachers, to cope with the challenges that these difficult students present.

Based on the scholarly and professional literature and on the findings from a large research study, the book suggests steps that teachers might take to help difficult students succeed at school. It begins by raising issues of role definition and inviting readers to assess their readiness and willingness to accept the challenges involved in seeking to resocialize difficult students (i.e., not merely to control their behavior but to help them develop more productive attitudes and coping strategies). Then, in the remainder of Chapter 1 and throughout Chapter 2, I draw from the literature on raising children at home and on managing students at school to suggest principles for establishing the classroom as a supportive learning community, encouraging students to develop desirable personal attributes, and resolving conflict productively. When implemented systematically, these principles nurture the development of a positive classroom climate and establish a strong base for teachers to work from in reaching out to difficult students. The focus is on teacher–student interaction, but with attention to collaborations with parents and with administrators, counselors, social workers, special education teachers, and other professional specialists at the school.

Having synthesized the views of scholarly researchers and treatment professionals in Chapters 1 and 2, I turn in Chapter 3 to the views of teachers, as expressed in the Classroom Strategy Study. For this research, elementary teachers were asked to describe their perceptions of and strategies for coping with each of 12 types of problem students. The first four problem-student types display unsatisfactory achievement progress: low achievers who make limited progress because of limited ability or readiness for the demands of the grade level; failure syndrome students who become so defeated by repeated frustrations that they eventually give up serious learning efforts; overly perfectionistic students who underachieve because they are more concerned about avoiding mistakes than about learning, so they become inhibited about classroom participation and counterproductively compulsive in their work habits; and alienated underachievers who see little or no value in what is taught at school, so they do only enough to get by rather than trying to do their best. The next three problem-student types display hostility: hostile–aggressive students who tend to bully or fight with peers; passive–aggressive students who are noncompliant and indirectly oppositional but stop short of direct defiance; and defiant students who directly challenge the teacher's authority through refusals to obey and overt provocations. The next three problem-student types display behavioral characteristics that make it difficult for them to adjust to the demands of the student role: hyperactive students who have difficulty meeting requirements for physical control and quiet; distractible students who have difficulty meeting requirements for sustained concentration; and immature students who have difficulty working independently, caring for themselves and their belongings, and "acting their age." Finally, the last two problem-student types display difficulties in their social interactions with peers: students who are rejected by their peers (they desire and seek friendships but are not accepted, perhaps but not necessarily because of their own negative personal qualities) and students who are shy or withdrawn (not actively rejected but socially isolated because they seldom initiate social interactions or respond effectively to the overtures of peers).

General information about the Classroom Strategy Study and about its findings that cut across problem-student types are presented in Chapter 3 and in the Appendix. Chapters 4–15 each focus on one of the 12 problem-student types. Each chapter begins by inviting readers to articulate their own current ideas about dealing with the problem type, then presents the views of selected teachers interviewed for the Classroom Strategy Study, and then presents a synthesis of the scholarly and professional literature. The chapters then continue with analyses of the teachers' responses to interviews concerning their perceptions of and strategies for coping with the problem-student type, along with their statements of how they would respond to each of two vignettes depicting behavior that the problem-student type might display in a particular situation at school. The interview and vignette data are analyzed both for general trends in the teachers' responses and for contrasts in response patterns between teachers who were rated as outstanding in their abilities to deal with problem students and teachers who were rated as average or typical in these abilities. Finally, Chapters 14 and 15 conclude with comparison of the strategies suggested by scholars and treatment professionals with the strategies suggested by teachers, as well as a summary of key ideas to keep in mind in dealing with the problem-student type.

Chapter 16 concludes the book by revisiting the role-definition issues raised in Chapter 1, commenting on recent trends affecting teachers' preparedness to manage classrooms and cope with problem students, and offering some final thoughts for readers seeking to prepare themselves to meet these challenges.

The book is intended to synthesize three sources of ideas about dealing with problem students that developed in isolation from one another and mostly remain so today: (1) The scholarly literature developed by researchers in child development and education, (2) the literature on helping strategies developed by treatment professionals, and (3) the wisdom of practice developed by classroom teachers. In deciding what to include from the first two bodies of literature, I have emphasized principles and strategies that are feasible for use by regular classroom teachers working under typical conditions. The book is intended to help such teachers to conduct realistic assessments of their current attitudes about and preparedness for meeting the needs of problem students and to begin to make specific self-improvement plans, as well as to equip them with basic principles and strategies. Numerous references (selected for relevance to teachers) are provided for readers who want more information about particular problem-student types or more details about the treatment strategies described.

Acknowledgments

The Classroom Strategy Study that provided the basis for this book was sponsored by the Institute for Research on Teaching, College of Education, Michigan State University. At the time, the study and the Institute were funded primarily by the Program for Teaching and Instruction of the National Institute of Education, United States Department of Education. The opinions expressed in this publication do not necessarily reflect the position, policy, or endorsement of the National Institute of Education (Contract No. 400-81-0014).

I thank Mary McCaslin (formerly known as Mary Rohrkemper) for her many contributions to the design, data collection, and data preparation phases of the Classroom Strategy Study, as well as her contributions to earlier data analysis and reporting phases (as communicated through several coauthored articles and reports referenced in this book). In a great many ways large and small, Dr. McCaslin's work helped to maximize the validity and reliability of the study's data collection and analyses.

I also thank June Benson for her careful tape transcription and other manuscript preparation work.

Other significant contributions to the Classroom Strategy Study were made by Jane Smith, Janice Elmore, Carolyn Rettke, Jean Medick, Lonnie McIntyre, Susan Rubenstein, Steven Katz, and Joanne Hite, who assisted in project planning and data collection; Jane Smith, Lynn Scott, Patricia Linton, Carolyn Wainwright, Linda Ripley, and Sheba Dunlap, who coded data; and Suwatana Sukpokakit, Neelam Kher, and Frank Jenkins, who assisted with data preparation and analysis.

This book was completed in part while I was on sabbatical from Michigan State University and in residence as a Fellow at the Center for Advanced Study in the Behavioral Sciences. I wish to thank both of these institutions for their financial support during that sabbatical year. In addition I which to thank the Spencer Foundation, which provided part of the funds for the support I received through the Center for Advanced Study in the Behavioral Sciences (Spencer Foundation Grant No. B-1074).

Finally, I thank Arlene Pintozzi Brophy, A.C.S.W., for carefully reading earlier drafts of the manuscript and offering a great deal of helpful feedback reflecting her perspective as a school social worker who collaborates with teachers in helping difficult students. This book is dedicated to her in recognition of that assistance and of the many forms of support that she has provided to me over the years.

Contents

1

General Principles and Techniques for Managing Classrooms and Coping with Problem Students

Teachers work with classes of 20 to 40 students. The students usually are similar in age, and their families often are similar in ethnicity and socioeconomic status. Even so, each student is an individual with particular personal qualities, interests, and needs. All teachers must plan for and interact with the class as a group, but the best teachers also personalize their instruction of individual students as much as they can.

This is not hard to do with some students—the ones who pay attention to lessons, apply themselves to their work, and seem comfortable and responsive to the teacher's instructional and social initiations. But other students lack these qualities or for other reasons are difficult, time-consuming, or frustrating to work with. These problem students may display very different combinations of personal attributes and behavior patterns. What they have in common is that they require much more of the teacher's time, energy, and patience than most of their classmates. For purposes of this book, I define "problem students" as students who possess one or more of the following characteristics:

Difficult: These students are difficult to teach because they are poorly adjusted or resistant to classroom routines and thus frequently disruptive. They may be surly or unresponsive when spoken to about their behavior.

Time-consuming: These students display chronic and serious problems that will not be eliminated in a single conference or other brief intervention. They may require specialized treatment sustained over several weeks or months.

Frustrating: Because they are difficult and time-consuming, and also because they may improve only very slowly and may be ungrateful for whatever help the teacher provides, these students can be particularly frustrating and unrewarding to teach.

This book brings together what various mental health experts and what elementary school teachers have to say about coping with problem students. It is divided into three parts. Part I introduces some basic issues and then presents theory and research on general principles involved in managing classrooms and coping with problem students. Next, Parts II through V offer chapters on 12 problem-student types, grouped into 4 clusters. Finally, Part III presents a synthesis of key findings and some concluding discussion.

Part I consists of three chapters. Chapter 1 introduces some key definitions, addresses some of the potential roles that teachers might take in interacting with problem students, and reviews research findings on managing classrooms and students. Chapter 2 summarizes research on principles and techniques for socializing the beliefs and attitudes and modifying the behavior of problem students. Finally, Chapter 3 presents general findings from a large study of elementary teachers' reported perceptions of and strategies for coping with problem students. More specific findings from this study are presented in subsequent chapters on particular problem-student types.

1

Choosing to Work with Problem Students and Creating a Context for Doing So Successfully

Teaching is not just curriculum and instruction. It's also managing the classroom, motivating students to learn, and meeting their individual needs, including the needs of students who display chronic personal or behavioral problems. These students frequently create situations such as the following:

- This morning, several students excitedly tell you that on the way to school they saw Tom beating up Sam and taking his lunch money. Tom is the class bully and has done things like this many times.
- Roger has been fooling around instead of working on his seatwork for several days now. Finally, you tell him that he has to finish or stay in during recess and work on it then. He says "I won't stay in!" and spends the rest of the period sulking. As the class begins to line up for recess, he quickly jumps up and heads for the door. You tell him that he has to stay inside and finish his assignment, but he just says "No, I don't!" and continues out the door to recess.
- Mary has the intelligence to succeed, if she applied herself, but she is convinced that she can't handle it. She gets frustrated and disgusted very easily, and then she gives up. Instead of trying to solve the problem another way, or coming to you for help, she skips the problem and moves on. Today she brings you her assignment, claiming to be finished, but you see that she has skipped many items.
- Nancy is oriented toward peers and social relationships, not schoolwork. She could be doing top-grade work, but instead she does just enough

to get by. She is often chatting or writing notes when she is supposed to be paying attention or working. During today's lesson, she
has repeatedly turned to students on each side of her to make remarks, and now she has a conversation going with several friends.

Teachers have always had to contend with problem students who require special management and motivational handling that goes beyond
what is needed for the class as a whole. In addition, Public Law 94-142
and related policy mandates have resulted in the mainstreaming of all
but the most extreme categories of special-needs students. Consequently,
most of these students now spend all or most of their time in regular classrooms. Lately, social and economic stresses and transitions have increased
the frequency and severity of such problems. This is most obvious in inner-
city schools, but it is also evident in suburban and rural schools and in
schools whose students mostly come from socioeconomically advantaged
families.

Chronically difficult students present serious challenges to teachers,
especially regular classroom teachers. These teachers must cope with special problems within the context of teaching classes of 20 to 40 students,
usually with little if any training in strategies and techniques for doing
so. These recent shifts in expectations for regular classroom teachers imply the need for better preservice and in-service teacher education to meet
the needs of problem students. They also raise questions such as the following:

1. How far should regular classroom teachers be expected to go, beyond what they do in managing and instructing the class as a whole,
   to try to meet the individual needs of chronically difficult students?
2. How can regular classroom teachers address these individual needs
   when they have continuing responsibilities for managing and
   teaching classes of 20 to 40 students?
3. What is the role of the regular classroom teacher in this regard,
   vis-à-vis the roles of the principal or other school administrators,
   counselors or social workers, or special education teachers?
4. To what extent, and in what ways, should regular classroom
   teachers attempt to work with problem students' parents?

Before reading further, take time to think about these teacher-role
definition issues and, if possible, discuss them with classmates or teaching colleagues. Jot down your ideas for reference at points when these
issues are addressed again in this book.

TEACHING ROLES

This book is about options that you as a teacher might pursue with problem students—those who require more intensive and personalized treatment than what is involved in everyday classroom management. To begin, let us consider four major *teaching functions:*

Instruction refers to actions taken to assist students in mastering the formal curriculum (presenting information, demonstrating skills, conducting lessons or activities, supervising work on assignments).

Classroom management refers to actions taken to create and maintain a learning environment conducive to successful instruction (arranging the physical environment of the classroom, establishing rules and procedures, maintaining attention to lessons and engagement in academic activities).

Disciplinary interventions are actions taken to elicit or compel changes in the behavior of students who fail to conform to expectations, especially misbehavior that is salient or sustained enough to disrupt your classroom management system.

Student socialization refers to actions taken to influence students' personal or social attitudes, beliefs, expectations, or behavior. Some socialization is done mostly with the class as a whole (articulating ideals, communicating expectations, and modeling, teaching, and reinforcing desirable behavior). Other socializing is done mostly with individual students (counseling, behavior modification, and other attempts to remediate poor personal or social adjustment).

All teachers are expected to be willing and able to handle the first three of these teaching functions as basic aspects of their job. However, expectations are less clear for the socialization function. Communities, principals, and teachers themselves vary considerably in their views on how much and what kind of socialization they should attempt with their students and, in particular, on the degree to which they should be expected to assume personal responsibility for resocializing problem students.

Views on the teacher's socialization role vary with differences in grade level and the availability of help from professional specialists. Different grade levels offer different opportunities and challenges to teachers in their roles as classroom managers and student socializers. Brophy and Evertson (1978) identified four stages in students' personal and social development that affect these roles:

1. *Kindergarten and the Early Elementary Grades.* In these grades, students are socialized into the student role. Teachers spend considerable time teaching them how to carry out basic routines and procedures, not just getting them to comply with familiar rules. Most younger students feel gratified when they please teachers and upset when they do not. They turn to teachers for directions, encouragement, solace, and personal attention.

2. *The Middle Elementary Grades.* This stage begins when basic socialization to the student role is completed and continues as long as most students remain adult-oriented and relatively compliant. Students are familiar with most school routines, and the serious disturbances seen frequently in later years are not yet common. Creating and maintaining an appropriate learning environment remain central to teaching success, but these tasks consume less time, and teachers are able to concentrate on instructing students in the formal curriculum.

3. *The Upper Elementary or Junior High School Grades.* As more and more students change their orientation from pleasing teachers to pleasing peers, they begin to resent teachers who act as authority figures. Some become more disturbed and harder to control than they used to be. As a result, classroom management once again becomes a prominent part of the teacher role. Now, however, the teacher's primary concern is motivating students to behave as they know they are supposed to, not instructing them in how to behave, as in the first stage.

4. *The Upper High School Grades.* As many of the most alienated students drop out of school and the rest become more mature, classrooms once again assume a more academic focus. Classroom management requires even less time than it did during the second stage, because students handle most student-role responsibilities on their own. Teaching at this level is mostly a matter of instructing students in the formal curriculum, although socialization occurs during informal, out-of-class contacts with individual students.

If you are not already established teaching at a particular level, you should consider these developmental aspects of classroom management when thinking about what grade level to teach. If you like to provide nurturance as well as instruction, enjoy working with young children, and have the patience and skills needed to socialize them to the student role, you would be especially effective in the primary grades. If you want to work in an elementary school but wish to concentrate mostly on instruction, you would be best placed in the middle grades. If you enjoy or at least are not bothered by "adolescent" behavior and see yourself as a socialization agent and model at least as much as an instructor, you would do well in grades 7 through 10. Finally, if you want to function mostly as a subject-matter specialist, you would be happiest in the upper high school grades.

At all four of the levels of schooling, there are problem students who require more intensive management and socialization than most of their classmates. Many of these students will have social–emotional needs that interfere with their attempts to meet the challenges of schooling. You will require knowledge and strategies for meeting these needs, not just to foster these students' social–emotional adjustment but also to enable them to make satisfactory academic progress. You may be expected to address their needs primarily on your own, especially if you work in an elementary school where you teach the same students all day long and have only limited access to social workers, counselors, or other professional specialists. Teachers are not expected to assume as much of the student socialization burden in high schools, where they usually see students for only one period each day. In fact, at most urban and suburban high schools, dealing with problem students has become more of a school-level function performed by administrators and professional specialists than a classroom-level function performed by teachers.

In between these two extremes of the elementary teacher/socializer expected to take full charge of the whole child and the secondary subject-matter specialist expected to concentrate on academics, there is a range of teaching situations and associated role expectations. If you teach at a middle school, a junior high, or even a high school, you may be expected to assume considerable socialization responsibilities if you work within a small team or a "school within a school" arrangement designed to ensure that you get to know your students as individuals. Or you may be expected to work closely with a school counselor or social worker in seeking to resocialize problem students. On the other hand, if you teach in a large, impersonal, and bureaucratic school, you may be expected only to refer "trouble makers" to the office for "discipline."

As a teacher, you will have to decide which problems you are prepared to handle on your own; which will require consultation with a school administrator, counselor, psychologist, social worker, or educational specialist; and which will require involvement of community agencies or resources beyond those available at your school. You also will need to work with parents, usually just to share information and perspectives on the problem and develop mutually acceptable plans for addressing it, although in some cases you will solicit their cooperation in arranging for assessment and potential specialized treatment by professionals who work at the school district (if available) or in the larger community.

This book is written primarily for teachers who are willing to invest significantly in the socialization role along with their other teaching roles, and thus to go the extra mile in working with problem students. It will be most relevant and useful to elementary teachers, both because they have more time to work with their students and because the teachers' views quoted throughout the book were obtained by interviewing teachers working in grades K through 6. Except where otherwise noted, however, the principles and techniques suggested here should be applicable at all grade levels. You can expect them to be effective if you consistently apply them as part of the systematic overall approach developed in Part I of the book. They are unlikely to do much good, however, if used as isolated gimmicks within an overall approach to classroom management that is inconsistent, authoritarian, or otherwise counterproductive to successful socialization of students.

CHOOSING YOUR ROLE

Regardless of the grade level you teach, the number of different students you teach each day, and your degree of access to professional specialists, you will need to decide how much you are willing to include student socialization responsibilities in defining your role as a teacher. This decision requires realistic self-assessment and thoughtful consideration of the responsibilities involved. If you want to commit yourself fully to the student socialization role, you will need to be prepared to:

1. Cultivate personal relationships with students that go beyond those needed for purely instructional purposes.
2. Spend time outside of school hours dealing with students and their families, without receiving extra financial compensation for your efforts.
3. Deal with complex problems that have developed over a period of years, without benefit of special training as a mental health professional.
4. Perhaps encounter some opposition from school administrators.
5. Perhaps encounter resentment or expressions of frustration from the students you are trying to help, their families, or others who may be involved in the situation.

Some teachers accept this challenge by addressing the full spectrum of responsibilities with determination to solve whatever problems come along. However, other teachers are philosophically opposed to this level of emphasis on student socialization, are not interested in it, believe that they are temperamentally unsuited to it, or are hesitant to engage in much of it without specialized training. I find these positions understandable and, to an extent, justified. Teachers who recognize their limitations and work within them probably will have more positive effects in the long run than they would have if they tried to do everything and ended up doing nothing very well.

However, there are limits to how much teachers can minimize their roles as authority figures and socializers of students. Research on school-wide approaches to managing disruptive behavior has shown that administrators and teachers work together in schools that respond effectively to problem students (Anderson, 1985; Gottfredson & Gottfredson, 1986; Metz, 1978). In contrast, there are more student misbehavior problems in schools where teachers place most discipline issues immediately into the hands of administrators and emphasize control and punishment over helping students to develop more productive behavior (Hawkins, Doueck, & Lishner, 1988; Wu et al., 1982). Jones (1988), after reviewing these studies, argued that teachers should assume responsibility at least for initial efforts at corrective intervention.

I'll go further by urging you to assume as much of the student socialization burden as you can handle effectively (with help from specialists available at your school). I will mention other reasons for doing so when revisiting the "defining your role as a teacher" issue in Chapter 16. For now, I will focus on just one reason because it is a recurring theme in the research findings to be presented: *Teachers have certain advantages over therapists or other mental health specialists in helping problem students.* True, teachers typically do not have special training in dealing with serious personality or behavior disorders. Nor do they have the luxury of interacting only with individuals or small groups and only within a therapeutic relationship. Instead, they must find ways to reach problem students while interacting with them as members of a class and continuing to function as an authority figure.

Yet teachers see their students every day and under a variety of conditions, so they have more and better information about them than most therapists have about their clients (therapists usually must rely on what their clients choose to tell them). Also, teachers are sometimes in a position to take direct action to help students cope with their problems, rather than just coaching them from afar. Even the authority-figure role has its advantages. Teachers can provide consequences (both rewards and punishments) to selected student behavior and, in the process, attempt to resocialize the students' beliefs and attitudes. Finally, teachers' interactions with their students are viewed by all concerned as normal forms of adult–child contact, so there is no reason for students to feel ashamed or identified as abnormal when their teachers talk with them about their problems.

GOOD CLASSROOM MANAGEMENT
ESTABLISHES A FAVORABLE CONTEXT FOR SOCIALIZING STUDENTS

To set the stage for effective student socialization work, you will need to apply the management principles involved in establishing a classroom as a successful learning environment. A well-managed classroom reveals organization, planning, and scheduling. The room is divided into distinct areas furnished and equipped for specific activities. Frequently used equipment is stored where it can be removed and replaced easily, and each item has its own place. Traffic patterns facilitate movement around the room and minimize crowding and bumping. Transitions between activities are accomplished efficiently following a brief signal or a few directions from the teacher, and students know where they are supposed to be, what they are supposed to be doing, and what equipment they will need. They are attentive to presentations and responsive to questions. Lessons and other group activities are structured so that subparts are discernible and separated by clear transitions. When students are released to work on their own or with classmates, they know what to do and settle quickly into doing it. Usually they continue the activity through to completion without difficulty and then turn to some new approved activity. If they need help, they can get it from the teacher or from some other source and then resume working.

To an observer who didn't know any better, this kind of learning environment seems to work automatically, without much teacher effort devoted to management. However, classroom research has established that such well-functioning classrooms result from consistent teacher efforts to create, maintain, and (occasionally) restore conditions that foster learning. The most successful teachers approach management as a process of establishing and maintaining effective learning environments. Less successful teachers approach it as a process of "establishing discipline."

Prior to the work of Kounin (1970), little research had been done on effective classroom management. Advice to teachers was of the "Don't smile until Christmas" variety, with emphasis on control or discipline. The guidelines amounted to a "bag of tricks" rather than an integrated set of principles. Kounin began his research by comparing the behaviors of effective and ineffective classroom managers. He videotaped activities in ideal learning environments such as those described above and also in poorly managed classrooms in which the teachers were continually struggling to "keep the lid on" and the students were regularly inattentive and frequently disruptive. Kounin initially focused on the teachers' handling of disruptive incidents and was surprised to find that his analyses failed to produce consistent results. That is, effective managers did not differ in systematic ways from ineffective managers *when they were responding to student misbehavior.*

However, Kounin noticed that effective managers differed from ineffective managers in other ways. Key behaviors shown by the effective managers included the following:

- *Withitness.* Remaining "with it" (aware of what is happening in all parts of the classroom at all times) by continuously scanning the classroom, even when working with small groups or individuals. Also, demonstrating this withitness to students by intervening promptly and accurately when inappropriate behavior threatens to become disruptive. This minimizes timing errors (failing to notice and intervene until an incident has already become disruptive) and target errors (mistakes in identifying the students responsible for the problem).
- *Overlapping.* Doing more than one thing at a time. In particular, responding to the needs of individuals while sustaining a group activity (using eye contact or physical proximity to restore inattentive students' attention to a lesson while continuing the lesson itself without interruption).
- *Signal Continuity and Momentum during Lessons.* Teaching well-prepared and well-paced lessons that focus students' attention by providing them with a continuous academic "signal" that is more compelling than the "noise" of competing distractions and also by sustaining the momentum of this academic signal throughout the duration of the lesson.
- *Challenge and Variety in Assignments.* Encouraging student engagement in seatwork by providing assignments pitched at the right level of difficulty (easy enough to ensure success with reasonable effort but new or difficult enough to provide challenge) and varied enough to sustain interest.

Kounin showed that effective managers succeed not so much because they are good at handling disruption when it occurs but because they are good at preventing disruption from occurring in the first place. However, they do not focus on preventing disruption; instead, they focus on establishing the classroom as an effective learning environment, preparing and teaching good lessons, and monitoring students as they work on good follow-up assignments.

Evertson and Emmer (1982) replicated and extended Kounin's findings in studies of how teachers establish an effective management system at the beginning of the year and sustain it thereafter. These studies demonstrated the importance of showing and telling students what to do. Clarity about rules and routines is crucial, supported if necessary by demonstration of desired behavior. In the lower grades, effective managers spend a great deal of time in the early weeks of school explaining expectations and modeling classroom routines and procedures. If necessary, they provide their students with opportunities to practice and receive feedback concerning such matters as when and how to use the pencil sharpener or how to manage the transitions between reading groups.

In the upper grades, there is less need to teach daily routines (the students are already familiar with most of them or can understand them sufficiently from verbal explanation), but it is just as important to be clear and detailed in describing expected behavior. At all grade levels, teachers need to ensure that students follow the desired procedures by providing additional reminders or feedback as needed. Effective managers consistently monitor compliance with rules, enforce accountability procedures and associated penalties for late or unacceptable work, and are prepared to punish students for repeated misconduct if necessary. However, their emphasis is positive and prescriptive, not threatening and punitive. Effective management primarily involves teaching students what to do before the fact rather than applying "discipline" following misconduct.

Subsequent studies have elaborated these findings about classroom management. Most of the existing knowledge base refers to the whole-class instruction/recitation/seatwork approach that has dominated traditional K through 12 teaching. Major management elements of this approach include preparing the classroom as a physical environment suited to the nature of the planned learning activities, developing and implementing a workable set of housekeeping procedures and conduct rules, maintaining students' attention to and participation in lessons and activities, and monitoring the quality of their engagement in assignments and their progress toward intended achievement outcomes. These broader management goals are accomplished through routines concerning such aspects as storing supplies and equipment, establishing traffic patterns, setting general expectations and rules at the beginning of the year, starting and ending each class period smoothly, managing transitions between activities, keeping activities going (once they are started) by stimulating involvement and minimizing interruptions, giving directions for and getting the class started on assignments, and meeting the needs of individual students during times when attention can be diverted from instructing or supervising the work of the class as a whole.

This book focuses on socializing problem students rather than on general management principles, so I will not elaborate the knowledge base on classroom management further here. For syntheses of the research findings see Bellon, Bellon, and Blank (1992); Brophy (1983a, 1988); Doyle (1986); Evertson and Harris (1992); Gettinger (1988); or Jones (1996). For detailed suggestions about practical applications, see Evertson and associates (1994), Good and Brophy (1995, 1997), Jones and Jones (1995), Larrivee (1992), or Weinstein and Mignano (1993).

SOCIALIZING STUDENT SELF-REGULATION
WITHIN A COLLABORATIVE LEARNING ENVIRONMENT

Research-based management principles are often described primarily as techniques for eliciting compliance with teachers' demands. This emphasis on compliance does not fit well with current emphases on learning through the social construction of knowledge and on teaching school subjects for understanding and higher-order thinking. Nor does it fit well with the notion of setting the stage for effective student socialization work. You will need to implement research-based principles for maximizing the time that students spend engaged in academic activities, but to do so in ways that encourage students to become thoughtful participants in a learning community and self-regulators of their own thinking and behavior.

Recently, views on good teaching and learning have shifted from a transmission view, in which teachers mostly explain and demonstrate and students mostly memorize or replicate, to a social construction or learning community view, in which teachers and students share responsibility for initiating and guiding learning efforts. Instead of drill and recitation designed to elicit correct answers to convergent questions, classroom discourse emphasizes reflective discussion of networks of connected knowledge. Questions are divergent but designed to develop understanding of powerful ideas that anchor these knowledge networks, and the focus is on eliciting students' thinking. Students strive to make sense of new input by relating it to their prior knowledge and by collaborating in dialogue with others. Instead of working mostly alone, practicing what has been transmitted to them, they act as a learning community that constructs shared understandings.

To establish such a learning community in your classroom, you will need to teach your students not only how to pay attention during lessons and work alone on assignments but also how to participate in collaborative dialogues and work together in cooperative learning activities. Collaborative knowledge construction means not only taking turns talking, listening politely, and keeping criticism constructive, but also responding thoughtfully to what others have said, making contributions that will advance the discussion, and citing relevant arguments and evidence to support one's position. When students work in pairs or small groups, collaboration includes making sure that everyone in the group understands the goals of the activity, participates in carrying it out, and gets the intended learning benefits from this participation.

In managing your students, emphasize thoughtful, goal-oriented learning, not mindless compliance with rules. Also, stress self-regulation by encouraging them to take increasing responsibility for organizing and directing their own learning (Corno, 1989; Rohrkemper McCaslin, 1989; Zimmerman & Schunk, 1989). The basic principle here is that management systems need to support instructional systems. A management system that orients students toward passivity and compliance with rigid rules will undercut the potential effects of an instructional system that is designed to emphasize active learning, higher-order thinking, and the social construction of knowledge (McCaslin & Good, 1992). Thus, it is important to increase students' capacity for goal setting, time management, collaboration with peers, and other aspects of self-regulation in the classroom.

Students have the potential to develop self-regulation, but this development must be stimulated through socialization by parents, teachers, and significant others. Most of the things that teachers can do to develop self-regulation in their students involve modeling and instruction rather than, or at least in addition to, propounding and enforcing rules.

Mature forms of self-regulation develop gradually (if at all) following passage through a series of less mature forms determined in part by children's levels of cognitive development and in part by the socialization they receive. Children depend on adults for concepts to use in making sense of their experience and for guidance about how to respond to it.

In infancy, the connections between language, thought, and behavior are loose, and cognitive control of behavior is very limited. Over the next several years, during what Jean Piaget called the preoperational period, cognitive abilities become more integrated with one another and with behavior. Gradually, the child becomes able to use thinking to plan and regulate behavior, particularly thinking that is mediated by inner speech or self-talk (Vygotsky, 1962). Such cognitive mediation is especially crucial in the social sphere, where not much of what occurs can be understood merely by observing people's physical movements. To understand and participate in social interaction, one must understand the language and associated concepts that make it meaningful.

Children's cognitive and linguistic abilities develop throughout the preoperational years (ages 2 through 7) and into the concrete operational years (ages 7 through adolescence). Even so, they remain heavily dependent on adult guidance as they learn to interpret and respond to their social environments. Preschool and early elementary school students tend to identify with and seek to please their parents and teachers. They tend to accept (even if they do not always follow) the conduct norms propounded by these adult authority figures, whom they want to please by "being good."

Children tend to accept what they are told about good behavior without much reflection or attempt at evaluation. They "introject" moral concepts and behavioral norms. That is, they acquire them directly from statements by adults ("Never tell a lie," "Be nice," "Wait your turn"), retain them in the concrete form in which they were communicated, and reproduce them in similar contexts in the future. They may come to think of these norms as things that they always knew or figured out for themselves.

Unfortunately, introjected moral norms do not contribute much to effective self-regulation of behavior. They tend to be isolated verbal responses — conditioned reactions to particular situations — rather than "words to live by" that have been adopted consciously as part of a general philosophy that guides behavior. Typically, children do not develop a moral philosophy of their own until they reach adolescence and enter Piaget's stage of formal operational thinking. Even then, great individual differences exist in the degree to which previously introjected norms are consciously examined and a more mature and functional set of norms is adopted, internalized, and developed into a consistent system. These individual differences are closely related to the degree and nature of the moral socialization to which the individuals have been exposed.

Characteristics of Successful Socialization

Most parents care about their children and attempt to socialize them in ways that they believe are appropriate, often the same ways in which they were socialized by their parents. However, some approaches to socialization are more effective than others. Research on child rearing suggests that successful socialization has two noteworthy characteristics. First, it is extensive in volume and rich in cognitive content. Effective parents spend a great deal of time interacting with their children in ways that stimulate the children's cognitive development. This includes time spent socializing the children's beliefs, attitudes, and expectations about morality, social conventions, rights, responsibilities, and related social issues. Effective parents supply their children not merely with behavioral norms but with concepts, labels, principles, and rationales that provide a context of meaning within which to interpret the norms. In short, such parents provide their children with a great deal of instruction, not merely with lists of dos and don'ts.

Second, effective socialization is what Baumrind (1971) called "authoritative" rather than "authoritarian" or "laissez-faire" (Dornbusch et al., 1987; Steinberg, Elmen, & Mounts, 1989). *Authoritative* parents accept their roles as authority figures responsible for socializing their children and therefore place demands and limits on the children. However, they routinely explain the rationales underlying these demands. This helps the children to appreciate that the demands are appropriate and motivated by a concern for people's (including the children's) rights and best interests.

Other patterns of parenting lack the balance and effectiveness of the authoritative pattern. *Laissez-faire* parents make few demands on their children. They tend to ignore them and let them do as they please, so long as they do not become destructive or annoying. This pattern requires children to make decisions about how to behave without first having equipped them with needed principles and concepts, so it entails a great deal of unnecessary and sometimes painful trial-and-error learning. It leads to insecurity, anxiety, or fear of failure in some children and to social incompetence or irresponsibility in others.

Authoritarian parents make little attempt to help their children understand the reasons for their demands. Instead, they "boss the children around" with a "you'll do it because I said so" attitude and a readiness to punish failure to comply. For their children, regulation of behavior becomes a matter of submitting to power exertion rather than regulating oneself using concepts of rights and responsibilities.

Authoritarian parents discourage thinking by demanding conformity and submission to their authority and by focusing on threat of punishment rather than moral justification in presenting their demands. If the parents succeed in breaking their child's will, the result will be a docile individual who obeys without questioning and is essentially externally controlled rather than self-regulated. If the parents fail to compel obedience, the result will be an oppositional individual who resists authority and is prone to delinquency and crime. Docile, intimidated children lack the emotional freedom to evaluate behavioral prescriptions because they have learned to view this as rebellion against powerful authority figures; oppositional children lack the motivation to do so because they have learned to equate behavioral prescriptions with arbitrary and oppressive exertion of power by authority figures.

The authoritative approach is the most likely to give children both the cognitive tools and the emotional freedom needed to think about and evaluate behavioral norms, to consciously adopt norms that make sense and use them to guide behavior, and to integrate them into a systematic and internally consistent moral philosophy (Hoffman, 1991; Lepper, 1983; Maccoby & Martin, 1983). In contrast to laissez-faire parents, authoritative parents provide their children with a well-articulated model of a systematic moral philosophy, which the children can learn and use as a base from which to develop their own moral thinking. In contrast to authoritarian parents, authoritative parents also provide their children with modeling and emotional freedom that encourage them to begin to think for themselves. They justify rules and demands by referring to the Golden

Rule (treat others as you would like to be treated yourself) or associated concepts of justice, fairness, or morality, rather than stressing the authority of a parent over a child. They encourage their children to think about why they behave as they do and to evaluate their behavior in terms of its effectiveness in attaining their goals and its consistency with basic values.

PROMOTING SELF-REGULATION IN THE CLASSROOM

These findings on socialization factors in the home that affect children's developing self-regulation capacities have implications for teachers' efforts to socialize students in classrooms. They suggest that research-based classroom management principles need to be adapted and supplemented as follows.

In setting limits and prescribing procedures, use an informational rather than a controlling style (Koestner, Ryan, Bernieri, & Holt, 1984). Stress the reasons for the limits and procedures, implying that these are reasonable and useful guidelines that students will want to follow because they will help them attain important academic or social goals. Even when acting as an authority figure, use a tone and manner that suggests that you are soliciting students' cooperation rather than issuing orders. Emphasize what to do and how this will yield desirable benefits rather than the consequences of failure to comply. Remember, your goal is to induce students to choose to adopt your guidelines for themselves and begin to use them as internal guides to behavior. The following are aspects of an informational style of presenting guidelines.

First, always give the reasons for the guideline in addition to the guideline itself. If it is not easy to show that the guideline is intended as a means toward a desirable end, something is probably wrong with the guideline.

Second, when correcting misbehavior, emphasize the desired behavior ("Talk quietly so as not to disturb those are who still working"). As much as possible, phrase corrections as friendly reminders rather than as power assertive commands, and encourage students to see themselves as regulating their own behavior rather than as being controlled externally ("You only have a few more minutes to finish your assignment" is better than "If you don't finish that assignment before the bell, you'll have to stay in during recess").

Third, if it becomes necessary to punish a student who has not responded to more positive approaches, announce the punishment with a tone of sadness and disappointment rather than vengefulness or righteous indignation. Help the student to understand that you do not want to punish but must do so because of his or her repeated misbehavior and failure to respond to your appeals. The punishment is not an arbitrary display of your authority; rather, it is an unfortunate but necessary consequence of the student's repeated misbehavior, and one that the student can avoid in the future if he or she chooses to do so.

Underlying this approach is the implication that students can and are expected to behave appropriately. It is primarily their own responsibility to regulate their behavior, rather than your responsibility to control them externally. Make it clear that you are a facilitator, not a prison warden, and that your students are well-intentioned, reasonable human beings, not sociopaths or weak individuals dominated by uncontrollable emotions or compulsions.

Finally, students will need individualized assistance in developing self-regulation. You can accomplish this with some of them by developing a personal relationship, presenting yourself as a resource person, and helping them to gain insight into the problem. Other students also may need explicit instruction in methods of self-regulation of behavior, as described in the next chapter.

CONCLUSION

Schooling is compulsory, and teachers must prescribe and control student behavior in order to establish the classroom as an effective learning environment. Even so, you can still stimulate self-regulation (not merely compliance) in your students by deemphasizing the authority figure aspects of your role and emphasizing the rationales that justify your demands, projecting positive expectations concerning students' desire to foster the common good, and encouraging them to view behavioral guidelines as reasonable and adopt them as their own. You will need to decide how much you are willing to include resocialization of problem students as part of your definition of your role as a teacher. This issue will be revisited in Chapter 16, following discussions of what experts who offer advice to teachers, as well as teachers themselves, have had to say about coping with problem students.

2

Socializing Students and Resolving Conflicts

roblem students need special help that goes beyond application of the research-based management principles summarized in the previous chapter. No comparable set of research findings exists regarding the teaching of students who present chronic personality or behavior problems. There have been few studies in which measures of particular teacher behaviors or implementations of particular student socialization programs were related to measures of change in student outcomes. Furthermore, most of the findings that do exist are from evaluations of behavior modification strategies. Until recently, these strategies were oriented toward exerting situational control over students' behavior rather than toward changing the students in more fundamental ways by helping them to develop better self-regulation.

Even in the absence of definitive classroom research, however, we have come a long way from 30 years ago, when most of the student socialization advice directed to teachers was based either on B. F. Skinner's applications of behavior analysis or on the ideas of Sigmund Freud, Alfred Adler, or Carl Rogers concerning psychotherapy techniques. It is now possible to identify a coherent set of concepts and strategies for socializing students that (1) reflects a consensus of the majority of mental health professionals concerning principles of effective practice and (2) is suitable for use by teachers working under normal classroom conditions. This conceptual base and its associated treatment strategies are compatible with the notion of the teacher as a professional who has particular expertise and specific but limited responsibilities to students and their parents, as well as certain rights as the instructional leader and authority figure in the classroom.

Major sources for this conceptual base include (1) the literature on child rearing, and in particular on parental orientations and behaviors that are associated with the development of desirable personal and social traits in children (Maccoby & Martin, 1983); (2) the literature on teaching through modeling, and especially on the attributes of models who are likely to be admired and imitated by others (Bandura, 1986); (3) the literature on expectation and social labeling effects, especially as it applies to developing desirable personal and social attributes (Dix, 1993; Good & Brophy, 1995, 1997); (4) the literature on cognitive-behavior modification and strategy training, with its emphasis on developing self-regulation mechanisms in students (Hughes, 1988; Hughes & Hall, 1989; Kendall, 1991; Kendall & Braswell, 1985), (5) suggestions contributed by mental health professionals who have adapted ideas used in therapy settings for use by teachers in classrooms, and (6) the literature on improving schools to make them more successful in meeting the needs of students in general and at-risk students in particular.

Key elements in a systematic approach to socializing the class as a whole include modeling and instruction, communicating positive expectations and social labels, and reinforcing desired behavior. *Modeling* is the most basic element, because teachers cannot hope to be successful socializers if they do not practice what they preach. When accompanied by thinking aloud—verbalizing the self-talk that guides behavior—modeling also is important as an instructional method. It is especially valuable for conveying the thinking and decision making that are involved in acting according to the Golden Rule and other guidelines for prosocial behavior.

Where prosocial behavior is difficult for students to learn, modeling may have to be supplemented with *instruction* (including practice exercises) in desirable social skills and coping strategies. The instruction should convey not only propositional knowledge (description of the skill and explanation of why it is desirable) but also procedural knowledge (how to implement the skill) and conditional knowledge (when and why to implement it).

Consistent *projection of positive expectations, attributions, and social labels* to students is important in fostering positive self-concepts and related motives that orient them toward prosocial behavior. If students are treated as well-intentioned individuals who respect themselves and others and who desire to act responsibly, morally, and prosocially, they are likely to develop these qualities.

Such development is even more likely if the students' positive qualities and behaviors are *reinforced,* not so much through material rewards as through expressions of appreciation. When delivered effectively, such reinforcement is likely to increase the students' tendencies to attribute their desirable behavior to their own desirable personal traits and to reinforce themselves for possessing these traits.

In functioning as the authority figure in the classroom, try to be *authoritative* rather than either authoritarian or laissez-faire. You have the right and the responsibility to exert leadership and impose control, but you will be more successful in doing so if you are understanding and supportive of students and if you make sure that students understand the reasons behind your demands in addition to stating the demands themselves. Focus on desired behavior (stressing what *to do* rather than what *not to do*). Follow up with cues and reminders, so as to minimize the need for scolding or threatening punishment. Be prepared to answer questions about your conduct guidelines. Instead of responding defensively, supply objectively good reasons for your behavioral demands.

Learn *basic socialization and helping skills* for working with students who display chronic problems in personal development or social adjustment. These basic skills include developing personal relationships with the students and reassuring them of your continued concern about their welfare despite their provocative behavior; monitoring them closely and intervening (when necessary) briefly and nondisruptively to keep them engaged in academic activities during class time; dealing with their problems in more sustained ways outside of class time; handling conflicts calmly without becoming engaged in power struggles; questioning them in ways that are likely to motivate them to talk freely; using active listening, reflection, interpretation, and related techniques for drawing them out and helping them to develop better insight into themselves and their behavior; negotiating agreements and behavior contracts; insisting that the students accept responsibility for controlling their own behavior while at the same time supportively helping them to do so; and developing productive relationships with their parents.

Using good instruction, management, and socialization techniques will go a long way toward minimizing the need for disciplinary interventions. Even so, situations calling for *disciplinary interventions* will arise, and it is important for you to handle them effectively. Some general principles for doing so can be identified: Minimize power struggles and face-saving gestures by discussing the incident with the student in private rather than in front of the class, question the student to determine his or her awareness of the behavior and explanation for it, make sure that the student understands why the behavior is inappropriate and cannot be tolerated, seek to get the student to accept responsibility for the behavior and to make a commitment to change, provide any needed modeling or instruction in better ways of coping, work with the student to develop a mutually agreeable plan for solving the problem, concentrate on developing self-regulation capacities through positive socialization and instruction rather than on controlling behavior through power assertion, and emphasize that the student can achieve desired outcomes and avoid negative consequences by choosing to act responsibly. If it does become necessary to punish, do so with an emphasis on pressuring the student to change future behavior rather than on exacting retribution for past misdeeds.

GENERAL ATTRIBUTES OF EFFECTIVE SOCIALIZERS

Good and Brophy (1995) identified some general attributes of teachers that contribute to their success in socializing students, based on the attributes of individuals who are effective as models or as parents. You should seek to develop these attributes to pave your way to success in socializing your students.

Social Attractiveness. You should be liked by your students. The characteristics that contribute to this are the same ones that make anyone well liked: a cheerful disposition, friendliness, emotional maturity, sincerity, and other qualities that indicate good mental health and personal adjustment.

Ego Strength. Certain qualities are essential when you act as the classroom authority figure. Cultivate an underlying self-confidence that will enable you to remain calm in a crisis, listen actively without becoming defensive, avoid win–lose conflicts, and maintain a problem-solving orientation rather than resort to withdrawal, blaming, hysteria, or other emotional overreactions.

Realistic Perceptions of Self and Students. It is important for you to see yourself and your students for what you are. Don't let your perceptions become clouded by romanticism, guilt, hostility, anxiety, or other threats to contact with reality.

Enjoyment of Students, but within a Teacher–Student Relationship. Enjoy spending time interacting with students and getting to know them as individuals, but maintain your identity as an adult, a teacher, and an authority figure. Be friendly without becoming overly familiar, comfortable with the group without becoming a group member.

Clarity about Roles and Comfort in Playing Them. To be consistent in your interactions with students, you need to be clear about your roles, your relationships with students, and the behaviors that you value and those that you will not tolerate. This will enable you to explain coherently to students what you expect, and to be comfortable in making these demands.

Patience and Determination. Some students persist in testing limits because they are accustomed to getting their way eventually if they keep at it long enough. You will need to convince these students that they will be required to fulfill their responsibilities and will have to suffer the consequences if they choose to continue the misbehavior. At the same time, make it clear that you will work with them to improve one step at a time if they need to build better self-control capacities.

Acceptance of the Individual, but Not All of His or Her Behavior. All of your students should know that they are accepted as individuals and welcomed as members of your class, but also that certain behaviors are inappropriate and will not be allowed.

Firm but Flexible Limits. State expectations clearly and reinforce them consistently, but keep them flexible and negotiable where possible. Keep rules to a minimum, and liberalize them as students become more capable of responsible self-regulation.

Modeling. Practice what you preach by modeling the ideals that you verbalize, particularly in areas such as politeness and good manners, friendliness and helpfulness, and consideration for the rights and feelings of others.

Projecting Positive Expectations. Treat students as basically good people who want to do the right thing and whose lapses are due to ignorance or forgetfulness. Avoid treating them as if they are inherently evil or under the control of powerful antisocial impulses. Even when admonishing, treat the student as a responsible person (or, at least, as one who will be responsible in this regard in the future). Often, children literally "don't know better" than to act as they do, so they need adults' help in learning to do the right thing. Therefore, emphasize guidelines for more appropriate behavior rather than personal criticism. Admonitions such as "John, be careful with that microscope—we wouldn't want to break it" or "Mary, I was surprised to hear you ridiculing Jean when you were talking to Janet today—how about trying to understand her better rather than just running her down?" (said in private) illustrate these principles. In contrast, consider comments such as "I don't know why you can't sit still" or "Do you think it's funny to make noises like that?" or "You are going to have to find some other way to take out your frustrations—we'll have no hitting in the classroom." These comments not only fail to provide positive guidance but also imply that no change in the students' behavior is really expected.

Developing these personal qualities and using research-based principles for managing the classroom will set the stage for your student socialization and conflict resolution efforts. The rest of this chapter provides overviews of three sets of techniques that you can apply to a great range of socialization and conflict resolution situations: behavior modification, strategy teaching, and counseling. More specific applications of these techniques are discussed in subsequent chapters dealing with particular problem-student types, along with additional techniques that focus on the problems addressed.

BEHAVIOR MODIFICATION

Behavior modification techniques (Kazdin, 1994; O'Leary & O'Leary, 1977; Schloss & Smith, 1994) may be helpful for dealing with habitual problem behavior that needs to be redirected. The well-known assertive discipline (Canter & Canter, 1992) approach to classroom management is built on behavior modification principles, as are other approaches that feature articulation of classroom rules and behavioral expectations, reinforcement of students' compliance, and time out or punishment as responses to misbehavior. Strategies for modifying behavior include methods for responding to behavioral deficits (by establishing and maintaining desired behavior) and methods for responding to behavioral excesses (by reducing the frequency of undesired behavior). Methods for establishing and maintaining desired behavior include cueing and reinforcement. Methods for reducing undesired behavior include satiation, extinction, and punishment. Negative reinforcement is a mixed method that includes elements of both reinforcement and punishment.

Cueing

When students have difficulty remembering to perform certain behaviors, you can help by cueing—providing a brief direction or reminder to cue their attention and behavior. Use these reminders for problem behaviors that occur repeatedly in specific situations, such as with students who get into squabbles over sharing equipment in a learning center.

Cueing is also useful to help students distinguish situations when certain behavior is appropriate from situations when it is not. For example, shouting would be inappropriate in the classroom at any time, but quiet conversational talk in designated areas might be allowed among students who have completed assignments, talk during work time might be confined to task-relevant collaboration, and so on. Students also must learn discriminations about when and how to move around the room, to approach you with an individual problem, or to call out comments during lessons. Deliver cues in ways that encourage students to see them as helpful reminders about behavior that is supposed to be produced, not as after-the-fact nagging or criticism. Fade out cueing as the need for it lessens.

Reinforcement

Behavioristic psychologists stress reinforcement as the primary mechanism for establishing and maintaining behavior. They define a reinforcer as anything that increases or maintains the frequency of a behavior when it is made contingent on performance of that behavior. This somewhat circular definition is needed because some people are not reinforced by things that most others find rewarding, and some people feel rewarded when they experience things that most others would prefer to avoid.

Reinforcers are either positive or negative. Positive reinforcers correspond roughly to what we usually call rewards. They include material rewards (food, money, prizes, or tokens that can be exchanged for something desired), social rewards (praise, grades, honors, status symbols, attention from the teacher or peers), and activity rewards (opportunities to engage in desired activities, use special equipment, or play games).

Negative reinforcement involves freeing students from some unpleasant state when desired behavior is performed. Although this technically involves increasing the rate of a desired behavior by reinforcing it, it also involves withholding reinforcement from students who do not meet demands, usually because they are misbehaving in some way. Consequently, negative reinforcement is discussed in a later section dealing with techniques for stopping undesired behavior.

Vicarious Reinforcement

Reinforcement may motivate not only the student who receives it but also other students who observe its delivery. In theory, you could motivate a student to work carefully not only by praising his or her careful work but also by praising the careful work done by others, especially peers with whom the student identifies. Vicarious reinforcement does not occur automatically, however, because not all students find the same consequences reinforcing (e.g., some value teacher praise, but some do not).

Fading of Reinforcement

In the early stages of trying to establish new behavior, it may be necessary to reinforce promptly and frequently, perhaps even 100 percent of the time. However, as the behavior becomes more established, it should become possible to delay reinforcement and to reduce its frequency or increase the intervals between deliveries. You can continue fading until you reach the minimal level of reinforcement needed to sustain the behavior. You also might want to shift from material or activity rewards to social rewards, and ultimately to wean students from dependence on your reinforcement by teaching them to reinforce themselves.

Shaping through Successive Approximations

For reinforcement to be effective, successful performance must occur often enough to be reinforced frequently. When bad habits are deeply ingrained, or when students have not yet established reliable cognitive control over the desired behavior, it may take some time before they can begin to produce this behavior frequently, even if the motivation to produce it exists. You can still use reinforcement to shape behavior, however, if you analyze the total task facing the student and divide it into subgoals that can be addressed in order of difficulty. Then you can reinforce students regularly as they approach the ultimate goal one step at a time. For example, hyperactive students who tend to leave their seats and roam the room can be reinforced initially for staying in their seats for 5 minutes at a time, then for 10 minutes, then for 20 minutes, and so on. As the student learns to stay seated for extended periods of time, you can begin to offer reinforcement for additional behavior such as working quietly without bothering classmates, and eventually for careful and successful work on assignments.

When changing the specifications of what behaviors qualify for reinforcement, you will need to ensure that students do not see you as failing to keep promises. Help students to recognize and appreciate the progress they have made and thus to see that higher expectations are now appropriate. Many teachers have found contingency contracting systems to be effective in communicating these perceptions.

Contingency Contracting

Contingency contracting involves conferring with the student about possible alternatives and then jointly drawing up a contract that specifies what the student will be expected to do in order to earn contingent rewards. The contract can be purely oral, although it helps to formalize it by having the student write down the details of the agreement. Contracts might call for students to complete a certain amount of work at a certain level of proficiency, or to improve their classroom behavior in specified ways, in order to earn specified rewards.

Contingency contracting helps students to see the relationship between their behavior and its consequences. Also, when they draw up the contracts themselves, they are more likely to make personal commitments that are real and meaningful to them because they express them in their own words. Contracts are especially useful for situations in which students know what they are supposed to do and are capable of doing it if they put their minds to it, but currently are not conscientious or motivated enough to do so consistently.

Contracting provides built-in opportunities for teacher–student collaboration in negotiating expectations and rewards. If perfect performance is currently an unreasonable expectation, the negotiation process might yield specifications calling for reinforcement of a level of improvement that the student views as reasonable and that you are willing to accept (at least for now). Contracting also provides opportunities to offer students choices of rewards, thus ensuring that the intended reinforcement is experienced as such.

Delivering Reinforcement Effectively

Early classroom applications of reinforcement methods involved delivering material reinforcers or tokens that could later be exchanged for selections made from a "reinforcement menu." These systems proved to be unwieldy except in classrooms with very low student:teacher ratios (Doyle, 1986; Ryan, 1979). Consequently, there has been a shift away from attempting to reinforce desired behaviors frequently and relatively continuously toward reinforcing major sequences of behavior that extend over significant periods of time. There also has been a shift away from material reinforcers toward activity reinforcers and (especially) social reinforcers.

Some educational theorists oppose reinforcement in principle, viewing it as bribing students for doing what they should be doing anyway because it is the right thing to do or because it is in their own best interest. For example, the use of rewards came under attack recently in a popular book (Kohn, 1993) claiming that their effectiveness has been exaggerated and that rewarding students for learning undermines their intrinsic interest in the material. Attribution theorists have developed research findings that support this view to some extent (attribution theorists are concerned about what happens when we try to explain our behavior to ourselves — when we *attribute* our behavior to causes). They have shown that if you begin to reward people for doing what they already were doing for their own reasons, you may decrease their intrinsic motivation to continue that behavior in the future (Deci & Ryan, 1985; Heckhausen, 1991; Lepper & Greene, 1978). Furthermore, to the extent that you focus their attention on the reward rather than on the task, their performance tends to deteriorate (Condry & Chambers, 1978). They develop a piecework mentality, doing whatever will garner them the most rewards with the least effort, rather than trying to do the job as well as they can in order to create a high-quality product.

For a time, it was thought that these undesirable effects were inherent in the use of extrinsic rewards, including teacher praise. More recently, it has become clear that the effects of reinforcement depend on the nature of the reinforcement used and especially on how it is presented (Cameron & Pierce, 1994; Chance, 1993). *Decreases* in performance quality and in intrinsic motivation to engage in the behavior are most likely when reinforcement has the following characteristics:

> *High salience* (the rewards are very attractive or presented in ways that call attention to them).
> *Noncontingency* (the rewards are given for mere participation in the activity, rather than being contingent on achieving specific goals).
> *Unnatural/unusual* (the rewards are artificially tied to behaviors as control devices, rather than being natural outcomes of the behaviors).

Thus, *reinforcement is likely to undermine students' intrinsic motivation when it implies that their behavior is controlled externally*—that they are engaging in an activity only because they must do so in order to earn a reward. You can reduce the danger of this by emphasizing social rewards over material and activity rewards, and by delivering the rewards in ways that encourage the student to value the behavior being reinforced. These principles are illustrated in the following discussion of teacher praise.

Praising Effectively

Praise is widely recommended as a way to reinforce students, although it does not always have this effect (Brophy, 1981). Sometimes a teacher's praise is not even intended to be reinforcing, as when it is used in an attempt to build a social relationship with an alienated student ("I like your new shirt, John"). Even when praise is intended to be reinforcing, some students will not perceive it that way. Public praise in particular may be more embarrassing than reinforcing, especially if it calls attention to conformity behavior rather than to some more noteworthy accomplishment. This is likely to be a problem when teachers try to shape the behavior of onlookers by praising peers ("I like the way that Susie is sitting up straight and ready to listen").

Effective praise expresses appreciation for students' efforts or admiration for their accomplishments, in ways that call attention to the efforts or accomplishments themselves rather than to their role in pleasing the teacher. This helps students learn to attribute their *efforts* to their own intrinsic motivation rather than to external manipulation by the teacher, and to attribute their *successes* to their own abilities and efforts rather than to external supports or pressures.

Effective praise is genuine. Brophy and Evertson (1981) found that teachers were credible and spontaneous when praising students whom they liked, often smiling as they spoke and praising genuine accomplishments. They praised students whom they disliked just as often, but usually without accompanying spontaneity and warmth and often with reference to appearance or conduct rather than accomplishments. Sometimes teachers praise poor responses as part of a well-intentioned attempt to encourage low achievers (Nafpaktitis, Mayer, & Butterworth, 1985; Natriello & Dornbusch, 1985). This tactic often backfires, however, because it undermines the teacher's credibility and confuses or depresses the students (to the extent that they realize they are being treated differently from their classmates).

Thus, praise is most likely to be effective when it is delivered simply and directly, in a natural voice, accompanied by nonverbal communication of approval but without gushing or dramatizing. Also, it specifies the particular accomplishment being praised and recognizes any noteworthy effort, care, or perseverance involved. Additional guidelines for effective praising are given in Table 2.1.

So far I have been discussing behavior modification techniques used to establish or shape desired behavior. I now shift to techniques used to reduce or eliminate undesired behavior.

Satiation

Satiation involves letting misbehavior run its course by allowing, or if necessary requiring, students to repeat the behavior until fatigue and boredom set in. It is most useful for behaviors that are not harmful and do not lead to powerful rewards, especially if they are recognized as counterproductive even by the students themselves (Krumboltz & Krumboltz, 1972). Such behaviors include throwing spitballs, making faces or noises, or almost any type of classroom clowning that is silly rather than genuinely funny.

Satiation is probably most effective if used sparingly and with a minimum of fanfare. Otherwise, it might become an enjoyable experience that reinforces the problem behavior or, if pursued too aggressively, might be perceived by students as an attempt to humiliate them.

Extinction

According to behavioristic theory, students will continue to produce undesirable behavior so long as that behavior continues to lead to attractive reinforcement. Such behavior can be extinguished through nonreinforcement, if the teacher controls the reinforcements that maintain it. The nonreinforcement technique most commonly recommended for classroom

TABLE 2.1. Guidelines for Effective Praise

Effective Praise	Ineffective Praise
1. Is delivered contingently.	1. Is delivered randomly or unsystematically.
2. Specifies the particulars of the accomplishment.	2. Is restricted to global positive reactions.
3. Shows spontaneity, variety, and other signs of credibility; suggests clear attention to the student's accomplishment.	3. Shows a bland uniformity that suggests a conditioned response made with minimal attention.
4. Rewards attainment of specified performance criteria (which can include effort criteria, however).	4. Rewards mere participation, without consideration of performance processes or outcomes.
5. Provides information to students about their competence or the value of their accomplishments.	5. Provides no information at all or gives students information about their status.
6. Orients students toward better appreciation of their own task-related behavior and thinking about problem solving.	6. Orients students toward comparing themselves with others and thinking about competing.
7. Uses student's own prior accomplishments as the context for describing present accomplishments.	7. Uses the accomplishments of peers as the context for describing student's present accomplishments.
8. Is given in recognition of noteworthy effort or success at difficult (for this student) tasks.	8. Is given without regard to the effort expended or the meaning of the accomplishment.
9. Attributes success to effort and ability, implying that similar success can be expected in the future.	9. Attributes success to ability alone or to external factors such as luck or (easy) task difficulty.
10. Fosters endogenous attributions (students believe that they expend effort on the task because they enjoy the task and/or want to develop task-relevant skills).	10. Fosters exogenous attributions (students believe that they expend effort on the task for external reasons—to please the teacher, win a competition or reward, etc.).
11. Focuses students' attention on their own task-relevant behavior.	11. Focuses students' attention on the teacher as an external authority figure who is manipulating them.
12. Fosters appreciation of, and desirable attributions about, task-relevant behavior after the process is completed.	12. Intrudes into the ongoing process, distracting attention from task-relevant behavior.

Note. From Brophy (1981). Reprinted by permission.

use is to ignore (and get classmates to ignore) misbehavior that appears to be motivated by a desire for attention. Some students will repeat any behavior that brings them attention, even negative attention involving disapproval.

However, extinction is not often feasible in the classroom. Certain misbehaviors are too disruptive or dangerous to be ignored, and some students assume that anything not explicitly disapproved is acceptable. Open defiance, obscenities, hostility directed specifically at you as the teacher, and similarly provocative behaviors demand response. Attempts to ignore them will confuse students or leave them with the impression that you are not aware of what is going on, are unable to cope with it, or don't care. Thus, ignoring is feasible only as a response to relatively minor misbehavior, and even then, it will need to be combined with techniques for shaping more desirable behavior.

Negative Reinforcement

Although behavioral psychologists define it as a technique for increasing desired behavior, negative reinforcement is discussed here among techniques for stopping misbehavior because you should use it only when students have been misbehaving persistently despite more positive attempts to get them to change. Negative reinforcement occurs when improved behavior brings about the termination of an aversive experience. For ethical reasons, you should not deliberately place students in aversive situations just so that you can use negative reinforcement by releasing them when their behavior improves. However, the natural consequences of many forms of misbehavior are aversive, and you can often arrange to let students escape some of these consequences by improving their behavior. Unruly classes can be kept after school until they become more cooperative and complete an activity acceptably, and students who have been removed from the class can be allowed to rejoin it if they make what appears to be a sincere commitment to begin behaving more appropriately.

Negative reinforcement is not punishment because it does not involve applying aversive consequences in response to misbehavior. Instead, it involves withholding reinforcement pending performance of desired behavior. The aversive condition exists solely because the students have not behaved appropriately, and they can terminate it at any time by changing their behavior. Negative reinforcement is probably most effective when you warn students about it in advance, to underscore that the students themselves will be responsible if reinforcement is not forthcoming. Ideally, such warnings stress the call for improved behavior rather than the withholding of reinforcement ("Class, I know you don't like to get out late, but you're going to stay until you settle down and pay attention to this announcement").

Punishment

Punishment reduces undesirable behavior by making aversive consequences contingent on that behavior. Its use should be minimized because (1) it is a stopgap measure that may temporarily suppress the overt performance of undesirable behavior but does not change students' underlying desires to misbehave or the reasons why those desires exist, (2) it does not provide guidance to students by indicating what they should do instead, and (3) it causes problems of its own by engendering resentment and damaging your relationship with students. The most effective forms of punishment are mild rather than severe, informative rather than merely punitive, and tailored to the specific misbehavior in ways likely to help the student see why the behavior is inappropriate.

Ineffective Forms of Punishment

Certain forms of punishment almost never work. Suspension from school, for example, removes disruptive students from class, but many of these students will welcome the "vacation" from school, all of them will lose class time and fall further behind in their work, and most will be resentful rather than contrite. Thus, except in extreme cases, school suspension is a mistake. The same is true of punishing students by forcing them to do extra academic work. By assigning schoolwork as punishment, you imply that the work is unpleasant.

Physical punishment is also generally ineffective, even where it is still legal. The best examples of its failure are antisocial delinquents and criminals, who almost always come from homes in which adults relied on physical punishment to socialize children. Also, physical punishment is a direct attack on the student, so it creates feelings of anger and resentment that are likely to be much stronger than any feelings of fear or contrition.

Finally, it is unwise to punish an entire class or group for the misbehavior of an individual, even though the peer pressure generated can be quite powerful. Group punishment forces students to choose between the teacher and one of their classmates. Many students will choose the classmate, uniting in sullen defiance of the teacher and refusing to blame the classmate for the group punishment.

Guidelines for Effective Punishment

When misbehavior persists despite repeated, positive attempts to stop it, mild forms of punishment may be necessary. Threat of punishment is usually even more effective than punishment itself, especially when phrased in a way that reminds students that it will be their own fault if punishment results. When punishment is used, it should be a deliberate, systematic method for suppressing misbehavior, not an involuntary emotional response, a way to get revenge, or a spontaneous reaction to provocation. The punishment should be as short and mild as possible but unpleasant enough to motivate the students to change their behavior.

Punishments should be combined with positive statements of expectations and rules, focusing more on what the students should be doing than on what they should not be doing. The students should be clear about why the rule exists, why their misbehavior cannot be tolerated, and why they have left you no alternative other than to administer punishment. Where possible, it is a good idea to combine punishment with negative reinforcement, so that students who do something positive to show good faith can escape punishment. For example, telling students that they will lose some privilege for a specific period of time is probably less effective than telling them that they will lose the privilege until their behavior improves sufficiently to warrant removal of the punishment.

Some of the most effective punishments are very mild, at least from a teacher's perspective. Merely keeping students after class to discuss a problem, for example, can have a punishing effect. A delay of even a few minutes may cause a student to have to go to the end of the lunch line or to go home alone instead of with friends. These may be more effective punishments for most students than being sent to an isolation area, sent to the principal, or physically punished.

Time Out

Students who are upset, angry, or out of control as a result of a particular situation, as well as hyperactive or aggressive students who are having bad days, may respond well to time out from regular classroom activities. You can ask them to move to an isolated part of the room, to a desk in the hall, or perhaps to the principal's office, where they will stay until they can collect themselves and behave appropriately. Time out usually works best if presented not as a punishment but as an opportunity for students to solve their own problems. Also, you should use it sparingly, because it embodies (on a smaller scale) the same disadvantages as suspending students from school (Harris, 1985; Jones & Jones, 1995).

Response Cost

Abuse of privileges is usually handled best with response cost — making it clear to students that costs will be attached to certain unacceptable behaviors and that if they do not heed fair warnings, they will have to pay these costs. Ideally, the costs are logically related to the offenses: Students who abuse library privileges will have them suspended, students who are persistently destructive with certain equipment will not get to use that equipment for a time, or students who start fights at recess will have to stay in or play alone.

Detention

Students who refuse to work on assignments usually are best handled by in-school or after-school detention during which they are required to complete the assignments. This shows them that attempts to escape responsibilities by refusing to work or creating diversions will result only in their having to spend extra time in school.

Making Problem Behavior Self-Defeating

Provocations and attention-getting behaviors are best handled through gentle and humorous put-downs. If these behaviors persist, punishment should be designed to frustrate the students' intended goals. For example, students who persist in shouting out obscenities can be required to copy them repeatedly during free time until they are satiated. Students who destroy property might be required to fix or replace what they have broken. If this is not possible, they might be required to perform some kind of service such as cleaning up the school grounds. In general, destructiveness is often handled best with methods that require the student not only to change behavior but also to make restitution by fixing or replacing damaged items.

In summary, punishment should be used only in response to *repeated* misbehavior. It is a treatment of last resort for students who persist in misbehaving despite continued expressions of concern and assistance. It is a way to exert control over students who will not control themselves. Thus, punishment is not appropriate for dealing with isolated incidents or with situations in which there is no reason to believe that the student will repeat the action. Even with repeated misbehavior, punishment should be minimized if students are trying to improve.

When you do find it necessary to punish students, use an appropriate tone and manner. Avoid dramatizing ("All right, that's the last straw!" "Now you've done it!") or implying a power struggle ("I'll show you who's boss"). State the need for punishment in a quiet, almost sorrowful voice and in a manner that communicates a combination of deep concern, puzzlement, and regret over the student's behavior. Whether or not you state it directly, you should imply the following message: "You have misbehaved continually. I have tried to help with reminders and explanations, but your misbehavior has persisted. I cannot allow this to continue. If it does, I will have to punish you. I don't want to, but I must if you leave me no choice."

Truly effective punishment does not leave students with revengeful attitudes. Instead, it leaves them feeling guilty, ashamed, frustrated, or embarrassed. They realize that they have gotten into trouble because of their own failures to respond to earlier, more positive attempts to curb their misbehavior.

STRATEGY TEACHING

Cueing, reinforcement, and other behavior modification methods are most useful when students already know what to do but currently do not do it consistently. To the extent that they create problems because they do not know how to cope with the situation more effectively, you will need to *teach them better strategies*.

One set of methods for doing so is called *cognitive-behavior modification* (Meichenbaum, 1977). Although it has its roots in behavioristic psychology, cognitive-behavior modification stresses developing self-regulation rather than imposing external controls, focuses on thinking and subjective experience more than on overt behavior, and relies on goal setting, planning, and self-instruction more than on reinforcement. In this approach, you go beyond telling students what to do. In addition, you model the process by verbalizing aloud the self-talk that you use to regulate your behavior while you carry out the activity (stating goals, reviewing strategies to be used in pursuing these goals, providing self-instructions at each step, monitoring and evaluating performance, taking corrective action when initial strategies have not succeeded, and reinforcing yourself for progress and success). Such modeling shows students how to regulate their own behavior by making visible the self-talk that guides effective action but usually remains invisible to observers.

In Meichenbaum's original version, a five-step approach was used to teach students to respond reflectively rather than impulsively to academic tasks: (1) The teacher models the task while speaking aloud (cognitive modeling); (2) the student performs the task under the teacher's instruction (overt, external guidance); (3) the student performs the task while verbalizing self-instructions aloud (overt self-guidance); (4) the student whispers self-instructions while doing the task (faded overt self-guidance); and (5) the student performs the task under self-guidance via private speech (covert self-instruction). Variations of this approach have been used to help socially isolated students learn to initiate activities with peers, to help aggressive students learn to control their anger and respond more effectively to frustration, and to help defeated students learn to respond to mistakes with problem-solving efforts rather than withdrawal or resignation. Assessments of cognitive-behavior modification treatments have yielded generally positive results (Durlak, Fuhrman, & Lampman, 1991; Dush, Hirt, & Schroeder, 1989; Forman, 1993).

Other cognitive-behavioral approaches to what is becoming known as *strategy training* have been developed by theorists working outside of the cognitive-behavior modification tradition. Some of these combine modeling with role playing or other simulation exercises (Sarason & Sarason, 1981). Others have been developed as ways to teach students strategies for reading with comprehension or for solving problems with clarity of purpose and conscious awareness of the strategies being applied (Manning, 1991). Stress inoculation programs (which help people to anticipate and prepare to cope more successfully with the stress induced by situations that they currently do not handle well) typically include important cognitive-behavioral components. So do rational–emotive treatments, which help people to stop producing "catastrophic" emotional reactions to stressful situations and begin generating more realistic and productive reactions.

Much strategy training involves *social skills training,* in which students are given modeling and instruction, then engaged in role play and other practical application exercises, to teach them better ways of interacting with peers and solving social problems. Social skills training programs have been used to teach strategies for initiating and maintaining social conversations, joining ongoing games or group activities, playing or learning cooperatively, and resolving conflicts through negotiation without resorting to aggression. Research indicates that social skills training can be effective for improving a wide range of student behaviors (DuPaul & Eckert, 1994; Gesten et al., 1987; Sabornie, 1991; Zaragoza, Vaughn, & McIntosh, 1991). For examples of classroom applications, see Adalbjarnardottir (1994); Cartledge and Milburn (1995); Elias and Clabby (1989); Foreman (1993); King and Kirschenbaum (1992); Matson and Ollendick (1988); Walker (1987); and Walker, Colvin, and Ramsey (1995).

Whenever problem behavior appears because students lack strategies for coping effectively with particular situations, you will need to *teach* them how to handle those situations better—not just *urge* them to do so. The most effective form of strategy teaching is likely to be modeling combined with verbalized self-instructions, because this demonstrates the processes directly for students. If you just provide them with an explanation, they will have to translate your directions into forms of self-talk that they can use to guide their behavior.

CRISIS INTERVENTION AND COUNSELING TECHNIQUES

Behavior modification and strategy training techniques have been developed primarily by experimental psychologists. Other techniques have been developed by mental health professionals for use in crisis intervention and personal counseling situations, and some of these have been adapted for use in the classroom. These techniques are designed to resocialize students' beliefs or attitudes, not just to modify their behavior. Their school applications have not been studied as extensively as those of behavior modification techniques, but the findings that do exist are encouraging (Emmer & Aussiker, 1990; Jones, 1996; Knoff, 1987).

Dreikurs and Interpretation of the Meanings of Behavior

Rudolph Dreikurs developed techniques for interpreting the goals of students' problem behavior and responding accordingly (Dreikurs, 1968; Dreikurs, Grunwald, & Pepper, 1982). Dreikurs stressed the importance of early family dynamics, tracing problems to sources such as parental overprotectiveness or sibling relationships that make certain children feel discouraged or inadequate. He saw children as compensating for feelings of inferiority by developing a style of life designed to protect self-esteem and avoid danger areas. He believed that children have strong needs for belonging, and that those who have not worked out a satisfactory personal adjustment and place in their peer group will strive to do so by pursuing one of the following four goals (listed in increasing order of disturbance): (1) attention, (2) power, (3) revenge, or (4) display of inferiority (in an attempt to gain attention or special treatment).

Dreikurs advised teachers to observe students, diagnose the meaning of their behavior, and then explain it to the students in private. The first step is to analyze problem behavior and determine what goal a student is pursuing. Attention seekers are disruptive and provocative, but they do not openly defy or challenge the teacher. Power seekers do challenge the teacher, but they do not seek to hurt or torment. Revenge seekers do both. Finally, the most seriously discouraged students stop even trying to cope and instead opt to display inferiority and helplessness. If unsure about which goal a student is pursuing, you might speculate aloud to the student to see if you strike a responsive note ("I wonder if you do that just to get attention").

Dreikurs believed that students become willing to abandon self-defeating goals and make more productive commitments once they develop insight into their behavior and its meanings. Therefore, rather than speculate about past causes of the problem behavior, try to make them understand the behavior's current goals. If necessary, confront them about their misbehavior and warn them of the natural consequences (i.e., not artificial punishments) that await them if the behavior does not improve. At the same time, express confidence in them and encourage their progress.

Life-Space Interviewing

Life-space interviewing was developed as a way to foster adjustment and obtain a degree of behavioral compliance from students by providing them with life-space relief (Wood & Long, 1991). Incidents of defiance or serious misbehavior often provide the impetus. In a life-space interview, you talk to a student privately, trying to elicit his or her perceptions of the incident and the events that led up to it. This provides an opportunity for the student to ventilate and for you to express a desire to be helpful.

As the interview proceeds, seek to obtain an accurate and detailed description of what happened and an indication of its meaning to the student. Communicate acceptance of the student's feelings without necessarily accepting the student's actions. Then shift to deciding what must be done, by analyzing to identify places where relief can be provided or changes made (How can the problems that led up to the incident be eliminated or reduced? What should be done if there is a repetition of the incident?). Attempt to provide the following kinds of help, as needed:

1. Help students see and accept reality and abandon defensive distortions.
2. Show them that inappropriate behavior is self-defeating.
3. Clarify values.
4. Suggest means to help them cope more effectively.
5. Help them think for themselves and avoid being led into trouble by peers.
6. Help them express anger by expressing sympathy and understanding.
7. Help them deal with emotions such as panic, rage, or guilt following emotional explosions.
8. Maintain open communication.
9. Provide friendly reminders.
10. Clarify thinking and facilitate decision making.

Glasser's 10-Step Model

William Glasser (1977) suggested a 10-step method for dealing with serious behavior and motivation problems. Thompson and Rudolph (1992) updated and elaborated this intervention model and reviewed research on its implementation in schools. They noted that the 10 steps are divided into three phases. The first phase, consisting of three steps, is designed to help you build a better relationship with the student.

1. Select a student for concentrated attention, and list your typical responses to the student's disruptive behavior. Determine which of your responses tend to be successful and which do not, and resolve not to repeat those that appear to be counterproductive. Often this alone (stopping ineffective interventions) will produce a positive change in the student's behavior.

2. If step 1 is unsuccessful, list and begin implementing change-of-pace interventions that might help break you and the student out of the rut that you have slipped into: "Catch the student being good," act surprised when the student repeats the typical misbehavior, and try not to do what the student expects you to do. Perhaps try a paradoxical intervention strategy such as asking the student to increase the behavior that you actually want to reduce.

3. If necessary, list and implement ways to improve your relationship with the student, and "help him have a better day tomorrow." For example, give the student some undivided, positive attention each day; ask him to run errands for you; give him choices about how to complete a task or assignment; ask his opinion about something relevant to both of you; give him an important classroom or household chore; or negotiate a few rules that you and the student think are fair to both of you. In general, take initiatives to show your concern and imply that things are going to improve.

One or more of the steps in the first phase often will be sufficient to eliminate the problem. Where this is not the case, move to phase 2. This phase also consists of three steps and is devoted to counseling the student.

4. Address the problem behavior more directly through one-line counseling approaches such as briefly (without "lecturing" or threatening) asking the student to stop the undesirable behavior, acknowledging his cooperative efforts (but not thanking him for behaving responsibly as if it were a favor to you), or speculating about the goal of the behavior (as suggested by Dreikurs).

5. Ask the student to describe what he has been doing. This will cause him to analyze the behavior, perhaps for the first time, and begin to see his own responsibility for it (although he may try to rationalize). Once the student describes the problem behavior accurately, simply ask him

to stop. Ordinarily, your questions will incorporate rules on which agreement was reached in a previous negotiation (What did you do? What is our rule? What were you supposed to do? What will you do in the future?).

6. If necessary, the sixth step also involves calling a conference and getting the student to focus on the misbehavior, but it includes announcing that a plan is needed to solve the problem. The plan must be more than a simple pledge to stop misbehavior, because such pledges have not been honored in the past. In effect, it will be a contract that states the problem, outlines a plan of action to address it, and indicates awareness of the positive consequences that will result if behavioral change promises are kept (as well as the negative consequences that will result if they are not). As much as possible, elicit rather than dictate the terms of the contract, helping the student by asking strategic questions (What did you do? How did it help you? What could you do that would help you? What will you do in the future?). If the contract is broken, allow the student to experience the consequences and then meet again to reaffirm the contract or shift to one that the student indicates an ability and willingness to meet and that you can accept. Build forward from there if necessary.

One or more of the four steps in the third phase may be required for students who continue to misbehave, especially if their misbehavior makes it difficult for you to teach and for classmates to learn. This phase emphasizes "time out" or isolation from the classroom at times when the student is not exercising adequate self-control.

7. The seventh step features in-class time out, in which the student is sent to a quiet corner, study carrel, or private work area. Students should understand that they have the choice of being with the group and behaving or misbehaving and being isolated. During their periods of isolation, they are charged with devising plans for ensuring that they follow the rules in the future. Isolation continues until the student devises a plan that meets with your approval and makes a commitment to follow it.

8. Some students may require in-school suspension, or time out outside the classroom. The procedure is basically the same one described in step 7, but now the student will have to deal with the principal or someone else other than yourself. However, this person will repeat earlier steps in the sequence and press for a plan that is acceptable.

9. The ninth step applies only to students who remain out of control during in-school suspension. It involves calling their parents to take them home and then starting over with them the next day.

10. The tenth step is removal from school and referral to another agency. Before this step is implemented, try to arrange for the student to learn about what will happen to him once he is caught up in the juvenile

justice system. Concrete realization of the consequences of continued mis-behavior may finally motivate commitment to change.

Glasser's 10-step approach is attractive to a great many teachers be-cause it provides a sequence of specific steps for dealing with students who have not responded to less formal methods. It also illustrates features common to several approaches that seem to be converging. One is insis-tence on minimal standards of in-school behavior, regardless of students' personal backgrounds. Another is insistence that students are respons-ible for their own behavior and will be held to that responsibility. Teachers will try to help students solve their problems, but they are the students' problems and not the teachers'. This approach may seem harsh, but it as-sumes that rules are reasonable and fairly administered and that teachers try to be helpful, cooperate with students in making feasible adjustments, and in general maintain a positive, problem-solving stance. When these assumptions do not hold, Glasser's methods, like any others, can be des-tructive. An authoritarian teacher, for instance, might concentrate more on building a case against a problem student than on trying to be helpful.

Gordon and "No-Lose" Agreements

Thomas Gordon (1974) developed Teacher Effectiveness Training (TET), a program that trains teachers to defuse conflicts by arranging no-lose agreements with students. The process starts with identification of *problem ownership*. Some problems are owned strictly by teachers, some strictly by students, and some by both teachers and students. Problem solving pro-ceeds more smoothly when all parties involved identify problem owner-ship accurately and respond accordingly.

Students own the problem when their needs are being frustrated but the teacher's are not. Examples of student-owned problems include anxi-ety, inhibition, and poor self-concept. For such problems, Gordon recom-mended door openers (invitations for students to talk about the problem), passive listening (showing that you hear and understand what students are saying), and especially active listening. Active listening goes beyond simply paying attention and showing that you understand; it includes providing feedback that responds to the underlying meanings of students' messages. Thus, when students express fears or negative statements about themselves, active listeners do not scoff at these statements or attempt to cheer the students up by praising or distracting them. Instead, they indi-cate that they heard what the student said, take it seriously, and are sym-pathetic ("So you would like to join in the game on the playground, but you hesitate to ask because you are afraid that the other kids might say 'No' ").

Active listening helps students to dissipate their feelings before getting down to work when something upsetting has happened, and it promotes smooth parent–teacher conferences. Through active listening, you help students not by assuming responsibility for their problems but by helping them to find their own solutions and become more independent, confident, and self-reliant.

When students own the problem, it is important for them to communicate and for teachers to be listeners and counselors. However, different responses are required when students create *teacher-owned problems* by behaving in ways that make teachers frustrated or angry. When the teacher owns the problem, the teacher does the communicating by sending messages to students and trying to influence them to change.

"I" and "You" Messages

Gordon listed ineffective techniques for trying to change students: statements that lead to confrontations, "solution" messages that induce only dependent and artificial compliance even when they do work, and put-down messages that breed resentment without bringing about constructive changes. He noted that most of these ineffective messages are "you" messages, used when the situation calls for "I" messages because the teacher has the problem and thus must do the communicating. "I" messages reveal feelings and vulnerabilities but in ways that pay off by fostering intimacy and describing the problem without imputing malevolent motives to the student.

"I" messages have three major parts. The first part indicates the specific behavior that leads to the problem ("When I get interrupted . . . "). The second specifies the effect on the teacher (". . . I have to start over and repeat things unnecessarily . . . "). The third part specifies feelings generated within the teacher (". . . and I become frustrated"). Taken together, the three parts link specific student behavior as the cause of a specific effect on the teacher, which in turn produces undesirable feelings in the teacher.

"No-Lose" Method of Problem Solving

Gordon maintained that combinations of environmental manipulation, active listening, and communication through "I" messages will solve most problems. Sometimes the needs motivating unacceptable student behavior are very strong, however, or the relationship with the teacher is very poor, and conflict will continue. Genuine conflict involves *problems owned by both students and teachers*. It must be approached in ways that avoid winning or losing and that meet the needs of all parties involved. Gordon's no-lose method is a process of searching until such a solution is found.

Prerequisites for use of the method include active listening (students must believe that their needs will be accepted if they are to risk serious negotiation), use of good "I" messages to state your needs clearly and honestly, and communication to students that this is a new and different approach (if you have not been using it previously). There are six steps: (1) Define the problem, (2) generate solutions, (3) evaluate these solutions, (4) decide which solution is best, (5) determine how to implement the solution, and (6) assess how well the solution is solving the problem.

Defining the problem includes accurately locating problem ownership and identifying only those people who are really part of the problem. This continues until everyone is agreed. It is vital that the problem be described in terms of conflicting needs, not competing solutions.

When generating solutions, simply list them. Do not evaluate them prematurely. Once evaluation starts, eliminate solutions that are objectionable to anyone for any reason. Decide which solution is best by searching for consensus without resorting to voting. Test proposed solutions by imagining their consequences. When agreement is reached, draw up specific implementation plans and responsibilities, including plans for later assessment. The result should be a no-lose agreement that everyone explicitly states satisfaction with and readiness to honor.

Not all agreements are honored, however. Agreements may be broken when students do not perceive the conflict in the first place, seeing their own problem but not the teacher's problem; do not believe that their needs have been heard and understood by the teacher; or agree to the solution only because of peer or teacher pressure. Gordon warned against using power when students break agreements. Instead, he suggested strong "I" messages to communicate your disappointment and indicate that now you share a new problem. However, he admitted that power assertion may be necessary when there is danger involved, when students do not understand the logic of your position, or when there is no time for more leisurely problem solving.

Quality Improvement Efforts in Schools

Additional principles for dealing with problem students have emerged from efforts to improve the overall quality and effectiveness of schooling, either for students in general or for at-risk students in particular. Along with better instruction in the formal curriculum, many of these improvement efforts have focused on school climate or other affective aspects of school quality.

William Glasser has continued to develop his ideas. His 10-step intervention model was originally developed as an application of a treatment approach called reality therapy. More recently, Glasser incorporated these and other notions into what he called control theory. He emphasized that people are responsible for their own goals, decisions, and general degree of happiness in their lives, and he described methods for taking control of one's life. In his book *Control Theory in the Classroom* (1986), he urged teachers to function as managers who motivate students by empowering them with the responsibility for learning. Drawing parallels to management practices that have been used successfully in business and industry, he suggested an emphasis on cooperative learning, in which students work in pairs and small groups to collaborate in the learning process.

More recently, in *The Quality School: Managing Students without Coercion*, he contrasted two managerial models: the boss manager and the lead manager. Boss managers motivate by punishment rather than reinforcement, telling rather than showing, overpowering rather than empowering, and emphasizing rule enforcement rather than cooperation. Lead managers do the reverse. Glasser emphasized that the lead manager approach is much more compatible with control theory notions of empowering students to take control of their lives at school, and that it is much more likely to be successful in eliciting their cooperation than the boss manager approach.

Complementary ideas about school and classroom management have been advanced by Carl Rogers and H. Jerome Freiberg (1994) in the book *Freedom to Learn*. They put forth a model of person-centered classrooms in which students are taught to develop self-discipline by making choices, organizing their time, setting goals and priorities, helping and caring about one another, listening, constructing a social fabric, being peacemakers when others engage in disputes, trusting one another, and engaging collaboratively in the learning process. They emphasized that creating a person-centered classroom is not merely a method but a philosophy: Unless you believe that your students can be trusted with the responsibilities involved, you won't be successful in granting them the freedom they need if they are to make their own choices (and mistakes). Moving from external discipline to self-discipline may take time, and you and your students may need to move toward it in small steps. Such movement may be well worth the effort, however. Classroom management interventions in inner-city schools that were derived from the person-centered classroom notion have produced remarkable improvements in both school climate and student achievement (Freiberg, Stein, & Huang, 1995).

The same has been true of interventions based on the school development model described by James Comer (1980) in his book *School Power*. Developed as a way to improve the educational experiences of poor minority youth, Comer's program emphasizes building supportive bonds among students, their parents, and the school staff in order to promote a positive school climate. It is designed to create a school environment where students feel comfortable, valued, and secure. In such an environment, they form positive emotional bonds with teachers and parents and a positive attitude toward school, which in turn facilitates their academic learning. Three principles underlie the process: (1) schools must review their problems in open discussion and a no-fault atmosphere; (2) collaborative working relationships must be developed among the principal, teachers, parents, community leaders, and mental and physical health care workers; and (3) all decisions must be reached by consensus rather than by decree (Haynes & Comer, 1993).

Each Comer school is governed by three teams: (1) The school planning and management team is headed by the principal but includes teachers, administrators, parents, support staff, and a child development specialist. This team is responsible for identifying targets for social and academic improvement, establishing policy guidelines, developing systematic school plans, responding to problems, and monitoring program activities. (2) The mental health team is also headed by the principal and includes teachers, administrators, psychologists, social workers, and nurses. It analyzes social and behavioral patterns within the school and determines how to solve chronic problems by applying principles of child development. (3) The parents' group tries to involve parents in all levels of school activity, from volunteering in the classroom to school governance.

In the context of dealing with problem students, application of child development principles within the Comer model implies communicating to the student something like the following: "We know that you are unhappy and that that is a big part of the reason that you are having trouble in school. We want you in our school, we like you, we know that you can learn and get along, and we want to help you do so. But we cannot tolerate your attacking other children and showing disrespect for your teacher. We know that you don't want to do these things either. We are going to go a step at a time in helping you to make it at school. When you are doing OK at a given step, you can move to the next. You let us know when you think you need more help. When you are not getting along well, we will hold you back. It's up to you. Do you have any ideas about how we can handle this whole thing better?"

This beginning would be followed by attempts to ignore minor misbehavior and encourage activities that would bring the student positive feedback and success. Where this was unsuccessful and the student increased misbehavior or began to lose inner control, interventions would be required. However, these would be conceived as attempts to prevent the student from hurting someone, engendering more disapproval, embarrassing himself, or increasing his general sense of failure. To prevent these outcomes, the student would be helped to leave the room gracefully by communicating messages such as the following: "I can see that you are having a tough time today. Before we have a big problem, I want you to go and sit in the principal's office for a while until you can pull your-self together. It's 1 P.M. now, and you ought to be able to do that by 1:30." If necessary, the teacher or another staff person trained for this task would speak to the student while he was out of the room, to talk about the problem, help him cool down, and help him begin to think about better ways to handle the situation. Throughout the process, the emphasis is on helping the student avoid embarrassment and stay in control, not on punishing misbehavior. On a "bad day," it is assumed that something is bothering the student, so he or she is invited to talk about it and is en-couraged and helped to reestablish self-control and productive behavior.

Developing Helping Skills in Teachers

Kottler and Kottler (1993) synthesized the helping skills developed over the years by school counselors and suggested ways in which teachers can use these skills with their students. They began by identifying helping at-titudes, which include being nonjudgmental in listening to students and developing relationships with them characterized by authenticity, genuine-ness, caring, respect, and compassion. Acts of helping are not mere ap-plications of skills and techniques but attempts to bring comfort and constructive input to students who are struggling or in great pain.

Common elements among the helping skills emphasized in various approaches to counseling include the following: bringing troubled stu-dents into a receptive mode by creating a favorable climate for change and projecting confidence and reassurance that you are prepared to help them; establishing a therapeutic relationship that features an alliance that is open, trusting, accepting, and safe for students who will be asked to take personal risks in facing up to their problems; creating opportunities for students to experience the cathartic processes that result when they are given the opportunity to talk without interruption about their fears and concerns; promoting self-understanding by increasing students' aware-ness of themselves and their relationships with others; providing instruc-tion, opportunities to practice, and feedback concerning improved coping skills; and encouraging them to try out these skills in everyday social contexts.

The counseling process itself involves a series of steps. First, the teacher develops an assessment of the problem by asking questions, reflect-ing the student's feelings, and clarifying the content of what is being presented. Once the problem is clarified, the teacher begins to dig deep-er, using reflective skills to help the student clarify thoughts and feelings. Where appropriate, there may be movement from empathy and reflec-tion to more active skills such as confrontation, interpretation, self-disclosure, and giving of information to help the student understand his own role in creating his problems. Once the problem is well understood, the focus shifts to action and the student gets opportunities to apply the insights that have been developed. Here, the teacher and student work together to set realistic goals, establish commitments to follow through on these plans, and arrange to evaluate progress and respond accordingly at a designated point in the future.

AN ECLECTIC YET COHERENT APPROACH

The research on effective classroom management and the advice on modifying behavior, teaching strategies, resolving conflicts, and socializing students within a positive school climate that has been summarized in the first two chapters can be synthesized by identifying an underlying common set of principles. These principles provide the elements for a comprehensive approach that is eclectic (it draws from various sources rather than just a single theory or line of research) yet also coherent (internally consistent, free from contradictions). The approach includes respect for student individuality and tolerance for individual differences, willingness to try to understand and assist students with special needs or problems, reliance on instruction and persuasion rather than power assertion, and modeling and encouragement of prosocial values. However, it also includes recognition that students have responsibilities along with their rights, and that they will have to suffer the consequences if they persist in failing to fulfill those responsibilities.

Good and Brophy (1995, 1997) drew on these common principles to suggest ways for you to observe and interview problem students in order to develop an understanding of why they behave as they do, as well as strategies for developing productive personal relationships with such students and working with them individually. They stressed the importance of supporting the positive elements of these students' self-concepts, projecting positive expectations about their willingness and ability to change behavior, setting realistic goals and monitoring progress toward attaining them, and emphasizing your role as a helper over your role as an authority figure (while still exerting that authority).

Gathering Information

When faced with a behavior problem, you first need to decide whether or not to gather information before taking action. Sometimes the situation is quite clear and no additional information is needed, as when a student calls out a provocative remark or creates a disturbance. Unless it is so serious as to require a conference, the situation can be handled with a brief response such as, "Cool it, John." Don't interrupt the lesson to ask unnecessary questions, especially not rhetorical questions such as "John, how many times do I have to tell you not to do that?"

When it is necessary to gather information, do so in ways that avoid causing any student to lose face. Talk with involved students in private and state that everything said during the discussion will be held in confidence (unless some explicit agreement to the contrary is made). Insist that students listen while their classmates speak, reassure them that they all will have a chance to give their versions, and proceed toward the truth gradually by asking questions and pointing out discrepancies in different versions. Concentrate on establishing exactly what happened and trying to determine the motives behind the actions. Eliciting motives is important because students often misinterpret one another's behavior, such as by interpreting accidents as deliberate provocations or minor teasing as serious insults.

Do not allow students to evade responsibility for their own behavior or project it onto others. Some students will attempt to excuse their behavior by giving reasons, such as "She started it," "People who leave money lying around like that *should* have it stolen," or "He looked at me funny." These students will need help in becoming more realistic in reflecting on their behavior.

Sometimes your efforts will reach an impasse because one or more students are lying or withholding part of the truth. Usually it is best to acknowledge this openly and express both disappointment that the whole truth is not being told and the expectation that it will be told. If further efforts still do not succeed, you will need to decide whether the discussion itself will end the matter or some follow up will be required.

Finding Solutions

Once all needed (or forthcoming) information is collected, the next step is to work out a solution. At this stage, focus attention on the future and on solving the problems that led to the conflict. Cut short attempts to rehash points already gone over by reminding students that everyone understands the problem now, so it is time to work out a solution.

Solutions should be perceived as positive, not punitive, in intent and effect. They should be acceptable to everyone, not just the majority, and should be considered tentative and subject to review at a designated future date.

You may have to limit the range of possible solutions by stating clearly that certain things cannot be done or are outside school rules. If students are unable to come up with realistic suggestions, you will have to make suggestions yourself. This should be open to comment and evaluation. If students endorse a proposed solution, ask them to think carefully be-

fore committing to it, again emphasizing that they must make the decision and will be responsible for abiding by it. Do not allow them to come
away from the meeting with the idea that you foisted a demand on them
that they did not really agree to.

If students simply refuse to cooperate in seeking acceptable solutions,
or if they persistently fail to follow through on their commitments, you
may need to involve the parents or seek help from a social worker, counselor, school psychologist, school administrator, or fellow teacher. The
titles held by these resource persons are less important than the quality
of their observations and advice. Discussing the problem with a good
resource person, preferably one who is familiar with the situation and
has observed in your classroom several times, may help you get new insights or specific suggestions.

You can set the stage for effective problem solving with parents by
developing collaborative relationships with them right from the beginning of the school year. Family involvement in children's education is associated with better attendance, more positive attitudes toward school,
and higher academic achievement.

If you choose to involve parents, bear in mind that your goal is to
find solutions for the problem, not to find someone to blame for it. The
parents are likely to be embarrassed about their child's problems and fearful of interacting with you because they believe that the problems are their
fault. Whether or not this is true, you will need to focus on problem solving rather than blaming if you want the parents to play a constructive role.

For example, you might contact the parents, arrange for a meeting
at the school (or by phone if necessary), and begin by saying something
like, "I'm seeing some concerns with Sarah in the classroom that I'd like
to share with you. I think that if we work together, we can help Sarah deal
with these problems successfully." Then describe your concerns in a nonjudgmental way and ask the parents if they are seeing any of these
problems in Sarah's behavior at home or in the neighborhood.

Sometimes these inquiries will yield information about stress factors
in the child's life (an impending divorce, a death or serious illness in the
family, etc.). Such information might help you to put the child's classroom
behavior into perspective (e.g., seeing it as preoccupation with or defense
against fears, and indirectly as a cry for help). This knowledge would make
you more informed and more able to express your concern directly in
private interactions with the student ("Sarah, I understand that your
brother is sick. I wondered if sometimes you think about this instead of
working on your assignments").

Merely informing parents about problems will not be helpful. If they
get the impression that they are expected to "do something," they might
just threaten or punish their child and let it go at that. Make suggestions
about how they might help their child, and if necessary, try to resocialize

their attitudes or beliefs about effective child rearing. In particular, emphasize the need to think of punishment as a last resort and the need for confidence and positive expectations. These are two principles that many parents violate when their children have problems.

If you call parents mostly just to get information, make this clear to them. State your observations about their child, and ask if they can add anything that might increase your understanding. Find out how much they know about the problem and what their explanation for it is. If some plan of action emerges, discuss and agree on its details.

If no parental action seems appropriate, bring the conference to some form of closure. ("I'm glad we've had a chance to talk about Jason today. You've given me a better understanding of him. I'll keep working with him in the classroom and let you know about his progress. Meanwhile, if anything comes up that I ought to know, please give me a call.") The parents should emerge from the conference knowing what to tell their child about it and what, if anything, you are requesting them to do.

If a serious problem persists despite the cooperative efforts of the parents, yourself, and other professionals at your school, you may need to work with the parents on getting help for the child through mental health agencies or treatment resources in the community. Parents are more likely to accept such suggestions and seek such help when they believe that their child's teacher is genuinely concerned about the child and the family. If parents believe that you like and respect them and their child, that you do not blame them for the problem, and that you have kept them informed and involved as you developed and implemented strategies for addressing the problem at school and at home, they will be more willing to seek professional help where it appears to be necessary, even though they may find the idea threatening to their pride or self-esteem. For more ideas about developing relationships with parents, see Christenson and Conoley (1992), Hoffman (1991), Kauffman and colleagues (1993), McCaslin and Good (1996), Swap (1993), and Weinstein and Mignano (1993).

CONCLUSION

Consistent use of the principles and techniques outlined in these first two chapters will help you to minimize behavior problems and deal effectively with the ones that do arise. You can then adapt and supplement this approach as needed to respond to the particulars of the situation.

Subsequent chapters explore some of the adaptations and supplementary techniques involved in responding to the 12 problem-student types addressed in the Classroom Strategy Study. Chapter 3 provides an overview of the study and a summary of its general findings.

3

Teachers' Ideas about Coping with Problem Students

Chapters 1 and 2 presented conclusions developed by researchers studying child rearing, behavior modification, or classroom management, as well as views on crisis intervention and student socialization expressed by mental health professionals. We now turn to the views of teachers, as expressed in statements about how they perceive and cope with problem students. These statements were gathered in a large interview study called the Classroom Strategy Study (CSS). The background, design, and general findings of this study are summarized briefly in this chapter and in more detail in the Appendix. More specific findings dealing with particular problem-student types are summarized in Chapters 4 through 15.

BACKGROUND AND RATIONALE OF THE CLASSROOM STRATEGY STUDY

The study was initiated as a response to requests by teachers for information about how to cope with students who are unusually time-consuming, difficult, or frustrating to teach. It was designed to describe and evaluate strategies that could be used by regular elementary teachers (i.e., not school psychologists, social workers, resource teachers, or other specialists), working within the constraints normally associated with the teacher role.

We asked the participating teachers to respond to descriptions of the 12 problem-student types (see Table 3.1) and to vignettes depicting incidents of troublesome behavior involving such students. The teachers were asked to tell us their general strategies for responding to each problem-

TABLE 3.1. The 12 Problem-Student Types

1. *Failure syndrome.* These children are convinced that they cannot do the work. They often avoid starting or give up easily. They expect to fail, even after succeeding.
   a. Easily frustrated
   b. Gives up easily
   c. Says, "I can't do it"

2. *Perfectionist.* These children are unduly anxious about making mistakes. Their self-imposed standards are unrealistically high, so that they are never satisfied with their work (when they should be).
   a. Too much of a "perfectionist"
   b. Often anxious/fearful/frustrated about quality of work
   c. Holds back from class participation unless sure of self

3. *Underachiever/alienated.* These children do a minimum to just "get by." They do not value schoolwork.
   a. Indifferent to school
   b. Minimum work output
   c. Not challenged by schoolwork; poorly motivated

4. *Low achiever.* These children have difficulty, even though they may be willing to work. Their problem is low potential or lack of readiness rather than poor motivation.
   a. Difficulty following directions
   b. Difficulty completing work
   c. Poor retention
   d. Progresses slowly

5. *Hostile–aggressive.* These children express hostility through direct, intense behaviors. They are not easily controlled.
   a. Intimidates and threatens
   b. Hits and pushes
   c. Damages property
   d. Antagonizes
   e. Hostile
   f. Easily angered

6. *Passive–aggressive.* These children express opposition and resistance to the teacher, but indirectly. It is often hard to tell whether they are resisting deliberately or not.
   a. Subtly oppositional and stubborn
   b. Tries to control
   c. Borderline compliance with rules
   d. Mars property rather than damages
   e. Disrupts surreptitiously
   f. Drags feet

(continued)

TABLE 3.1. (cont.)

---

7. *Defiant.* These children resist authority and carry on a power struggle with the teacher. They want to have their way and not be told what to do.
   a. Resists verbally
      (1) "You can't make me"
      (2) "You can't tell me what to do"
      (3) Makes derogatory statements about teacher to others
   b. Resists nonverbally
      (1) Frowns, grimaces, mimics teacher
      (2) Arms folded, hands on hips, foot stomping
      (3) Looks away when being spoken to
      (4) Laughs at inappropriate times
      (5) May be physically violent toward teacher
      (6) Deliberately does what teacher says not to do

8. *Hyperactive.* These children show excessive and almost constant movement, even when sitting. Often their movements appear to be without purpose.
   a. Squirms, wiggles, jiggles, scratches
   b. Easily excitable
   c. Blurts out answers and comments
   d. Often out of seat
   e. Bothers other children with noises, movements
   f. Energetic but poorly directed
   g. Excessively touches objects or people

9. *Distractible.* These children have short attention spans. They seem unable to sustain attention and concentration. They are easily distracted by sounds, sights, or speech.
   a. Has difficulty adjusting to changes
   b. Rarely completes tasks
   c. Easily distracted

10. *Immature.* These children have poorly developed emotional stability, self-control, self-care abilities, social skills, and/or responsibility.
    a. Often exhibits behavior normal for younger children
    b. May cry easily
    c. Loses belongings
    d. Frequently appears helpless, incompetent, and/or dependent

11. *Peer rejected.* These children seek peer interaction but are rejected, ignored, or excluded.
    a. Forced to work and play alone
    b. Lacks social skills
    c. Often picked on or teased

12. *Shy/withdrawn.* These children avoid personal interaction, are quiet and unobtrusive, and do not respond well to others.
    a. Quiet and sober
    b. Does not initiate or volunteer
    c. Does not call attention to self

---

student type and their more specific strategies for responding to the incidents depicted in the vignettes.

The 12 patterns are defined so as to be mutually exclusive, but several could exist in the same student. For example, distractibility and hyperactivity are often seen in the same individuals, and either or both of these could be combined with underachievement or hostile–aggressive behavior. Even where different patterns exist in the same student, however, teachers use different strategies to address the different behavior problems. Consequently, the teachers were asked to consider each behavior pattern separately.

The 12 problem-student types included four subgroups: (1) problems in achievement progress (low achiever, failure syndrome, perfectionist, underachiever/alienated), (2) hostility problems (hostile–aggressive, passive–aggressive, defiant), (3) problems in meeting student-role requirements (hyperactive, distractible, immature), and (4) social isolation problems (peer rejected, shy/withdrawn). These four subgroups of problem types are addressed, respectively, in Parts II, III, IV, and V of this book.

IDENTIFYING AND INTERVIEWING TEACHERS

Ideas about coping with problem students were solicited from teachers who had been nominated by their principals for participation in our study. All of these teachers had at least 3 years of experience, and most had 10 years or more. We interviewed 98 teachers, of whom 54 taught in a small city school system and 44 taught in inner-city schools operated by one of our nation's largest cities. The teachers were distributed roughly evenly across grades K through 6.

Teachers were identified through their principals' ratings of their success in coping with problem students. Some had been nominated by their principals as "truly outstanding in handling difficult students—minimizing their problem behavior and responding to it effectively when it does occur." The rest had been nominated as average or typical in their abilities to handle problem students—falling between the 10 percent or so who are outstanding and the 10 percent or so who are overwhelmed with problems and cannot cope with difficult students. In characterizing this second group of teachers to the principals, we said that "we seek the 80 percent or so of teachers who are neither outstandingly effective nor notably ineffective in this regard—teachers who maintain satisfactory classroom control and who usually can cope with the problems that difficult students present, even though they are not as outstanding as the teachers named above."

We recruited teachers by first obtaining a commitment from an "out-

standing" teacher and then recruiting a paired teacher for the comparison group. If possible, we paired the outstanding teacher with another
teacher working at the same grade in the same school. Otherwise, the outstanding teacher was paired with a teacher working at an adjacent grade
in the same school or at the same grade in a nearby school serving similar students.

Participating teachers were observed and interviewed by research assistants who did not know how the teachers had been rated by their principals. The teachers were asked about how they might respond to each
of the 12 problem-student types and to each of 24 vignettes (2 for each
problem student type) that depicted common examples of the kinds of
troublesome behavior that these problem students present. Four of these
vignettes were shown at the beginning of Chapter 1; the complete set is
given in Table A.1 in the Appendix.

The behavior problems depicted in the vignettes were described within contexts and in terms familiar to elementary teachers. There were no
references to student age, grade, geographic location, or other context
factors that might apply to certain teachers but not to others. However,
the depicted students were given common names that identified them as
male or female. This was because teachers found it easy and natural to
talk about "Tom" or "Mary" but not about someone described only as "a
student."

Interviewing began with the vignettes because we wanted teachers
to respond to them "cold," without having had a chance to think about
them beforehand. The vignettes were presented one at a time, and teachers
were asked to read them and then tell us what they would say and do in
the depicted situations. Thus, the vignettes elicited teachers' immediate,
reactive responses to events initiated by problem students, whereas the
subsequent interviews elicited their more general strategies for dealing
with each problem-student type. These strategies tended to be more
proactive—planned and initiated by the teachers themselves.

After completing the 24 vignettes, teachers were given the 12 problem-
type descriptions shown in Table 3.1 and asked to take them home and
think about how they handled such problem students. They were given
at least a week to prepare for the interview and were encouraged to make
notes. However, we explained that we wanted their personal experience-
based knowledge, so that they should not consult books, colleagues, or
resource persons. We wanted them to draw on their knowledge and teaching experience in order to tell how to handle each of these 12 types of
problem students, by first explaining their general philosophy about dealing with each type of student and then listing specific strategies they would
use. They also would be invited to explain the reasons for their views and
strategy preferences, to indicate any qualifications on when or how cer-

tain strategies might need to be implemented, and to identify strategies that they had found to be unsuccessful.

DATA CODING AND ANALYSIS

The vignette and interview responses were transcribed and coded into categories that describe the teachers' perceptions of and strategies for coping with problem students. For example, the interview responses were coded into one or more of eight categories describing general approaches to the problem: (1) controlling or suppressing problem behavior without doing any of the things described in categories 2 through 8, (2) shaping improved behavior through successive approximations, (3) providing instruction or other help designed to enable the student to recognize and eliminate the problem, (4) teaching the student strategies for coping with the problem (as opposed to eliminating it), (5) identifying and eliminating an assumed underlying cause of the problem, (6) counseling or other techniques for increasing the student's insight, (7) trying to change the student's beliefs or attitudes (and thus behavior) through persuasion or appeal to reason, or (8) providing encouragement or other supportive treatment designed to develop greater confidence and a more positive self-concept.

Interview responses also were coded for more specific problem-solving strategies such as breaking tension with a humorous or distracting remark, attempting to inhibit undesirable behavior or to communicate support through physical proximity or tone of voice, using time-out procedures (either as punishment or as a way to give the student a chance to settle down and regain composure), rule reminders, performance contracts, modeling of desired behavior, praise or criticism, temporary special consideration ("kid gloves treatment") to students who had become upset or frustrated, changing the student's assignment or working conditions, providing academic help, or involving peers, parents, school administrators, or other professionals to support or pressure the student. Responses also were coded for such distinctions as whether or not they included long-term prevention or solution strategies in addition to immediate reactions to problem behavior, whether the teacher recognized the possibility of different subtypes of the problem and suggested different strategies for handling them, and the different teacher motives that were stated or implied.

Scores from this coding were subjected to statistical analyses that yielded two general types of information: (1) descriptive data indicating the relative frequency of each response in the sample of teachers as a whole and in various subsamples, and (2) correlational data indicating relationships between these responses and ratings of the teachers' effectiveness in coping with problem students. For more details about the study's design, data collection, procedures, and statistical analyses, see the Appendix of this book, Brophy and McCaslin (1992), or Brophy (1995).

SOME GENERAL FINDINGS

General trends in the teachers' responses indicated a tendency to emphasize brief verbal responses that could be made on the spot (possibly backed by a conference later) over responses that were more time-consuming. The teachers also preferred neutral or supportive methods over punitive methods (although this varied dramatically with the type of problem behavior involved). Finally, the responses tended to be based on common sense and personal experience rather than expert advice or well-articulated theories of diagnosis and intervention.

Other than a few ideas and techniques picked up through brief inservice workshops or individual reading, the teachers' responses showed little familiarity with theoretical concepts and treatment principles. What they said about controlling behavior through reward and punishment usually fell short of systematic knowledge about behavior modification, and what they said about using personal relationships and talking to students about their problems usually fell short of systematic knowledge about counseling and psychotherapy.

Given that few of these teachers had had courses in classroom management, let alone in methods of diagnosing and treating problem students, these trends are not surprising. However, they do verify that even teachers considered experts at dealing with problem students are usually working from rules of thumb developed through experience rather than from well-articulated knowledge developed through formal education.

Response trends varied with the nature of the problem behavior depicted. The teachers tended to respond with concern and attempts to help when the depicted problems were purely academic (low achievers) or confined to anxiety or difficulty in coping with the demands of school (failure syndrome, perfectionist, rejected by peers). However, the teachers tended to respond with rejection and an orientation toward control or punishment when the depicted problems were disruptive or threatening to their authority (defiant, hostile–aggressive). These findings are consistent with other findings indicating that adults tend to respond with concern, assistance, and attempts at long-term solution when children's problems do not threaten or irritate them, but often respond with anger, rejection, and emphasis on short-term control or punishment when they do.

Response trends also varied with differences among the teachers. Teachers who worked in inner-city schools, teachers who worked in the upper grades, and teachers who emphasized the instructor role over the socializer role were more likely to restrict their responses to brief, impersonal calls for behavior change backed by threat of punishment if necessary. In contrast, teachers who worked in the smaller city, teachers who worked in the lower grades, and teachers who emphasized the socializer role over the instructor role frequently offered more personalized, extended, and supportive responses that called for a greater variety of problem-solving strategies.

Differences between higher rated and lower rated teachers were identified through correlations with the principals' ratings or with combination scores that reflected both the principals' ratings and ratings made by the research assistants who observed and interviewed the teachers. In general, these analyses indicated that higher rated teachers showed more willingness to become personally involved in working with problem students, expressed more confidence in their ability to elicit significant improvement, and provided richer descriptions of long-term prevention or solution strategies (developing personal relationships, providing support and encouragement, teaching or modeling coping skills, resocializing attitudes and beliefs). However, there were interesting qualifications and elaborations on these general patterns in the findings for each problem-student type, as well as interesting contrasts in findings within each pair of vignettes. These findings, detailed in Chapters 4 through 15, illustrate how general strategies interact with situational factors when teachers respond to particular incidents.

II

Students with Achievement Problems

Among students who show unsatisfactory achievement progress, we studied four subtypes: low achievers and three types of underachievers. *Low achievers* are students who make limited progress because of limited ability or readiness rather than because of motivation problems (although motivation problems are likely to develop in most such students if they continually experience failure and frustration). Low achievers' slow progress may reflect the level of success that can be expected from them given their limited abilities, In contrast, *underachievers* work below their abilities. Some underachieve because of *low self-concept/failure syndrome/learned helplessness* reasons: They become so defeated that they eventually give up serious learning efforts. Others underachieve because of neurotic *perfectionism:* They are more concerned about avoiding mistakes than about learning, so they are inhibited about classroom participation and counterproductively compulsive in their work habits. Finally, some students underachieve because of *alienation:* They see little or no value in what is taught at school, so they do only enough to get by rather than trying to do their best.

Findings concerning these four student types are presented in Chapters 4 through 7, beginning in Chapter 4 with low achievers. Unlike the other 11 problem-student types addressed, low achievers' problems are rooted primarily in limited academic abilities rather than disturbances in personal adjustment generally or in adaptation to the role of student at school.

4

Low-Achieving Students

ow achievers were described to the teachers as follows: These children have difficulty, even though they may be willing to work. Their problem is low potential or lack of readiness rather than poor motivation. They:

1. Have difficulty following directions
2. Have difficulty completing work
3. Display poor retention
4. Progress slowly

What special strategies might you use to minimize such problems and help these students to function more successfully in your classroom? Before reading further, take time to think about this and make notes about your ideas.

CSS INTERVIEW EXCERPTS

Here is what three of the CSS teachers had to say about teaching low achievers.

A LOWER RATED TEACHER

"I have a little girl like this right now. These children could be immature. They could not be ready for first-grade work at all. They may need to go back to kindergarten. The first thing I would do is call the parent right away and find out if this child has had problems before. They probably have. We could look in the cumulative file. If we had the other teacher in the building, we could talk to her or him

and then check with the parent. I would think that this child probably was not ready for this grade, and maybe the best thing would be
to repeat kindergarten. Or they might have a learning disability, so
we could check them for that. We could also talk with the counselor
about him and then possibly have her check this child. I think this
type of child would have trouble all year. It sounds like they wouldn't
fit in a regular classroom, although lots of times we have to keep them
in our room. My goal would be to put this child where they could
do something, have a learning experience, but by staying in this room
you would have to design a special program for them that would be
a lot easier than the one that most of the children are ready for. Then
at the end of the year, hopefully the parents would let the kids stay
in the same grade, or if possible they could have gone back to kindergarten."

This teacher seemed oriented more toward removing low achievers
from her[1] classroom than toward finding ways to instruct them successfully. She was influenced heavily by diagnostic labels and notions of readiness, so that even when she did speak of individualizing instruction to
meet low achievers' needs, she spoke of giving them easy work rather than
of helping them to make forward progress.

A HIGHER RATED TEACHER

"When they have difficulty in following directions, I would give them
only one or two directions at a time and gradually build up on following directions until they were able to do it with more competen-
cy. When they are having difficulty completing work, if the work is
definitely too hard, I would cut down the workload and put them
into a situation where they can meet more successes. I often have other
children work with them on reading. The reverse of this is that these
children make excellent tutors to other children who are at about
the same ability level. Not only are they teaching other children, but
they are getting the material themselves and have to understand it
before they can explain it to someone else. This has been extremely
successful in dealing with a couple of cases that I have had. If I find
the child isn't making any headway whatsoever, I would think that

[1] I have minimized the use of gendered pronouns by pluralizing most references to teachers
or students. Where pluralizing was unfeasible or potentially confusing, I have usually referred
to both genders (he or she, him or her). Even this convention was not always suitable, however,
so I occasionally found it necessary to refer to a teacher or student in the singular case.
In these instances, I have used female pronouns to refer to teachers and male pronouns
to refer to students.

he probably has more severe learning difficulties than what I could cope with alone in the classroom. I would refer him to our special services where he would be evaluated. If it proved that this child was of just plain low ability, I would see about getting a university student to tutor the child on Tuesdays and Thursdays when they come in. My general thought about a child like this is that you have his motivation and you have his bodily presence within the classroom, and because he is so willing, there has to be a method in which you can deal with him. He needs to meet successes so that he doesn't become completely turned off by school. My most successful strategy in working with this child has been having them tutor children of the same ability. Probably one of the least successful things would be to send them back to their seat and say, 'Oh, go ahead and do it, you can do it' or 'Do as much as you can.' It's better to set a specific goal and say, 'Why don't you try to complete this much, because these are things we have talked about. At the end of that time, bring it back to me,' so that he can have an immediate reward for it. It sounds very structured to always set goals for a child, but I think children having a lot of difficulty need to have specific limitations set on them and to see that they are actually able to do it. . . . My math program is completely individualized, as well as spelling and some of the other areas, so they would be working in a book that they are able to meet successes in. It would be almost impossible and completely deflating to them to have to compete with a child who is able to do things readily and quickly."

This teacher spoke not just of adjusting assignments to students' levels but also of helping them to move forward from those levels by progressing through successive approximations. She spoke of referring them for assessment and special education services if her own attempts to meet their needs had not been successful, but she viewed special education services as supplementary to her own efforts rather than as a mechanism for getting the child out of her room. Her emphasis was on using and building on what low achievers brought to the learning situation (and to their potential roles as tutors of other students), not on their supposed limitations.

ANOTHER HIGHER RATED TEACHER

"With a student like this, the first problem is to ascertain what their actual abilities may be and to have expectations and work that will stretch them to achieve their potential but will not be at a frustration level. We have done something this year that might be of interest. We had a group of six students who were all 9 and 10 years old and had been held back at least one year and repeated a grade. They were all reading at beginning first-grade level. My aide, who is a former teacher of first grade, and I decided that we would go right back to that level in working with them. She came up with some very creative ideas for these students, and we are very pleased with the results. They are showing real progress and actually at ages of 9 and 10 are achieving what they should have achieved at 6 had they been in a state of readiness for it. When it comes to actual mental impairment, it is, as far as I am concerned, the same sort of thing. The student is asked to do everything that he is capable of without reaching the frustration level. Usually they respond very readily to this and will work perhaps to the point of being an overachiever if you can handle the problem in this manner. For other strategies, I would mention much warm support, much individual help, one-to-one tutoring whenever possible, encouragement at all times, praise for all work done well, and getting the help of specialists in the building whenever possible. The sort of things that would work for a child who gives up easily, who experiences failure, would pretty much be what I would do for this sort of student. . . . I guess it is as simple as the old cliché, taking the student where he is and working from that point in a very supportive manner. By your attitude, make it a very normal thing in your classroom that you have some people working on a first-grade level in reading and some on a fifth-grade level, that we all have our strengths and weaknesses. We don't trumpet it to the skies that Andy is reading at a first-grade level, but we don't try to hide it because everybody with normal intelligence is going to know very soon that Andy is reading at the first-grade level and that perhaps Brian who is at the fifth-grade level is far above him. But then we point out that Andy's artwork is simply beautiful, and he has a real talent there, where Brian is all thumbs and will admit it himself. You try to emphasize each child's special abilities. They all have some, even if it is the best kickball artist in the room. When you do this, the class as a whole is very supportive toward students who are having academic difficulties. Often they will volunteer: 'Could I help Andy with this work? He is having some trouble with it.' . . . You have to be satisfied with very small progresses, maybe not even measure on a day-to-day basis, but week-to-week or maybe even month-to-month. Certainly these children are not going to amaze you with their flamboyant records set within a week or even 2 weeks. If you can keep records of the student as he came entered in the fall and then review them in the spring, that's where the satisfaction will come, when you see the progress that has been made over the school year."

This teacher also emphasized moving low achievers forward through successive approximations, using a great deal of encouragement and a variety of instructional strategies. Note her insights about challenging these students to achieve up to their capabilities, yet minimizing frustration and providing a great deal of support.

WHAT THE SCHOLARLY LITERATURE SAYS

Low achievement was the only problem addressed in our study that would not be described primarily as a problem in personal or behavioral adjustment. It was included as a way to call teachers' attention to the difference between unsatisfactory achievement progress due to limited ability and unsatisfactory achievement progress due to motivational problems (failure syndrome, perfectionism, alienation from school). The teachers suggested quite different strategies for responding to these different types of achievement progress problems.

Low achievers have difficulty keeping up with their classmates because of limitations in academic ability and background knowledge. Their IQ and achievement test scores are relatively low, although within the normal range. They are not profoundly retarded children who cannot function in regular classrooms; nor are they students hampered by specific learning disabilities that can be diagnosed and addressed using specific special education techniques. Perhaps they are best described simply as slow learners who are not progressing at a normal rate and thus are not keeping up with the class. For example, many students can decode reasonably well but cannot read with enough efficiency to allow them to understand and remember what they read. These students may seem to make at least minimally satisfactory progress in the early grades when the curriculum concentrates on the basics of the three R's. However, as they move into the third and fourth grades, the curricular emphasis shifts more toward comprehension and the use of basic skills for thinking and problem solving. Textbooks and teaching methods begin to assume that they have attained functional literacy and can learn through independent study. Instead of being able to handle 70 or 80 percent of the academic demands made on them, slow learners' effective mastery now begins to drop much lower. The value of many activities is lost to them because they do not understand the directions or cannot comprehend enough of the text to be able to follow it.

Similarly, their problems in mathematics become magnified when the instructional emphasis shifts from memorizing basic computation facts to working on more difficult problems that assume this earlier knowledge as a basis. As slow learners fall further behind, it becomes more difficult to teach them using instructional materials and methods developed for the grade level. Some slow learners may still be able to keep up with the class if provided with tutoring or other forms of special help, but others may begin to require individualized materials and instruction.

Given sufficient instructional support, slow learners may make steady progress and achieve enough to satisfy both their teachers and themselves, even though they may remain at or near the bottom of the class in overall achievement. However, if they should become frustrated too often because they can't handle tasks and can't get the help they need when they need it, or if they frequently feel humiliated because they are not keeping up with their classmates, they may begin to show symptoms of failure syndrome (Chapter 5). That is, they may lose their motivation to persist with their learning efforts and instead begin to give up quickly at the first sign of frustration. Or they may become more concerned with covering up their confusion than with learning what the task is intended to teach. The latter students may begin to show symptoms of alienation (Chapter 7). They may begin to withdraw into passivity rather than participate in lessons, leave items blank or simply guess the answers instead of seeking help, or become behavior problems. At this point, the teacher is faced not only with low achievement due to limited academic ability, but also with underachievement due to motivational problems.

Suggested Strategies for Teaching Low Achievers

For most teachers, low achievement by slower learners is an enduring dilemma that they must cope with as best they can, not simply a problem that they can solve in any permanent sense. Teachers must teach classes of 20 to 40 students who usually differ considerably in general academic abilities and in specific readiness for what will be taught at their grade level, so it is to be expected that some students will achieve more/faster than others. Experts disagree on issues such as how much can be expected from slow learners and how much teachers should focus on their slow learners' needs (rather than the needs of other subgroups in the class). However, they tend to suggest similar strategies, especially providing tutorial help to slow learners and individualizing their assignments.

For example, McIntyre (1989) culled suggestions for teaching low achievers from a variety of sources. Many of the suggestions involved individualizing these students' activities or assignments by downgrading the difficulty of the task, using multisensory input sources to reduce the emphasis on learning by studying texts, building assignments around the student's interests, teaching through the student's strongest learning modality, making sure that assignments are well structured and within the range of the student's ability level, keeping assignments short, and making sure that the first part of the assignment is easy or familiar to provide initial success experiences. A second group of suggestions focused on providing directions to structure tasks for the student: Have the student repeat instructions to you to make sure that he or she knows what is supposed to be done; model task performance while thinking out loud and train the student in methods of self-instructional guidance; outline for the student exactly what must be done to achieve the desired level of accomplishment; and set time limits within which the work should be done, preferably longer limits than necessary so that the student can "beat the clock."

A third set of suggestions focused on providing the student with task assistance or remedial tutoring: Provide such help yourself or arrange for tutoring by an aide, adult volunteer, older student, or classmate; set up a "study buddy" system to encourage the student to collaborate with a neighborhood friend during study sessions at their homes; reassure the student that help is available if needed; sit the student among higher achieving classmates with whom the student enjoys friendly relationships, and ask these classmates to help keep the student "on track" by making sure that he writes down assignments and due dates and by providing task assistance; rephrase questions or provide hints when the student is unable to respond; praise the student when he or she responds acceptably; and have the student revise work that is unacceptable.

Finally, some of the strategies focused on maintaining the student's motivation: Provide encouragement and positive comments on papers, assist the student in setting realistic goals and evaluating accomplishments, call attention to successes and send positive notes home, encourage the student to focus on trying to do better than the previous day's or week's performance rather than to compete with classmates, use contracting methods, and give marks and report card grades on the basis of effort and production rather than in relation to the rest of the class.

Abbott (1978) published a similar collection of strategies. She included many of those mentioned by McIntyre, along with some additional ones: Keep directions simple, if necessary dividing the task into parts rather than providing lengthy directions that the student may not be able to remember; seat the student toward the front of the class and maintain frequent eye contact; provide extra assignments that address learning needs and allow the student to earn extra credit toward grades; and keep in close communication with the person or persons who tutor the student, to make sure that the tutoring focuses on the student's primary needs and that you are kept abreast of progress and problems.

Good and Brophy (1997) reviewed research indicating that low achievers need frequent monitoring and supplementary tutoring from the teacher (or an adequate substitute), not just exposure to so-called individualized instructional materials (too many of these materials are restricted to low-level, repetitive tasks that amount to busywork rather than truly remedial instruction). Also, low achievers often need to be retaught using varied and enriched forms of instruction, not just to be recycled through the original instruction followed by additional drill and practice. Other strategies mentioned by Good and Brophy included the following: Collect books and instructional materials that address content taught at your grade but are written at easier reading levels; tutor slow learners in independent reading and study skills, not just in subject-matter content; identify the most basic and necessary learnings embedded in each curriculum unit, and make sure that the slow learners master those, even if they do not learn some of the less necessary things that their classmates may be learning; provide them with study guides and related learning supports; combine empathy for slow learners with determination to see that they meet established learning goals, rather than misdirecting your efforts by making sure that these students are happy in school but not making sure that they are learning; and to the extent that frustration or other motivational problems arise, reinforce instructional strategies with motivational strategies (such as those emphasized in Chapter 5 for dealing with failure syndrome problems).

ANALYSIS OF INTERVIEW RESPONSES

Here and elsewhere in Chapters 4 through 15, I provide brief, nontechnical summaries of the Classroom Strategy Study's findings (for details, see Brophy, 1995). Each of these sections begins with descriptive data on the numbers of teachers who were coded for the various response alternatives described. As you read these numbers, bear in mind that we interviewed 98 (i.e., almost 100) teachers, so that the numbers also correspond approximately to percentages. Following presentation of descriptive data, each of these sections describes the similarities and differences that emerged between the higher rated and the lower rated teachers.

All of the teachers said that they would provide academic help to low achievers. Many added that they would arrange for additional help from an aide, student teacher, or adult volunteer (38), one or more classmates (31), a resource teacher or other educational specialist (30), the parents (19), or older students acting as tutors (11).

Most (72) of the teachers spoke of personally providing sustained help to low achievers in the form of tutoring, task assistance, and review or reteaching. In addition or instead, some spoke of beginning remediation efforts by assigning work at these students' current achievement levels (40), making sure that they get off to a good start when they begin work on assignments (36), arranging for extra drill or practice (31), reducing expectations by giving shorter assignments or easier work (26), using concrete materials or learning games (23), enlisting parental support and task assistance at home (16), and dividing the work into shorter segments or arranging to monitor the students' progress more frequently so as to keep them working productively (14). Thus, the majority of the teachers would take it upon themselves to decide what their low achievers needed and then attempt to meet these needs personally with help from aides, parents, or classmates. However, a minority would seek outside professional help by arranging for the student to be taught by a resource teacher or other specialist (31) or by arranging for diagnostic testing and then seeking to implement the treatment suggestions resulting from it (19).

Along with providing academic help, 75 of the teachers mentioned strategies that would address motivation. Given our description of low achievers, motivational strategies would be appropriate if they focused on preventing or remediating academic self-concept problems and related reactions to continued failure. However, they would be less appropriate if they were based on the idea that these students were lazy and needed to be encouraged or prodded into working harder. Most of the motivational strategies mentioned involved providing support: Encourage and reassure low achievers or reinforce their accomplishments (46), help them to recognize and appreciate their progress (25), praise their accomplishments (24), change the tasks or materials if necessary to allow them to achieve success (14), and provide extra, personalized attention (13). However, a minority of teachers mentioned emphasizing to low achievers that they need to work hard (12) or offering them rewards or contracts to increase their motivation to do so (11).

Higher rated teachers did not mention a significantly greater range of strategies for working with low achievers than lower rated teachers. However, they were more likely to mention different strategies for different subtypes of low achievers, and they expressed more ideas about ineffective strategies to be avoided. They also were more likely to speak of relying on their own observation of the student as a way to get more information about the problem, and to speak of dividing work into shorter segments or monitoring progress more frequently as a way to ensure that the students' work remained productive.

Lower rated teachers mentioned most of the same strategies for providing academic help to low achievers, but they were more likely to raise issues of achievement expectations or student motivation, and in ways that appeared counterproductive. These teachers were more likely to cite developmental lags as possible causes for low achievement and to stress the need to avoid overly high expectations. Some lower rated teachers were prone to underestimate what low achievers could accomplish in their classrooms, and thus to expect less from them than they could achieve. Surprisingly, lower rated teachers also were more likely to speak of attempting to boost low achievers' motivation by praising their accomplishments or encouraging them to work harder. Perhaps the teachers who emphasized these strategies were overly focused on student motivation and did not provide enough emphasis on the academic help strategies that address low achievers' needs most directly.

In summary, higher rated teachers tended to identify the problem correctly as rooted in limited academic abilities and therefore to address it with primary emphasis on academic help strategies and only secondary emphasis on motivational strategies. Some lower rated teachers similarly emphasized academic help strategies, but others spoke of developmental lags and limited expectations or emphasized motivational strategies that do not address low achievers' need for academic help.

Vignette: Jeff

Jeff tries hard but is the lowest achiever in the class. This week you taught an important sequence of lessons. You spent a lot of extra time with Jeff and thought he understood the material. Today you are reviewing. All the other students answer your questions with ease, but when you call on Jeff, he is obviously lost.

Before reading further, take time to think about how you might respond to this incident. Make notes about your ideas.

CSS Vignette Response Excerpts

Here is what four of the CSS teachers had to say.

A LOWER RATED TEACHER

"He is totally not paying attention to anything that's going on in the classroom. I would just ask him where he has been all this time that we have been going through these lessons. I'd probably say, 'This week you will not have any free time, you will not go to gym like you would like to do, you will not go to art, which you love to do, and you definitely will not go to music, since you seem to enjoy that music class. I'll just keep you here until you have accomplished these objectives I've set out for you.'"

A HIGHER RATED TEACHER

" 'Jeff, I see that you are having some difficulty with some of the material we went over the other day. That's all right. I know that sometimes you need a little bit more work on it, and there is no problem with that. We will talk about the problem after school, and possibly I can give you some material to take home. I'll talk with your parents, and they might be able to help you with the difficulties you are having. So don't worry about it. We'll just work a little harder on that and see if we can maybe present it in a different way so that you can understand it.' My goal would be to try to make him not feel uncomfortable in that situation but to try to give him encouragement so that he would perhaps work on it again and work on it together to try to overcome some of the obstacles. So the goal would be to get him to learn the material, possibly by working again on where he is having difficulty. My rationale would be that it is important not to embarrass him any further or make him feel less capable, but to work with him individually when other children aren't around to see the difficulty he is having."

ANOTHER HIGHER RATED TEACHER

"After I had called on Jeff and he was unable to answer my question, I would just quickly call on another child and immediately take him out of the spotlight, because as the lowest achiever in the classroom, I'm sure he is very aware of it and he doesn't need to be put in the situation where he is feeling very awkward. I would try later in the day to take Jeff aside and on a one-to-one basis go over the material again and maybe ask him the questions by himself when he would be more comfortable. He might even have known the answer to the question, but being put on the spot, he might have frozen. [What would your goal be then?] To not let him get discouraged by the fact that he couldn't answer in front of the class and as soon as possible get back to him and go through the lesson and try to bolster him up again, because he might have been somewhat frustrated and couldn't answer in front of the other children. Help him to keep on trying. Let him know that it is important that he does try hard and that I understand that even though he tries hard, he still has problems learning. But the effort is appreciated, and half of learning is the effort you go through to try to learn."

ANOTHER HIGHER RATED TEACHER

"If Jeff is lost in spite of all the instruction he has had, I would not deal with his problem on the spot because I think he is so far along that you need to start from square one again. I would continue reviewing with the class and then perhaps give them an assignment that would be a part of the review that would keep them going for 15 or 20 minutes. I would then work with Jeff one-to-one and start again at the beginning and find out just where he began to lose out, whether it was the first lesson or the second or the third and begin to build on that. Then I would probably give him some work at the point where he understands, so that he is reassured that he does know something, and then I would establish with him some times that either he and I would get together or he and a teacher aide would get together and go through the sequence again more slowly and in smaller steps until he began to have a better idea of the whole concept. I would deal with Jeff one-to-one because I think it would be too embarrassing for him to try to stop and explain something to him, in particular when the rest of the class understands much more than he does. Also it would be very hard for the other children to be patient with him. It would also call attention to the fact that he doesn't get it, and this probably happens more than once so that it would then again be calling attention to his low achievement in the class. By working with him one-to-one, I think the two of us could find something that he does know and build on that until he was a little more confident. I think it is important that he has some kind of success. He may not reach the goal that you had set for the whole class, but it is important that he still continue to learn. I would characterize him as a very slow learner or one that is rather dull."

Despite the wording of the vignette, the lower rated teacher interpreted Jeff's difficulty as resulting from failure to pay attention to the lesson, and spoke of responding punitively. In contrast, all three of the higher rated teachers interpreted the problem accurately and suggested responses that combined minimizing Jeff's embarrassment in the depicted incident and following up with support, encouragement, and special tutorial instruction.

Analysis of Responses to Jeff

Commonly mentioned strategies for responding to Jeff focused on providing tutorial assistance or other special instruction (61), helping him deal with frustration and other emotional responses to failure (44), reducing demands or changing the task if necessary (37), peer support (31), providing "kid gloves" treatment during incidents like the one depicted in the vignette (27), arranging for assistance from a resource teacher or other professional specialist (27), arranging for diagnostic workup (20), and enlisting parental support and assistance at home (15).

A majority of the teachers spoke of responding to Jeff's larger achievement problem, not just to the incident depicted in the vignette. Only 29 would confine their response to reviewing a few specific questions or problems (thus ignoring the fact that Jeff was described as totally lost). Instead, 40 would provide sustained and extensive reteaching or tutoring, and 14 would arrange for specialized placement or treatment of Jeff on a continuing basis.

Most teachers spoke of dealing with Jeff in a nonemotional, matter-of-fact manner, but 23 said that they enjoyed the challenge of working with students like Jeff, and 21 spoke of feeling discouraged, frustrated, or angered by these students' slow response to instruction. Only 40 teachers attended to Jeff's impending motivational problems and discouragement. Of those, 20 reported that they would make sure that Jeff experienced success and was praised for it, 8 would switch to materials that Jeff found more interesting, and 7 would encourage him to keep trying because his efforts would eventually pay off.

The higher rated teachers tended to give more complete responses that included strategies for responding to Jeff's failure in the immediate situation, following up with academic help to address his larger problem of unsatisfactory achievement progress, and keeping him motivated over the long term by ensuring that he had sufficient success experiences. These teachers' responses were more likely to include mention of personal counseling for Jeff, attempts to help him develop insight into his problem, or attempts to provide him with comfort and reassurance following failures.

The lower rated teachers did not have much confidence that they could bring about generalized improvements in Jeff's achievement levels. The forms of academic help that they mentioned were more likely to be minimal situational responses than sustained long-term improvement efforts, and the motivational attempts that they mentioned tended toward exhortation ("You can do it if you try") rather than more supportive forms of reassurance. Higher rated teachers were more likely to speak of working intensively with Jeff personally and enjoying the challenge of doing so, but lower rated teachers were more likely to talk about the frustrations of working with students like Jeff and about passing his problem along to a resource teacher or other educational specialist. For many lower rated teachers, primary impediments to success with Jeff would be a lack of patience with his slow progress and an inability to derive satisfaction from working with him, not a lack of ideas about how to help him.

Vignette: Tim

Tim is a poor student. He has a low potential for schoolwork and also lacks the basic experiences that help a child function in the classroom. You have just presented a new lesson to the class and have assigned related seatwork. You look over the class and see that Tim is upset. When you ask him if something is wrong, he tells you that he can't do it — it's too hard.

Before reading further, take time to think about how you might respond to this incident. Make notes about your ideas.

CSS Vignette Response Excerpts

Here is what four of the CSS teachers had to say.

A LOWER RATED TEACHER

" 'Tim, come to my table and I'll help you. But you must try. The aide helped you yesterday, and you did just fine. Remember how pleased you were?' Tim has a very low IQ. He needs a one-to-one ratio whenever possible. Also, he needs much encouragement and support and praise."

A HIGHER RATED TEACHER

"I would pull up a chair to Tim and say, 'I would like to help you with this, Tim.' I think I would begin with the first thing in the seatwork and then talk through the high points of the lesson in relation to that seatwork and work through it with him. I may have to do the whole thing with him that day and then follow up with him personally or have an aide follow up with him on subsequent activities so that he would begin to get an idea of what the lesson was about. [What exactly would you say to him?] 'Tim, I noticed that you're upset about this assignment. You say that it's too hard, so I guess that you weren't able to understand everything I was telling the class. I would like to help you with this now, and we can do this together today.' I may even reduce the assignment, have him do two or three together, and then try one on his own rather than 10 or 15 like the rest of the class would be doing. I think it would be important to get back to him at another time that day and then proceed to the next lesson so that he would begin to get a little background on the subject, perhaps begin to see some patterns and kind of get the idea. This child is probably at the low end of the intelligence scale because of his lack of basic experiences, but with concerted effort, he may be able to at least have success if he's got one-to-one attention and new information. I think it's important that Tim feel some success in anything that is presented to the class as a whole, and I think that this is possible with any child unless they are truly mentally retarded. I think that it simply takes reexplanation in different ways and more individual help. Tim will feel better about himself and other students will feel better about Tim in the class if he is able to have some success with what the rest of the class is doing."

ANOTHER HIGHER RATED TEACHER

"In looking at Tim's situation and looking over the assignment, if I felt that it is something Tim is able to do, I would go over to him and say, 'I would like you to work with Joe.' In that case, Joe might be a student of the same capabilities, but the two of them could help each other through the assignment. Very often I will assign a lower achiever as a helper to a child who is of equal ability level, so that at least he is having successes in seeing that other children are in the same boat that he is. And as he goes over his lessons and tasks with the other child, he can see that there are things that he is able to do and also teach the other child."

ANOTHER HIGHER RATED TEACHER

"First of all, I would make sure that the type of work being handed to Tim is within his range of capabilities. If indeed he has been given work within his range, then my approach would be to give him all the support that he needs, such as, 'I'll be over in just a moment to sit down beside you and help you get started,' or 'I will assign Jenny to come over and read the portion that is hard for you to help you with any words you need and get you started,' or 'We have a roving student helping today [and give the name]. Just raise your hand, and he will be over to help you.' I would approach this situation as purely supportive in every aspect, because once he realizes he can master something with help, you know that before long he is going to try it on his own without asking for any help and will find that indeed he can accomplish some tasks that other people are doing in the classroom by themselves. Of course, that will snowball into self-confidence, and so on. My goal would be to see that Tim becomes self-sufficient in being able to accomplish his work without outside help but, meanwhile, to give him every sort of help from either students or adults in the classroom until he does feel confident."

In this case, all four of the quoted teachers recommended a combination of support and assistance for Tim. However, the lower rated teacher's response was brief and somewhat perfunctory, and it was implicitly critical of Tim as well as supportive. The three higher rated teachers all cast themselves more clearly as benign, supportive helpers and did not suggest impatience with Tim or criticism for lack of effort.

Analysis of Responses to Tim

The teachers' responses to Tim were quite similar to their responses to Jeff. Commonly mentioned strategies for responding to the depicted behavior included providing task assistance (76), reducing expectations or changing Tim's work assignments (54), helping Tim deal with the emotional consequences of failure (41), involving peers (24), providing encouragement (20) or "kid gloves" treatment (17), involving resource teachers or other school professionals (17), and referring him for a diagnostic workup (11).

All of the teachers mentioned at least one strategy for helping Tim cope with his work. The most frequently mentioned strategy was to provide sustained help and tutoring (63), mostly individual (54). Tutorial help would come from the teacher (81), a classmate (18), or an educational specialist (15). Only four teachers mentioned involving Tim's parents in helping him at home, perhaps because the vignette described Tim as suffering from a lack of basic educational experiences. However, six teachers mentioned giving Tim special remedial work to do at home.

Other strategies for helping Tim complete assignments successfully included reducing expectations and substituting easier work (51), reexplaining directions and walking him through several problems to help him get started (27), arranging for diagnostic testing and/or special placement (19), and subdividing his work into smaller segments or providing more frequent monitoring and feedback (13). The 51 teachers who would reduce expectations or substitute easier work for Tim represented by far the largest number of teachers who mentioned this strategy in connection with any of our vignettes. Essentially, these teachers said that Tim had been misplaced and needed to be given more appropriate work.

All of the teachers spoke of providing academic help to Tim. In addition, about half (49) mentioned strategies for improving his motivation or attitude. The most commonly mentioned strategy was to encourage and reassure Tim that his efforts were appreciated and that the teacher realized he was doing his best (30). Other strategies included stating demands and articulating expectations that Tim meet his responsibilities (14) and providing proof to Tim that he could handle at least part of the work (14). Only two teachers suggested rewards or contracts.

Higher rated teachers were more likely to state that they enjoyed the challenge of working with students like Tim and were more confident that they could bring about significant improvement that would generalize beyond their classrooms. Along with the academic helping strategies mentioned by most teachers, higher rated teachers were more likely to mention involving peers to assist Tim and giving him special work to do at home.

Higher rated teachers' responses also were noteworthy for their greater emphasis on counseling strategies and attempts to improve Tim's coping skills. Individual elements in the larger pattern that showed significant correlations with effectiveness ratings included modeling or prescribing better ways for Tim to cope with his problem, trying to build his self-concept, and supporting his motivation by proving to him that he could handle the work. Lower rated teachers made less mention of these strategies and were more likely to state that students like Tim are frustrating to work with or that goals need to be limited because one can only expect so much from Tim.

COMPARISON OF RESPONSES TO JEFF AND TO TIM

The two vignettes yielded similar response patterns. In each case, a majority of the teachers responded to the problem primarily as one of academic ability rather than motivation. Of these teachers, one minority saw the problem as a relatively minor one that could be solved with brief and limited help (get the student started on work, divide work into segments and monitor as needed, show him that he can do the work by displaying his earlier successes). Another minority saw the problem as so serious as to require diagnostic testing and possible placement of the student into a resource room. The majority were in between, calling for intensive reteaching or tutoring.

The remaining teachers dealt with Jeff and/or Tim more as motivation problems than academic ability problems. These teachers were split between those who stressed demands for greater effort and those who stressed encouragement and success experiences. The latter teachers typically spoke of providing encouragement to Tim in the context of helping him handle his assignments, rather than relying on encouragement alone without giving academic help.

The few contrasts in patterns of response to the two vignettes were related either to differences in the depicted settings (a public lesson vs. a private seatwork interaction) or to the fact that Tim was described as lacking basic educational experiences and complaining that the work was too hard for him. The teachers were more comfortable with the idea of working with Tim than with Jeff, and more likely to talk about addressing his problem personally rather than seeking to place him in a resource room. They also were more likely to talk about self-concept support and other attempts to improve Tim's motivation. Finally, they were much more willing to reduce expectations or provide easier work for Tim than for Jeff. Although indicative of greater empathy for Tim, this response would not necessarily be in his best interests, compared to strategies for helping him learn to cope with work demands more successfully (see Chapter 5).

QUALITATIVE IMPRESSIONS AND EXAMPLES

Teachers' responses to interview questions about low achievers were less diverse than their interview responses concerning other problem-student types. Most teachers focused on the same few popular themes, without much mention of creative alternatives or even interesting elaborations of commonly mentioned strategies. Early grade teachers tended to say that low achievers will make steady progress if you give them material that they can handle, extra instruction and monitoring, and praise for their accomplishments. Many of them, however, especially first-grade teachers, spoke of retaining these students in grade for another year if they made slow progress. Upper grade teachers tended to emphasize that low achievers know how far behind they are and are likely to have self-concept problems no matter how encouraging you try to be.

Many responses, especially from Big City, were long on description of symptoms but short on description of what teachers might do about these symptoms. Also, responses coded into some categories were less impressive in the original than the coding category label might suggest. For example, many of the suggested interventions coded as tutoring or reteaching called for leading the student through repetitive drill work without providing much actual instruction, let alone remedial instruction that involved teaching the material more thoroughly or in a different way than it was taught originally.

Many of the Big City teachers called for having low achievers tested. In some cases this was part of a strategy for getting these students out of their classes, but in many cases it reflected these teachers' belief that testing would pinpoint the students' problems and lead to prescriptions for what kind of instruction they needed. Whether or not they mentioned testing, however, a great many Big City teachers said in one way or another that low achievers need individual attention but that such attention cannot be provided consistently in large classes, so the only real hope for them is placement in resource rooms that have much lower student:teacher ratios. Some of these teachers flatly stated that slow learners who cannot keep up do not belong in regular classrooms. Several expressed irritation with parents who refused to allow their child to be tested and moved out of the regular class. One even expressed moral outrage, both at the system (for allowing these students in regular classes) and at the parents (whom the teacher viewed as inconsiderate of their child's best interests).

Several teachers noted that parents of low achievers need help in learning to accept their child's limitations, yet provide support and assistance. They suggested that unless the teacher takes the initiative, some parents will be too embarrassed to talk about the problem, either with the teacher or with the child, so that everyone pretends that it doesn't exist. Worse, some parents will call their child stupid or exacerbate the problem in other ways.

Among teachers who spoke of providing more task structure for low achievers, several noted the need to give simplified and oral instructions because these students usually cannot read well. Others spoke of not only segmenting tasks into smaller bits for these students but helping them to set goals for accomplishing successive approximations of the final task, and then rewarding them for doing so.

Several teachers noted that you usually have a number of students like this in each class, so that you can make a group of them as a way to give them more special attention without going to an individual level that you do not have time to sustain. Some noted that the group is a reassuring mechanism for a student who otherwise might feel alone in being so far behind. Several teachers also mentioned the value of keeping the number of students in lower groups smaller than the number in higher groups (again, as a way to provide more individualized attention). Finally, although many teachers recommended assigning a buddy or peer tutor, some of them warned that you shouldn't overuse this strategy or select the wrong peers because they may express frustration with the low achiever's slow progress. A few teachers said that they avoided peer tutoring for this reason.

One teacher maintained a "catch up" corner in the room that she used to run through lessons one more time for students who needed it. She also kept a collection of flash cards and worksheet activities that were good for sending home to involve parents in extra tutoring or practice activities. Another teacher reported a similar approach but emphasized educational games rather than flash cards. She said that parents do not enjoy using flash cards with their children but are much more willing to play educational games with them, and both the parents and the children enjoy it more. Other teachers who mentioned games for low achievers cited not only their motivational value but the idea that participation in the games helps students to remember material that they might forget otherwise.

One fourth-grade teacher reported meeting with her high reading group for only a few minutes each day and concentrating on the lower readers. She ran two 15–20-minute reading groups with the low readers each day and also made time to tutor individuals. This quote from her captures both the frustrations and the potential rewards involved in working with low achievers: "You have to find out what level they are at and then just go at it day after day after day. Sometimes they read so slowly, it's torture, but as long as they are excited about what they are doing, they are not noticing that you are sitting there bored or sending someone for a cup of coffee. It's slow, it's frustrating, but I have had success with kids like this. They are a challenge to me as a teacher. To get movement out of them pleases me. They do grow and learn. It just takes time."

One teacher noted that in rewarding slow learners, you have to emphasize effort and quality of work rather than how much work they complete successfully. Otherwise, you will either encourage them to just guess at answers or cause them to get fewer rewards than their classmates even though they are working up to their own abilities.

One teacher reported some interesting strategies for building low achievers' confidence in their ability to handle more challenging work. One method was to give these students work that looked more difficult than it really was (long words that are easy to spell because they are compound words or are spelled just like they sound; addition problems that involve four or five columns but no carrying). Another was to actually expose the students to higher-level challenges occasionally, such as by encouraging them to check out difficult (for them) books on subjects that interest them "because it won't hurt them to try to read something higher-level and because they are probably bored with the stories in the readers by now."

One teacher noted that low achievers can become confused, as well as miss some important things in class, if they are taken out too frequently for pull-out instruction (especially if this is done without advance notice). Anticipating many recent concerns about pull-out programs, this teacher suggested that "maybe too many people are working with these kids."

One teacher noted that although the auditory mode is often recommended for slow learners, she found that most commercial tape and worksheet programs made for use in listening centers move too quickly for these students. Consequently, she made her own tapes that proceeded at a slower pace. Finally, a fifth-grade teacher reported working on direction-following and test-taking skills with low achievers, not just subject matter.

The teachers' responses to the vignettes were more varied and interesting than their responses to the general strategies interview. With Jeff and especially Tim, several teachers said that it would be their own fault if the work was too difficult for the student. They would tell this to the student as part of an effort to reassure him that corrections would be made and he would be able to achieve success if he kept applying himself. Several also said that they would avoid letter grades and conspicuous marking of wrong answers. Instead, they would use check marks, happy faces, plus signs, or encouraging written feedback, even if it was nothing more than recognition that the child was willing to try. One teacher reported using a three-smiley-face system in giving students feedback on their papers. They got one for completing part of the paper, two for completing all of it, and three for completing all of it correctly. This enabled even the slowest learners to get at least one smiley face, which the teacher said was important to them because they fretted if they got nothing.

Among teachers who spoke of helping the student do the work in class, several mentioned that they would write "done with teacher help" on these pages as a way to alert parents to areas in which their child was behind. Many Big City teachers talked about getting these students to express themselves through artwork, constructions, or nonverbal or non-written means. Some justified this as an alternative way for the child to get practice and for the teacher to assess what was learned, but others justified it on affective grounds by saying that low achievers need to be able to spend time in school doing things that they enjoy or are good at besides struggling with learning.

Responses to Jeff often reflected teachers' conflict between their desire to help him and their need to get on with the lesson. Several said that they would ask Jeff if he remembered anything from the lesson and then allow him to state what he remembered and move on. Others would avoid this situation by not calling on Jeff to answer questions in front of the whole class unless they were certain that he could respond successfully. Finally, several teachers said that they would speak to Jeff later to try to determine whether he really didn't know the answer or was afraid to speak up in front of the class. One teacher said that once she realized that Jeff was lost, she would first back up and direct questions to other students who could answer them and then come back to Jeff with one of these questions "to see if that would pull him back together." Later she would review the material with him to see if that helped. If the problem persisted, she would send extra work home for the parents to go over with him. Another teacher would tell Jeff that he didn't know the answer because "I haven't taught you enough yet." Her intention was to communicate that the problem is not Jeff's fault, and that she realized that he was working hard.

Among teachers who spoke of trying to avoid further embarrassment to Jeff, some suggested strategies that seem counterproductive (stating that his answer is wrong and asking someone to help him; taking the entire class through the line of questions all over again "to help Jeff remember some of these"). Finally, one teacher would grade Jeff on individual standards (perhaps third-grade level instead of fifth), but would explain this to the parents and the principal and would make a note in his permanent record so that future teachers could interpret the grades accurately.

In talking about how they might respond to Tim, several teachers indicated that they assumed he was crying. One who said that she would work with him individually also said that she would first move him to a corner of the room where other students wouldn't see that he is upset. Another would try to avoid this problem by using group and individualized methods to make sure that students were never given work that they couldn't handle. Other responses to Tim mentioned by individual teachers included offering to read the questions to him (thinking that his reading limitations might be the problem); modeling and attempting to teach Tim self-monitoring and self-evaluation skills to use when he studies; and varying the degree of help given to Tim depending on the nature of the task (for an ungraded task, concentrate on trying to provide a success experience for Tim, but for an important graded task or a test, be careful not to do the work for him).

DISCUSSION

Most teachers were empathetic and eager to be helpful to low achievers. They tended to be realistic in recognizing that goals for these students would have to be limited, but they were quite willing to work with them, or arrange for others to do so, for as long as was necessary. However, very few teachers mentioned remedial techniques that involved new teaching *methods* or *materials* (as opposed to new *people*), or the use of concrete manipulables, learning games, or other special approaches. The emphasis was on continuing to lead low achievers through the same basic drill work, without introducing much curricular variety or many adjustments in instructional approach. Thus, although with few exceptions the teachers' commitment and desire to help low achievers seemed clear, most of them would have benefited from more information about how to help low-ability students learn.

Most responses centered around a basic set of principles that appear likely to be effective: Focus on providing academic help; supplement this with counseling or motivational support if needed; provide extra monitoring, feedback, and tutoring; enlist help from peers, parents, or other students or adults; and view low achievers as challenges to your professionalism as a teacher rather than as candidates for retention in grade or removal from your classroom. These principles appear to apply across grade levels and student populations.

The following are some important elaborations on these principles for dealing with low achievers. First, try to accept the situation and make the best of it. Set and follow through on realistic goals. Identify essential objectives, and make sure that low achievers learn these, even if this means skipping other things. Also, help low achievers to view their situation realistically, yet still try to progress as best they can. Let them know that their work will be acceptable to you so long as they apply themselves, even if they are unable to keep up with most classmates. Elicit their commitment to establishing and working on feasible goals. Let them know that extra practice and repetition are necessary for them, even if frustrating. You empathize, but you want to see them learn too.

Low achievers will need extra help, especially individualized help provided during tutoring interactions. However, you and any other helpers will need to be patient and caring. If you use peer or cross-age tutoring, make sure that tutors understand this. Also, arrange for low achievers to tutor peers or younger students. This will help them to master material more thoroughly and also avoid making them always the receivers but never the givers of help.

As soon as possible after getting the class as a whole settled into an assignment, give personal attention to low achievers to make sure that they understand what to do and get off to a good start. Don't let them "practice errors" or end up turning in completed papers that are "all wrong." If they are not ready for pencil-and-paper work, build toward it with readiness work. If they can't read, help them learn to do so and at other times engage them in worthwhile learning activities that do not require significant reading skills or that can be explained to them orally. In mathematics, use concrete manipulables and other specialized instructional materials designed to help them grasp basic concepts. In language arts and content subjects, ask them many questions that focus on key ideas and require them to compose thoughtful oral or written responses. In providing feedback, focus on their grasp of key ideas rather than on the formal correctness of their language or writing.

In effect, "cut a deal" with low achievers: It's OK if they can't keep up with the rest of the class, but you have special goals and activities for them. You will be pleased if they accomplish these goals and are prepared to help them do so, but they will have to work hard and hold up their end too. You are demanding effort and progress, but not necessarily the attainment of grade-level norms or the performance of the class as a whole.

5

Failure Syndrome Students

ailure syndrome students display the following characteristics: These children are convinced that they cannot do the work. They often avoid starting or give up easily. They expect to fail, even after succeeding. They:

1. Are easily frustrated
2. Give up easily
3. Say, "I can't do it"

What special strategies might you use to minimize such problems and help these students to function more successfully in your classroom? Before reading further, take time to think about this and make notes about your ideas.

CSS INTERVIEW EXCERPTS

Here is what three of the CSS teachers had to say about teaching failure syndrome students.

A LOWER RATED TEACHER

"These children have been convinced that they can't do a good job. Evidently it has been going on for a period of time. They have a low self-concept. I would start off by evaluating them to be sure that they can handle the work that I am trying to give them. I would work with them or see that they have other supervision at least to get started. I'd give a lot of praise for all of the success they have accomplished, and I would cut their work into small amounts so that they can have success. . . . I would talk with them, I would encourage them, I'd say, 'You can handle it. You have the ability, and I'm sure you don't feel good being behind. You have a chance to bring yourself up. Why don't you get busy.' I might even try some rewards. It could be a verbal reward, or it could be a treat or something, maybe a few extra minutes for games or some drawing time or some time to do nothing if they want."

This teacher showed concern about failure syndrome students and suggested several useful strategies: making sure that their work is appropriate in level of difficulty, praise and encouragement, and rewards for completed work. However, she did not elaborate these ideas very much or indicate that her efforts with these students would be very extensive. Beyond helping them to get started on assignments and providing some extra praise or reward if they kept at it and completed the work, she would leave her failure syndrome students mostly on their own.

A HIGHER RATED TEACHER

"These children need a lot of praise and encouragement. I don't think you can talk them into working just by saying that something is easy; you have to feel it through with them. They are a very hard group to work with because you have to be so patient. It's a very slow process with these children, and I try not to hurry, not to apply too much pressure, but to try to work things through with them. Sometimes just give them a limited amount of work to do, and set very small goals. Maybe we'll plan to work 15 minutes and see what they can get accomplished. Sometimes they do need easier work. You really need to know what their background is: what kinds of problems they might have at home or in the classroom (if somebody has always put them down or not given them the chance to work something themselves). It's easy for a teacher to try to do things for this type of child and not let them be successful on their own. . . . It's important of course to make them feel successful; whenever they do something successfully say, 'Yes, this is right,' and 'You're doing a fine job.' Usually I like to start with a child that way, and sometimes I will get another child to work with them, a child that works well with other children, that is reinforcing, that will be patient, that will just try to help them understand. And I have had quite a few instances where this has worked well. And it has gotten the child to have a special kind of friend. This has bolstered their ego, too, and made them feel that 'with someone encouraging me and if they think I can do it, I guess I really can do it.' But I think you have to give them small amounts of work at a time so that they don't look over something and say, 'Oh, it's way overwhelming. It's too much.' Another thing is to say, 'How many problems do you think you can do today?' because generally they don't have to do a whole page in order to show their knowledge. And let *them* make some choices like 'Well, I think I can do five problems and do them successfully.' Or start out and increase. I think it's very important, too, when they *do* finish, to put a star on their paper or give them some other immediate reinforcement that they can take home, that they can show to somebody else that will really make them proud. . . . These children need to know that you're always there, that they can come to you for help if they do become frustrated. Maybe you can't help right at that moment, but you can say, 'I want to help you. Let's plan some time where we can work quietly together.' Lots of times I have stayed after school to help, and I know children appreciate it. They become more frustrated when they need your help right then and you can't give it to them. If you can, just say, 'Why don't you put that away right now, and let's do it when we're alone when I can give you my full attention.' This close contact—with them knowing that they have your support and that you're not going to be angry with them, that you're going to be patient with them—works best in the long run. Rewards can work well for a while, but it's your relationship with the child that's most important in the long run."

This teacher recommended the same general lines of approach as the lower rated teacher, but with several important elaborations. First, she implied that she would spend much more time with these students, structuring and scaffolding tasks for them and frequently working with them rather than just getting them started and then moving away. Second, she emphasized the need for patience in moving them through successive approximations toward ultimate goals. Finally, she viewed these students as needing consistent help and encouragement in building up their confidence, not merely a brief statement to the effect that they could do the work if they tried.

ANOTHER HIGHER RATED TEACHER

"The child that's convinced they cannot do the work might be the child who has had everything done for them. Or maybe they've been so put down, when they do something that's not up to what the parents expect, that they don't feel they can do anything. This is the way they cope. They just give up or say, 'I can't do it.' First of all, we give the child work that we know they can do, even if it's simpler than the others are doing. Then if they still just say, 'I can't do it' before they even look at it, you go to them and you start them and say, 'Is there anything on the page that you have done before that might help you?'

Usually this will get the child started. We do have them work on their own level rather than have them trying to do things with the whole group, if they're a child who cannot do that. If the teacher's busy, you may ask another child to help the child get going. Or give them a feeling of security and say, 'You look at the paper, and then if you really feel you can't do it, you ask somebody to get you started,' and you name a person that you know is reliable and won't do it for the child but will get them started. Then when they do start doing the work, you give them a little praise and try to go out of your way and go over and say, 'Oh, you're doing a great job! I think you're going to get that done!' Then kind of help them along in praising them. Then when they've really done a good job, you give them stars on their paper and so on, so that they really begin to feel good about themselves. But it's not going to happen overnight. They're going to continue, but after a while they gradually come out of it if you're consistent about doing this—getting them started, then giving them the rewards by praise and stars, and so on, and keeping it within their realm. What you do is preteach everything before they ever get the paper.... This will not happen overnight. Usually it takes several months to really get the child going and feeling good about themselves. You have to continually build up their self-esteem."

Like the previous teacher, this teacher elaborated on the basic strategies in important ways. She also spoke of providing failure syndrome children with various forms of help in addition to praise and encouragement, arranging for classmates to help at times when she could not, and patiently working to build up these students' self-confidence and skills for coping with confusion or frustration in their work on assignments.

WHAT THE SCHOLARLY LITERATURE SAYS

"Failure syndrome" is one of several terms that teachers commonly use (others include "low self-concept," "defeated," and "frustrated") to describe students who approach assignments with very low expectations of success and who tend to give up at the first sign of difficulty. Psychologists have given the term "learned helplessness" a slightly more technical definition, but it refers to a similar pattern of behavior. Unlike low achievers, who often fail despite their best efforts, failure syndrome students often fail needlessly because they do not invest their best efforts: They begin tasks halfheartedly and simply give up when they encounter difficulty. Butkowsky and Willows (1980) observed the following tendencies in learned helplessness students confronted with challenging reading tasks: (1) has low initial expectancies for success, (2) gives up quickly in the face of difficulty, (3) attributes failures to uncontrollable causes (lack of ability) rather than to controllable causes (insufficient effort or use of an inappropriate strategy), (4) attributes successes to external and uncontrollable causes (luck, easy task) rather than to personal abilities and efforts, and (5) following failure, makes unusually severe reductions in estimates of future success probabilities.

Some students, especially in the early grades, show failure syndrome tendencies as part of larger patterns of emotional immaturity (low frustration tolerance; avoidance, inhibition, or adult dependency as reactions to stress). They may focus more on dependency-related desires for attention from the teacher than on trying to learn what an academic activity is designed to teach. Dreikurs (1968) described this pattern as a defense mechanism exhibited by some children (especially youngest children) who feel unable to compete with successful siblings or who have been pampered to the point that they lack confidence in their own abilities.

Other students originally acquire failure expectations from their parents or teachers. Parents sometimes lead their children to believe that school will be difficult for them or that they have only limited academic potential, especially if the child's first few report cards contain low grades (Entwisle & Hayduk, 1982). Teachers may communicate low expectations through a variety of direct and indirect means (Brophy, 1983b; Dusek, 1985), especially to students who have been assigned labels such as "learning impaired."

However, most failure syndrome symptoms develop through social learning mechanisms centered around experiences with failure. Most children begin school with enthusiasm, but many begin to find it anxiety-provoking and psychologically threatening. As students, they are accountable for responding to teachers' questions, completing assignments, and taking tests. Furthermore, their performance is monitored, graded, and reported to their parents. These accountability pressures might be tolerable under conditions of privacy and consistent success, but they become threatening in classrooms where failure carries the danger of public humiliation.

Given these conditions, it is not surprising that some students, especially those who have experienced a continuing history of failure or a recent progressive cycle of failure, begin to believe that they lack the ability to succeed. Once this belief takes root, failure expectations and other self-conscious thoughts begin to disrupt their concentration and limit their coping abilities. Eventually such students abandon serious attempts to master tasks and begin to concentrate instead on preserving their self-esteem in their own eyes and their reputations in the eyes of others (Ames, 1987; Butkowsky & Willows, 1980; Clifford, 1984; Diener & Dweck, 1978, 1980; Phillips, 1984; Rohrkemper & Corno, 1988).

Among failure syndrome patterns, Dweck and Elliott (1983) distinguished learned helplessness from high evaluation anxiety (often called test anxiety). *High evaluation anxiety* is a more generalized and chronic condition in which anxiety, low expectations, and fear of failure are triggered by evaluative cues (e.g., cues indicating that one will be required to perform and that the performance will be evaluated). In contrast, *learned helplessness* is a more acute and situational condition characterized by plunging expectancies in response to perceived failure.

Students who suffer from high evaluation anxiety in school tend to be low achievers who experience failure routinely, whereas students who develop learned helplessness reactions can be found at all levels of academic ability. These students do not routinely develop high anxiety in response to evaluation cues or begin tasks with failure expectations. As long as they do not question their ability to succeed, they may be able to handle even challenging activities smoothly and successfully. However, they are prone to develop "catastrophic" reactions when they encounter serious frustration, followed by progressive deterioration in the quality of their coping once they have *begun* to fail. Fincham, Hokoda, and Sanders (1989) found that symptoms of learned helplessness noted in third grade were correlated with achievement problems seen later in fifth grade. Their article includes checklists for teachers to use in assessing their students for learned helplessness symptoms.

Suggested Strategies for Coping with Failure Syndrome Students

Common sense suggests that failure syndrome students need assistance in regaining self-confidence in their academic abilities and in developing strategies for coping with failure and persisting with problem-solving efforts when they experience difficulties. Wlodkowski (1978) suggested that teachers (1) guarantee that these students experience success (by seeing that they know what to do before asking them to do it independently, providing immediate feedback to their responses, and making sure that they know the criteria by which their learning will be evaluated); (2) encourage their learning efforts (by giving recognition for real effort, showing appreciation for progress, and projecting positive expectations); (3) emphasize personal causation in their learning (by allowing them to plan and set goals, make choices, and use self-evaluation procedures to check progress); and (4) use group process methods to enhance positive self-concepts (activities that orient students toward appreciating their positive qualities and getting feedback about these qualities from their peers).

Swift and Spivack (1975) suggested most of these same strategies. In addition, they recommended exploring with these students which classroom situations they find comfortable and which they find anxiety-provoking (and why), helping them to gain better insight into and sense of control over their anxieties, and reassuring them of your willingness to help. Forms of help included minimizing emphasis on evaluation and competition, marking and grading with emphasis on noting successes rather than failures, using individualized instructional materials, and calling on the child only when he or she volunteers (or, alternatively, only when the child has been prepared through advance warning and study or rehearsal suggestions).

Good and Brophy (1995, 1997) suggested (1) programming students for success and calling their attention to it as it is achieved; (2) ensuring that they know what to do and can do it successfully if they invest reasonable effort; (3) teaching them goal setting, performance appraisal, and self-reinforcement skills; and (4) helping them to recognize linkages between their efforts and their learning outcomes. For particularly discouraged students, they recommended the attribution retraining approaches described below as well as mastery learning approaches that virtually guarantee success and thus build confidence and increase willingness to take the risks involved in committing oneself to challenging goals (see Grabe, 1985).

McIntyre (1989) suggested reading and discussing with these students *The Little Engine That Could* (Piper, 1991), praising them for attempting difficult tasks as well as for whatever success they achieve, requiring them to complete (or at least make a serious attempt to complete) a certain portion of the assignment before asking you for help, pointing out similarities between the present task and work completed successfully earlier, and allowing them extra time if necessary but insisting that their work must be completed.

More specific and elaborated suggestions have emerged from research on particular theoretical concepts or treatment approaches. Many of these involve what Ames (1987) has called "cognition retraining." Three of the more prominent approaches to cognition retraining are attribution retraining, efficacy training, and strategy training.

Attribution retraining involves inducing changes in students' tendencies to attribute failure to lack of ability rather than to a remediable cause such as insufficient effort or use of an inappropriate strategy. Typically, attribution retraining treatments involve exposing students to a planned series of experiences, couched within an achievement context, in which modeling, socialization, practice, and feedback are used to teach them to (1) concentrate on the task at hand rather than worry about failing, (2) cope with failures by retracing their steps to find their mistake or by analyzing the problem to find another approach, and (3) attribute their failures to insufficient effort, lack of information, or use of ineffective strategies rather than to lack of ability (Andrews & Debus, 1978; Chapin & Dyck, 1976; Craske, 1985; Dweck & Elliott, 1983; Forman, 1993; Fowler & Peterson, 1981; Kennelly, Dietz, & Benson, 1985; Medway & Venino, 1982;

Relich, Debus, & Walker, 1986; Shelton, Anastopoulos, & Linden, 1985; Thomas & Pashley, 1982; Tollefson, Tracy, Johnsen, Farmer, & Buenning, 1984).

This line of work represents a significant advance over the common-sense idea of programming students for success because it has shown that success alone is not enough: Even a steady diet of success will not change an established pattern of learned helplessness (Dweck & Elliott, 1983). In fact, a key to successful attribution retraining is controlled exposure to failure. Rather than being exposed only to "success models" who handle the task with ease, students are exposed to "coping models" who struggle to overcome mistakes before finally succeeding, and who model constructive responses to such mistakes as they occur (by verbalizing continued confidence, attributing failures to remediable causes, and coping by first diagnosing the source of the problem and then responding by correcting mistakes or approaching the problem in a different way). Following exposure to such modeling, students begin to work on the tasks themselves. Conditions are arranged so that they will sometimes experience difficulty or failure, and the instructor's comments will encourage them to respond constructively rather than becoming frustrated and giving up.

These treatments involving controlled exposure to failure experiences reflect the growing recognition that successful student socialization includes attention to frustration tolerance, persistence in the face of difficulties, and related aspects of constructive response to failure, rather than trying to avoid failure experiences altogether (Clifford, 1984; Rohrkemper & Corno, 1988).

Early attribution retraining programs stressed attribution of failure to insufficient effort ("I didn't try hard enough or concentrate carefully enough"). More recently, programs have stressed attribution of failure to use of an ineffective strategy ("I went about the problem in the wrong way"; "I misunderstood the directions"; "I made a mistake at a certain point that negated my efforts thereafter"; etc.). This shift recognizes the fact that most students at least subjectively put forth their best efforts, so that failure results not so much from lack of effort as from a limited repertoire of relevant knowledge and coping strategies. That is, they do everything they know how to do but still don't succeed, and they don't know how to diagnose and overcome the problem on their own.

Thus, most classroom applications involve teaching easily frustrated students how to resist the temptation to give up and instead persist in attempting to cope with the task by analyzing to see where they may have gone wrong, looking to earlier problems or relevant text sections for clues about what to do, noting what information is given and what is needed, or trying to determine what it is that they don't understand (and then getting help if necessary).

Efficacy training programs also involve exposing students to a planned set of experiences within an achievement context and providing them with modeling, instruction, and feedback. However, whereas attribution retraining programs were developed specifically for learned helplessness students and thus focus on teaching constructive response to failure, efficacy training programs were developed primarily for low achievers who have become accustomed to failure and have developed generalized low self-concepts of ability. Consequently, efficacy training helps students to set realistic goals and pursue them with the recognition that they have the ability (efficacy) needed to reach those goals if they apply reasonable effort.

Efficacy training is based on Bandura's theorizing about the role of self-efficacy perceptions in determining effort investment and performance levels in achievement tasks (Bandura, 1982; Bandura & Schunk, 1981). Schunk (1985) identified the following practices as effective for increasing students' self-efficacy perceptions (and, indirectly, their task persistence and achievement levels): (1) cognitive modeling that includes verbalization of task strategies, intentions to persist despite problems, and expressions of confidence in achieving eventual success; (2) explicit training in strategies for accomplishing the task; (3) performance feedback that points out correct operations, remedies errors, and reassures students that they are developing mastery; (4) attributional feedback that emphasizes the successes being achieved and attributes these to a combination of ability and effort (the student has the needed ability and will succeed with reasonable effort); (5) encouraging students to set goals prior to working on tasks (goals that are challenging but attainable, phrased in terms of specific performance standards, and oriented toward immediate short-term outcomes); (6) focusing feedback on how students' present performance surpasses their prior attainments rather than on how they compare with other students; and (7) supplying rewards contingent on actual accomplishment (not just task participation).

In *strategy training,* modeling and instruction are used to teach problem-solving strategies and related self-talk that students will need to handle tasks successfully. Strategy training is a component of good cognitive skills instruction to all students; it is not primarily a remedial technique. However, it is especially important for use with frustrated students who have not developed effective learning and problem-solving strategies on their own but who can learn them through modeling and explicit instruction.

Poor readers, for example, can be taught reading comprehension strategies such as identifying the purpose of the assignment and keeping it in mind when reading; activating relevant background knowledge; identifying major points and attending to the outline and flow of content; monitoring understanding by generating and attempting to answer questions about the content; and drawing and testing inferences by making interpretations, predictions, and conclusions (Duffy & Roehler, 1989; Palincsar & Brown, 1984; Raphael, 1984). Two keys to effective strategy training are that (1) it includes attention not just to propositional knowledge (what to do) but also to procedural knowledge (how to do it) and conditional knowledge (when and why to do it) and that (2) it includes cognitive modeling (thinking out loud that makes visible the covert thought processes that guide problem solving).

Programs have been developed for training students in general study skills (Devine, 1987) and in learning strategies such as rehearsal (repeating material to remember it more effectively), elaboration (putting material into one's own words and relating it to prior knowledge), organization (outlining material to highlight its structure and remember it), comprehension monitoring (keeping track of the strategies used and the degree of success achieved with them, and adjusting strategies accordingly), and maintenance of appropriate affect (maintaining concentration and task focus, minimizing performance anxiety and fear of failure) (Good & Brophy, 1995; Weinstein & Mayer, 1986). The affective management components that have been suggested for inclusion in general strategy training programs (McCombs, 1984; Rohrkemper & Bershon, 1984; Rohrkemper & Corno, 1988) are similar to those included in attribution retraining and efficacy training programs. Thus, a comprehensive cognition retraining program for failure syndrome students will include attention to both the cognitive and the affective aspects of task engagement and persistence.

Ames (1987) noted that the cognitive retraining approaches discussed so far are oriented toward individual students and do not take into account the social aspects of the classroom and the reward structures in effect there. Citing findings that an emphasis on competition and social comparison will increase performance anxiety, Ames recommended emphasizing private rather than public feedback, phrasing such feedback in terms of progress beyond the individual's own previous levels rather than comparisons with classmates, and avoiding such practices as publicly grading on a curve or posting students' achievement scores.

Dweck and Elliott (1983) have shown that normal students view intellectual ability as a repertoire of skills that can be increased incrementally through effort (you can develop the ability to do something through working at it, even if you do not possess the ability now). In contrast, learned helplessness students view intellectual ability as a global and stable entity that one possesses to a fixed degree. Therefore, they view failure at a particular task as a sign that they lack ability to succeed at that kind of task, and they respond to such failure by giving up rather than by seeking to overcome it through increased efforts or development of more effective problem-solving strategies.

Dweck and Elliott identified the following as teacher behaviors that encourage incremental rather than entity views of ability: acting more as resource persons than as judges, focusing students more on learning processes than on outcomes, reacting to errors as natural and useful parts of the learning process rather than as evidence of failure, stressing effort over ability and personal standards over normative standards when giving feedback, and attempting to stimulate achievement efforts through primarily intrinsic rather than extrinsic motivational strategies.

Dweck and Elliott (1983) added that students who have developed an *entity* view of ability (seeing it as fixed and limited) stand to benefit from direct training designed to shift them to an *incremental* view (seeing it as something that can be developed through practice). Similarly, Clifford (1984) argued the value of creating expectancies not merely for success on particular tasks but for more generalized levels of performance improvement as abilities are learned and solidified. Rohrkemper and Corno (1988) argued that teachers should provide both support and challenge/push to failure syndrome students, not merely ensure their consistent success by lowering your levels of demand.

Finally, additional approaches to cognitive restructuring have been developed as part of rational–emotive education (Knaus, 1974), which focuses on eliminating irrational beliefs that cause students to behave inappropriately. Irrational beliefs involved in failure syndrome problems are "catastrophic" reactions to failure ("I'm not getting it—I can't do it—there's no use in trying"). Once such irrational themes are identified, the teacher challenges and analyzes them with the student to replace them with more rational ones, such as that errors are a natural and expected part of the learning process and that deeper understanding and improved performance can be expected with persistent efforts.

ANALYSIS OF INTERVIEW RESPONSES

Responses concerning failure syndrome students were concentrated in just two of the categories for general problem-solving approaches. A large majority (78) of the teachers mentioned attempts to encourage, reassure, build self-concept, or provide support. In addition or instead, 38 teachers mentioned attempts to shape greater persistence and task completion through successive approximations. There was little or no emphasis on threat or punishment, teaching the students how to cope with anxiety or failure, treating external causes, developing insight, or trying to change attitudes through appeal or persuasion.

These same trends can be seen in the teachers' more specific problem-solving strategies. The ones mentioned by more than half of the teachers were building self-concept (67), encouraging increased effort or improved completion rates (62), providing tutoring or other academic help (59), changing the task to make the work easier (56), providing for frequent success experiences (52), and praising the student's efforts or successes (52).

Other commonly mentioned strategies included providing encouragement or expressing positive expectations (37); providing extra attention or support for motivational reasons (36); offering or delivering rewards (35); making sure that the student gets off to a good start on assignments (32); minimizing the time that the student must work independently by subdividing goals, giving work in smaller segments, or monitoring more closely (25); charting or demonstrating the student's progress or success levels (24); involving the parents (20) or school-based professionals (20) for support or problem solving; reducing expectations by giving fewer or shorter assignments (20) or easier work (20); diagnosing learning problems and then following up with more precise teaching (19); starting at the student's current level and moving forward from there (18); and assigning peers to provide academic help or motivational support (18).

Only about a third of the teachers mentioned methods of socializing attitudes and beliefs. The most common were encouraging the students to develop realistic expectations and acceptance of their strengths and weaknesses (12), trying to convince them that struggle and frustration are normal parts of learning and that they will need to learn to persist in the face of difficulties (12), and helping them to notice relative improvement and to think of such improvement as success even if it falls short of perfection (9).

Among strategies that the teachers rejected as ineffective, the most frequently mentioned were scolding or criticizing (22); pep talks, verbal buildups, or attempts to deny the problem (14); pushing the student to do better (13); continuing to give the student work that is too difficult or frustrating (10); persisting with expectations that are too high (7); and punishing (6).

Most of the teachers recommended praise, encouragement, self-concept support, programming for success, and tutorial assistance. However, the higher rated teachers mentioned a broader range of strategies: suggesting guidelines for coping with anxiety or discouragement (in addition to guidelines for responding to the task), starting at the student's current level of understanding, not only helping students to achieve success but allowing them opportunities to publicly demonstrate this success in group situations, and gradually phasing out special treatment when it was no longer needed.

In identifying reasons why students develop failure syndrome problems, the higher rated teachers were more likely to mention a past history featuring frequent failure experiences, whereas the lower rated teachers were more likely to mention assignments that are too difficult. Perhaps the latter teachers experienced difficulty in matching assignments to their students' needs. Finally, lower rated teachers were more likely to try to socialize failure syndrome students by convincing them that it is normal to struggle with assignments but they should persist nevertheless. Teachers who emphasized this response apparently were among the minority who did not emphasize the frequently mentioned strategies.

In summary, responses to the interviews concerning failure syndrome students converged on a set of commonly mentioned (and apparently effective) strategies: praise, encouragement, self-concept support, programming for success experiences, and tutorial help with assignments. The higher rated teachers were more systematic and detailed, but the lower rated teachers tended to emphasize the same basic ideas.

Vignette: Joe

Joe could be a capable student, but his self-concept is so poor that he actually describes himself as stupid. He makes no serious effort to learn, shrugging off responsibility by saying "that stuff" is too hard for him. Right now he is dawdling instead of getting started on an assignment that you know he can do. You know that if you approach him, he will begin to complain that the assignment is too hard and that he can't do it.

Before reading further, take time to think about how you might respond to this incident. Make notes about your ideas.

CSS Vignette Response Excerpts

Here is what four of the CSS teachers had to say.

A LOWER RATED TEACHER

" 'What grade level are you working at, Joe? Do you think you can do the work at this grade level? Are you really trying to do the work?' Joe probably lacks self-motivation more than anything. I would expect him to be able to do sixth-grade work. Remember, we're talking about someone who is capable of doing the work. We're not talking about someone who isn't capable; someone who is incapable would have to be dealt with differently. In other words, I would have to be sarcastic if I had to go down to a lower level of work with Joe. I would say, 'OK, then, I'll put you back in fifth grade, and we'll see what you're gonna do with fifth-grade work.' . . . Motivation is not there. A lazy streak is probably one of the worst things that many teachers cope with. They don't want to work unless someone gives them the answer. Joe is typical of that."

"My objective first would be to raise Joe's self-concept and try to get him to have enough self-pride to try assignments that he thinks might be too hard for him. I would concentrate on the pride angle, praising Joe for whatever good he did, and stressing that he had to do more and giving him the individual help to see that he did more work each day until he completed assignments without dawdling. So number one, for a day Joe would have to be the center of my attention. As soon as the lesson is introduced to the group, I would see that Joe understood the assignment in the first place, put his name on the paper, and got started. If there was a title to be written, I'd say, 'You didn't write the title of the lesson (or the date or whatever the heading was to be).' When he did it, give him some praise. 'That's very good. Now, how did we say that we would do the example?' Have Joe do another example. While the rest of the class understood the example and are working, Joe is pretending that he can't, so let's do another example. 'I'm going to help you.' If Joe still seems confused, we would do another example. Maybe for the first few days, Joe would need my help. If with my help he got half of the job done that the rest of his group was completing, he should feel better about himself in a few days and then would go on and attempt to finish an assignment. When he got part of it done, I would always have a mark that I would give him saying that you're getting better. I would use that kind of a stamp to do this, the kind that says, 'You've tried, keep on trying,' a happy face saying, 'Better today.' If he didn't complete it, I'd use a stamp that said "Incomplete" but with a little note. All of the notes would be positive rather than a lot of marks that would be depressing and defeating to a child who is having a problem, although he has the ability and could be a capable student. I prefer a positive approach, like 'You only got half of it done today, Joe, but tomorrow we're going to see if we can do two-thirds of it, because you can do it. I like what you did today.' My comments would be like that, rather than letter grades, some positive comments showing him what is good and what he needs to work on, saying, 'This is much better than yesterday.' This kind of thing, from my experience, helps Joe to know that I'm concerned, not that he gets the 100 percent or the 'A' like Andy over here always does, but 'I'm pleased that you are making progress, aren't you? We did better because I helped you. I want to see if you can tell me what I said, and show me. If you don't understand, I'll help you again.' Then we get a certain amount done. 'Now see if you can finish it.' Give him the positive comments then, the grading that would be Joe's and my grading system. He's making progress rather than have Joe compare with the class and feel defeated right off and say, 'I can't do that stuff. It's too hard for me.' 'It's not too hard for you, and if you work a little harder and with my help, and it's my job to help you, we're going to get it.' I feel that child would soon stop complaining and dawdling and would begin to do a little more because he feels that I am watching his progress as an individual and letting him know that he's growing and he should see growth after a few days. He should feel that he is capable, which he is."

ANOTHER HIGHER RATED TEACHER

"The first thing I would say to Joe is to ask him why he feels that what is in front of him is too difficult. Then I'd work through one of whatever he is doing and then watch him do another one, and if he is still not confident, I'd sit with him while he does yet another. Then let him do it on his own, with directions to bring his work to me when he is finished so that we can go over it together to see how he has done. If we use the example of a math problem, I would talk through the problem using the mathematical language and do it with him and have him write the answer. Then I would say, 'All right now, what are you going to do to begin this next one?' If he is unable to tell me, tell him again and have him tell it back to me. I would want to make sure that he can tell me what he has to do, and then I can reassure him that 'OK, you know what to do, and I want you to try it on your own.' . . . I think by working with him, you can begin to show him that you want to help him, so that he can feel that if he needs help, there is a place to go and get it. Also, you can help him work through it so he begins to gain a little confidence in whatever procedure he has undertaken. Give him the out that if he has trouble, or when he is finished, he can show it to me directly, so that we can look at it right away and he won't have delayed reinforcement. I see him as a student who for some reason has decided that he can't do what he is supposed to be able to do, and therefore he has a very poor self-concept."

ANOTHER HIGHER RATED TEACHER

"I would say to Joe that he has the assignment ahead of him and that he must do it. I would take no arguments as long as he has understood the directions and I know that he is capable of doing it and can do it. I would say that he has the choice of getting it done right at that particular time, and if he makes a choice of not doing it then, I would have him stay in to do it at recess or after school and work with him on it. I would do this because I feel that a child really needs to do their assignments. I try to give them assignments that could be completed in the time that they have in the classroom to do it, and they need to know that they make their own choices and are responsible for their own actions as far as either putting off an assignment or getting it completed. It is very important for them to know that they must complete an assignment, to know that this is one of the top priorities in the classroom. Being able to work independently is another goal of mine. So I try to work with a student to make them understand these goals, and I try to give them enough encouragement so that they know they can do it and enough help so that they would be able to complete their assignments."

Despite the wording of our vignette, the lower rated teacher interpreted Joe's behavior as evidence of laziness and therefore suggested a punitive rather than a helpful response. In contrast, the three higher rated teachers recognized the need to develop Joe's confidence and coping skills, so they spoke of encouraging him and working with him rather than just making demands and threatening sanctions. Even the last teacher, who expressed less sympathy for Joe than the previous two higher rated teachers, still emphasized the need to encourage him and to spend time helping him see that he could succeed.

Analysis of Responses to Joe

The teachers emphasized encouragement and shaping strategies in their responses to Joe. Most (94) mentioned at least one supportive behavior, especially instruction (75) and encouragement (51). The most frequently mentioned specific strategies were attempting to build up his self-concept (69), prescribing or modeling better coping strategies (66), offering rewards for task persistence or completion (23), and attempting to develop his insight into the problem (19).

The most commonly mentioned strategies for boosting Joe's motivation were motivating by helping (54) and providing reassurance or encouragement (44). Other methods included personal appeals or attempts to cajole Joe into renewed effort (18), offers of incentives for specified improvement (14), and demanding or insisting on better effort (10).

In summary, most of the teachers recommended strategies that featured support, encouragement, instructional assistance, and shaping through successive approximations. Only a minority would prod or pressure Joe, and even fewer would go so far as to threaten him with punishment.

Higher rated teachers were more likely to mention encouragement as a supportive behavior, making improvement demands on Joe and appealing to his pride or positive self-concept when doing so, providing him with brief supportive help as a way to motivate him to get to work or persist on tasks, giving him extra help in getting started on tasks, and offering behavior contracts. Their approach involved making improvement demands on Joe but at the same time providing him with support, encouragement, and assistance designed to ensure that he could meet such demands. In contrast, the lower rated teachers were more likely to report either making no improvement demands at all (e.g., by lowering their expectations for Joe or by providing him with praise or encouragement that was not contingent on actual performance) or else attempting to pressure him without providing much special support and assistance.

In summary, higher rated teachers were highly confident in their abilities to intervene successfully with Joe, using strategies that combined demands for improved persistence and task completion with provision of support, encouragement, and task assistance. Many lower rated teachers would take the same general approach but implement it less comprehensively or systematically, although some either would fail to make serious attempts to improve Joe's behavior or would confine their efforts to pressuring Joe without at the same time providing him with needed support, encouragement, and assistance.

Vignette: Mary

Mary has the intelligence to succeed, if she applied herself, but she is convinced that she can't handle it. She gets frustrated and disgusted very easily, and then she gives up. Instead of trying to solve the problem another way, or coming to you for help, she skips the problem and moves on. Today she brings you her assignment, claiming to be finished, but you see that she has skipped many items.

Before reading further, take time to think about how you might respond to this incident. Make notes about your ideas.

CSS Vignette Response Excerpts

Here is what four of the CSS teachers had to say.

A LOWER RATED TEACHER

" 'Mary, I see that you still have some problems here that you did not finish. Why did you skip them? You couldn't do them? If you need help, I'll help you. OK?' Mary can do the work, but she gets frustrated easily, and my goal is to get her not to be frustrated but to come to me for help if she can't do it on her own. She is the type of student who gives up very easily."

A Higher Rated Teacher

"Mary needs a lot of encouragement. Even though she gets through her work somehow, she is frustrated, she's disgusted, and she easily gives up. Well, this is a sign that she is not really understanding what she is doing, so one of the ways I could handle this is to first give her a lot of encouragement. Try to get her to feel better about herself. Try to get her to feel that she can achieve. At the moment, it appears that her feeling is 'I can't do it.' I might even say to her the very words 'Mary, you can do it.' Then I will go through enough of the work to allow her to feel that she understands how to go ahead with it. She might not, but I will go through enough of it so she will feel that she can. Then, it is likely that Mary is going to come to me many times, but I am not going to let her become dependent on me. I am going to say, 'Mary, you must think for yourself,' and I am going to give her an opportunity to do that. If she gets stuck on something where she just can't handle it, then I will go and give her assistance. But I am not going to let her become totally dependent on me. That won't help her any. I am going to do enough for her to give her something to begin with, and from there we will work, trying to give her self-confidence and the belief that she can do it."

Another Higher Rated Teacher

" 'Mary, I see looking through your paper that you haven't completed all the items on it. Perhaps we can go through these items together. Would you like to read the first item out loud to me?' I guess I would go through it. Sometimes children can be really bright but lack confidence in themselves. I wouldn't make a big deal about the fact that she said it was finished when it wasn't finished. I would just say, 'Oh, I see that you have skipped some things. Let's see if we can go through it together and you can get the answers down.' I think at this point she needs to build herself up. She needs to be able to feel that she can handle it. Sometimes you have to go along and do it with them for a little bit and give them a pat on the back or a little praise and let them know you like how they are trying, doing a good job, good thinking on this one. If you do it that way rather than getting all over her case for not having finished the paper, she is more likely to attempt the next paper. . . . My goal would be to help her see that she can do it, that she is able to do it. It would be me helping her and then gradually withdrawing much of that help until she could actually see for herself that she could do it on her own. If she really comes across something that she can't solve on her own, she could come to me for some help, rather than just skipping it."

" 'Mary, in looking over your assignment, it appears that you're not finished and that you really need to go back and take a look at all the items that you have skipped. What seems to be your difficulty with these? Do you have no idea what the answers are, or are they ones that you just skimmed over and didn't feel like answering, or are they things that perhaps you just didn't see?' At this point, I would have her go back to her seat, and if she did have any questions on them, make sure that she asked. If she turned it in again and it still wasn't finished, I would have her go item by item and ask new questions on them as far as what the difficulty was in doing them. She needs to have a paper that is complete at the end, otherwise she will turn in every paper without items completed. Since Mary has the intelligence to succeed, and it appears that she needs a lot of extra help, I might plan an afternoon session with her, not as a disciplinary measure or punishment to her, but to sit down with her and actually go through the assignment completely with her and be working on my own papers side by side, at her desk. Every time she comes to a point where she can't handle something, I would insist that she ask questions on it."

All four of the quoted teachers realized that Mary would need help. However, the lower rated teacher spoke of making a rather perfunctory invitation to Mary to come and get help when she needed it, whereas the three higher rated teachers suggested more specific and detailed plans for interacting with Mary regularly and moving her out of her failure syndrome pattern. In addition, two of them emphasized providing Mary with encouragement as well as help.

Analysis of Responses to Mary

General approaches for Mary were similar to those for Joe, but with more emphasis on shaping strategies and less emphasis on provision of encouragement, support, or assistance. Most of the teachers mentioned supportive behaviors, especially instruction (68), encouragement (38), specific praise (12), kid gloves treatment (12), and involving peers to support or help (12).

The most commonly mentioned specific strategies were prescribing or modeling better coping strategies (82), trying to build up Mary's self-concept (47), and trying to develop her insight into the problem (21). By far the most frequent response to Mary was to instruct her in more desirable responses to classroom tasks (e.g., to tell her to persist in trying to figure out difficult items and then to seek help from the teacher if necessary, but not to skip the item or just record a wild guess). This instruction was often accompanied by encouragement or self-concept support.

The most commonly mentioned methods for boosting Mary's motivation were providing her with attention or help (60) or with reassurance or encouragement (48). Only a minority of the teachers mentioned follow-up methods, most commonly providing Mary with self-concept support (13) or tutorial help (11).

The overwhelming majority of the teachers, regardless of effectiveness rating, stated that they would respond to Mary by explaining that it was not acceptable, or in her own best interests, for her to skip items and turn in incomplete work. Instead, she would be expected to be more persistent in trying to solve problems on her own, seeking help only if her efforts still had not succeeded. Most of the teachers would also attempt to motivate Mary by helping her with the work, by reassuring or encouraging her, or by providing self-concept support. The higher rated teachers were more likely to supplement this pattern with attempts to develop Mary's insight into her behavior and its consequences or with praise of her progress in completing assignments successfully.

In summary, most of the teachers recognized Mary's behavior as a failure syndrome problem rather than interpreting it as evidence of a deliberate attempt to shirk her responsibilities as a student, so that they would provide her with instructional support and assistance. Even so, they would also explain to Mary that it was not acceptable for her to skip items and that she would be expected to work more persistently when she encountered difficulties and to come to the teacher for help rather than turn in incomplete work. A majority of the teachers would supplement this instruction and socialization with encouragement and self-concept support for Mary, but a significant minority would be forceful and insistent in demanding improved performance from her.

COMPARISON OF RESPONSES TO JOE AND TO MARY

The teachers reported similar response strategies to the two vignettes, featuring assistance with assignments and clarification about expected behavior, usually accompanied by attempts at encouragement or self-concept support. A majority emphasized shaping improved behavior through successive approximations, gradually reducing instructional support as the student gained confidence in his or her ability to handle the work. Most of the teachers viewed task assistance as important not only for the instructional support it provided but also for its motivational role in reassuring the student that help would be available if needed and in redirecting attention from discouragement toward renewed task engagement.

One set of contrasts undergirded most of the noteworthy differences: The teachers saw Joe as a victim and mentioned supplementing task assistance with encouragement or self-concept support, but they were more likely to view Mary as needing to be pressured or prodded to improve her behavior. They responded to Joe primarily in terms of attempts to repair a damaged self-concept, whereas they responded to Mary primarily in terms of correcting bad work habits through socialization. However, even the teachers who would demand improved performance from Mary usually would do so in the context of reassuring her that she would be able to meet these demands and providing task assistance to help her do so.

QUALITATIVE IMPRESSIONS AND EXAMPLES

Unlike teachers in the upper grades, who tended to emphasize relatively impersonal task assistance and clarification of expectations, teachers in the lower grades often stressed providing emotional support to failure syndrome students. They spoke of getting physically close to these students, working together with them on assignments, showing appreciation for their efforts, and providing encouragement and reinforcement designed to build their confidence. This sympathetic and supportive stance probably helped such teachers to get off to a good start in working with failure syndrome students.

Good intentions are not enough by themselves, however, and the strategic thinking of some of the most warmly sympathetic teachers appeared to be too scattered to be very effective. Once they began talking about helping students with academic difficulties, some of these teachers would drift away from failure syndrome problems toward other problems such as perfectionism or limited ability. Such teachers sometimes included strategies that were overreactions to the defined problem (such as giving failure syndrome students shorter or easier assignments rather than helping them to see that they were capable of completing the regular assignments successfully). Or they would talk about implementing potentially helpful strategies in ways that would limit their effectiveness (such as praising students' clothing or appearance instead of their work accomplishments).

Several teachers working in kindergarten or first grade observed that severe failure syndrome problems are relatively rare in these early grades, although they become more common later. As one teacher put it, the children's self-concepts have not been "beaten down enough" yet. Another reason is that most young children have positive self-concepts of ability and optimistic performance expectations as part of the egocentrism of the preoperational years (until about age 6 or 7). As they begin to become

more operational in their thinking, they begin to make increasingly frequent and accurate comparisons between themselves and their peers. As
a result, unrealistically positive self-concepts and expectations begin to
give way to more realistic (or, in the case of failure syndrome students,
unjustifiably pessimistic) perceptions (Stipek, 1984). It appears that failure
syndrome problems are more serious and difficult to change in older students than in younger ones.

Some teachers working in kindergarten and first grade also mentioned that certain students superficially appear to have failure syndrome
problems in that they are prone to whine or say, "I can't do it" in response
to assignments. However, instead of genuinely suffering from shattered
confidence, they are merely seeking more attention from the teacher or
are unaccustomed to having demands made on them because they have
been babied at home. These socially immature students do not so much
need reassurance and task assistance as they need supportive yet firm limit
setting.

The following are noteworthy elaborations of commonly mentioned
strategies or unique suggestions made by individual teachers.

Causes. One teacher suggested that failure syndrome problems are
likely among grade repeaters who have become convinced that they are
stupid because they are repeating the grade. Another suggested that such
problems are likely in students who are learning English as a second language, and it is helpful to speak to these students in their native language
when giving them individualized task assistance.

Task Simplification Strategies. One teacher would briefly help failure
syndrome students, and then tell them to continue working a specified
set of problems on their own and to raise their hand when they were ready
for her to check their work and get them started on the next set. Another
would tell such students to give unobtrusive signals (such as folding their
arms) when they had finished part of the work and needed to speak to
the teacher before going on. Another would mark "C" next to correct
answers on the page, and then place a line farther down the page and
ask the child to try to get that far by the time she got back.

Problem Redefinition Strategies. A few teachers spoke of defining the
problem to the student in ways that made it seem less serious. For example, one would define Mary's problem as a tendency to rush through the
work too quickly and thus would tell her to go back, take her time and
finish carefully, and then bring up the assignment for review. Another
would tell Mary that she had inadvertently (i.e., not deliberately) skipped
some of the items and return the paper to her for completion.

Peer Involvement. One teacher would appoint another student to be
a designated helper for Mary. Mary could come to the peer to get help

in getting started, but the peer helper wouldn't do the work for her. Several teachers mentioned that having failure syndrome students act as tutors to peers or younger children was helpful in building up their confidence in their own knowledge.

Miscellaneous Suggestions. One teacher mentioned that computerized instruction or programmed learning allows the student to get feedback privately and thus is especially helpful for students who are concerned about being monitored or about having others see them make mistakes. Several mentioned the value of letting parents know that it is important to provide encouragement and reinforcement for their child's academic efforts and also not to call the child stupid or to allow peers or siblings to do so. Finally, one would identify certain work as "practice" that would not be graded (at least not in the same sense that the regular work was graded). This teacher would also tell the student that "there's nothing wrong with making a mistake. That's why there are erasers on pencils!"

DISCUSSION

The teachers were unusually confident about their abilities to intervene successfully with failure syndrome students. They tended to mention similar response strategies regardless of their grade level, location, or effectiveness ratings. A few spoke of providing support and encouragement to such students without making any demands on them, a few others spoke of making demands without providing special support or assistance, but most suggested a combination of support, encouragement, and task assistance to shape gradual improvement in work habits.

These teachers would make it clear to failure syndrome students that they were expected to work conscientiously and persistently so as to turn in work done completely and correctly, but they would also provide help if needed, reassure them that they would not be given work that they could not do, monitor their progress and provide any needed assistance, and reinforce them by praising their successes, calling attention to their progress, and providing them with opportunities to display their accomplishments publicly. This special treatment would be faded gradually (over a period typically expected to last several months) as the students gained confidence and began to work more persistently and independently.

This typical response pattern, especially in its more systematic versions given by higher rated teachers, appears well suited to the needs of failure syndrome students. It is particularly adequate from the standpoint of efficacy training. Although none of the teachers were familiar with this term, most of them intuitively favored the strategies stressed in efficacy training programs (negotiating agreement to strive to meet specific proximal goals and giving feedback that stresses the student's ability to suc-ceed). The typical response pattern appears less satisfactory from the stand-point of attribution retraining and remediation of learned helplessness. Most teachers mentioned support, encouragement, and instructional as-sistance but did not say much about learned helplessness symptoms (catas-trophic reactions to frustration, attribution of failure to lack of ability, giving up quickly). Nor was there much mention of modeling to teach better coping strategies or of teaching the student how to persist in the face of difficulty. It appears, then, that the strategies for responding to failure syndrome students that teachers develop intuitively through class-room experience could be augmented significantly by teaching them about self-efficacy training and attribution retraining as responses to learned helplessness problems.

Certain aspects of the typical response pattern are worth noting be-cause they go beyond the methods developed by psychologists for treat-ing learned helplessness problems, and in ways that take advantage of the continuing relationship that teachers share with their students. Helping the students to meet curricular goals is basic to the teacher's role, and the teacher can exert control over both the difficulty of the work assigned to students and the amount of extra help they receive. This puts teachers in a position not only to offer instruction or modeling in better coping strategies and to help failure syndrome students understand that they have the ability to handle the work but also to reassure them that they will give them work that they can handle in the first place and will provide whatever task assistance they need. Teachers can "create reality" for students who are beginning to develop failure syndrome problems. They may be able to short-circuit what otherwise might be a long, slow process by inform-ing failure syndrome students that they have been misinterpreting the situation and showing them how to respond to it in the future.

In summary, although teachers have not been exposed to the research literature on failure syndrome students, most of them develop ideas about the nature and causes of failure syndrome problems, as well as strategies for coping with these problems, that as far as they go reflect the major research findings. Teachers' effectiveness would probably be enhanced, however, if they learned to use modeling to teach coping strategies, espe-cially techniques for persisting in the face of frustration or failure.

6

Overly Perfectionistic Students

erfectionistic students display the following characteristics: These children are unduly anxious about making mistakes. Their self-imposed standards are unrealistically high, so that they are never satisfied with their work (when they should be). They:

1. Are too much of a "perfectionist"
2. Are often anxious/fearful/frustrated about the quality of their work
3. Hold back from class participation unless sure of themselves

What special strategies might you use to minimize such problems and help these students to function more successfully in your classroom? Before reading further, take time to think about this and make notes about your ideas.

CSS INTERVIEW EXCERPTS

Here is what three of the CSS teachers had to say about teaching perfectionistic students.

A LOWER RATED TEACHER

"They are fearful of making mistakes and should be told not to be afraid, that everybody makes mistakes and this is how we learn. 'I make mistakes, the principal makes mistakes, and you should at least try and not be afraid of making a mistake. If you do make a mistake, fine. This is the way you are going to learn.' Sometimes you have to be a little bit firm and say, 'You have to do it.' But keep telling them not to be afraid of making mistakes."

This teacher's response was confined to a socialization message (it's OK to make mistakes). Although intended to be sympathetic and reassuring, it sounds almost like a "lecture," and it was not accompanied by mention of any other forms of helping these students overcome their problems.

A HIGHER RATED TEACHER

"My general philosophy is to make them more accepting of the fact that they're fallible. They're so afraid about making mistakes, so afraid of criticism for not doing what they think they are expected to do. I can relate to this because I'm like this myself, and I really have to work at it. I would start on a one-to-one basis, just talking to them about the fact that we all make mistakes, and that rather than getting upset about it, we should look at it as a learning experience. What have I learned from this? How can I profit from it and go on? I can imagine this child having headaches or upset stomachs a lot, and counseling might be in order just to help them be more accepting of the way they are. I would probably also talk to the parents and, as tactfully as possible, ask them how they handle it when their child makes a mistake. Perhaps the child is helping wash the dishes and breaks a dish. How does the parent deal with this, because I think it all comes back to how the parents have dealt with the child making errors, or perhaps how their first new teachers dealt with errors. Another thing that I have done is have the class just talk about times when they've made mistakes, when things haven't turned out quite right, and how they felt about it and how they handled it. That frequently helps other children to know that they're not alone, that they're all in the same boat, that we're not perfect. . . . Also, I help them to differentiate between mistakes that are made when you're trying real hard and thoughtless kinds of mistakes, that if you're putting forth your best effort, it's OK if you're still having difficulty; just ask for some help."

This teacher also wanted to help perfectionists come to understand that mistakes are a natural part of the learning process, but she suggested doing so in more varied and likely effective ways than the first teacher. In part, this was because she had special insight into the problem since she suffered from it herself. Note that instead of confining her response to brief verbal reassurance, this teacher would engage in more extensive and informative discussion with perfectionistic students, work on their coping skills as well as their attitudes, and speak to their parents about avoiding counterproductive responses to their children's mistakes.

ANOTHER HIGHER RATED TEACHER

"My philosophy with this kind of child is that I think they need to feel comfortable with what they can do. They should be taught to set realistic goals, and they need to feel comfortable with goal setting. This is what I try to work toward with this type of child. Right at the very beginning of school, we talk about how important it is to set realistic goals. We note that you don't set a goal for a baby that they're going to walk in 2 months or that they're going to talk in just a few weeks; this kind of development comes gradually. When one thing develops, we begin to look and say, 'Well, see if we can improve on this, or can we set a higher goal.' And I try to have children write down goals at the beginning of the year. One thing that helps me with all of this is getting to know children and how they feel about themselves, and one way I can begin to spot this before I really find out from their work is to have them write something about themselves. I introduce myself to them, and I want them to tell me as much as they can about themselves so I can get to know them and understand them, to let them know that I'm interested in them. Sometimes something might come out that would show that they do something but it's never good enough or doesn't please somebody. They think that they need to do it perfectly for the teacher or the parent. 'Even though I do it as well as I can, she (Mom) doesn't accept it.' So another thing I ask them to do, a few weeks later as they're working along and know what we're going to be doing, is to set some goals for themselves — some short-term goals, maybe something that they're going to do within that week, for instance, that they were going to complete their assignments and have them in on time. That might be a goal. Now, when I begin to see that there is a child that is not pleased with what they're doing, even though I am accepting of it, they still don't feel that it's good enough, I would sit down with them, and we would talk about 'Well, are you setting too high a goal for yourself? Sometimes this is something that we do, and we can't achieve it.' I try to give them some concrete examples, you know, not related to academic work, perhaps out of my own experience, like if I wanted to lose weight, 10 pounds in 2 weeks would be too high a goal and I would become frustrated. I also would ask about their feelings: 'How do you feel when you do a paper and you don't think it's good enough and you want to throw it away and start over again?' Then they begin to think that this just makes things worse. I've had children say, 'Well, then I try to do it and it still doesn't work out, and then I don't want to do it at all.' I think they begin to become very frustrated and see that they are trying to do something that's just *too* good. I think this is a really hard line to tread because you want them to work to certain standards, and I *do* tell the class that I *do* expect certain things. I try to go a little beyond saying, 'I want you to do your very best' by giving them some definite things that I expect of them. 'I expect neatness in your work, I expect you to proofread your work and to try to find your errors, and I expect you to read directions and try to do it without coming to the teacher for help.' I am trying to work toward independency in their work. I have had children come back to me and always want approval. They feel it's not good enough. Sometimes these are not real perfectionists; they just want some kind of approval and praise, and want *you* to say that it is good enough.... Right at the beginning of the year I tell them that in this classroom it's permissible to make some mistakes, and very often this is the only way to learn. Don't be afraid to speak in class. We want to hear everybody's ideas, and they're all worth something. Try to make the children feel comfortable when they make mistakes, to have other children be accepting.... Be very accepting of what they do and yet not lower your standards either. This is hard to do because you don't want them to lower their standards, and yet you don't want them to be so much of a perfectionist that it makes them frustrated. I think you have to move very slowly with this child too. Very often, before general class participation, I might have small groups of children working on one particular topic, maybe three children that I feel would work well together in sharing ideas. I try not to have one in this particular child's group that always wants to carry the ball of the conversation, but there might be one that's a little stronger than the others but won't just take over. They can all share some kinds of ideas and often work maybe on a newspaper current event where they report to the class. I think if you can get them to do this, very gradually they feel much more at ease. There are some that just always have trouble if it's their own idea. They are very much afraid to offer, but again, I have found it best just being accepting of what they do say and *never* putting a child down or using sarcasm. Also you should never force the child. For instance, with reporting to the class, don't force them into getting in front of the class and don't call on them if they are not offering, because once you do this, you really shut them off. That doesn't work."

This teacher emphasized goal setting in socializing her students. She would work within this goal-setting emphasis to help perfectionistic students learn to think in terms of improvement through successive approximations rather than feeling that they need to be perfect the first time they try to do something. She also expressed several other ideas about actions to emphasize or to avoid in dealing with perfectionists, and like the previously quoted higher rated teacher, she emphasized helping these students learn to recognize the nature and implications of different kinds of mistakes.

WHAT THE SCHOLARLY LITERATURE SAYS

Perfectionists show unsatisfactory achievement progress because they are more concerned about avoiding mistakes than about learning. They are inhibited about classroom participation and counterproductively compulsive in their work habits.

Varieties and Causes of Perfectionism

Perfectionists are not satisfied with merely doing well or even with doing better than their peers. Instead, they are satisfied only if they have done a job perfectly, so that the result reveals no blemishes or weaknesses. To the extent that perfectionism involves striving for difficult but reachable goals, it includes the success-seeking aspects of healthy achievement motivation and functions as an asset to the student and an ally to the teacher. Even a *success-seeking* version of perfectionism, however, can become a problem to the extent that the student begins to focus not so much on meeting personal goals as on winning competitions against classmates (Furtwengler & Konnert, 1982).

More serious problems are associated with forms of perfectionism that focus on *avoiding failure* (Burns, 1980). Fear of failure (or of blame, rejection, or other anticipated social consequences of failure) can be extremely destructive to achievement motivation, especially if it is powerful and persistent. Victims of such fear typically try to avoid or escape as quickly as possible from achievement situations in which their performance will be judged according to standards of excellence. When this is not possible, they try to protect their self-esteem by either expressing very low aspirations that will be easy to fulfill or expressing impossibly high aspirations that they have no serious intention of striving to fulfill. In the school setting, many such students eventually become alienated underachievers.

Other students who are obsessed with avoiding failure do not simply follow the path of least resistance by avoiding achievement situations or minimizing their personal investment in them. These students have a powerful sense of responsibility for doing as well as they can on assignments. Thus, they are caught between a strong drive for perfection and a continuing preoccupation with avoiding failure. To the extent that their failure avoidance concerns become rigid and preponderant, they will undermine the potentially positive aspects of "normal" perfectionism and result in what Hamachek (1978) called "neurotic" perfectionism. Such students become driven. They rarely feel that they have done things well enough to warrant a sense of satisfaction, and they do not experience satisfaction for long even when they succeed in meeting their perfectionistic standards.

Pacht (1984) listed the following as symptoms of neurotic perfectionism: impossibly high and rigid performance standards, motivated more by fear of failure than by seeking after success, tendency to measure one's own worth entirely in terms of productivity and accomplishment, all-or-nothing evaluations that label anything other than perfection as failure, difficulty in taking credit or pleasure even when success is achieved because such achievement is merely what is expected, seeking to avoid being judged for fear of being found wanting and thus being rejected, procrastination in getting started on work that will be judged, and continually starting things over again or taking a long time to do them because the work must be perfect right from the beginning and continue to be perfect as one goes along. Symptoms commonly observed in students include unwillingness to volunteer to respond to questions unless certain of the correct answer, overly emotional and "catastrophic" reactions to minor failures, and low productivity due to procrastination or excessive "start overs."

Low productivity problems with perfectionistic students are especially likely to develop around written work. Writing creates a lasting product that is (or at least seems) more vulnerable to criticism than fleeting verbal responses. Also, the writing process presents numerous opportunities to procrastinate by wondering if each word is the right word, if it's spelled correctly, if the sentence is punctuated properly, and so on.

The causes of perfectionism problems in elementary students are usually traced to parent–child dynamics. Hamachek (1978) suggested that such students come from homes in which they receive either (1) nonapproval or inconsistent approval, so that they never learn how to please the parent, or (2) only conditional approval that is contingent on doing things perfectly. Pacht (1984) hypothesized similar causes, suggesting that neurotic perfectionists are continually trying to convince their parents that they are lovable by being perfect. Other possible causes, compatible with those already mentioned, include modeling by parents who are similarly perfectionistic themselves and impose perfectionistic expectations on the child, attempts to compete with a "perfect" sibling, and a tendency of current or past teachers to overstress perfect work and criticize imperfections.

Suggested Strategies for Coping with Perfectionistic Students

Common sense suggests that these students need resocialization concerning performance norms and work expectations. They need to learn that (1) schools are places to *learn* knowledge and skills, not merely to *demonstrate* them; (2) errors are normal, expected, and often necessary aspects of the learning process; (3) everyone makes mistakes, including the teacher;

(4) there is no reason to devalue oneself or fear rejection or punishment just because one has made a mistake; and (5) it is usually more helpful to think in terms of making progress from where one is now rather than comparing oneself with peers or with ideals of perfection.

Swift and Spivack (1975) emphasized that resocialization attempts with perfectionists need to be couched within a context of acceptance of their motivation to achieve and their need to feel satisfied with their accomplishments. Thus, instead of just dismissing their concerns as unfounded (and expecting them to accept this view), teachers should use active listening methods to encourage these students to express their concerns, make it clear that they take those concerns seriously, and engage in collaborative planning with the student concerning steps that might alleviate the problem.

As Pacht (1984) put it, the goal is to help perfectionist students achieve a 20- or 30-degree change rather than a 180-degree turnaround. We want them to retain their dispositions toward aiming high and putting forth their best efforts, but to learn to do so in ways that are more realistic and productive, less rigid and compulsive. Because their problems are rooted in their own attitudes, beliefs, and expectations, intervention efforts are likely to feature some form of cognitive restructuring. Two of the better known approaches are rational–emotive education and cognitive-behavior modification.

Rational–emotive education (Hajzler & Bernard, 1991; Knaus, 1974; Vernon, 1989) focuses on eliminating irrational beliefs that cause students to behave inappropriately. Common irrational beliefs related to perfectionism include rigid expectations and "catastrophic" reactions to failure. ("I expected to get all of them right. This is awful! I should have done better. I am worthless and no good.") The teacher challenges, questions, and logically analyzes such irrational themes with the student in order to replace them with more rational ones. Thus, the idea that mistakes are horrible and crippling catastrophes would be replaced with the idea that they are minor setbacks to be overcome. Similarly, the idea that poor performance implies that one is a bad person would be replaced with the idea that one's worth as a person is tied much more closely to enduring character traits than to performance on particular tasks.

Cognitive-behavior modification strategies focus on developing effective coping responses to stressful situations. Meichenbaum (1977) used a three-stage process: (1) Teach clients to become good observers of their own thoughts, feelings, and behaviors; (2) make the process of self-observation the occasion for emitting adaptive cognitions and behaviors; (3) alter the person's internal dialogues so that changes can be generalized. Problem situations are role played so that the person can practice using coping statements before, during, and after these situations. With perfectionists, the problem situations would center around failure experiences, and the training would teach them to replace catastrophic emotional reactions focused on the self with task-focused thinking that will help them to profit from the mistake by identifying the reasons for it and taking corrective action.

Burns (1980) recommended cognitive-behavior therapy for perfectionists. This method begins by asking clients to list the advantages and disadvantages of their perfectionism, partly to acknowledge its productive aspects but mostly to make them aware, often for the first time, that their perfectionism causes them to be both less accomplished and less happy than they should be. After this consciousness-raising, the treatment proceeds to exercises designed to help the clients begin to set more realistic goals, to be flexible rather than all-or-nothing in evaluating levels of success, to recognize when their work on a task has passed the point of diminishing returns (so it is time to wrap it up), and to take satisfaction in achievements that are solid even if not perfect.

Barrow and Moore (1983) developed group interventions for perfectionists that involved both rational–emotive education and cognitive-behavior modification. Group members were taught to (1) become more discriminating in setting standards and goals, (2) develop more tolerance for the inevitable times when goals are not met, (3) differentiate self-worth from task performance, and (4) develop a cognitive coping process to moderate and control initial perfectionistic responses.

The cognitive restructuring techniques that therapists have developed for use with their clients could also be used by teachers with their students. Teachers are in a position to use other techniques as well. As authority figures who both demand performance from students and judge the quality of that performance, teachers are in a position to communicate performance standards that students can use for judging their levels of success. In the case of perfectionists, the teacher's standards are likely to be more lenient (e.g., realistic) than the students', so that teacher clarity and consistency in articulating these standards may reduce the tendency of such students to set themselves up for failure. Similarly, teachers may help such students become more task-focused and less self-focused by reminding them that a particular exercise is intended as a learning experience where mistakes are expected. They also can help the students to make better use of work time by clarifying the primary purposes of activities (e.g., explaining that students should concentrate on the content and flow of ideas in developing first drafts of compositions, postponing concern about spelling and punctuation until later drafts).

Teachers also are in a position to assist by reassuring perfectionists of their interest in seeing them succeed and their willingness to help them do so, by providing consistent encouragement and support, by monitoring them closely so as to be able to intervene quickly when they start to become frustrated, and by providing assistance when they are having trouble getting started or have become flustered by mistakes. Such techniques will be most effective, of course, if they are merely personalized elaborations on more general efforts to establish the classroom as a collaborative learning community. In such a classroom, all of the students learn to view the teacher as a helper and resource person, to focus on working together to learn rather than on competing with others or displaying superiority, and to become comfortable in taking intellectual risks and making mistakes as part of the learning process.

McIntyre (1989) suggested these and several other teacher strategies for working with perfectionists: "Give permission" to make mistakes or divide assignments into outline, rough draft, and final draft stages, with perfection promoted only for the final drafts; discuss with the student appropriate reactions to making mistakes; and frequently use ungraded assignments or assignments that call for creative and individual responses rather than correct answers. If necessary, place limits on perfectionistic procrastination by limiting the time that can be spent on an assignment or the amount of erasing allowed.

Teachers must be careful to be sure that the assistance they provide does not make these students overly dependent on them to the point that they seek teacher clarification and approval of every step of their work. The goal is to gradually wean the student toward a more independent work posture.

ANALYSIS OF INTERVIEW RESPONSES

A majority (56) of the teachers mentioned some attempt to appeal to, persuade, or change the attitudes of perfectionistic students. In addition or instead, 32 mentioned attempts to encourage, reassure, build self-concept, or support these students; and 20 mentioned providing instruction, training, modeling, or help designed to eliminate the problem. Thus, persuasion, encouragement, and assistance were the most frequently mentioned responses to neurotic perfectionism.

The most commonly mentioned specific problem-solving strategies were appeal or persuasion (50), prescribing/telling/instructing/eliciting guidelines for improved coping (41), pressuring the student to complete assignments even if they are not done perfectly (38), showing the student that the teacher makes mistakes too (33), praising the student's accomplishments (31), proscribing by imposing limits or stating rules (e.g., about turning in work completed and on time) (30), attempting to build self-concept (26), and indirect modeling of appropriate attitudes about and effective coping responses to failure (25).

Three-fourths of the teachers mentioned methods of socializing attitudes and beliefs. More than half (52) would try to get the student to see that everyone makes mistakes, no one is perfect, mistakes are no big deal, we learn from them, and so on. Other socialization attempts included explaining how perfectionism is counterproductive for the student (24), trying to teach the student to set more realistic or individualized goals (18), communicating the teacher's standards more clearly or forcefully in an attempt to get the student to use these standards rather than his or her own more rigid standards (17), and explaining that perfect performance is an ultimate goal to be approached gradually in small steps rather than something to be expected on the first try (10).

More than half of the teachers mentioned methods of reducing the pressures experienced by perfectionistic students, most commonly articulating expectations that stress learning and improvement over 100 percent perfect performance on assignments (43). Other methods included allowing the student to redo the work until pleased with it (13); accommodating to the student's needs by marking the correct answers rather than incorrect ones or by making tiny correction marks that could be erased easily when the answer was corrected, so that the student would end up with a perfect paper (12); and reducing time pressures by allowing the student to complete tasks at home or after school (6).

Of the strategies that the teachers rejected as ineffective, the most frequently mentioned (by 33 teachers) involved criticizing or nagging the student, insisting on improved behavior, or threatening punishment for failure to improve. Other strategies mentioned as ineffective included simply ignoring the problem (8) and giving pep talks that have the effect of denying the problem rather than confronting it (6).

Taken together, the frequency data indicate that most of the teachers would respond to perfectionism with some combination of strategies that emphasized persuasion or attitude change (designed to get the student to adopt more realistic goals and to see that everyone makes mistakes and one should not overreact to them), encouragement and self-concept support, and assistance (making sure that the student gets off to a good start on assignments and monitoring closely so as to be able to provide assistance when necessary). More than a third of the teachers also mentioned pressuring perfectionistic students on the issue of timely completion of assignments, but usually with emphasis on encouragement and assistance (rather than threats of punishment). Finally, in addition to describing reactive strategies for responding to already developed perfectionism problems, many teachers stressed proactive strategies for preventing the development of such problems by building a friendly and supportive learning environment, establishing the expectation that mistakes are a normal part of the learning process, and presenting themselves as helpful instructors concerned primarily with promoting student learning rather than as forbidding authority figures concerned primarily with evaluating student performance.

The correlational data indicated (1) a negative relationship with effectiveness ratings for teacher responses that were confined to attempts to control or suppress the problem behavior; (2) no significant relationship for the most popular response of trying to change the student's attitudes through appeal or persuasion; and (3) positive relationships for offering instruction, training, modeling, or help designed to assist the student in eliminating the problem and for attempting to be supportive by providing encouragement or reassurance, building the student's self-concept, or establishing the classroom as a supportive learning environment.

Except for the 10 teachers who confined themselves to control or suppression strategies, responses to perfectionistic students emphasized empathy, concern, and attempts to be helpful. However, the higher rated teachers generally mentioned more strategies and included more elaboration concerning their implementation. In particular, they were more likely to mention instruction/help or encouragement/support strategies in addition to or instead of appeal/persuasion strategies. Higher rated teachers also were more likely to mention strategies for preventing perfectionism problems from occurring in the first place and to speak of providing patient and personalized assistance that might extend over a considerable time period to students who did develop such problems.

These data suggest, however, that any positive effects that persuasion and socialization strategies may have on perfectionistic students are insufficient to accomplish significant improvement—that these students need sustained support and assistance, not just brief doses of well-intentioned advice. Related findings include a negative relationship for attempting to encourage by expressing positive expectations, coupled with positive relationships for building self-concept, providing tutoring or other academic help, seeing that the student gets off to a good start on assignments, and monitoring the student closely so as to be able to give assistance if needed. These data indicate that teachers who provide only verbal and somewhat empty reassurances ("Don't worry, you'll get it, everything will turn out fine in the end") are less likely to be effective with perfectionistic students than teachers who provide these students with academic help (thus making sure that they succeed) or who present them with objective evidence of their progress or accomplishments (thus providing them with good reasons for accepting the teacher's reassurances).

Most teachers would assume an empathetic and helpful stance in response to perfectionistic students, even when cautioning them against undesirable behavior. In contrast to their reported responses to alienated underachievers, which often involved demands for timely work completion backed by threats of punishment for noncompliance, the teachers mentioned work completion expectations and deadlines to perfectionistic students as part of attempts to help them succeed by providing structure and assistance (i.e., as friendly reminders rather than as threats).

Higher rated teachers tended to assume that students in general would be vulnerable to anxiety about their abilities to meet performance expectations, so they often spoke of the need to establish the classroom as a supportive learning environment and themselves as supportive helpers right from the beginning of the year. These teachers defined acceptable performance in terms of consistent good efforts and steady progress rather than in terms of comparisons with ideal standards or the performance of peers, and they spoke of communicating appreciation for effort and valuing of contributions whether correct or incorrect. To the extent that it proved necessary to do so, they then would supplement these strategies for socializing the class as a whole with group meetings or individualized treatments designed to counteract neurotic perfectionism, fear of failure, test anxiety, and related problems.

Higher rated teachers were more disposed than lower rated teachers to take perfectionistic students' high performance standards and related anxieties seriously. They were prepared to deal with them in ways that required considerable empathy and patience and involved providing intensive and personalized help, as well as special considerations such as marking only correct responses or marking incorrect answers in ways that could be erased easily.

Most of the variables that failed to correlate significantly with effectiveness ratings were not directly responsive to the problem. For example, offering rewards for better performance might be appropriate for students who lacked incentives, but it does not address perfectionistic students' performance anxiety. Similarly, arranging for positive classroom participation experiences or for opportunities to demonstrate success in public might have some marginal value, but these students suffer primarily from their own self-imposed rigid performance standards rather than from overconcern about how classmates view them. Also, kid gloves treatment or attempts to provide comfort or reassurance when the student is upset might help the student through stressful situations, but by themselves they do nothing to address the underlying perfectionism problem that produces these stressful situations in the first place.

In summary, the vast majority of the teachers would emphasize empathy and help in response to perfectionism problems. Mention of attempts to change beliefs or attitudes through appeal or persuasion was the most common response, but this response did not differentiate higher rated from lower rated teachers. Instead, higher rated teachers were notable for their more frequent mention of preventive measures designed to establish the classroom as a supportive learning environment and of patient, personalized, and sustained efforts to assist perfectionistic students by providing them with (1) academic monitoring and help to ensure that they could meet performance demands and (2) self-concept support in the form of credible reassurance that they were making acceptable progress and could be expected to continue to do so. The higher rated teachers also said that they would strive to help perfectionistic students learn to set more realistic goals and to cope more effectively with failure, but they mentioned these socialization attempts in addition to rather than instead of attempts to provide academic help and self-concept support.

Vignette: Beth

Beth has average ability for schoolwork, but she is so anxious about the quality of her work that she seldom finishes an assignment because of all her "start-overs." This morning you have asked the children to make pictures to decorate the room. The time allocated to art has almost run out, and Beth is far from finished with her picture. You ask her about it and find out she has "made mistakes" on the other ones and this is her third attempt at a "good picture."

Before reading further, take time to think about how you might respond to this incident. Make notes about your ideas.

CSS Vignette Response Excerpts

Here is what four of the CSS teachers had to say.

A LOWER RATED TEACHER

"We talk a lot about conservation of our materials, and we have a quota of how many times you can start over, so she would know automatically that she wasn't supposed to start over that many times without permission. They can get permission, but at least it makes them stop and think before they start over again. . . . I might suggest that she start over on the back and then just say to her that we have to be through at such and such a time and that this will have to be her finished product. Sometimes you have to put limits on children or they'll never stop."

A HIGHER RATED TEACHER

" 'Beth, let's take a look at these other pictures that you started. Tell me what you think didn't go right.' I would wait for her to give me an explanation, and I would say, 'Beth, whenever people make things or do things, nobody is perfect, and we all make mistakes. Every time you do something, you'll get a little bit better, but you have to try and take something and complete it because just the act of doing it, just trying to do it, will make the next time you do it a little easier.' I would probably give her an example of something where I had made a mistake but had then gone ahead. Help her to know that other people feel the same way when they make things that don't come out just right, but you accept it as a learning experience, that you are being unfair to yourself if you always want things to be perfect. I would tell Beth that her attempts have been fine, that it's OK if your picture doesn't come out exactly how you expected it to, and that you have to accept it. That is the way it is. When you go through life, it's partly the mistakes in the doing that help you learn to become more capable. . . . My goal would be to help her accept the fact that it is OK to make a mistake because things don't have to be perfect, to be more accepting of what she is able to do. Maybe the person next to her is really artistic, but she should understand that she is Beth and this is what Beth can do, and you shouldn't expect to do exactly what the other person can do."

ANOTHER HIGHER RATED TEACHER

"I would begin by asking Beth what she wanted to make in her picture and why she felt that the others were mistakes. If we could find others in the wastepaper basket where she put them, we could look at all of them and talk about what she had done. She is frustrated apparently by her inability to make pictures the way she wants to, but maybe she is expecting too much from herself. I am not sure that we can solve this problem in one session, but I think Beth and I could talk about what she expects of herself, and is that really something that she can do now or is it something that she can work toward? She may not be able to finish the picture at that time. She may want to finish it later. I would certainly encourage her to finish it later, and if she did so, we would talk about it again and notice the things that she liked about it and maybe the things that she felt weren't good enough and what she might have to try to work on to make it up to par as far as she is concerned. I would also talk to her about the fact that it is good that she sets high goals for herself, but she needs to consider more what she is able to do at this time. She cannot expect everything to be perfect. I think that this child is a perfectionist, and she may have to fight this problem for a long time before she works it out with herself as far as her expectations and what she is actually capable of doing."

" 'Beth, this is your third attempt, and you have not completed your pictures because you have made mistakes on the other ones. I wish that you would bring up your first one to me when you think you make mistakes, and we could look it over. Maybe you are just being too critical of what you do. Don't try to compare yourself to what all the other boys and girls are doing. You are an individual, and if you're doing the best job that you can, that's all anyone should ask of you and you should be happy with that. You should try to do your best and try to be happy with what you come up with. I'm sure that what you have done is a very good picture. If you keep throwing things away, then you never get anything completed. I think you would like to have your work displayed with the rest of the children. If the time has run out and you want to complete something, maybe you could stay a few minutes after school and complete it then. There wouldn't be anyone else around, and maybe you would find that you could get it done during that time. But I certainly think that you should try to complete your work and try to be happy with what you have done.' My goal would be to have her start something, to try to look at what they have done and not be so critical, not to compare themselves with the other children in the room, possibly to work by themselves later on so that there aren't other children around who are looking at their things and being critical of what they are doing."

The lower rated teacher spoke of dealing with Beth mostly as an irritating child who was using too much paper. In contrast, the higher rated teachers focused on Beth's perfectionism problem and suggested attempting to socialize her toward more realistic goal setting and more productive responding to mistakes.

Analysis of Responses to Beth

The teachers tended to see Beth as a victim of her own rigid standards and expectations. Half (47) advocated the general approach of shaping through successive approximations by first providing Beth with heavy doses of structuring, encouragement, and assistance, and then gradually reducing the frequency and intensity of these personalized interventions as she became more able to cope effectively with failure and work productively on her own.

All but seven of the teachers mentioned at least one supportive behavior, most frequently instruction (54), encouragement (36), specific behavioral praise (24), comfort or reassurance when Beth was upset (19), and kid gloves treatment to help Beth through difficult periods (19).

Most of the commonly mentioned specific strategies involved providing Beth with some form of support or assistance: prescribing or modeling better ways of coping with the task (70), attempting to build up her self-concept (40) or develop her insight into the problem (38), proscribing by stating rules, limits, or expectations (20), attempting to eliminate an external source of the problem (20), and brief management responses designed to deal with the incident in only a minimal way and then get Beth back to work quickly (15).

All but 16 of the teachers mentioned at least one strategy for resocializing Beth's perfectionism concerns. The most frequently mentioned was to reject her perception that the pictures were unacceptable and to relabel all or part of them as successful or at least as a good start (36). Other resocialization strategies included attributing her problems to poor goal setting and planning skills rather than to lack of artistic talent and then helping her to plan by asking questions or making suggestions (24), rejecting her claim that she could not do the task and trying to cajole, demand, or encourage her to do it (24), reassuring her that whatever picture she turned in would be acceptable (22), reassuring her that mistakes are normal and expected (20), accepting her criticism of her work but labeling her expectations as too high or rigid (16), and cautioning her not to worry about what peers were doing or to judge her work by comparing it with theirs (6).

Strategies for getting Beth started again included encouraging her to finish or appealing to her using personalized or logical arguments (36), pressuring her to complete the picture by noting time constraints or limited paper supplies (27), helping her to plan how to salvage one of her existing efforts (15), and staying with her to work with her continuously to finish the picture (7). Strategies for dealing with the time constraints involved allowing Beth to continue to work on the picture after the time limit or to complete it later (39), pressuring her to finish quickly (24), and ordering her to turn in whatever she had finished when the time ran out, even if it were not completed (12). Rationales offered as justifications for behavior change demands made on Beth usually involved citing rules (typically those limiting the use of paper or requiring that students turn in their work at specified times) (34).

Twenty-four teachers did not mention any attempt to work on the larger perfectionism problem, so that their goals were confined to the immediate situation and centered around getting Beth to complete the task. Broader goals mentioned or implied by the other teachers included arranging for Beth to experience success frequently or trying to get her to redefine her work as successful by praising it frequently (34), and trying to teach her to set more realistic goals (28), to think and act in terms of completing what she starts (16), or to plan her work before beginning and to adjust plans in order to salvage what has been accomplished so far (16).

In summary, a majority of the teachers were confident that they could intervene successfully with Beth, and most would do so using strategies that featured support, encouragement, instructional assistance, and shaping of more efficient task completion rates through successive approximations.

Higher rated teachers generally mentioned more strategies and gave more elaboration about implementing those strategies. They also called for more intensive and personalized treatment that would extend over a longer time period. Lower rated teachers focused on getting Beth to complete the picture (often by pressuring her to do so), with little or no mention of working on the larger perfectionism problem, dealing with her perfectionism concerns at the moment, supportive behavior, or follow-up strategies. Some of these teachers responded as if this were simply a case of dawdling, or else treated it primarily as an occasion for restating classroom rules (students are allowed only one piece of paper for drawing pictures; students are required to turn in their work at the end of the period even if it is not completed). Teachers who gave these kinds of responses appeared to be oblivious or at least insensitive to Beth's perfectionism problem. Other lower rated teachers were sensitive to the problem and spoke of addressing it at least to the extent of suggesting better coping strategies and providing some form of encouragement or self-concept support, but their responses usually were less systematic and detailed than those of higher rated teachers.

Higher rated teachers' strategies for responding to Beth usually included considerable instructional input. Some of this was focused on the immediate task completion problem and involved sitting down to work with Beth or give her suggestions about how to salvage one of her existing efforts (or to plan a new picture in sufficient detail to allow her to work smoothly through to completion). To the extent that these teachers were concerned about task completion or time constraints, they might place light pressures on Beth by appealing to her sense of pride or positive self-concept or by reminding her that she would have to turn in whatever she had completed when the time period ran out. However, any such pressures were likely to be applied within a larger context of support, encouragement, and reassurance to Beth that both she and her work were acceptable. The teachers in general, and the higher rated teachers in particular, usually did not want to make an issue out of the drawing assignment by insisting that Beth turn in an acceptable picture complete and/or on time (many teachers mentioned that they might do so if this had been an academic assignment instead of an art activity).

Other instructional input that higher rated teachers said they would provide to Beth would be directed at her perfectionistic attitudes and be-havior, either in general or in relation to the task at hand. These teachers would try to develop Beth's insight into the problem by helping her to set more realistic goals, to realize that everyone makes mistakes, or to recognize that her perfectionism was keeping her from achieving her potential.

Higher rated teachers also were more likely to speak of providing Beth with support and encouragement. They would accentuate the posi-tive in their comments to Beth about her efforts so far, pointing out aspects that they liked, reassuring her that one or more of her efforts were sal-vageable or that a newly planned effort would result in a good picture, reassuring her that she had the ability to create good pictures but was simply going about it in the wrong way, and offering assistance. To help Beth experience the success that she craved, they would structure tasks more completely for her (break them into smaller segments, provide more detailed instructions, etc.).

Finally, higher rated teachers were more likely to state that they would hang Beth's picture on the wall for display. This would provide oppor-tunities for Beth to get peer recognition for her efforts and would rein-force the teacher's verbal reassurances to Beth that her work was good. However, several teachers cautioned that this technique can do more harm than good if the student does not want the work displayed or is not proud of it (a problem that is especially likely to occur with perfectionistic stu-dents), so they would get the student's permission before displaying the work publicly.

Like the interview data, these vignette data suggest that teacher sup-port, encouragement, and assistance designed to ensure that the student can both be and feel successful are more crucial to effective response to perfectionism problems than attempts to change the student's perfectionis-tic beliefs and attitudes through persuasion and appeal. Apparently it is not enough for students to realize that others, including the teacher, make mistakes and that mistakes can be useful learning experiences. These stu-dents need to feel that they can and will be successful, both now and in the future.

Vignette: Chris

Chris is a capable student who is exceptionally anxious about making mistakes. He doesn't contribute to class discussions or recitation unless he is absolutely sure he is right. You recognize his anxiety and try to call on him only when you are reasonably sure he can handle it. When you do this today, he blanches and stumbles through an incorrect answer. He is clearly upset.

Before reading further, take time to think about how you might respond to this incident. Make notes about your ideas.

CSS Vignette Response Excerpts

Here is what four of the CSS teachers had to say.

A LOWER RATED TEACHER

"If I see that Chris is already upset, then I definitely wouldn't call on him that day. I'd just let him be. Maybe that afternoon I could pick up and ask him questions. Maybe time will cure whatever the problem is. If he's clearly upset, then I definitely wouldn't call on him because it would make matters worse. Later I could try to encourage him not to try to be so perfect. 'We all make mistakes. I made a couple myself, which is not the worst thing in the world. I'm not perfect you know.' I'd say that type of thing. Maybe he will ease up and be willing to try and not be so anxious about this."

A HIGHER RATED TEACHER

"I guess I would say, 'Chris had a little bit of trouble with the answer. Is there anybody who can help him out? Let's see what the right answer is.' First of all, he is upset because he doesn't want to be wrong in front of the other children, and so I wouldn't make too big a deal of it. I would say, 'Is there anybody that can help out with this answer or perhaps give us a better answer?' I would try to talk to Chris as soon after that lesson as possible to help him understand that it's OK to make mistakes, that every time you open your mouth you don't have to be right, that I make mistakes. I probably would give a case in point where I have made a mistake. Something else I have tried, and it's worked reasonably well, is to say, 'Class, was it OK that Chris made a mistake?' Most of the time the kids will say, 'Yes,' and then I might add, 'Can somebody give me an example of a time that they made a mistake?' I have used that technique and found it has worked several times. So there are two possible ways I would handle it. One would be to just quickly ask if there is somebody who can answer the question and talk to Chris afterward. The other would be to help him realize that mistakes are OK, that everybody makes mistakes, and that his class will accept the fact that he makes mistakes. We are all here learning, and in the process of learning you make mistakes and you learn by them. You just keep going on."

ANOTHER HIGHER RATED TEACHER

"I would let it go at the time—just go on to another child and then talk to him separately later. I would try to get him to tell me why he thinks he has to have the right answer all the time or only the right answer when he volunteers. Then I would ask him if he knows if I ever make mistakes, and because I don't ever hide this in the class-room, I would hope that he would be able to think of a time when I had. Then I would talk to him about the fact that it is OK to make mistakes and that nobody is right all the time. Chris needs to learn that he is still going to be acceptable to his friends and the adults around him even though he makes mistakes, and he needs to accept himself when he is making errors. [What would you say to him?] 'Hey, Chris, I noticed that you were a little upset when I asked you the question today and you had an answer that wasn't right. Why does that bother you so much? Do you think it is wrong to make a mistake? Why? I make mistakes, your parents make mistakes, and other people in the class make mistakes. I don't think that people are dumb or think less of them because they answer things incorrectly or if they are not right all the time, because I'm not right all the time. I want you to be able to not feel so badly about yourself when you make a mistake, because I don't feel badly about you. That's something that happens to everybody.'"

ANOTHER HIGHER RATED TEACHER

" 'Chris, I am so pleased that you stumbled through and gave me an incorrect answer, that I can't even begin to tell you how delighted I am.' A child like this undoubtedly has got a complex as far as being the perfect child all the time. He is always praised for doing perfect things and completely makes sure that whatever he does has to be 100 percent. Every child must learn that in life, whatever they do, there are going to be times when they can be perfect and there are going to be times when they fall flat on their faces. And the sooner they learn that, the better. I very often tell a child (I don't want to say *tease*, but it's very close to teasing), 'Just once, can you give me a wrong answer? Why are you doing everything so perfectly?'"

All four quoted teachers emphasized attempts to resocialize Chris to make him more realistic in his expectations and more accepting of im-perfections. However, the lower rated teacher seemed to lack confidence in this approach and spoke as if she would implement it only tentatively. In contrast, the first two of the higher rated teachers would undertake resocialization of Chris with more confidence, and they suggested approaches that seem likely to have more credibility with Chris than the brief message suggested by the lower rated teacher. Finally, the last higher rated teacher felt confident enough to suggest a humorous or teasing approach. When used under the right circumstances, this response might be quite effective as a way to help perfectionistic students relax and put their mistakes into perspective. However, in situations where these students were still upset or were shaky in their confidence about their abilities, a more clearly sympathetic and helpful response might be preferable to teasing.

Analysis of Responses to Chris

All but one of the teachers mentioned strategies for supporting Chris, including comfort/reassurance (56), kid gloves treatment (44), instruction in better means of coping (37), encouragement (26), specific praise (11), and involving the peers (11) or parents (6) in providing support or assistance.

Most (70) of the teachers mentioned some attempt to develop Chris's insight into his problem (i.e., he was overreacting to mistakes). Other frequently mentioned strategies included suggesting better coping strategies (39), attempting to build up Chris's self-concept (33), and humor or other tension release comments designed to defuse his embarrassment (20). Twelve teachers spoke of minimizing or postponing any attempt to respond to Chris's embarrassment because they believed that trying to deal with it publicly in the middle of the lesson would only make the situation more traumatic for him. This was a common perception, in fact; most of the teachers' reported interactions with Chris concerning the depicted incident would occur later on in private conversation. Comments made to Chris on the spot usually would be confined to a sentence or two designed to provide brief emotional support and then get him refocused on the lesson.

In responding to Chris's mistake, a majority (54) of the teachers would simply tell him that his answer was not correct and then go on to give him the answer, provide another chance to respond, or invite response from someone else. Other teachers would be more solicitous of Chris's need for success experiences. They favored such strategies as softening the impact of their negative feedback by telling Chris that his answer was "not quite" or "not exactly" correct (14), responding only to the part of his answer that was correct (9), and rephrasing the question or giving clues in such a way as to virtually ensure a correct answer on the second try (7).

In responding to Chris's anxiety or embarrassment in the situation, a majority (55) of the teachers would reassure him that his input is valued whether right or wrong, that we all make mistakes, and so on. In addition or instead, 39 would try to get Chris "off the spot" quickly by giving the answer or making a minimal response and then moving on to someone else, 12 would try to create an immediate success experience by repeating the question or asking a new question, 12 would rely on humor to help Chris be able to laugh at his mistake and feel less anxious about it, and 7 would move on quickly for now but get back to him soon with a response opportunity that he could handle successfully.

A majority (54) of the teachers mentioned one or more methods for following up on the depicted incident. These included attempts to resocialize Chris's attitudes and beliefs (35), attempts to make sure that Chris enjoyed frequent success experiences (13), scheduling a conference with his parents (10), and trying to teach him better emotional coping skills (7).

Most of the teachers spoke of communicating some form of socialization message to Chris, although 11 would avoid speaking to him about the problem because they believed that any such discussion would only make it worse (even a private discussion held subsequent to the depicted incident). The most common socialization message (71) was that no one is perfect and we all make mistakes. Other socialization messages included communicating that it is understandable for Chris to be upset and that he has permission to leave the group until he recovers if he wishes to do so (9), trying to show Chris that he is hurting himself by maintaining overly rigid expectations (8), communicating sympathy for his embarrassment (7), trying to instruct him in emotional coping strategies for use in such situations (7), and trying to convince him that he did not really make an error at all (6).

In summary, the vast majority of the teachers were confident that they could intervene successfully with Chris, whom they saw as a victim needing empathy, support, encouragement, and assistance. A few would minimize their response to the depicted incident, both by moving on with the lesson quickly and by avoiding any subsequent discussion of the problem with Chris, because they believed that calling attention to the problem would only make it worse. Most, however, would at least take time to communicate to Chris that mistakes are expected and that he should not overreact to them. Many would also attempt to provide emotional support to Chris by moving quickly to get him "off the spot," by reassuring him that his input is appreciated whether correct or not, by communicating support and encouragement ("That's OK, you'll get the next one"), or by creating success experiences for him during or shortly following the depicted incident.

Most teachers, regardless of their effectiveness ratings, attributed the problem to similar causes, felt confident in being able to intervene effectively, and emphasized insight-oriented communications (especially the idea that we all make mistakes and should not overreact to them) and communications of support and reassurance, but not pressure or demands for behavioral change. Lower rated teachers generally suggested the same kinds of strategies as higher rated teachers, although typically with less comprehensiveness and elaboration.

Higher rated teachers not only mentioned trying to get Chris to understand that we all make mistakes and should not overreact to them but also mentioned providing instructional input in the form of suggestions for better ways of coping with failure situations, providing emotional support by reassuring Chris that he and his performance are acceptable and that his input is valued whether right or wrong, and seeing that he achieves success and feels successful (not just that he learns to tolerate mistakes). They also were more likely to mention involving peers in providing support or help for Chris.

COMPARISON OF RESPONSES TO BETH AND TO CHRIS

The two vignettes produced teacher response patterns and correlations with effectiveness ratings that were similar both to each other and to the patterns produced by the interview. Still, there were several interesting differences. These occurred mostly because Chris was portrayed as visibly upset and nothing in his behavior could be seen as objectionable, whereas Beth was portrayed more as frustrated than upset and as engaging in behavior that would leave her open to criticism by some teachers (using too much paper, failing to create a finished product within the time allotted). Also, Chris's traumatic experience occurred during a public lesson (where the presence of onlookers increased the potential for embarrassment to Chris and where the teacher's options were limited by the need to get on with the lesson), whereas Beth's problem occurred during an individualized art activity (so that the teacher could interact with her privately and could take more time to deal with the problem on the spot).

The teachers saw the two problems as stable, generalized, and caused by similar factors. Yet 41 saw Beth as able to control the problem behavior if she chose to do so, whereas only 3 believed that Chris had such control. Also, 12 implied that Beth might be misbehaving intentionally, whereas only 2 implied this about Chris.

There was relatively more emphasis on shaping through successive approximations and praise and encouragement in the responses to Beth, but on comfort, reassurance, and kid gloves treatment in the responses to Chris. Beth's problem was primarily behavioral (at least in its overt manifestations) and thus called for techniques designed to change behavior, whereas Chris's problem was primarily emotional and thus called for provision of emotional support and attempts to improve coping skills.

QUALITATIVE IMPRESSIONS AND EXAMPLES

The typical response to the general strategies interview was expression of concern about the problem coupled with descriptions of attempts to help. Also frequent were statements that the problem was common and familiar, that progress would have to occur slowly over a significant time period, and that perfectionists are difficult to work with because they are so anxious. Many teachers noted that some aspects of perfectionism are desirable and should be reinforced even while you try to change the undesirable aspects. Many also mentioned that they are or were perfectionistic themselves.

Almost all teachers expressed concerns about Chris's emotional trauma, but many were much less concerned about Beth. In particular, many Big City teachers viewed Beth as a student with high standards who wanted to work at her own pace. They not only saw no problem with this but would facilitate it by telling her that she could finish her work at home and turn it in the next day. Several of these Big City teachers said that they welcomed perfectionism (short of the extremes depicted in the vignettes) and would like to see more of it in their students.

One teacher believed that perfectionism problems like Beth's are seen more often in girls than boys and are especially likely to occur with respect to penmanship. This teacher also claimed that perfectionism problems do not occur as often in individualized programs because all of the students work at a challenging level (for them individually) so that they become accustomed to making mistakes, whereas under the traditional system the "A" students often are able to enjoy relatively continuous easy success so that they are prone to becoming upset when they do encounter difficulties.

Several teachers said that they would make a point of retrieving a paper that Beth had crumpled and thrown in the wastebasket, smoothing it out again, and then showing her how her rejected effort could be salvaged (turned into a good picture). In some cases, this was because limited paper supplies required them to restrict each child to one piece of paper for artwork. Students who were dissatisfied with their efforts could turn over the paper and use the other side, but could not get more paper. Several teachers also mentioned using the clock to pace Beth ("When the big hand gets to the 3, you will have to turn it in").

Other strategies for coping with erasures and "start-overs" included (1) compromising by telling students that they will be "allowed" a specified number of lines that contain erasures but will be required to turn in the other lines without erasures (crossing out incorrect material rather than erasing it); (2) changing the task to something easier, such as switching from painting to work with clay, which one teacher described as "not quite as 'perfect' as paint"; (3) trying to talk the student into crossing out rather than erasing because erasing only makes the paper look worse and will eventually tear holes in it; (4) suggesting that the student sketch the intended drawing on scrap paper before attempting a final version (or get composition ideas down in first drafts written on scrap paper, without worrying yet about spelling or appearance); (5) letting students use the teacher's big art gum eraser when they are frustrated about mistakes, to distract them from their frustration; (6) showing the child mistakes made in a book or newspaper to help underscore the message that everyone makes mistakes; and (7) making a game or challenge out of trying to avoid erasing by creatively hiding mistakes and incorporating them into the picture.

Many of the responses to Chris included strategies for minimizing the emotional trauma depicted in the incident. Teachers suggested such techniques as (1) thanking Chris for his information and then going on to someone else without giving feedback as to its correctness; (2) appearing to accept the answer but then asking someone else, "What is another aspect of that?"; (3) saying, "That's one answer, but can you think of another one that might be a little better?"; (4) saying, "I'll get back to you later" and then going on to someone else; and (5) moving on quickly at the time but then coming back to Chris later and saying, "I knew that you had the answer to that question, but you just couldn't think of it at the time." One teacher attempted to minimize such problems by training students to say "I don't know" when they don't know an answer, making it clear to them that this is perfectly acceptable behavior under the circumstances (and preferable to making a wild guess).

Several teachers mentioned methods of responding to perfectionistic students' needs for a feeling of success. One would put a happy face or sticker on their papers regardless of how many answers were correct, so that these students would know that their work was acceptable even if not always perfect. Another would encourage these students to cross out mistakes and move on with their work, and then later would put smiley faces next to the responses that looked best or ask the student to decide which looked best and then mark accordingly.

The following strategies calling for involvement of peers or work with groups were mentioned: (1) teaching these students in smaller groups as much as possible so that they feel less pressured when stuck for answers; (2) group sharing activities in which the students talk about occasions in which they made big mistakes in public (the teacher would describe such experiences too); (3) having perfectionists work with peer partners so that they get immersed in the activity and are less likely to obsess about failures; (4) reading and discussion of the book *I'm Not Perfect;* (5) singing and discussion of the song "Free to Be You and Me"; (6) sending perfectionists to tutor younger students; and (7) leading a class discussion on mistakes in which participants would take turns telling about the biggest mistakes they ever made, so that everyone could laugh about them.

Preventive or follow-up strategies mentioned included (1) saving work done early in the year (or following a difficult assignment with an easy one that would have been difficult early in the year), to show students how they have progressed; (2) asking perfectionists relatively easy questions, or giving them enough clues to make the questions easy, in order to create consistent success experiences (however, some teachers objected to this strategy and favored getting the student to learn to accept mistakes rather than artificially creating success experiences for them); (3) scheduling speed drills or exposing students to tasks that they have not been fully prepared for, so as to create situations where perfectionists cannot possibly get perfect scores and yet can be praised for doing X percent correctly, which would be defined as grade "A" performance; (4) talking about how Christopher Columbus set out to find spices and jewels for the queen as a way to make the point that one must make the best of one's mistakes; and (5) taking every opportunity to call on perfectionists to respond to opinion questions or other questions for which there are no clear-cut right or wrong answers.

Several teachers mentioned attempts to use humor, both as a way to make a point and as a way to put perfectionists at ease. One said that if she thought the student would respond positively to it, she would say, "I want you to turn in this paper with at least two mistakes on it. You decide which two mistakes you want to make." Another suggested responding to Chris by saying, "Well, that's your goof for today. You don't get any more of those!" If a mistake had provoked laughter because it was funny, another teacher would encourage the victim to laugh at it too ("Come on, laugh with us"). Finally, another teacher suggested humorous role play for overly anxious and dependent students. Specifically, she would switch roles with the student by working on an assignment but frequently interrupting to come and ask, "Is this all right? . . . Is this good? . . . etc."

Finally, teachers mentioned the following sayings for use with perfectionists: (1) Making mistakes is part of being human, so if you don't make mistakes, you're not human; (2) the only way to avoid not doing anything wrong is to not do anything at all; (3) we all make mistakes—that's why they put erasers on pencils; (4) it's OK to make mistakes—just don't make the same ones over and over again; (5) if we were all perfect, we wouldn't have anything to strive for; and (6) don't reach for Mars until you have reached the moon.

Most of these unique suggestions seem insightful and likely to be helpful, although a few could be counterproductive (e.g., leading the student to believe that a wrong answer is correct) and several (e.g., role switching, attempts at humor) would have to be implemented carefully and only with certain students.

DISCUSSION

Most of the teachers were familiar with perfectionism problems, were confident that they could alleviate them (especially higher rated teachers), although improvements might occur only slowly over a long time frame, and were oriented toward sympathetic responses featuring support, encouragement, assistance, and attempts at cognitive restructuring. The teachers intuitively recognized that the most fundamental aspects of perfectionism problems are subjective cognitive and emotional reactions to failure cues, not overt behavioral symptoms. Consequently, their reported strategies stressed attempts at cognitive restructuring and provision of support and assistance rather than attempts at behavior modification featuring offers of reward or threats of punishment. Although none of the teachers had had training in reality therapy, cognitive-behavior modification, or other systematic approaches to cognitive restructuring with perfectionistic students, most of the socialization and instruction strategies that they mentioned involved pursuing similar goals with similar methods. To the extent that such socialization and instruction efforts are more extensive than a brief "we all make mistakes, don't worry about it" statement, they should help move the student toward more realistic goal setting, more balanced and differentiated performance assessment, and greater tendency to respond to mistakes with diagnostic thinking and coping strategies rather than catastrophic emotional reactions.

Nevertheless, cognitive structuring/socialization/persuasion strategies, even if well implemented, would constitute only part of an optimal response to perfectionism problems in classrooms. Teacher support, encouragement, and assistance appear to be crucial elements as well. Our data suggest that the most effective teachers not only seek to establish more realistic goal setting and more effective coping with failure experiences but also provide perfectionistic students with whatever support and assistance they may need in order to achieve success and reassure them that they are progressing acceptably despite imperfections in their work.

These additional treatment elements tend not to be featured in programs developed by therapists for use with perfectionistic adults. They reflect the fact that, rather than being confined to the role of outside coach or resource person, teachers can work with the problem directly by interacting with perfectionistic students to help them shape their thinking as they set goals and expectations prior to tasks, cope with the events that occur as they work on the tasks, and evaluate their performance as it unfolds.

The most effective teachers honor the subjective experience of perfectionistic students by taking them seriously and trying to meet their needs (halfway, at least). They do not take lightly or attempt to brush off the students' catastrophic emotional reactions. Rather than blithely tell-ing them to relax and not worry about mistakes, they communicate un-derstanding and approval of the students' desire to do well and empathize with their feelings of embarrassment or frustration. Also, they honor the students' achievement motivation. Rather than just talk in terms of lower-ing goals and being satisfied with less-than-perfect performance, they re-assure perfectionistic students that they will get whatever help they need to achieve success, follow through by providing this help, and communi-cate their approval of the students' progress and accomplishments. Thus, in addition to attacking unrealistic expectations, they take steps to max-imize these students' objective levels of achievement and also their sub-jective appreciation of their attainments. In this way, they support and reinforce the success-seeking aspects of achievement motivation even while working to reduce unrealistic goal setting, either–or thinking in evaluat-ing success or failure, catastrophic emotional response to mistakes, and the other symptoms associated with neurotic perfectionism.

7

Underachieving Students

Underachievers display the following characteristics: These children do a minimum to just "get by." They do not value schoolwork. They:

1. Are indifferent to school
2. Do minimum amounts of work
3. Are not challenged by schoolwork and are poorly motivated

What special strategies might you use to minimize such problems and help these students to function more successfully in your classroom? Before reading further, take time to think about this and make notes about your ideas.

CSS INTERVIEW EXCERPTS

Here is what three of the CSS teachers had to say about teaching underachieving students.

A LOWER RATED TEACHER

"These boys and girls are underachievers because there's nothing that you want them to do that they're going to do. You can do everything you want, but if a child does not want to learn—does not want to do something—he's not going to do it. I don't care what you do, what rewards, what punishments, whatever you want to offer in any kind of answer; you just are not going to get it unless a child wants to do it. Now, when you see this indifference to school and poor motivation, I think also you've got to look at what the home life's like. If it's indifference to school, then nobody at home cares about what's going on. It's almost obvious that there is nothing really being done at home to push this child, because there's something that has to be done at home to make the boys and girls understand the importance of school. When they're not challenged by schoolwork, it's because they don't want to do it; that's why it's not a challenge. They won't even try to do it."

This teacher communicated despair and impotence. She described the student's problem and noted home background factors that might have contributed to its development, but she had no constructive suggestions about how it might be addressed. Her basic message was that nothing could be done.

A HIGHER RATED TEACHER

"This kind of a child needs to be sat down within a conference and gone over as far as why he doesn't value his schoolwork, why he's indifferent. Most of the time, when you run into a child like this, you are dealing not only with a situation in school but he's very much like this in situations he doesn't care for at home. A good way to start out with a child like this is to set certain goals for him to complete within an allotted amount of time and then immediately reward him with something that he really enjoys doing. This might include going back to a game corner and spending 20 minutes playing certain games that he likes. It might include taking the attendance around or any kind of immediate reward that would get him on the right track.

"His indifference to school is something that's been ingrained from the start of kindergarten all the way up to the present grade level, and it's for sure that I would not be able to deal with the situation in 1 year. Very often I would call in a parent and explain what the problem is at school and find out their attitudes toward school, because often these children are parodying their parents' actions at home. ('I never did well in school. I didn't care for this, and I only wanted to do so much.') Consequently, the child, no matter what you do, just isn't going to be able to change his frame of mind if he has one situation to deal with in school and then goes home and listens to just the opposite. I would need to sit down and explain to the parents the harm that can come from talking down about school. Children enjoy and like to please parents as well as they do teachers most of the time, and I don't think that parents realize what they are doing.

"My dealing with this child is definitely based on the reward system. There can be rewards that are material such as getting so many coupons to buy things from the store or some kind of food or just odd jobs around the room that the child enjoys doing. The success rate on this is fairly high. There are children that it definitely does not work with. Periodically I will run into a child who not only is indifferent to school but is very belligerent insofar as my loading him on goals and the student not wanting to do them. Consequently, in a case like this, I would have to call in outside help. Whether it would be a counselor or the principal, it would not be in a reprimanding sense. It would be more or less sifting out and filtering just what we are going to do to make this the most pleasurable situation for the child until the end of the school year. Very often the principal does have time to deal with a child like this. He may at that time impose certain goals for the child to complete within the classroom, and there would be feedback every week into the principal's office.

"Strategies that have never worked with this kind of situation are anger on my part or disciplining the child and saying, 'Well, because you can't do this, you'll miss recess' or 'Go sit in the hall until you have gotten this done.' This has never worked."

This higher rated teacher characterized the underachieving child and his home situation in much the same way as the lower rated teacher quoted previously. Rather than conclude that nothing could be done, however, this teacher spoke of addressing the problem through strategies aimed at both the child and the parents. She claimed generally good success with her approach, although she noted that she would get help from a counselor or the principal in cases where it was not working satisfactorily.

ANOTHER HIGHER RATED TEACHER

"It is important to try to get the child to gain more of a positive feeling toward schoolwork, try to make learning enjoyable for them so that they will become more motivated to do it. One thing that I think is very important is to try to find out the reason why. If you can't see a particular reason, talk with the parent as soon as possible to let them know that the child is just getting by and is not very well motivated. Very often the parent has the same attitude toward schoolwork. They feel that school is not that important, and they give the same attitude to the children. So I think it is very good to find out first of all if that is one of the causes. Then maybe you can understand it better and deal with it. I would talk to the parent and just see if they could shed some light so I could understand why the children feel this way. Also, I would try to find out what interests the child. I might give an interest survey and see the kinds of things that they like and maybe change the curriculum in a way that would interest them. Very often when there is a project that is of particular interest, it will motivate the child more. They will be enjoying something in school, and this will tend to follow through into other areas also, so that they will just get a better feeling toward school in general. Sometimes it helps to let the child go to another room to tutor children in an area in which he is poorly motivated. All of a sudden he has become kind of excited about school. He enjoys this very much, and he finds out that the only way he is going to keep doing this is if he continues with the work in the classroom also. One other thing that has seemed to motivate these children is putting their own book together. One of the other things I do is talk with them in a conference arrangement, not scold them or talk about the poor work they are doing or that they are not motivated, but just talk about work in general. Talk about the value of work, why these things are important to do, and do they think they are, just try to get their general feelings. This is good to do right when you start seeing this kind of thing. Just to sit down, let the child know that you are interested in what they are doing, that you care about their success in school. Again, I would give recognition to these children, especially for extra work. I give them a lot of choices for extra things that could be done. One other thing is pairing them with another child who is highly motivated, who does enjoy school, and having them work together on something specific. Often this gets the other person geared up and wanting to do more. Sometimes it becomes competitive; they want to do as much as the other person. Another thing is to give them responsibility, like being the head of a committee or having them arrange a puppet show or a play. This tends to get them more motivated. I think anytime you get them interested in some kind of activity, it begins to reflect in their schoolwork. They become more interested in school in general. I think this is what you have got to do for these children — change things enough so that you give them something that they can become interested in."

This higher rated teacher also spoke of working with the parents as well as the child. In contrast to the reward or behavioral contract approach suggested by the previous teacher, she would try to make the curriculum more interesting to the student, ask him to tutor other students as a way to increase his own interest in schoolwork, and develop a good relationship with the student and then work within it to socialize him toward more productive attitudes.

WHAT THE SCHOLARLY LITERATURE SAYS

Over the years, many psychologists and educators have referred to *under-achieving* students, but not always with the same meaning. Different writers have applied the term to each of the problem syndromes described in Chapters 4, 5, 6, and 7 of this book, as well as to students who combine low achievement with hyperactivity, aggression, or defiance. These multiple meanings make it difficult to synthesize and draw conclusions from the literature on underachievement. Several reviewers remarked that underachievers are a heterogeneous group or that each underachiever has his or her own unique pattern of symptoms and causal factors. One even suggested that the term be dropped from further use (Plewis, 1991). Others have used the term but qualified it with one or more adjectives, as we did by speaking of *alienated underachievers* in our study.

We used this term to describe students who are not oriented toward academic achievement and thus do the minimum required of them rather than their best work. This is close to the original meaning of underachievement, which was defined as a consistent discrepancy between academic abilities (measured by IQ or aptitude tests) and achievement in school (as reflected in grades). It also is close to the syndrome that recent reviewers of the literature have identified as the prototype of underachievement: a persistent tendency to work below one's abilities, motivated (often with little or no conscious awareness) by an unwillingness to accept the increased responsibilities and raised expectations that higher achievement would bring. Thus, whereas failure syndrome and perfectionistic students underachieve because they fear failure, alienated underachievers underachieve because they fear (or at least seek to avoid) success.

McCall, Evahn, and Kratzer (1992) listed 23 personal and behavioral characteristics that have been linked to underachievement, including low self-concept, low perception of abilities, unrealistic goal setting, lack of persistence, responding impulsively rather than thoughtfully to assignments, social immaturity and poor peer relationships, oppositional and aggressive response to authority, and a tendency to make excuses for continued underachievement rather than accept responsibility and make a serious commitment to change. The parents of these students are often described as either indifferent or overly preoccupied with their child's achievement. Another common theme is parental tendencies toward either an authoritarian, restrictive, and rejecting style (especially by the father) or a style that features extreme permissiveness and freedom, bordering on neglect.

McCall and his colleagues completed the largest study of underachievers done to date, starting when they were still in school but following them into adulthood. They concluded that underachievement in school is part of a larger syndrome of underachievement that is characterized by failure to persist in the face of challenge, whether that challenge is educational, occupational, or marital. They also found that the underachievement syndrome persists if left untreated. The underachievers followed in their study were less likely to complete college and to display job and marital stability than comparison groups, including a group that earned similar grades but had lower aptitude scores than the under-achievers. Thus, there is no reason to believe that the problem will take care of itself once underachievers "find what interests them" or "leave school and enter the work world."

Whitmore (1980) suggested that the majority of underachievers are aggressive—disruptive, talkative, clowning in class, rebellious, and hostile. However, she also noted that some are withdrawn—uninterested, bored, failing to participate or try hard on assignments—and some combine these two sets of traits. She described underachievers as students who have found academic activities unrewarding and thus seek their rewards elsewhere. They usually cannot avoid school demands completely, but they minimize them through strategies such as avoiding participation as much as possible, complying only grudgingly when they do comply, finding compensatory relief through disrupting the class or performing assignments in unique ways, projecting blame for their failures on the teacher or other people, and protecting their self-concepts by devaluing achievement ("Who cares, anyway?").

Mandel and Marcus (1988) suggested that underachievement is part of a broader symptom pattern that begins when certain children become fixated at a particular stage instead of continuing to develop normally. They identified five categories of underachievers whose different characteristics depend on the stage at which fixation occurred. In one of these patterns, which they called the nonachievement syndrome, the primary symptom is underachievement without complication by anxiety, self-concept problems, oppositional defiance, or various conduct problems. Mandel and Marcus claimed that these underachievers are consistently described by parents, teachers, and even themselves as lazy and unmotivated procrastinators who could do better in school if only they would try harder. At almost any age after 10, these individuals seem to "coast, cruise, and float" through life, appearing to lack a sense of purpose or meaning in their lives. Except for their underachievement pattern, they appear to be personally and socially well adjusted. They recognize their underachievement problem and readily agree that all they need to do is try harder and their grades will improve, but instead of doing so, they procrastinate, give up easily at the first sign of difficulty, and avoid following through on most tasks. To explain this, they offer an endless series of rationalizations or excuses, such as forgetting books, studying the wrong material for tests, not being good in that subject, being lazy, getting bored with the subject, losing interest, having trouble concentrating, failing to take good notes, making stupid mistakes on tests, etc.

Analyzing these students more closely, Mandel and Marcus suggested that they are not unmotivated but in fact highly motivated — to sustain their pattern of poor or mediocre performance and to avoid consistently working up to their potential. They convince themselves that their lack of motivation is beyond their understanding, so they can't do anything about it. However, their real motivation is the desire to avoid or at least continue to postpone the expectation that they will consistently do the things that students need to do in order to work up to their potential.

Bruns (1992) reported a similar pattern of behavioral symptoms in students whom he described as "work inhibited"—unable to engage consistently in the work of school unless an adult is standing over them and helping. Bruns stated that work-inhibited students "are not tough or resilient" and that they "lack the emotional fitness to stay the course when faced with difficult tasks." Like Mandel and Marcus, Bruns traced this syndrome to disturbances in personality development, although he described it more as a pattern of immaturity and dependence on adults than as a pattern of unconscious motivation to delay or avoid responsibilities.

Schaefer and Millman (1981) described underachievers as children who do not see personal meaning in the school curriculum or who have not developed achievement motivation and related goal setting and success-seeking behaviors. Among contributing factors they identified parental lack of interest in the child or overpermissiveness about conduct limits, parental expectations that are either too low or too high and perfectionistic, parental overprotectiveness that makes their children immature and unwilling to accept challenges, and teachers who treat the child in ways that resemble one of the unproductive patterns noted in parents.

Karlin and Berger (1972) offered a similar description of the nature and causes of underachievement, noting that an additional contributor to the problem might be that the underachiever has never learned how to study. Borkowski and associates (1990) and Krouse and Krouse (1981) also cited deficiencies in study skills and self-regulation abilities along with problems in motivation and other personality characteristics. Finally Rimm (1986) described four types of underachievers, along with each type's likely predisposing home and school experiences. Her analyses included most of the symptom descriptions and predisposing factors mentioned above.

Suggested Strategies for Coping with Underachievers

Given the variety of behavioral symptoms and presumed predisposing causes mentioned in connection with underachievement, it is not surprising that the literature on treatment contains a great range of strategies. McCall, Evahn, and Kratzer (1992) reviewed this literature and concluded that most treatment programs have shown at least some success in remediating targeted symptoms. However, many programs failed to improve achievement because they targeted peripheral symptoms such as self-esteem or social relations but not the core symptoms of low achievement motivation and the desire to avoid increased expectations and responsibilities. The best results have been obtained with comprehensive programs that address the full range of symptoms observed in the student and include treatment elements aimed at parents and teachers as well as students.

McCall and his colleagues found no data on the effectiveness of commercially available tutoring programs or specialized psychoeducational therapies. Nor did they find remedial programs focused directly on lack of persistence in the face of challenge, which they identified as the core symptom of underachievement. They did report that the most commonly used approach is teacher–parent collaboration in using behavior modification strategies. That is, the teacher sends home a daily or weekly report of the student's achievement efforts and accomplishments, and the parents withhold or dispense privileges or other rewards contingent on their child's achievement of previously specified academic and behavioral goals.

Mandel and Marcus (1988) developed treatment strategies for each of the five underachievement patterns that they described. Their strategy for the nonachievement syndrome focused on pressuring these underachievers to stop generating excuses to explain away their continued failure to apply themselves and instead begin to take responsibility for doing so. Mandel and Marcus believed that less confrontive strategies, such as providing a lot of encouragement or making the work easier or more interesting, will not lead to any fundamental change because these students are motivated to continue their underachievement pattern so as to avoid increased expectations and responsibilities. They claimed that their approach has been successful but that it requires the treatment agent to resist the temptation to try to "take over" (by telling the student how to solve problems), to recognize that the student will not necessarily follow through on seemingly sincere commitments, and to patiently work through the student's excuses and resistance strategies.

The first step is to ask the underachiever if he or she wants to get better grades in school (as opposed to announcing that you are going to help the student do so). For the overwhelming majority of students who respond positively to this initial question, the relationship has now been structured such that it is the responsibility of the student to set goals, whereas your role is to help the student achieve them. Step 2 involves taking detailed stock of current progress and problems in each subject, along with any plans that the student may have for addressing the problems. At this point, your role is to elicit information nonjudgmentally, without giving any interpretations or recommendations.

Step 3 involves focusing on specific problem areas and isolating the student's excuses for these respective problems. You ask what problems are getting in the way of better grades, probe for specifics when the student offers only vague generalizations, and if necessary challenge questionable claims. For example, the student might claim to spend an hour every day studying, but specific questions about how much he or she has studied in the last few days might establish that the real average study time is more like 10 or 20 minutes per day. Step 4 involves linking each excuse to its natural consequence by describing (or, better yet, eliciting from the student) what will happen if the student does not address this problem effectively. Step 5 involves asking the student to suggest solutions for each identified hindrance to success and then engaging the student in a detailed discussion of potential solutions in order to clarify their practicality, anticipate snags, and refine plans. Here, you need to be careful to elicit plans from the student rather than tell the student what to do. Once the student "owns" the goal of better grades, has recognized the connection between the current problem and future consequences, and has developed a specific and workable solution, there is no way to "unrecognize" these connections again. The student must accept personal responsibility for the grades.

Step 6 is a call for action (saying, "OK, now what do you propose to do?" followed by questions about specifics). Step 7 is follow-up to assess whether or not the student has implemented the plan and eliminated the problem. Given the student's motivation to continue to underachieve, it is likely that the assessment will indicate that the student either continued to underachieve but simply dropped this one excuse and substituted another one or else began to achieve in just the one area but not in others. This leads to a possibly lengthy step 8, which involves repeating steps 3 through 7 with one different excuse each time. Eventually, the student will run out of excuses and be forced to accept personal responsibility for academic performance. When this occurs, there may be accompanying reactions such as panic, depression, anxiety, anger, regret, energy toward achievement, confusion, changes in social relationships, or intense introspection. At this point, your role shifts from taking away excuses and pressing for acceptance of responsibility to becoming a supportive, nonjudgmental listener and resource person who helps the student begin to express and struggle with questions such as, "Why did I allow myself to get such poor grades?" and "What do I want my future to be?"

The strategy outlined by Mandel and Marcus is consistent with their view of underachievers as motivated to sustain their underachievement pattern. Bruns (1992) outlined a different strategy for dealing with work-inhibited students, whom he depicted more as immature and adult-dependent than as determined to persist with their pattern of underachievement. He recommended that teachers help these students by establishing friendly and supportive relationships with them, encouraging them to stay on task and persist in the face of challenges, moving them gradually through successive approximations from partial to completed work on assignments, varying the nature and difficulty level of their assignments, setting goals with them and charting their progress, arranging for them to work with one or more peers or to tutor younger students with similar weaknesses, praising their genuine accomplishments, and providing them with opportunities to develop their strengths and feel empowered. He also argued against persistently assigning types of homework that work-inhibited students do not complete, retaining these students in the grade for failure to complete assignments, or punishing them by denying recess or access to extracurricular activities.

More general sources of advice to teachers about coping with underachievers mention a great many strategies that range between the primarily confrontive approach represented by Mandel and Marcus and the primarily supportive approach represented by Bruns. Schaefer and Millman (1981) suggested both preventive strategies and treatment strategies. Preventive strategies included encouraging students to do their best but also being accepting and supportive when they fail, reassuring them that frustration and mistakes are part of the learning process, helping them to set realistic goals, teaching and modeling active learning and problem-solving strategies, and rewarding interest in learning and academic achievement. Treatment strategies included parent–teacher collaboration in establishing and implementing a performance-contingent reward system; teaching students to monitor, evaluate, and reinforce their own performance; and making the classroom as stimulating and rewarding as possible.

Summarizing recommendations gleaned from school psychologists, Blanco and Bogacki (1988) mentioned peer and cross-age tutoring, contracting approaches featuring collaboration with the student in setting goals and with the parents in withholding or providing performance-contingent rewards, counseling sessions designed to allow underachievers to ventilate their concerns but also to pressure them to accept responsibility for their performance and commit themselves to realistic goals, and requiring students to make up missed homework assignments during recess or after school. Recommendations concerning involving parents were mixed. They favored eliciting parents' collaboration in providing their children with an appropriate place to study at home, making sure that they do so, and following through on implementation of a contract system. However, they cautioned against overinvolvement by parents who may have been pushing their child to live up to overly ambitious expectations or expressing their concerns about the child's underachievement through counterproductive means.

McIntyre (1989) emphasized many of the same strategies after culling the literature on underachievers, especially contracts and reward systems, collaborative learning with peers, increasing performance gradually through successive approximations, and requiring the student to redo shoddy work and complete unfinished assignments. Other suggestions included using small-group cooperative learning methods in which each individual has a unique function to perform to enable the group to achieve its goals (thus creating peer pressure on underachievers to do their part); monitoring these students closely and checking back with them frequently to make sure that they stay on task during work times; instructing them in study habits and self-regulation skills; making their work as interesting as possible and helping them to see its current or future application potential, but at the same time making it clear that they have the responsibility to apply themselves to accomplish all curricular goals (boredom is not a valid excuse); letting them do extra credit work in areas of interest; discussing their occupational plans and then helping them to see that academic skills are required in those occupations; and soliciting their suggestions about how you might be helpful to them and following through on those that are feasible.

Thompson and Rudolph (1992) also developed a similar list and included the following strategies: Increase work production gradually through escalating contracts; avoid lecturing, nagging, or threatening the child; solicit ideas from underachievers themselves about how the problem might be addressed; where feasible, have underachievers study with or at least talk about study habits with a friend of theirs who models motivation to learn and conscientious work on assignments; reinforce and build on current accomplishments rather than emphasizing past faults and failures; and structure their work by providing clear instructions and identifying specific goals.

Krouse and Krouse (1981) identified four groups among treatments assessed prior to 1980: (1) academic remediation, including teaching general study skills and attempting to remediate specific skill deficits (results mixed); (2) psychotherapy (results inconsistent); (3) promoting self-regulation through self-monitoring, self-reinforcement, and stimulus control (results mixed); and (4) reducing test anxiety (successful, but not always accompanied by improved academic performance).

Certain individual studies are worth noting because of the positive results they achieved. Markle, Rinn, and Goodwin (1980) succeeded in raising students' grade point averages through counseling sessions that combined an emphasis on study skills with an emphasis on achievement motivation training (teaching students about the goal-oriented thinking and self-regulation that are involved when tasks are approached with motivation to achieve, and giving them practice in doing so). Jackson,

Cleveland, and Mirenda (1975) produced higher grades and other lasting achievement-related improvements through an approach that focused more on parents and teachers than on the underachieving students themselves. These investigators assessed students individually to determine the factors that may have been involved in causing or sustaining their underachievement syndrome, and then met with parents and teachers periodically to suggest ways that they (individually and in collaboration) could change how they thought about and interacted with the child. They emphasized turning around negative views of the child and mobilizing all concerned to develop more positive expectations and work toward improvement goals, to become more aware of strengths and potential in the child, and to provide any needed individualized or remedial educational opportunities.

Butler-Por (1987) reported improvements in attitudes and achievement of 9- to 12-year-old underachievers through an intervention that consisted of the following four steps: (1) Teachers were provided with diagnostic profiles of the underachievers in their classrooms. These were designed to help the teacher accept these students and to guide her in enabling the students to recognize the need for change. (2) A preliminary meeting between the teacher and each individual student was held, in which the need for changing was recognized and the joint responsibility for effecting change was accepted. This was operationalized in the form of a contract in which the student set tasks for the coming week and selected rewards to serve as reinforcers. Tasks included improved classroom conduct and social behavior as well as improved learning efforts. (3) Subsequent meetings were devoted to discussion, evaluation, and reinforcement of the previous week's accomplishments and setting new tasks and rewards for the coming week. (4) The program culminated in a final meeting in which the teacher and student evaluated the success of their joint efforts and agreed that progress could be maintained in the future without structured meetings. The student accepted responsibility for maintaining the change process, while the teacher accepted responsibility for following and encouraging progress in the classroom. In addition to its successful results, this study is noteworthy for the authors' finding that individual differences in levels of success achieved were closely related to the teacher's enthusiasm for the project and, especially, the teacher's confidence or degree of positive expectation that the treatment would be successful.

In summary, the literature on underachievers shows less agreement than the literature on most other problem-student types. One reason is that the term has been applied to many different kinds of achievement-related problems, so that when some sources speak of underachievers, they actually refer to students described here as failure syndrome students or hostile–aggressive students. Even with this factor taken into account, however, there are disagreements on such issues as the degree to which teachers should enlist help from parents of underachievers and the roles that the parents might play if they become involved in the treatment, whether or not it is helpful to require underachievers to finish incomplete assignments or redo sloppily done work during recess or after school, and, more generally, the degree to which treatment should focus primarily on support, encouragement, and help to underachievers or should also feature significant elements of pressure and coercion.

ANALYSIS OF INTERVIEW RESPONSES

Teachers' responses to questions about underachievers reflected the differences of opinion seen in the scholarly literature. Unlike responses to the low achiever, failure syndrome, and perfectionist interviews, which showed broad agreement on a single primary approach, responses to the underachiever interview revealed contrasts among teachers who favored distinctly different approaches. The most commonly mentioned general problem-solving strategy — an attempt to change underachievers' attitudes through appeal or persuasion — was suggested by only 28 teachers. Other commonly mentioned general approaches included restriction of response to control and suppression techniques (25); offering encouragement, reassurance, and self-concept support (20); attempting to shape improvement through successive approximations (19); and attempting to identify and treat external causes (18).

Several specific strategies were mentioned much more frequently. This indicates that teachers pursuing different general approaches would use some of the same strategies, although probably with differing emphases. More than two-thirds of the teachers would include strategies for improving the student's effort level, performance quality, or task completion rate (67), and more than half would offer rewards as incentives (49). Other commonly mentioned specific strategies included gathering information about the student's interests and then attempting to build these into the curriculum in general or into the tasks assigned to that student in particular (36), changing assignments in an attempt to make them more appealing (35), using learning games or more varied instructional materials (27), attempting to reason with or persuade the student (27), threatening or punishing (26), reemphasizing limits and expectations (25), involving the parents for support or help (23), attempting to identify and eliminate the source of the problem (21), attempting to build up the student's self-concept (19), providing academic help (18), and getting underachievers diagnosed in the hope that this would lead to recommendations about how to teach them more effectively (18).

The remaining strategies mentioned by more than 5 teachers were mostly general pressure or support strategies. Surprisingly, only 7 teachers mentioned contracts, although 13 mentioned charting or demonstrating the student's progress over time. Finally, 7 teachers mentioned only minimal intervention or redirection strategies. These teachers minimized the seriousness of the problem and suggested that they would not do much so long as the student continued to meet minimum requirements.

A majority of the teachers included some attempt to socialize the underachievers' attitudes or to rationalize their own demands for improved performance. Most of these teachers said that they would elaborate on their expectations concerning attention to lessons and work on assignments (38) or that they would try to help the student see the connections between current schoolwork and future success in school or applications to life outside of school (28). Only 6 teachers would attempt to convey that the learning would enrich the student's life or have other self-actualization value. Also, only 8 would convey a "You can do it if you try" message. Apparently, most teachers assumed that underachievers already know this and that this knowledge does not motivate them to work harder.

The teachers frequently mentioned involving particular peers or the class as a whole in attempting to improve the work of underachievers. The most commonly mentioned method was the indirect approach of publicly displaying examples of excellent work by the underachiever (22). Other methods included involving peers to provide academic or motivational support or modeling (17), holding class meetings to discuss the problem (10), or involving peers to pressure the underachiever (6).

Among teachers who mentioned using rewards, 33 said that they would reward the underachiever for completing assignments, 26 would do so for good performance or high achievement, and only 10 would reward them for good effort. Among teachers who would focus on increasing the underachiever's effort level, 17 would be primarily encouraging but 25 would be primarily demanding.

A minority of teachers talked about changing their relationship with the underachieving student. Most of these talked about improving the relationship by trying to make it better or closer (11), by inviting the student to participate in special activities with them (6), or by providing extra attention and friendly interactions in class (6). However, 14 teachers spoke of becoming firmer with the underachiever.

About a third of the teachers spoke of contacting the parents. Of these, 14 would only gather information about the problem and possible solutions, 13 would ask the parents to pressure the student to work harder, and 9 would ask them to help with work at home. Fourteen teachers stated that parental support or help would be crucial in changing the student.

Among strategies rejected as ineffective, 28 teachers mentioned criticizing/demanding/threatening/punishing, 11 mentioned ignoring the problem, 8 mentioned involving parents, and 7 mentioned offering rewards for improvement.

Our correlational data favor the patient and supportive approach to underachievers over the demanding and threatening approach. Lower rated teachers were more likely to emphasize control and suppression as their general problem-solving strategy, but higher rated teachers were more likely to suggest other strategies, especially attempts to shape improvement through successive approximation or to provide encouragement, reassurance, and self-concept support. They also were more likely to include long-term prevention or solution strategies in their responses, to anticipate that improvement would occur only slowly over a long period of time, and to say that parental support or help would be crucial.

Higher rated teachers were more likely to include attempts to socialize underachievers' attitudes and beliefs and, in particular, attempts to reason with the student instead of just elaborating expectations concerning attention to lessons and work on assignments. They favored appeals that involved relating schoolwork to the student's current or future needs or stressing the work's potential for enriching the student's life. Higher rated teachers were more likely to mention attempts to build the student's self-concept, including the technique of charting or demonstrating progress over time to help the student appreciate it. They also were more likely to suggest involving the student's peers or parents in positive ways. Peer strategies included attempting to improve the underachievers' social roles in the classroom, enlisting peer support in helping them to improve their achievement, and posting their best work to publicly demonstrate their capabilities. Among teachers who mentioned home contacts, higher rated teachers were more likely to speak of intensive work with or counseling of the parents, whereas lower rated teachers were more likely to speak of asking the parents to place more pressure on their child.

Among teachers who focused on improving underachievers' effort levels, higher rated teachers were more likely to speak of encouraging these students to work harder, whereas lower rated teachers were more likely to speak of demanding better work and threatening punishment for failure to produce it. Higher rated teachers were more likely to say that they dispensed rewards for good effort, but lower rated teachers were more likely to say that they dispensed rewards for good performance.

Vignette: Carl

Carl can do good work, but he seldom does. He will try to get out of work. When you speak to him about this, he makes a show of looking serious and pledging reform, but his behavior doesn't change. Just now, you see a typical scene: Carl is making paper airplanes when he is supposed to be working.

Before reading further, take time to think about how you might respond to this incident. Make notes about your ideas.

CSS Vignette Response Excerpts

Here is what four of the CSS teachers had to say.

A LOWER RATED TEACHER

"I would simply take no excuse from this child at all. I would just put that assignment in front of him and, if I have to, stand there with a ruler in my hand and say, 'You are going to do this assignment, and I don't want to hear any of your complaints or anything. Take that serious look off your face, cause I don't even want to see that. You're going to do this today.' He wants someone to notice him and to put it to him, 'Ooh teacher, he is making an airplane, he is making this, he is doing this, and he is not doing his work.' This sort of thing."

A HIGHER RATED TEACHER

"I would assume that prior to this incident of Carl making paper airplanes, I would have spoken to him kindly, reassuringly: 'Carl, I know you can do better work than this, I know you can finish this, and I know you can make this more neat' (or whatever the particular problem was). Since being nice guy hadn't worked, I would then get very firm and tell him, 'Carl, I am really angry, because I know that you can do better than this. I have seen you do better than this, and I want a change now. I want you to stop making paper airplanes. I want this to be done and done neatly and correctly. If you are having trouble, I will help you, but I want you to try.' And I would tell him at that time that if it still wasn't what I expected from him, he would have to do it over again, so hopefully that would put enough pressure on him to do it correctly the first time. I would do that because I think Carl needs to know he cannot get by with knowing he can do it but not actually producing any work. He must know that good work is expected of him and that people care enough, that I care enough about him doing good work that I am going to check up and make certain that he does his work. I would characterize him as a child who perhaps is a little bit lazy. Maybe he likes to play more than work."

ANOTHER HIGHER RATED TEACHER

" 'Carl, why don't you bring the paper airplanes that you are making and show them to me.' After he shows them to me, I would probably say, 'If you complete this much on the lesson that you are supposed to be doing, you may sit and make other airplanes.' In the long run, I would make a graph and post it right on his desk and have it by subject, and as Carl completes the part of each subject that he has been assigned to do or that he feels he can make the commitment to do, then I would probably give him a smiley face on it. This appears to be the kind of child that you need to sit down with and ask him just how much he feels that he can do that day, and as he meets these goals, reinforce them. I would lessen the amount of work for him, but give him a specific amount to do so that he can meet that, because Carl has the capability for doing work but he doesn't. He is the kind of child who is not able to set goals for himself."

ANOTHER HIGHER RATED TEACHER

"I would go over to Carl and say, 'Hey Carl, what's happening? I thought I told you to start your reading paper. If you finish your work and you do a good job and want to make some paper airplanes afterward, that's fine with me. If you have some free time and the other children are still working, there is a book in the library that has some neat paper airplane designs. You might want to go down there and check it out and then come back and make some paper airplanes and share them with the rest of the class.' My rationale would be to get him to do the work that I know he is able to do and try to get him started. Obviously he is interested in making the paper airplanes, so you say, 'After you have done your work and have done a good job, tried hard, the reward would be to make the airplanes.' Making airplanes is sort of a distraction to the rest of the children in the class. If he wants to share it so much, give him the opportunity afterward. If he is a reasonably bright child, he could probably go to the library and look up some information and maybe come up with some neat designs to share with other children. So capitalize on the fact that he is a good student. It's almost like letting him do something extra or beyond. Maybe he is bored, and it's a good way to channel his behavior. I would definitely get on his case about not doing his work, and I would say to him, 'You come to school first to work. Like it or not, that's the way it is. We come to school to do our schoolwork first, but if you have some free time, I don't mind if you make the paper airplanes.'"

The lower rated teacher suggested an authoritarian, even hostile, response to Carl. In contrast, the higher rated teachers were much less inclined to take Carl's misbehavior personally and respond angrily. They appeared to be less concerned about this particular incident than about the larger underachievement pattern that Carl displayed, and their responses focused on increasing his appreciation for the value of school-work or, failing that, at least making him understand that he is responsible for completing his assignments and must give them first priority during class time.

Analysis of Responses to Carl

Heavy majorities of the teachers viewed Carl's misbehavior as not only controllable (83) but intentional (80). Therefore, it is not surprising that 71 teachers featured exercising control through threat or punishment as a major goal of their influence attempt. In addition or instead, 47 teachers mentioned shaping improvement through successive approximations, and 14 mentioned improving Carl's mental hygiene or coping skills.

Punishment was the most frequently mentioned specific strategy for responding to Carl (58). Other commonly mentioned strategies included reward (33), reviewing expectations or otherwise prescribing desired behavior (32), proscribing against misbehavior (22), attempting to identify and eliminate the source of the problem (20), brief management responses (19), and involving the parents (14).

The most frequently mentioned method for stopping Carl from continuing to work on paper airplanes was to remind him that he was supposed to be working on an assignment at the moment (30). Other methods included confiscating the paper airplanes (20), telling Carl to put them away (16), and requiring him to continue making them until he became satiated with the activity (5).

The most commonly mentioned method of returning Carl to the task was to remind him of rules or expectations (43), typically by telling him that he was supposed to be working on his assignment now. Other methods included providing additional task structuring and monitoring him closely thereafter (19), simply requesting or demanding that he get back to work (15), asking if he was having some problem with the work (7), and attempting to elicit from Carl himself the statement that he should be working on the assignment (6).

The most commonly mentioned method for keeping Carl on task (once he was returned to it) was to direct him to work on it until he finished. The majority of teachers would issue such orders to Carl, although only 17 of them would rely on directives alone. Of the rest, 42 also would threaten punishment for noncompliance, and 14 would promise a reward for compliance. Other methods for keeping Carl on task included providing close supervision and help if necessary (12), changing his seat (9), and making an attempt to help him see the value in the work (7).

Three-fourths of the teachers would include some sort of socialization message to Carl. A majority (46) of these would just restate rules and expectations. In addition or instead, 22 would propose contracts or in some other way attempt to strike a bargain with Carl to secure his agreement to do the work, and 10 would try to impress Carl with the value of the activity.

The majority of the teachers would initiate some follow-up with Carl. Most would either institute contracts involving reward and/or punishment (35) or contact his parents (34). Other responses included attempting to provide him with work related to airplanes or in other ways capitalize on his airplane interest (10), holding a work motivation conference (9), changing his work (8), or holding a goal-setting conference (6).

In general, the majority of teachers would act *on* rather than *with* Carl, relying heavily on power assertion backed by threat of punishment. In addition or instead, a minority would attempt to motivate Carl by helping him to see the value in the assignment, by changing his assignment, or by offering him rewards if he fulfilled some contract or agreement.

Lower rated teachers were likely to rely on power assertion backed by threats of punishment, but higher rated teachers, instead or at least in addition, were likely to mention more positive problem-solving strategies. Higher rated teachers were more likely to include prevention or (especially) follow-up strategies in addition to strategies for responding to the immediate situation, and their goals were more likely to include shaping improvement through successive approximations or resocializing Carl's attitudes or self-regulation capabilities instead of just exerting situational control over his behavior. Higher rated teachers were more confident, particularly concerning their prospects for inducing stable improvement. They were more likely to speak of eliminating the source of the problem, scheduling work motivation conferences, prescriptively clarifying what they expected from Carl, and attempting to help Carl to see that his misbehavior was not in his own best interests.

Vignette: Nancy

Nancy is oriented toward peers and social relationships, not schoolwork. She could be doing top-grade work, but instead she does just enough to get by. She is often chatting or writing notes when she is supposed to be paying attention or working. During today's lesson, she has repeatedly turned to students on each side of her to make remarks, and now she has a conversation going with several friends.

Before reading further, take time to think about how you might respond to this incident. Make notes about your ideas.

CSS Vignette Response Excerpts

Here is what four of the CSS teachers had to say.

A LOWER RATED TEACHER

" 'Stop interrupting by turning to the other students and talking.' If she was having problems with this, I would have to remove her from the class and have her stand outside the door and let her know that this is stopping the class process. We're wasting time and we can't have it, so stand outside of the room. When she's ready to join the class, have her apologize and come back in. Further I would have to let her mother know in the parent–teacher conference how Nancy spends her day and that she could be doing top-grade work. Instead she's spending her time chatting with her friends. It's just a waste. 'Look at Nancy's grades, and let's do something about these. She can bring her grades up, and perhaps you have some means of letting her know that you're disappointed and expect more out of her and see that she gives you her best.' Go from there, and let the mother be concerned and work on that. Even though you talk yourself, some of this support has to come from the home."

A HIGHER RATED TEACHER

"I would go over to Nancy, and first of all, to give her a fair chance, I would say, 'Nancy are you perhaps helping these other children with their schoolwork?' Kids being honest, she probably would tell me, 'No.' Then I would say, 'Nancy, I'm really sorry, but since you seem to be unable to do your lesson sitting next to other children, I would like for you to sit at the table in the back of the room. When you are finished with your lesson, you may go back to your regular desk. I'm really sorry that you found it necessary to be doing so much talking and carrying on when you had work to do.' My goal would be to help her realize that peer and social relationships are important, but when you are given a particular task, your first responsibility is to that task. The social interaction is going to have to come after. Also, if she cannot control the socializing, then she is going to have to be physically placed in a situation where she can't interact with other children until the work is completed."

ANOTHER HIGHER RATED TEACHER

" 'Nancy, I want you to get out the work that you are supposed to be doing right now. I want the talking stopped immediately. You have work to be done, and you are bothering and interrupting. Other chil-

dren are concerned with what you are saying, and they are not getting their work done. You must work at your seat without talking.
If this is not possible, then I want you to go to the back of the room
and take a seat there and continue with your work so that you do
not interrupt and bother other people around you.' My goal is to get
Nancy to stop her talking, to complete her work without delay, and
also to have her not interrupt the other children. I think that you
should not plead with her to do this. You should make it very definite
that this is what they have to do, and they make their own choice.
If they choose not to do the work there, they will have to do it in
another place or at another time."

ANOTHER HIGHER RATED TEACHER

"I would talk to Nancy and tell her that I am concerned about the
fact that her schoolwork is not what it should be, because I know that
she's able to do better than that. I would also ask her how she thinks
the children around her feel about her talking to them a lot. Are they
able to get their work done? If she doesn't know the answer to that,
I would ask some of the people that sit close to her to join us in a
discussion about how well they think they can work with people talking around them. Does Nancy's talking bother them? Perhaps she
doesn't realize that she is having an effect on the other students. I
would ask her what she thinks would help her to not talk during the
work periods, and I would hope to come up with something like a
friend who would ask her, 'Please, don't talk now, I'm working,' or
maybe she could write a note or put a sign on her desk like 'Work,
don't talk,' or 'Work before you talk,' or something to that effect. She
is concerned about social relationships and peers, so maybe having
a peer tell her that she is bothering them will have a good effect on
Nancy, because I think that she would not want to be diminished in
the eyes of her peers for talking. If she thinks that she can be raised
in their esteem by not talking and doing her work and not bothering
others, she will probably try to go along with that. I would describe
her as immature if she is not concerned with the schoolwork."

The lower rated teacher would remove Nancy from class and lecture
her about her conduct, as well as seek to get her mother to pressure her
to apply herself better at school. Her response was confined to
threat/pressure strategies. The higher rated teachers also would emphasize to Nancy that she is responsible for completing her assignments and
for respecting prohibitions against disturbing classmates during work
times. However, they would take less authoritarian, more informative and
likely-to-be-successful approaches to communicating these understandings.

By placing less emphasis on punishing or embarrassing Nancy and more emphasis on "getting through" to her, they would increase their chances of doing so successfully.

Analysis of Responses to Nancy

The teachers viewed Nancy as less blameworthy than Carl. Although 70 of them saw her problem behavior as controllable, only 19 saw it as intentional. Even so, 75 teachers said that their response to Nancy would include attempts to control her behavior through threat or punishment. In addition or instead, 28 would attempt to shape improvements through successive approximations, and 23 would attempt to improve her mental hygiene or coping skills.

Punishment was the most frequently mentioned specific strategy (47). Others included changing Nancy's seat (31), limit setting and other proscriptions against her misbehavior (30), rule reminders and other prescriptions of desired behavior (24), attempting to develop Nancy's insight (23), attempting to identify and eliminate the source of the problem (14), brief management responses (13), rewards (13), self-concept support (8), involving Nancy's parents (7), and removal or isolation (7).

Among teachers who would attempt to develop Nancy's insight, 18 would focus on her own behavior or its consequences, and 7 would focus on the teacher's goals or feelings. Among teachers who provided rationales or justifications for the demands they would make on Nancy, 32 mentioned logical analysis linking Nancy's behavior to its consequences, 23 would cite class rules, 19 would attempt to induce empathy (usually by suggesting that Nancy was interfering with her classmates' opportunities to learn), 7 would appeal to her pride or self-concept, and 6 would make a personal appeal (asking her to improve her behavior to please the teacher).

All but one of the teachers said that they would intervene in the situation, usually by reminding Nancy of rules and expectations (63), changing her seat (53), or simply telling her to pay attention (14). In addition, all but 12 would follow up with some attempt to resocialize Nancy's attitudes and behavior. The most commonly mentioned socialization content included reminding Nancy of her responsibilities as a student (35), telling her that her behavior was unfair to her classmates because it interfered with their learning opportunities (30), offering rewards or (especially) threatening punishments (26), telling Nancy that she was being unfair to herself by denying herself learning opportunities (15), telling her that she was being unfair to the teacher by interfering with instruction (9), telling her that the work is important (8), and appealing to her self-interest by explaining what she would gain by paying better attention or what she will lose by failing to pay attention (7).

Most teachers also mentioned prevention or follow-up strategies. These included punishing Nancy if necessary (27), changing her seat (22), having a discussion about her behavior (17), parent contact (14), and trying to solve some problem presumed to underlie her behavior (lack of acceptance in the peer group, need for more structure or direction in her work, need for more appropriate work) (12).

Once again, lower rated teachers emphasized demand, pressure, and punishment strategies. They were more likely than higher rated teachers to view Nancy's disruptive behavior as intentional and to speak of punishing her or isolating her from her classmates (rather than merely changing her seat). They also were less likely to mention supportive behavior or attempts to resocialize Nancy.

Higher rated teachers were less likely to speak of threatening or invoking punishment in the process of intervening on the spot. Instead, either then or as follow-up later, they were more likely to talk about resocializing Nancy's attitudes or providing her with some form of assistance (in addressing an underlying cause of her problem). These teachers were more likely to mention holding a follow-up conference or discussion, enlisting the help of classmates, explaining their own goals or feelings in an attempt to develop Nancy's insight into the consequences of her behavior, and telling Nancy that she was not being fair to her classmates by interfering with their learning opportunities. Thus, higher rated teachers spoke of attempts to "get through to" Nancy along with controlling her behavior, whereas the lower rated teachers tended to focus only on control.

COMPARISON OF RESPONSES TO CARL AND TO NANCY

Both vignettes portray underachievers engaging in situationally inappropriate behavior instead of paying attention to a lesson (Nancy) or working on an assignment (Carl). In each case, most teachers' responses called for immediate intervention designed to restore the student to appropriate task engagement. Sometimes these interventions would involve only a brief directive ("Pay attention, Nancy"). More typically, they would involve rule reminders or elaboration of expectations, often accompanied by punishment (or threat of punishment for further noncompliance). Lower rated teachers favored demanding and threatening versions of this general response, often without mentioning any additional strategies. Higher rated teachers favored less punitive versions and tended to mention more preventive or follow-up strategies such as conferences with the student, attempts to resocialize attitudes, or attempts to address causal factors.

Even though both students were described as chronic underachievers who were displaying situationally inappropriate behavior, and even though Nancy's misbehavior disrupted a lesson, the teachers were more likely to view Carl as misbehaving intentionally and thus to mention threatening or invoking punishment as part of their response to him. One reason for this was that many teachers, especially in the early grades, treated the second vignette as a situational problem (Nancy is chatting with her friends when she should be paying attention to the lesson) rather than as a symptom of a more chronic syndrome (Nancy does this sort of thing all the time and is underachieving because of it). These teachers often suggested an easy situational solution (moving Nancy to another seat) without speaking of socialization, problem solving, or other attempts to address the larger underachievement syndrome. However, those teachers who did speak of follow-up with Nancy mentioned a variety of strategies, whereas most of the follow-up strategies mentioned for Carl involved contracts/shaping or contacting his parents.

The most obvious difference in response to the two vignettes was that 53 teachers spoke of changing Nancy's seat as a way to isolate her from classmates with whom she socialized regularly. In contrast, only 9 teachers mentioned changing Carl's seat, and this was to get him closer to them so that he could be monitored more consistently.

QUALITATIVE IMPRESSIONS AND EXAMPLES

Several teachers noted that underachievement problems do not so much indicate alienation from work but rather show a lack of positive value concerning it, which leads to a "do as little as you can get away with" attitude. Reward and punishment systems can control work output, but socialization is needed to change the student's attitude. Thus, the goal is not just to get underachievers to perform more acceptably but to build their motivation by teaching them to see benefit in schoolwork and take pride in their effort and successes. A variation on the same idea, expressed frequently by teachers working in the early grades, is that underachievers aren't so much alienated or unsocialized but rather lacking in direction. They need imposition of responsibilities and expectations, at home as well as at school.

Many teachers began this interview by talking about how the problem stems from the home, usually because parents disparage school or fail to make sufficient demands on their child. These teachers believed that underachievers need to know that both their parents and their teachers care about what they do and intend to check on their progress. In this regard, one teacher said that enlisting parental assistance was her most powerful strategy for addressing underachievement problems. The parents always agree to cooperate because she begins by saying that she knows that they want their children to do well in school and are eager to be helpful. She also makes it clear that she is eager to be helpful and is not picking on their child.

Another teacher invited parents to come to class, either to observe their children or to work together with them on certain activities. Observational visits help to provide pressure on underachieving children; cooperative work helps to enhance the attitudes of both the parents and the children toward school and schoolwork.

Teachers reported following up on parent contacts in various ways. Some would attempt to keep things positive by sending home examples of the students' best work, so that successes achieved in the classroom could be reinforced at home as well. Others would use both supportive and pressuring strategies, typically by sending home daily or weekly reports to keep parents informed. Often these reports would be the basis for delivering or withholding rewards as part of a formal contract or an informal agreement that the teacher had negotiated with the parents. Finally, one teacher would follow up by throwing underachievers' poor papers into the trash and making them do the papers over again, telling them that both she and their parents want their very best work.

Several teachers mentioned strategies for making students more conscious of the potential value of what they study in school. Often these strategies were connected with career education. For example, one teacher arranged for visits by adults involved in various occupations and asked them to emphasize during their presentation that academic skills are needed in their work. Another teacher arranged for students whom she had taught 2 years previously to visit her current class and tell her students about things that they learned in her room that are useful to them now. Where relevant, she also encouraged the visitors to tell her students about things they need now that they wish they had studied more carefully when they were in her class. Another teacher tried to help her students to understand that what they learn in school is useful not only for jobs but for increasing their quality of life, bringing more to their relationships with other people, and other self-actualization reasons. She told them that "you don't do things for rewards, you do them to make yourself a better person." Finally, one teacher would tell her students that her husband is a high school teacher and reports that his students are starting to see that their life chances have been limited and that they now wish they had developed their basic skills better when they were younger.

One teacher said that you need to use reward systems with underachievers in the early grades because they are not yet old enough to appreciate arguments based on the use of academic skills in adult occupations. As students move into the middle grades, however, she would favor asking them about what they would like to be as adults and then following up by making them realize that they will need academic skills in order to do what they want to do. Many other teachers appeared to share this view, in that teachers in the early grades often mentioned reward systems as an effective approach to underachievers, whereas teachers in the upper grades were more likely to mention persuasion attempts and other strategies designed to change students' attitudes toward schoolwork. In addition, several first-grade teachers claimed that problems of indifference to school are infrequent among first-graders, who tend to look forward to schooling in general and learning to read in particular.

Several teachers mentioned that, at least until underachievers begin to value the work itself, it is important to make sure that they value whatever rewards you offer them for working up to their potential. One told of an attempt to use a contract approach with an underachiever that failed because the reward offered was not attractive to the student. She stressed the need to talk to the student first and determine what kinds of rewards would be effective. Many teachers, especially in the early grades, used a classroom management system that automatically allowed students to engage in various alternative activities when they completed their assignments acceptably. Others did not do this routinely but said that they would institute something like it for underachievers.

Another teacher stated that praise does not work well with underachievers but reward systems do. She tried to move underachievers toward their potential through successive approximations by gradually increasing what was required of them to qualify for rewards. She also worked to interest them in the material, although she believed that quietly raising expectations so as to get these students to work closer to their potential without even realizing it was more effective than confronting them about their underachievement.

One teacher assigned each student a place along the wall to post work samples under his or her photo and name. She reported that this exerted some pressure on underachievers to do a good job because they wanted to have nice work samples hanging under their photos. Another teacher would not only post papers in the classroom but send students to show their papers to the principal, and the principal would display some of these in the hall near the entrance to the school.

One teacher listed several strategies for trying to make underachievers care about the quality of their work: stating that she wants her students to do good work that they can be proud of, pointing out that the skills they are learning will be needed later on the job or to pass a driving test, and posting unusually good papers from another class as an example of what other students are doing (then encouraging her own students to do as well).

In an attempt to develop achievement motivation, one teacher would show the film version of *The Little Engine That Could* (Piper, 1991) and would read and discuss excerpts from self-improvement books such as *Yes I Can* by Sammy Davis, Jr. (Davis & Boyer, 1990), or *I'll Fix Anthony* by Judith Viorst (1988).

The most impressive responses combined use of incentives, attempts to build on the student's interests, attempts to raise consciousness or resocialize attitudes, and other positive strategies with firm demands for more conscientious work, backed if necessary by the threat of negative consequences such as loss of privileges or having to redo assignments during recess or after school. Several teachers' responses seemed unlikely to be effective because they were limited to strategies that did not address underachievers' failure to work conscientiously on a continuing basis.

For example, some teachers would rely on finding especially meaningful activities for these students and hoping that these good experiences would carry over into their work on regular assignments. Others suggested that the problem might be boredom or resentment by underachievers who already knew how to do the work, so they prescribed more challenging assignments for them. Others spoke of using art, sports, or other nonacademic activities as ways to make sure that the student enjoys at least something about school. One suggested involving underachievers in drama, sports, choral reading, or other activities that require discipline in terms of holding up your end as a member of a group or team (somehow hoping that this would transfer to the student's work as an individual learner in the classroom). Finally, several teachers mentioned getting books from the library in underachievers' areas of interest so that these students could read what they wanted as they developed skills. They also would allow these students to use their areas of interest as content bases for research and writing assignments. All of these strategies seem likely to be marginally helpful by making school a more positive experience for underachievers, but they do not address the core problem of persistent failure to work up to potential.

Several teachers mentioned involving underachievers in competitions as a way to increase their motivation to achieve. Usually they would apply this strategy subtly rather than directly. For example, several mentioned using the students' need to be part of a group by putting them in group situations where they would have to hold up their end, praising nearby peers for working persistently, publishing charts showing group and individual progress, and so on. One teacher would place high-ability underachievers into a group with other high-ability students so that they no longer could do well without putting out much effort. Another teacher spoke of pairing underachievers with students of similar ability who work harder and therefore produce more and better work, thus inducing some competition indirectly. This teacher also mentioned the risky strategy of posting poor efforts by underachievers as a way to embarrass them into working more conscientiously.

Teachers who viewed underachievers as lazy or seeking to do minimum work tended to talk about applying constant pressure to these students by checking on them frequently and making it clear that their demands for good work would be enforced. One clarified that, whereas with low achievers you check back often to provide encouragement and help, with underachievers you check back often to set goals and demands, see that they are being met, and show that you care and will continue to monitor and apply accountability pressures. Another noted that if you take a punitive approach (tell underachievers that they must finish their work or else lose recess time), you must be consistent in following through on threats and also must make sure that these students can do the work on time if they apply themselves (so that it is their choice if they do not). Rather than being more sharply demanding or more clearly punitive in following through on threats, one teacher would say something like "Why don't you stay after school and help me wash the board, and we'll finish up your paper." Several suggested that contracts, goal setting, and other approaches that involve eliciting the student's commitment to goals are preferable to making demands because they require the student to take responsibility for seeing that the work is done.

Many of the noteworthy elements in the teachers' responses to the vignettes elaborated on the same themes noted in their responses to the interview. For example, several teachers noted that their response to Carl would be routine because they had a system in place that automatically requires students to use free periods or to stay after school to finish work that wasn't done when it was supposed to be. Also, several teachers mentioned using proximity control when underachievers are not paying attention to the lesson or doing their work. They would move near to Carl or Nancy, and in the case of Carl, they would take away his airplane unobtrusively. Among the least impressive responses were those from teachers who would simply call the parent immediately when a problem arose, without trying any strategies of their own first. Typically, their basic message would be that the parent should force the child to behave.

One teacher suggested the following response to repeated excuses: "I'm sorry, but I have heard this before, and you haven't changed, but today you are going to change. This is not going to continue. Today is the first day of the rest of your life." Another teacher would show her grade book to underachievers, to impress on them that she grades them according to what they do, not what they are capable of doing, and that they are headed for low or failing grades if they don't begin to work more conscientiously.

Pressuring strategies were mentioned frequently as responses to Carl.

One teacher would tell him to put his paper airplane in the wastebasket and then put his head down on his desk and keep it there until he was ready to work. If necessary, she would keep him in to do the work at recess, saying "If we play when we are supposed to work, then we are going to have to work when other people get to play."

Several teachers spoke of using contracting approaches with Carl. However, some would not so much negotiate a contract collaboratively with Carl but rather announce an imposed contingency (if he doesn't get a certain amount accomplished by a certain time, he will suffer some negative consequence).

There were some supportive responses to Carl. One teacher would post a graph or chart on his desk and put smiley faces on it as he completed work that he had made a commitment to do. Another would suggest that he keep an eye on the clock as a way to focus, perhaps planning in terms of getting a certain amount of the task done by a certain time. Finally, one teacher would compliment Carl on his paper airplanes before telling him that right now he is supposed to be working on his assignment. This would lighten the tone of the interaction and avoid more direct power assertion.

Almost all of the teachers described Carl as an underachiever, but many described Nancy as a talker or social butterfly. Some suggested responses based on Nancy's sociability. For example, several teachers said that they would show Nancy some good work done by one or more of her friends and then ask her to try to do the same. Others would take advantage of her social interests by seating her apart from her classmates and telling her that she would have to remain isolated until she showed that she could work continuously on her assignments and do them well. Still others would make Nancy's sociability the basis of sarcastic remarks to her (such as referring to her talking with neighbors as "romancing" or "holding a summit conference").

Some of the least effective responses to Nancy were simply punitive. Often these were directed at her note writing, which, like Carl's airplane making, seemed to bother certain teachers more than her social chatting. One teacher would intercept one of Nancy's notes, pin it on her, and make her wear it the rest of the day. Two others would give up trying to change Nancy directly and instead begin threatening her friends. For example, one would announce that peers seen talking to Nancy or accepting notes from her would be punished instead of Nancy, "because I have tried to help Nancy. I have talked to her, and Nancy just doesn't cooperate, so in order for Nancy to cooperate, everyone in the class is going to have to help. You are going to have to ignore her and not take part in the things that she is doing that she shouldn't be doing. Outside it is different. You may do this, but in the classroom I'd like to have you just ignore her. If she calls your name, just sit there, and eventually I will hear her calling you."

Finally, one teacher had a much more positive response to note passing, claiming that it had worked well in the past. She would write note-passers a note explaining the problems that their behavior causes. Her note would close with a question that required a written response from the student. This approach avoids a public and disruptive intervention and is likely to lead to an improved personal relationship with the student (along with a solution to the particular problem behavior involved).

DISCUSSION

To the extent that they viewed underachievement as a problem and possessed ideas about how to address it, most teachers focused on its core symptoms. Typically, they suggested rewards, natural consequences, or punishment as tools for manipulating underachievers' overt behavior. Often, they also suggested some form of socialization as a strategy for addressing these students' underlying attitudes and beliefs. In addition or instead, some teachers suggested other response strategies that were linked to their views on the nature and causes of the underachievement syndrome. For example, teachers who believed that the student's tendency to devalue schoolwork was reflecting attitudes modeled at home tended to speak of working with the parents, whereas teachers who thought the problem was lack of interest tended to speak of making changes in the curriculum.

Compared to our findings for other problem-student types, the data on underachievers showed noteworthy contrasts between responses to the interview and responses to the vignettes. The problem-type description used as the basis for the interview emphasized underachievers' lack of achievement motivation and interest in schoolwork. However, it did not depict them as engaging in provocative behaviors that create teacher-owned problems, as did the vignettes. Apparently for this reason, the interview responses emphasized supportive attempts to encourage and assist underachievers, while the vignette responses emphasized demands and pressuring strategies. This was especially the case with Carl, whose construction of paper airplanes was viewed as more provocative than Nancy's socializing. When confronted with the behaviors depicted in the vignettes, many teachers, especially lower rated teachers, confined their response to power assertive interventions without mentioning any of the supportive strategies or long-term prevention or solution strategies that most of them discussed in the interview.

As far as they went, the teachers' responses reflected the diversity found in the scholarly literature concerning contrasting underachievement syndromes, their nature and causes, and potential strategies for addressing them. The correlations of response strategies with effectiveness ratings supported the patient, supportive, and instructive strategies recommended in the literature over the limit-setting and pressuring strategies. One basic reason for this was that the latter strategies often were the only types mentioned by lower rated teachers. Also, among teachers who emphasized the latter strategies, some (again, lower rated teachers in particular) described implementations that seemed likely to be counterproductive. These teachers' responses depicted impulsive or vengeful applications of punishment instead of a more goal-oriented use of threat of punishment as part of a larger treatment package designed to both encourage and pressure underachievers to change their attitudes and behavior.

These findings can also be interpreted from a child development perspective. Themes noted both in the scholarly literature and in the teachers' interview responses suggest that, until they reach age 10 or so, most underachievers do not settle into the pattern of systematic avoidance of responsibility as described by Mandel and Marcus (1988) or failure to persist in the face of challenge as described by McCall, Evahn, and Kratzer (1992). Even when younger underachievers are drifting toward this pattern, it usually hasn't "hardened" yet. Most younger underachievers appear to be more like the children that Bruns (1992) described as work-inhibited—adult-dependent, attention-seeking, unprepared to assume responsibilities, or otherwise immature, but not systematically working below their potential because they are consciously or unconsciously motivated to do so.

To the extent that these developmental hypotheses are valid, they imply that encouraging and instructional strategies might be more effective with younger underachievers, whereas confrontive and persuasive strategies might be more effective with older ones. This implication has not been tested directly. However, it is consistent with the fact that the findings from our study favoring supportive strategies were obtained from elementary teachers, whereas findings supporting confrontive strategies tend to come from studies done in junior and senior high schools. Thus, in the elementary grades, and especially in the primary grades, it may be best to avoid treating underachievers as "hardened" cases unless there is clear evidence that they have become so. Instead, it is probably better to give them the benefit of the doubt and treat them as well meaning but in need of socialization and instruction concerning what they will need to do in order to get the most out of lessons and assignments. In short, you will need to teach these students about motivation to learn (Brophy, in press; Good & Brophy, 1995, 1997).

I view the readiness to engage in academic activities with motivation to learn as a schema—a network of connected insights, skills, values, and dispositions that enable students to understand what it means to engage in academic activities with the intention of accomplishing their learning goals and with metacognitive awareness of the strategies they use as they attempt to do so. Many underachievers, especially those who do not so much resist schoolwork but rather fail to find meaning in it, are children who have not had much exposure to the motivation-to-learn schema. *You can socialize students to the value elements of the motivation-to-learn schema* by modeling interest in learning, encouraging your students to develop positive concepts of themselves as learners, and helping them to appreciate that growth in knowledge and skills is empowering (it enables you to do more without relying on others) and life-enhancing (it stimulates your mind and makes your everyday experiences more meaningful).

You also can instruct your students in the knowledge and skills aspects of the motivation-to-learn schema. This involves teaching them to approach learning activities with an awareness of purposes and goals, to monitor their comprehension by asking themselves questions about what they are learning and paraphrasing it into their own words, to make connections to applications and examples, to keep track of the strategies they use as they engage in learning activities, to adjust these strategies as needed, and to reinforce themselves and experience the satisfactions involved in working toward and achieving learning goals. In short, the notion of learning (including school learning) as a meaningful and worthwhile activity that leads to important personal payoffs when pursued with these goals in mind is simply foreign to many underachievers (and often to their parents as well). Consequently, it is left primarily to teachers to help these students acquire understanding of the motivation-to-learn schema and appreciation of its power to enhance their lives.

III

Students with Hostility Problems

P art III addresses three types of students whose problems feature hostility. In planning the Classroom Strategy Study, we originally separated problems involving hostility into just two types, according to whether the negative emotion was directed at the teacher (*defiant*) or at peers (*hostile–aggressive*). However, pilot interviews revealed that teachers distinguished between students who defied them overtly and students who were noncompliant and oppositional in various ways but stopped short of direct defiance. The term "passive-aggressive" was borrowed from the psychological literature to refer to the latter students.

Part III consists of three chapters. Chapter 8 addresses hostile–aggressive students, Chapter 9 discusses passive–aggressive students, and Chapter 10 covers defiant students.

8

Hostile–Aggressive Students

ostile–aggressive students display the following characteristics: These children express hostility through direct, intense behaviors. They are not easily controlled. They:

1. Intimidate
2. Hit and push
3. Damage property
4. Antagonize
5. Are easily angered

What special strategies might you use to minimize such problems and help these students to function more successfully in your classroom? Before reading further, take time to think about this and make notes about your ideas.

CSS INTERVIEW EXCERPTS

Here is what three of the CSS teachers had to say about teaching hostile–aggressive students.

A Lower Rated Teacher

"First, I call the mother to see if I can enlist her help. Now the type of child that hits, pushes, intimidates, threatens, damages property, antagonizes, etc., usually has a mother who couldn't care less. But you do try in that area. Then I go back, and if he has been a former student in our school, I check him back right through to kindergarten. If the hostility has been there since then, I am in trouble. Nothing

I do is going to change this behavior pattern. If he has not been that way since kindergarten but is building year by year, then we may be dealing with a home problem, and there again, we can't get hold of the mother. So what you do is build a case. We have these attendance sheets, and every time he does something, you write him up, and every time he is really out of line . . . like he is in a fight . . . as a rule of thumb I take care of all the fights in my classroom unless there is blood. Blood automatically goes to the office because that is an accident report. But if the child is already in the fourth grade and these are becoming vicious, I kick him out to the office. After the second or third time, the office gets disgusted and calls the mother. And eventually we get to a situation like I had last week where the child is suspended until the mother comes to school. And usually my boss sticks a social worker's form right under her nose and says, 'Sign.' The funny thing is, if the kid is an LD and he is a behavior problem, the LD rooms won't take him. But we have to see what we are dealing with, and often the psychological testing is a big help. Also the social worker is very good in our school, and she works with the parents and the child. But if you have an antagonistic mother or father, you are definitely not going to get through. Except for keeping the peace in your room, there is not too much you can do. If you are able to isolate them—usually they like to show off their behaviors—if you can isolate them, beautiful, but usually not in our classrooms that are so crowded. It is really difficult to isolate them. [If you are forced to just keep peace in your classroom, how do you go about doing that?] Well, it depends on the child. Sometimes they threaten, but they have to be near somebody to threaten. If you can isolate them somewhat, they don't like that, and they will straighten up because they can't hit anybody if they aren't near anybody, so they want to be within the mainstream. So they will straighten up to a certain degree. Also a reward situation sometimes works: 'If you can stay in your seat for half an hour with your mouth shut, you will get a star on your paper.' 'If you can stay in your seat and keep your mouth shut for an hour and not touch anybody, then I will have a surprise for you at the end of the day.' It could be a balloon, a stick of gum, a piece of candy. It doesn't even have to be a lot. But sometimes this child doesn't even care for a reward. He still wants the fun and games of hitting. Of course, if you are bigger than he is and you can hurt harder, sometimes that will work. But most of these children have been hit so many times that hitting won't do a bit of good. . . . There isn't too much you can do. You just try different methods. Sometimes they work; sometimes they don't. And sometimes the child is so bad that taking away a privilege, isolation, nothing is going to work. That sounds very poor.

I do think we need elementary school counselors. Not only that, but I think we need a cooling-off room. If you have a child and you know his temper is beginning to climb and you know you are going to have a fight in 5 minutes, grab him and send him down to someplace where he can just sit down and cool off away from his class. Then maybe he will be able to function . . . once he gets the anger out of his system. These are angry children. These are angry, frustrated children, and teachers aren't psychologists. We aren't God. We just try to do the best we can, but you can't do everything for every child."

This interview and others like it are heartbreaking to read. The teacher intended to be helpful, but her potential for success with hostile–aggressive students was minimized by her lack of strategies and low level of expectation that approached hopelessness. Her immediate response was to refer the problem to the parent, the principal, or the school counselor or social worker. More generally, her response focused on building a case against the student as a basis for removing him from her classroom and placing him in a special education setting, rather than on building a relationship with the student and trying to resocialize his attitudes and behavior.

A Higher Rated Teacher

"My first strategy is to find out what caused the problem. If I am able to identify it, it would be through parent conferences or telephone calls to the parent, in other words, close contact with the home. Sometimes after talking to the parents the teacher can identify quite easily what is going wrong at home. Sometimes it is beyond the help of the teacher or the parents—it could be a crisis situation—but lots of times it is an ongoing thing that the parents unknowingly are doing or not doing that causes this sort of behavior. You will often have parents say, 'Yes, we have this at home. What would you recommend?' At this point, you have an opportunity to give them some good suggestions that might reduce this sort of behavior. My own experience indicates that it can be minimized greatly within the classroom through strategies that the teacher uses. If you find out that there has been too strong discipline in the home, too violent or whatever, you certainly don't want to repeat those mistakes at school. You have to study the child quite carefully. Observe when he becomes threatening or hostile. What sort of things provoke him? Steer around those or avoid them if possible. When he does break a rule or injure another child or whatever, you have to be very careful in how you approach any so-called punishment. One strategy that works well is to take the student outside the room and sit down with him on a one-to-one basis and talk to him about his behavior. Try to be completely nonthreatening so that he will open up and perhaps express some resentments or feelings that he has. I always ask if it is something here at school first and try to get them to feel so nonthreatened that they will be honest about their feelings. If it is nothing that I can control here, then I try to help them deal with the situation at home. Perhaps they can't change. In most cases they can't, but I can at least help them to learn how to deal with it. I think one of the major problems that a teacher has today is to deal with hostility and to teach children how to deal with their own angers and hostilities in a nonthreatening way, a nonaggressive manner. This behavior can be greatly minimized by teacher modeling and teacher interaction not only with the student involved but with the rest of the class, perhaps when that student is absent. Sometimes after repeated incidents, one has to take action of a punitive sort, and I feel that in the case of property damage a child should be made to pay for at least part of the damage he has caused even if he makes a small contribution by earning money at home, by maybe working here at school. If he has injured another child, I ask him to think about whether an apology is due. I do not say whether he has to apologize. I ask him to think about it. In a rare occasion, I have him call the parents of the child who has been injured and explain what he has done. This is a very difficult thing for a child to do, but I think it teaches a lasting lesson. I often have him call his own parents with me standing by and tell them that he is in the office and why he is in the office and what he has done. I think as often as possible, have the child deal with the problem directly, taking the responsibility for his own actions. So many of these students have never seen a relationship of cause and effect when it comes to lashing out at people through poorly controlled tempers, this sort of thing. I think the sooner they can take responsibility for their own actions, the better they will be able to progress both in and out of school."

Although mindful of the difficulties involved in dealing with entrenched hostile–aggressive behavior, this teacher emphasized problem-solving efforts (directed not only at the student but at the parents as well). She emphasized helping these students to understand that their behavior is seriously wrong and to develop skills for managing anger and handling conflicts more productively.

ANOTHER HIGHER RATED TEACHER

"I think these children are very angry. They probably come from a home where anger often is expressed outwardly, and they may be the victim of that anger quite often. The first thing that needs to be done is to stop them either verbally or physically when they are going to hurt someone else, so you need to be very aware of where they are in a group situation, and you need to be able to read body language and facial expressions about when they are upset and stop them at that point. Then they need to be able to tell you what it is that is bothering them. This should be done away from the rest of the class, so that attention is not called to them. If they don't volunteer information, then the teacher should suggest some possibilities of things that may have induced them to anger. They need to realize the results of their actions and own up to them. If they hurt another child, they need to hear about it from that child. The hurt child needs to say how they feel. This should be done every time that their actions result in hurting someone else. This child needs to think about what alternatives they can have as an outlet for their anger. If they are not able to think of any, then I would suggest things, like writing down or drawing a picture of what is bothering them. They would probably want to show it to the person who is bothering them, or to someone, and if the picture or the note is an alternative that they can choose, then the other children need to become aware by the class discussion that this is what this angered child is going to do. When they get angry, they are going to draw a picture, or they are going to write a note, and that is not cause for someone else to start slugging but to start talking about what is causing the anger. This child also will have to learn to read his own body when he feels himself getting angry, maybe have to walk out of the room and go down the hall and get a drink, go to the bathroom, and then come back when they feel more calm. This would probably be a step after the drawing or writing, because physically removing yourself is more difficult than staying there and expressing your anger on paper with drawings. This anger is something that takes a very long time to try to control, and maybe within a school year the child would not get past the point of drawing a picture. Even shouting at another person would be better than hitting. But they need to be constantly reminded by classmates how their behavior is affecting other children. Over time they may become more sensitive to what is happening and develop an interest in forming some friendships that would make them want to negate their hostile and angry behavior, make them not want to do that. Some of the strategies that don't work are sending the child from the classroom simply to cool off and sending them to the office on a repeated basis. That's not going to help them get control of their behavior. They need to learn how to cool off themselves, either by excusing themselves or getting it out in some other way. Simply getting mad with that child is not going to help them."

This teacher also emphasized the need to sensitize hostile–aggressive students to the inappropriateness of their behavior and help them learn to manage frustration and conflict more productively. In contrast to the lower rated teacher, the two higher rated teachers would try to "reach" hostile–aggressive students emotionally and to teach them more effective coping strategies. Also, although they spoke of applying powerful consequences, they did so with an emphasis on requiring aggressive students to recognize and take responsibility for their behavior as an initial step in moving toward long-term change, not on getting rid of these students or using punishment to impose penalties on them.

WHAT THE SCHOLARLY LITERATURE SAYS

Chronically aggressive, bullying behavior against peers typically is part of a more general conduct disorder: an antisocial and rule-breaking syndrome that also includes aggression directed toward parents, teachers, and siblings. Hostile–aggressive students typically are characterized by impulsivity and strong needs to dominate others. They have a more positive attitude toward the use of violence than other students, and they have little empathy with their victims. Their aggression usually is not compensation for anxiety, insecurity, or low self-esteem. Instead, it is instrumental—a tool that they have learned to use as a way to get what they want (Besag, 1989; Olweus, 1994; Patterson, Reid, & Dishion, 1992).

Hostility and aggression against peers are among the most serious problems confronting teachers and also among the most difficult to handle effectively. Physical attacks, bullying, fights, and arguments disrupt the academic focus of the classroom and threaten the physical safety and psychological security of everyone in it. School administrators and teachers cannot allow aggression to become commonplace if they expect their schools to remain viable as educational institutions.

Once established, antisocial and aggressive patterns of behavior tend to persist, and hostile–aggressive children are likely to become maladjusted adults (Furlong & Smith, 1994; Heusmann, 1994; Loeber, 1982). Generalized patterns of aggressive behavior develop gradually but are increasingly self-sustaining as they become more entrenched.

Causes of Aggression

Aggressive children have been pictured as frustrated and angry individuals who have learned to "take it out on" others. Early theorizing concentrated on *deprivation* or other *frustration* that made them angry in the first place. Psychoanalytically oriented writers usually stressed emotional dynamics (rejection by one or both parents) or frustrating events (displacement by a newborn sibling) occurring in the family. Early social learning theorists cited a broader range of causes, both generalized (social rejection due to unattractiveness; humiliation due to persistent school failure) and specific (being attacked or insulted; losing a competition). These early formulations included the notions that some sort of deprivation or frustration induced rage, which in turn led either to direct retaliation or to displaced aggression against some substitute object (human, animal, or inanimate). In theory, the buildup of rage would act as a drive predisposing frustrated people to "act it out" or "express" it, and creating increasingly intolerable tension until they did so. Acting out would induce tension release or *catharsis,* allowing them to calm down and resume a more normal mode of functioning.

There are several problems with this formulation (Eron, 1994). For one, people respond differently to frustration. Instead of anger, some people respond with disappointment or with a relatively unemotional attempt to analyze what went wrong and how it can be remediated. Furthermore, only some of those who do develop anger will develop intense rage, and only some of those who experience intense rage will become aggressive. Another problem is that, contrary to the catharsis hypothesis, aggression against substitute objects tends to increase rather than decrease subsequent rates of aggressive behavior (Berkowitz, 1993; Parke & Slaby, 1983). Instead of helping aggressive students learn to respond more maturely to frustration, encouraging them to act out their anger against substitute objects (1) reinforces the idea that extreme anger is expected as the normal response to frustration; (2) reinforces the expectation that whenever they have angry feelings they will need to act them out behaviorally; and (3) provides an inappropriate model for the rest of the class, increasing the likelihood that the problem will spread to them too. The problem is that the connection "I need to act out angry feelings—I can release them through catharsis" is merely the end point in a chain of reactions. The connections "frustration—angry feelings" and "angry feelings—act out" precede the cathartic end point. Every time the end point of the chain is reinforced, the whole chain that led up to it is reinforced. The student is reinforced not only for expressing extreme anger harmlessly but also for building up extreme anger in the first place and for believing that this emotion requires or justifies aggressive behavior.

Investigation of why only certain individuals develop generalized patterns of aggressive response to frustration led to discovery of additional factors that might explain hostile–aggressive behavior patterns. One is *modeling,* particularly by the parents. A large proportion of aggressive individuals come from strife-ridden homes in which the parents are aggressive toward each other (or one is aggressive and the other is passive), and the children are frequently treated with hostility, abuse, and physical punishment. Children growing up in such homes not only suffer frustration and deprivation but are continually exposed to the modeling of aggression as normal behavior. They are likely to become hostile and aggressive themselves, especially if they are not consistently exposed to better alternatives (by a significant individual in their lives who consistently preaches and practices more mature responses to frustration and more effective methods for resolving conflicts).

The *consequences of aggression* are also important. One consequence factor is the response of adults to the aggression that children exhibit toward their peers. If adults express disapproval of such aggression, it is likely to decrease, but if adults approve of it, it is likely to increase. The same is true even if the adults should merely observe without disapproving overtly, because children will tend to respond to a lack of overt disapproval as if it were approval (Berkowitz, 1993).

Another consequence factor, and perhaps the most important, is *the degree to which the child is reinforced for aggressive actions.* Children who have learned to enjoy or profit from aggression (because they gain some material advantage, take something away from a peer, or just enjoy making the peer cry or run away) are likely to continue such behavior unless adults intervene to prevent it or change the reinforcement contingencies that sustain it.

Patterson (1982) found that all of these causes are usually present in the backgrounds of extremely antisocial children. Even where the parents are not particularly rejecting or aggressive themselves, child rearing tends to be marked by poor monitoring of the child's activities and inadequate or inconsistent discipline. The parents come to accept aggressive behavior from their child and often unwittingly encourage it by labeling the child as deviant (e.g., as hot-tempered, a bully, etc.).

Peterson's model best fits bullies—children who learn to use aggression in a proactive way as an instrument for accomplishing their goals. Dodge (1991) suggested that many children develop a different form of aggression, which is more reactive and characterized by emotional and behavioral reactions to perceived mistreatment by others. He described two fictitious boys who represent the prototypes for proactive and reactive aggression:

> The first boy, Billy, is 12 years old and has been arrested four times for vandalism, theft, and similar offenses. He is reported to be a major behavioral problem in school. He is a bully among peers, in that he regularly coerces other boys to deferring to him. He teases peers, threatens them, dominates them, laughs at them, and starts fights with them. Billy would most likely fit criteria as socially rejected (highly rejected and

not at all liked by peers). His background is fairly underprivileged. His father has been in and out of prison, and he has grown up in a "tough" neighborhood, without close monitoring or guidance from adults.

The second boy, Reid, is also 12 years old. He has been arrested for assault on his teacher. One day following her ridicule of him for failing an exam, he pulled a knife on her in the school parking lot and cut her in the arm. He is also considered highly aggressive and socially rejected among peers, but he doesn't seem to start fights as much as he escalates conflicts and can't avoid them. He overreacts to minor provocations and is viewed as volatile and short-tempered. Nobody wants to get too close to Reid because he might strike at any time. During the case manager's inquiry into this boy's background, it was determined that he had been abused physically as a young child. (p. 201)

Research by Dodge and others has shown that reactively aggressive children tend to be paranoid—prone to interpret neutral or even prosocial behavior of peers as aggressive in intent. Once they interpret hostile intent, they are more likely than other children to respond aggressively. Finally, they tend to be unrepentant for such behavior, relying on defense mechanisms that depersonalize blame, rationalize their own actions, or even blame the victim. Attempts to change these reactively aggressive children need to include elements designed to combat their paranoia and help them learn to test their social perceptions before acting on them.

In summary, children who develop generalized patterns of hostile, antisocial, and aggressive behavior tend to come from homes where similar emotions and behavior are modeled by at least one parent. Also, such children tend to be "undersocialized"—poorly monitored and inconsistently or otherwise inadequately disciplined—so that their aggressive behavior is reinforced rather than replaced with more acceptable methods of meeting needs and solving conflicts. If such behavior patterns are allowed to become well established, and especially if the child is labeled as deviant, they can become very difficult to change (Besag, 1989; Furlong & Smith, 1994; Parke & Slaby, 1983).

Cognitive Deficits in Aggressive Children

Along with explaining aggression as instrumental behavior learned through modeling and sustained through reinforcement, recent research has focused on deficits in the cognitive processes that aggressive children use to regulate their behavior (Dodge, 1993; Hudley, 1994; Perry, Perry, & Boldizar, 1990). Dodge has incorporated many of these findings into a 5-step model of the cognitive self-regulation activities needed to respond competently to a social situation.

The first step is the *encoding* of social cues, which involves searching for and focusing attention on relevant information (such as facial expressions and voice tones that provide cues to a peer's intentions in an ambiguous situation). Aggressive children tend to be impulsive in encoding social information, jumping quickly to conclusions (such as inferring hostile intentions) before considering all of the available evidence. The second step is an *interpretation* of the cues that have been considered (such as determining whether actions are accidental, hostile, or well-intended). Aggressive children are more likely to infer hostile intent in situations where other children would not. The third step is *response search*, in which the child generates possible responses to the situation. Aggressive children tend to generate fewer possible responses than other children, and these responses are likely to be aggressive rather than prosocial or cooperative. The fourth step is *response decision*, which involves choosing a response after evaluating the potential consequences of each possibility considered. Aggressive children are more likely to evaluate aggressive responses favorably and to believe that they will be successful. They concentrate on the positive outcomes that they seek for themselves, without paying much attention to potential negative outcomes of aggression (such as causing suffering to the victim or being rejected by the peer group). The fifth step is *enactment* of the response evaluated most favorably. Aggressive children often lack the skills needed to gain what they want through prosocial or cooperative methods, so they may not be able to enact these methods even when they recognize that they are preferable to aggressive alternatives. These findings on cognitive deficits in aggressive children indicate the need for attention to their information-processing and self-regulation skills along with setting limits on and attempting to modify their behavior.

Suggested Strategies for Coping with Aggression

Suggested guidelines for teachers usually do call for attempts to resocialize aggressive students' attitudes and beliefs as well as to modify their behavior (Blanco & Bogacki, 1988; Cohen & Fish, 1993; Thompson & Rudolph, 1992). Roedell, Slaby, and Robinson (1976) suggested modeling and expecting students to exhibit a reasoned, nonaggressive approach to solving conflicts; reinforcing cooperative statements and behavior; teaching students how to solve conflicts verbally and cooperatively; attending primarily to the victim following aggressive acts; making sure that the aggressor does not benefit from such acts; teaching potential victims assertive strategies for discouraging aggression against them; and avoiding physically punishing aggressive students or encouraging them to act out aggression against inanimate objects. Parke and Slaby (1983) added that eliciting and reinforcing prosocial behaviors that are incompatible with aggression is a promising response to it, and one that avoids the undesirable side effects of punitive approaches. They recommended engaging aggressive students in prosocial and cooperative activities whenever possible and reinforcing them for behaving desirably. They also suggested that reinforcement strategies are best suited to use with younger students, whereas coaching or other strategies that rely heavily on verbal and conceptual abilities are more suited to older students.

Berkowitz (1993) cautioned that punitive approaches are not likely to be helpful, both because aggression-prone individuals are less affected by threat of punishment than most other people and because punishment tends to be successful only under a complicated set of conditions that are difficult if not impossible to sustain in the classroom setting. He recommended that aggressive students be treated using a combination of willingness to listen sympathetically to their concerns (but not allow or condone their violent behavior), making sure that their aggression is not reinforced, and teaching them better ways of controlling their anger and solving social problems constructively.

Good and Brophy (1997) stressed the need to make it clear that aggressive behavior will not be tolerated, while at the same time showing a willingness to try to help aggressive students by listening to them sympathetically, attempting to resocialize their beliefs and attitudes through modeling and persuasion, and teaching them more effective ways of interacting with others and solving conflicts. In particular, they stressed helping such students to monitor their emotional reactions (not all anger is justified) and distinguish emotions from behavior (even justified anger does not legitimize physical aggression), avoiding labels such as "deviant," and finding ways for them to interact prosocially and cooperatively with peers.

Direct socialization based on appeal to reason would seem to be a useful strategy for dealing with aggressive children, but it has not received much systematic study. Zahavi and Asher (1978) reported a reduction in aggression and an increase in cooperation among aggressive preschoolers who were instructed about the harm that results from aggression, its ineffectiveness as an interpersonal strategy, and the value of constructive alternatives such as cooperation and sharing.

Behavioral and Cognitive-Behavioral Treatments

As theory and research on aggression have developed, they have focused more and more on social learning causal explanations and treatment approaches. Most of the treatment elements studied have been examples or combinations of four treatment approaches identified by Coie, Underwood, and Lochman (1991) as behavior management, emotional control strategies, social skill training, or social information processing.

Behavior Management

Behavior management approaches developed out of applied behavior analysis theory that called for determining whether a problem represents a behavioral deficit or a behavioral excess and then using techniques for either increasing or decreasing relevant behaviors. This approach conceptualizes aggression as a problem of behavioral excess. It addresses it by stating clear limits on acceptable behavior, reinforcing students when they do behave acceptably but withholding reinforcement when they do not, using response-contingent time-out to prevent students from deriving reinforcement from aggressive acts, and using response cost (punishment) procedures if necessary (O'Leary & O'Leary, 1977; Patterson, 1982). To the extent that it succeeds in preventing aggressors from obtaining the reinforcements that they seek, the behavior management approach is an appropriate response to aggression that is used as an instrument to attain goals.

More recently developed approaches are based on the notion that aggression involves deficits in addition to behavioral excesses. These deficits are cognitive, but they have behavioral consequences, as outlined in Dodge's five-step model. Aggressive students who show basic attentional and information-processing deficits often fail to analyze social situations carefully enough to develop accurate perceptions, so they are prone to jump to erroneous conclusions about what others are doing or thinking and then act on these conclusions in aggressive ways. They are often unaware of their own behavior, how it is perceived by others, and the unintended side effects that it has, so that they overvalue the potential benefits and underappreciate the potential costs of acting aggressively. Finally, they often are unaware of or do not know how to implement more effective methods of responding to touchy social situations, so they often resort to aggression for lack of better alternatives. Recognition of these deficits has led to development of various cognitive-behavioral and social cognitive approaches to treatment of aggressive students (Furlong & Smith, 1994; Hughes, 1988; Pepler & Rubin, 1991).

Teaching Emotional Control Strategies

This approach involves helping children learn to recognize their angry emotions and aggressive impulses and gain control of them before they lead to aggressive behavior. Several techniques have been developed to address these cognitive deficits (Goodwin & Mahoney, 1975; Kettlewell & Kausch, 1983; Stewart & Ashby, 1981).

Some are quite imaginative. Novaco (1975), for example, used cognitive restructuring (teaching the person to view stressful situations in more productive ways), self-instruction, and problem-solving techniques to "inoculate" aggressive individuals against stress and equip them with better coping mechanisms. In this method, a counselor helps the aggressive person to consider hypothetical stressful situations and generate self-instructions for (1) preparing for possible provocations, (2) dealing with the impact and confrontation, (3) coping with emotional arousal, and (4) reflecting on the experience subsequently. The person is taught to retain control over behavior through cognitive self-instruction (self-talk).

Robin, Schneider, and Dolnick (1976) developed the "turtle technique" for helping angry children to control their emotions and behavior. These children were taught to imagine themselves as turtles who go into their shells when angry instead of lashing out. They learned to sit down, place their heads in their arms, relax physically, take time to calm down, and then think of nonaggressive ways to respond to the situation.

Camp and associates (1977) developed the "Think Aloud" program for aggressive elementary school boys, combining techniques taken from Spivack and Shure's (1974) problem-solving training program and ideas developed by Meichenbaum (1977) and others for using modeling and verbalized self-instructions to improve control over behavior. The children were taught to think about four basic questions in developing responses to problems: What is my problem? What is my plan? Am I using my plan? How did I do?

Unfortunately, although these programs have improved aggressive students' performance on various cognitive measures, they have not been very effective in reducing aggressive behavior. However, Lochman and colleagues (1984) developed an anger control program that did yield significant decreases in disruptive and aggressive behavior in the classroom and at home. The treatment principles from this study were incorporated in treatments used by Coie, Underwood, and Lochman (1991) that also reduced students' aggression. The anger-coping aspects of these treatments involve helping children to control strong negative feelings by teaching them how to identify and curtail impulsive responses, to use self-statements to regulate their behavior, and to reframe the ways that they think about who "wins" in interpersonal situations. Taking advantage of reactively aggressive children's concerns about looking weak or being taken advantage of, the reframing aspects of the treatment involved convincing such children that when they become angry or aggressive, they have been manipulated by others into losing control of themselves, and that if they want to look good in front of others, they need to learn to handle conflict situations more maturely.

Social Skills Training

To the extent that aggressive students are unaware of or unskilled at implementing alternatives to aggression, a complete treatment package would include training in positive interaction skills or social problem-solving skills. For example, Coie, Underwood, and Lochman (1991) trained aggressive children in social skills, such as entering a group situation smoothly and playing with peers cooperatively, as well as in social problem-solving skills, such as recognizing problem situations, articulating goals in these situations, inhibiting impulsive reactions, considering alternative responses and their consequences, and developing solutions through negotiation rather than aggression.

Goldstein and his coworkers (1980) developed a complete curriculum for teaching social skills to students who need to learn them. One unit dealt with skill alternatives to aggression (asking permission, sharing, helping others, negotiating, using self-control, standing up for your rights, responding to teasing, avoiding trouble with others, and keeping out of fights). Another unit taught skills for dealing with stressful situations (making a complaint, answering a complaint, showing sportsmanship after a game, dealing with embarrassment, dealing with being left out, standing up for a friend, responding to persuasion attempts by others, dealing with failure, dealing with contradictory messages, dealing with accusations, getting ready for a difficult conversation, and dealing with group pressure).

Since then, Goldstein and his colleagues have extended and refined their approach, developing "skillstreaming" treatments that involve modeling the skill to be taught (broken into steps), having students role play the skill in realistic situation simulations, providing feedback and improvement suggestions, and then engaging the students in activities designed to promote maintenance and transfer of the skills they are learning. These include "homework" assignments in which the students try out their new skills in actual social situations, reflect on and evaluate their performance, and then discuss it with the group and perhaps design or role play better alternatives.

Eventually Goldstein and his coworkers developed a treatment program specifically for hostile–aggressive students called Aggression Replacement Training. This program combines the 50 social skills taught in the skillstreaming program with lessons in anger control and moral education (Goldstein & Glick, 1987). Subsequently, they developed an even more comprehensive program called The Prepare Curriculum (Goldstein, 1988). Most of the Goldstein programs are designed for use with adolescents, but elementary teachers can adapt the lessons outlined in *Skillstreaming the Elementary School Child* (McGinnis & Goldstein, 1984).

Several other programs featuring lessons, role playing, and other techniques for teaching anger control, social skills, and social problem solving are also available for use by teachers (Forman, 1993; Larson, 1994; Morrison & Sandowicz, 1994; Walker, Colvin, & Ramsey, 1995), most notably the ACCEPTS program (A Children's Curriculum for Effective Peer and Teacher Skills; Walker et al., 1983) developed for elementary grades. Designed originally to prepare socially handicapped students for mainstreaming, the ACCEPTS program focuses on skills for making friends, getting along with others, and coping with social conflict.

Social Information Processing

Treatment efforts in this category attempt to reduce aggression by reducing reactively aggressive students' tendencies to infer hostile intent in ambiguous social situations. A successful example is the BrainPower program (Hudley, 1994; Hudley & Graham, 1993) that involves group meetings held twice weekly for 6 weeks. The first lesson introduces the program, and the twelfth lesson reviews it. The lessons in between address the three components of the intervention. Lessons 2 through 6 are designed to strengthen aggressive students' abilities to detect intentionality accurately. Through role playing, discussion of personal experiences, and other activities, they learn to distinguish between prosocial, accidental, ambiguous, and hostile peer intentions. Lessons 7 through 9 are designed to increase the likelihood that aggressive students will make attributions to nonhostile intent during ambiguous social encounters, such as when a peer spills milk on them in the lunchroom. Lessons 10 and 11 teach the students to make more appropriate (nonhostile) behavioral responses in these ambiguous social situations, rather than assuming that the peer acted from hostile intentions and then reacting aggressively themselves. An evaluation of this program with boys in grades 4 through 6 indicated that it was successful both in changing their attributional tendencies and in reducing their aggressive behavior.

Comprehensive Approaches

Reviewers agree that comprehensive treatment packages that combine several elements are more likely to be effective than treatments based on a single approach. The most comprehensive approaches target not only aggressive students but their parents and teachers as well. The students receive some combination of the treatments just reviewed; the parents and teachers receive training in ways to implement the treatments or at least make sure that the students are no longer reinforced for behaving aggressively. Ideally, the treatment elements aimed at students will be individualized to the nature of their aggressive patterns. For example, treatment would emphasize changing reinforcement contingencies so that aggression would no longer pay off for bullies who use it instrumentally. On the other hand, the approach would focus on anger management and attribution retraining for reactively aggressive students who are prone to retaliate against what they perceive as hostile actions of others.

The most ambitious attempt to reduce aggression in school that has been attempted to date, and also one of the most successful, was a national campaign against bullying conducted in Norway. There were several components to this program. First, a booklet was prepared for school personnel describing what was known about bully/victim problems and giving detailed suggestions about what teachers and the school could do to prevent and counteract such problems. This book was sent to all primary and junior high schools in the country. Second, a brochure with information and advice to parents was distributed by each school to all parents. Third, a videocassette was prepared showing episodes from the everyday lives of two bullied children, a 10-year-old boy and a 14-year-old girl. Fourth, a short questionnaire was filled out anonymously by students, addressing the frequency of bully/victim problems in their school and the readiness of teachers and students to do something about them.

Interested schools participated in a more intensive aggression reduction program that built on these initial procedures. The program involved trying to create a school and, ideally, also a home environment characterized by warmth, positive interest in the child, and involvement from adults, but also firm limits to unacceptable behavior. In cases of violation of limits and rules, nonhostile, nonphysical sanctions would be applied consistently. The adults would monitor the students' activities in and out of school to make sure that they became aware of any bullying problems quickly and then followed up appropriately. Along with raising students' awareness of and concern about bully/victim problems, measures taken at the schools included better supervision during recess, increased staff–parents communication relating to such problems, class rules against bullying, class meetings to discuss bullying problems if they arose, and serious talks with bullies, victims, and their parents following serious incidents. This program has been remarkably successful at reducing bullying in Norwegian schools (Olweus, 1994). It is questionable whether a similar national program could be implemented in the United States, but the program could certainly be implemented at the local school or district level. For a summary of the principles involved and information about the program, see Olweus (1993).

ANALYSIS OF INTERVIEW RESPONSES

The CSS data indicated that 38 teachers would confine their responses to attempts to suppress aggressive behavior, but the majority would do something in addition or instead. The typical response was to reassert prohibitions against aggression and the intention to be firm in enforcing them, but then also to try to establish and work within a personal relationship with these students to resocialize their attitudes and beliefs, shape more desirable forms of behavior, or develop more effective coping skills through instruction or counseling. Less typical patterns involved either purely punitive reactions or purely supportive ones.

Lower rated teachers often had little to suggest beyond speaking with aggressors about their behavior and perhaps threatening punishment. Lacking strategies, they often spoke of referring the problems to the parents or the principal.

Higher rated teachers usually combined firm limit setting with willingness to try to resocialize aggressive students or help them learn to cope with frustration more effectively. On the one hand, they would be firm in warning that continued aggression would be punished. They might seat aggressive students nearby or move near them frequently, monitoring them closely so as to become aware of potentially explosive situations early and intervene quickly before the problem could escalate. In short, the higher rated teachers would be assertive in reaffirming limits on aggressive students, making it clear that they were serious about these limits and prepared to enforce them with sanctions if necessary. Their aggressive students would have to accept responsibility and take the consequences for aggressive behavior.

On the other hand, most of these teachers also would reach out to aggressive students by building closer personal relationships with them, trying to resocialize their attitudes and beliefs, and helping them learn better methods of coping with frustration and resolving conflicts. Many would try to avoid publicly singling out or blaming aggressive students, especially in response to minor incidents that could be handled with strategies that would minimize stress or embarrassment to the student. Also, many would use time-out as an enabling mechanism (an opportunity for an upset student to calm down, reflect, and regain control before returning to the group), rather than as a punitive mechanism.

Higher rated teachers also would instruct aggressive students in strategies for solving or at least coping better with social problems. Although none mentioned cognitive-behavior modification or self-control training explicitly, many mentioned the self-talk involved in coping effectively with problem situations and emphasized the use of time-out to provide opportunities for aggressive students to reflect on their behavior and think about ways they could have handled the situation more effectively.

Two additional strategies that correlated positively with effectiveness ratings were directly expressing positive affect toward or positive perceptions of the student (18) and enlisting one or more peers to act as a buddy by helping the aggressive student calm down during tense situations or providing assistance and support (7). These findings underscore the point that higher rated teachers would treat aggressive students as continuing members of the classroom group and try to build on their capacities for exercising self-control and interacting prosocially with peers, instead of treating them as outcasts who needed to be isolated from peers and controlled through threat of punishment. Rather than give up on aggressive students, higher rated teachers would try to resocialize them. They recognized that physical or verbal assault on the student would not be helpful, and several also mentioned that demanding, lecturing, nagging, and so forth, would be ineffective as well.

Vignette: Tom

This morning, several students excitedly tell you that on the way to school they saw Tom beating up Sam and taking his lunch money. Tom is the class bully and has done things like this many times.

Before reading further, take time to think about how you might respond to this incident. Make notes about your ideas.

CSS Vignette Response Excerpts

Here is what four of the CSS teachers had to say.

A LOWER RATED TEACHER

"Immediately I would pull Tom out and have a talk with him, and since he has done this thing many times before, I would definitely have him excluded for 3 days. 'I think you need a rest. You just don't go around bullying people and taking their lunch money, because they need to eat just as you do.' [Can you describe how you would see a kid like that?] Maybe he's trying to get more attention from the adults, wanting to be loved, you know."

A HIGHER RATED TEACHER

" 'Tom, I hear that you had some difficulties on the way to school, and I would like to talk to you.' I would take him out into the hall. 'Tom, I was really sorry to hear that on the way to school you were beating Sam up and you took his lunch money. I'm going to call Sam out, and I would like you to please give him back his money and tell him that you sometimes have a little trouble controlling yourself, and you will try not to have this thing happen again. I know that sometimes people have things that you want, or sometimes when a person is smaller than you are, to make yourself look good or big, you have to act like this. But in the long run if you can try to be a little more thoughtful of other people, you are going to have more friends. This sort of behavior doesn't help you. It makes other children not want to be around you. Another thing is that if this sort of behavior continues, I'm going to have to call your mother in to discuss it with her. If you are having difficulty getting to school and taking care of yourself at the same time, there will have to be some arrangement made so that other children are not intimidated by you.'"

ANOTHER HIGHER RATED TEACHER

" 'Tom, I would like to see you out in the hall after the other children have started on their work.' When I take Tom out in the hall, I would say, 'Tom, I had a report from the students that you had a problem on the way to school this morning. Would you like to tell me about it?' If he did not tell me about it, I would say, 'Tom, the problem apparently was that you were beating up Sam and taking his lunch money. This is something that we can't put up with. Sam has a right to come to school without being interfered with. He should certainly be able to keep his lunch money if he needs it, and he doesn't need anybody taking it from him. It is very important to him that he has that. I believe you have lunch money of your own, and it isn't necessary for you to get some from someone else. If this happened, I would like to have you give the lunch money back to Sam. If you feel so inclined, talk it over with him and decide that this is not something you are going to do anymore, and let Sam know so that he won't be fearful that you are going to trouble him. If this is not possible, then I think we should go down and make a phone call to home and talk with your parents.' I think it is very important that children respect other people's belongings, that they don't interfere with them going and coming from school, threaten them in any way, or intimidate them. Everyone has the right to come to school without being bothered. This is very important. Hopefully, there is something otherwise bothering Tom so that he feels he has to assert himself in this way. Either a child must have some problems with making friends or maybe somebody has bothered him in the past. Perhaps there is a problem at home, and he isn't getting the money or some situation like that. I think it would be the time to discuss this with his parents and see if they could come up with some solutions."

ANOTHER HIGHER RATED TEACHER

"As soon as Tom came in the door, I would take him aside and say, 'I have had several reports that you were beating up Sam and you took his lunch money. I want to hear your story about why this happened.' Hopefully he would tell me what he was doing and why he did it. If he didn't, then I would give him three options: (1) He could tell me then (I was still ready to listen), (2) he could take a few minutes to get his thoughts together and then tell me at that time, or (3) he could go to the office and talk to the principal. I guess if he admitted beating up Sam and taking his lunch money, or even part of it, the next step would be to get Sam and Tom together with me away from everyone else and ask Sam to tell me his side of the story. Then if Tom has any refutation, he would have a turn, and so on, until a collaborated story was arrived at. Then we could go about the process of getting the lunch money back, if that was possible. If not, then I would ask Tom what his ideas are about solving the problem in the future. How is he going to make up the lunch money to Sam, or was he going to give him his lunch money for that day, or just what was he going to do? Tom is a person who does this frequently, so it is important to make him own his own problem. If this is something he has done, then he has got to admit it and come up with a solution that is going to work. If he doesn't, then I will suggest some alternatives and he can choose from them, but I would first give him the chance to come up with a solution by himself. If this is an ongoing problem with Tom, then he needs to face up to it and start dealing with it. He should also be able to listen to how Sam feels, and maybe he can relate to the feelings in some other situation, or perhaps something that I have seen I can relate to him — another situation where he might have felt like Sam. Only by stepping into another person's shoes after actually solving a problem is he going to have any improvement in behavior. I would characterize Tom as someone who is very unhappy, and he is feeling like somebody isn't treating him fairly."

Despite ascribing Tom's behavior to a desire to get attention or love from adults, the lower rated teacher would respond with a lecture and a 3-day suspension. In contrast, the first higher rated teacher's response alluded to potentially serious consequences but did not invoke them yet, and it included socialization content that seems more likely to "get through" to Tom than the response suggested by the lower rated teacher. The other two higher rated teachers also suggested responses that focused more on "getting through" to Tom than on invoking punishment. Also, all three of the higher rated teachers suggested actions designed to accommodate Sam's needs, not only for return of his lunch money but for reassurance that he would not continue to be victimized.

Analysis of Responses to Tom

Most (78) teachers mentioned attempting to control Tom through threat or punishment, although in addition or instead, 42 mentioned trying to improve Tom's coping skills. Beyond punishing him for the depicted incident, the most commonly reported responses to Tom involved communicating strong messages about his conduct — prescribing guidelines for expected behavior and trying to get him to understand the seriousness and consequences of aggression. These responses involved more power assertion and less supportive counseling or socialization than was seen for most of the other problem-student types.

Most teachers would provide socialization to Tom in the form of instruction (26), Golden Rule/empathy appeals (21), or moralizing (18). Only 56 teachers mentioned providing help to Sam in addition to dealing with Tom. Most of these limited themselves to seeing that Sam got his lunch or money to buy it. Only 13 teachers mentioned trying to protect Sam or reassure him that the problem would not recur.

Most lower rated teachers would not do much other than speak to Tom about his behavior and then punish him either personally or by informing the principal or parents. Perhaps these teachers had no other ideas about how to resocialize Tom, or perhaps they did not believe that their efforts could succeed.

Higher rated teachers believed that they could improve Tom's behavior and thus spoke of attempting to change it rather than merely control it. A minority would try to "reach" Tom by delivering a stern lecture on the unacceptability of aggression. This approach is not optimal, but it is preferable to the resignation shown by lower rated teachers in that it illustrates the teacher's belief that change is possible and a willingness to try to bring it about.

The majority of higher rated teachers, however, reported trying to counsel Tom or instruct him in better means of coping with frustration and handling conflict. Many also would create a general climate of support for Tom by enlisting the help of the peers or parents and by stressing improvement rather than threat of punishment.

Higher rated teachers also were more likely to recognize and try to meet Sam's needs — not only by seeing that Sam got his lunch money but by reassuring him that the situation would be handled effectively and that he would not have to face further abuse from Tom.

In summary, higher rated teachers would attempt to "reach" Tom and resocialize him rather than merely control his aggression through threats of punishment. A few would rely on severe scolding or berating, but most would use individual or group counseling that included prescription, modeling, or instruction in better self-control or coping strategies.

Vignette: Ron

Class is disrupted by a scuffle. You look up to see that Ron has left his seat and gone to Phil's desk, where he is punching and shouting at Phil. Phil is not so much fighting back as trying to protect himself. You don't know how this started, but you do know that Phil gets along well with the other students and that Ron often starts fights and arguments without provocation.

Before reading further, take time to think about how you might respond to this incident. Make notes about your ideas.

CSS Vignette Response Excerpts

Here is what four of the CSS teachers had to say.

A LOWER RATED TEACHER

" 'One of these days, Ron, you might run up on someone who is a little tougher. They may be mild and sit back and seem less aggressive than you, but you don't always play that number.... You might be a bully, but you might run into a bull one day. You may get what you are asking for.' I'm getting to the bottom of it, and I am going to punish him for it. I am going to let him know I don't want this to happen in the classroom again."

A HIGHER RATED TEACHER

"Since it is Ron who has left his seat . . . I would remove him immediately from the room and talk to him and find out the problem. I would say, 'Ron, you were out of your seat and hitting Phil. Could you tell me why you were doing it?' and find out his rationale. If he thinks Phil has done something, I would have Phil come out and give his side of it. Make Ron listen. I would not accept anything from Ron. I would let Ron hear Phil and then let Ron talk, and let Phil hear Ron to see what could happen. I would see if I could learn something that I did not know because it is so easy to jump in and not know all the facts or where the children are coming from. The main thing is to find out what started it. Why is he doing this? If it is consistent with Ron doing this and fighting and so on, we would talk. I would begin to talk to Ron about ways he can cope with this rather than fighting and hitting. 'What could you do that wouldn't hurt anybody? I know you are feeling angry.' So you let the child know how you think he is feeling, and that gives him a chance to say, 'Yes, I am angry and mad because so and so did so and so.' So you do try to have the child know that you understand where they are coming from and how they are feeling, and you accept it. But how could they cope with it in another way? You are going to have to start working with Ron if this is a consistent thing. To stop it right then and there you would remove him from the room and find out why.... We are going to start exploring ways of dealing with feelings."

ANOTHER HIGHER RATED TEACHER

"I would immediately go over to Phil's desk and separate the boys and just tell them to try and get themselves together. Then I would take them out into the hall. First I would ask Phil, 'What were you doing when Ron came to your desk and started hitting you?' I would let Phil give some explanation, and then I would ask Ron, 'Why did you come over to Phil's desk, and why were you hitting him? Try to see if you can understand why you did it.' Sometimes children who are really physically aggressive don't understand why they are doing it. It's like an impulse, and it comes. They might be angry about something totally unrelated to the child they are hitting. It's like the nearest available person gets the aggression. Once I had settled it with Phil, and if it was an instance where Phil had done absolutely nothing to provoke the situation, I would send Phil back into the classroom and try to help Ron get a handle on himself. When he starts feeling really angry and aggressive inside, rather than taking it out on someone else, perhaps he could come and talk to me, and I could tell him to go run around the playground three times, just some other way to get it out. Try to stop his aggressions against other people and, maybe with my help, redirect it. Help him to know that we all have angry feelings, we all feel like hitting somebody at some point, and it's just a matter of whether you act on it or not. The feelings that he has aren't wrong, but he could deal with them in a better way. Try to help him find a better way to handle them."

ANOTHER HIGHER RATED TEACHER

"I would take both Ron and Phil into the hall and say to Ron, 'Why were you hitting Phil?' If he didn't have anything to say, then I would turn to Phil and say, 'Phil, can you tell me what happened?' I am assuming that since Phil was the victim in this case, or seems to be, he would be able to tell me what exactly Ron had done. Perhaps hearing Phil telling about this would make Ron angry enough to then want to tell his side of the story. I would certainly want to hear both sides of the story and would keep encouraging Phil to talk until Ron did. Then if it was a problem of no provocation on Phil's part, I would excuse Phil and talk alone with Ron and ask him why he had done it. Actually I probably would have asked him that first when Phil was there, and if he said he didn't know or if Phil didn't seem to be at fault, then I would excuse Phil. If Ron doesn't seem to have a reason or doesn't seem to know why, I might suggest some things like 'Was Phil looking at you? Was Phil doing something that bothered you? Did Phil do something today before school?' Ron may be a child who carries over a grudge for a long time and may have recalled something on the spur of the moment that Phil had done that bothered him. At that point, if I feel that Phil needs to get involved again, I would call him back and talk with the two or have the two tell each other what they felt about the situation. Phil might tell how he feels about Ron coming over and starting a fight, or about Ron's reason for fighting him, especially if it is a leftover from another day or another week, and Ron should have his turn to tell Phil his feelings. Then I would talk to them both if there was a joint fault or to Ron alone if it seemed to be merely his problem, about other ways he could have handled his anger. Could he have told Phil what was bothering him, and could they have talked it out, or could he have told me that there was something Phil had done that bothered him? In any case, Ron should be able to come up with two or three alternatives that he could use. Then, if he has at least thought of them, perhaps over time Ron would be able to recall these alternatives and eventually begin to use them. I would characterize Ron as being very angry and unhappy."

The lower rated teacher's response was threatening and punitive, focused more on retaliation than on serious attempts to resocialize Ron's attitudes or change his behavior. In contrast, the three higher rated teachers all spoke of talking with both boys to find out what led to the incident and then following up by attempting to teach Ron better ways of handling conflict.

Analysis of Responses to Ron

As with Tom, most (72) teachers mentioned trying to control Ron through threat or punishment, but in addition or instead, 35 mentioned trying to improve his coping skills. A majority of the teachers would threaten or punish Ron, typically by informing his parents or the principal or by isolating Ron from his classmates. In addition or instead, 31 would provide instruction in better coping skills, 27 would moralize or lecture, and 17 would urge him to come to them in the future for solution of interpersonal conflicts rather than try to solve such conflicts on his own. Again, these general trends indicate more power assertion and less counseling or socialization than is seen in responses to most other vignettes.

Responses to Ron resembled responses to Tom in most respects, although with Ron there was more willingness to suspend judgment and hear both sides before determining guilt or taking action, less informing of the principal or the parents, and mention of a greater variety of strategies designed to resocialize attitudes and beliefs in addition to controlling behavior.

Lower rated teachers generally lacked coherent ideas about how to respond to Ron's aggressive behavior. Some doubted their abilities to cope with Ron effectively at all, so they spoke of delegating the problem to another authority or referring Ron to the principal or the parents for punishment. Others spoke vaguely of addressing Ron's unmet needs, but did not have much to say about how to do this. Their responses often were limited to punishment or to strategies that suggest failure to appreciate the seriousness of the problem (e.g., changing seat assignments).

Instead of viewing Ron as incorrigibly aggressive, higher rated teachers were more likely to view him as not yet able to control his aggressive impulses because he had not yet learned strategies for doing so. They were more confident of their abilities to achieve significant improvements in Ron's behavior, and they tended to emphasize instruction over attempts to control through threat of punishment. A few would rely on "third-degree" methods, but most would use more positive approaches featuring either behavioral change demands phrased as personal appeals or backed by explanations of why change was needed, or else attempts to instruct Ron in strategies for controlling his temper or expressing anger in more acceptable ways (e.g., communicating verbally rather than hitting).

Higher rated teachers would try to settle the depicted incident, especially by having the boys talk out their problem. They would not invoke a rule calling for automatic punishment of participants in a classroom fight. In following up on the incident with Ron, they would stress resocialization and instruction strategies rather than threat or punishment.

COMPARISON OF RESPONSES TO TOM AND TO RON

The findings from the two vignettes are more similar than different, so they suggest similar conclusions regarding effective handling of incidents of aggression between students. Common findings suggest the need to settle the incident (not just to separate the students in order to break up the fight for the moment) and to take action to resocialize the aggressive student or at least pressure him to exert better control over his impulses.

Responses concentrated on interactions with the aggressors (Tom, Ron) rather than the victims (Sam, Phil). However, the higher rated teachers made more mention of actions taken to attend to the well-being of the victims and to ensure that the incident was settled (so that the victims did not have to fear another attack).

Higher rated teachers treated outbreaks of aggression as serious incidents calling for strong responses designed to make it clear that aggression would not be tolerated. Some would confine their response to such forceful limit setting, but most would also attempt to resocialize aggressive students through counseling or instruction designed to teach them to control themselves more effectively or to express their anger through more acceptable means. In contrast, lower rated teachers would often try to pass along the problem to the principal or a parent. To the extent that they spoke of taking action themselves, they tended to make vague comments about getting to the bottom of the problem or meeting unmet needs, giving the student a brief "talking to," or using strategies of limited scope and intensity (offering incentives for improved behavior, changing seat assignments).

The teachers tended to see Ron's aggression problem as less serious than Tom's and to feel greater confidence in their ability to improve Ron's behavior. They were more likely to speak of dealing with Ron themselves and less likely to involve classmates, his parents, or other adults. They were also less likely to interpret Ron's aggression as deliberate or intentional (e.g., premeditated) and more willing to hear both sides before drawing conclusions about guilt or responsibility. Most teachers assumed that Tom had committed premeditated assault and robbery against blameless Sam, but many preferred to investigate to find out whether Phil or other students might have provoked Ron.

The teachers reported a greater number and variety of strategies for resocializing and controlling the behavior of Ron than of Tom. In addition to more brief management responses, there was more mention of time-out and physical isolation, logical and personal appeals, catharsis, and instruction in acceptable ways of expressing aggression. In short, Ron was seen more as a boy with a temper problem who needed help in learning to control his aggressive impulses, whereas Tom was seen more as an incipient criminal who needed to be controlled through vigilance and punishment.

QUALITATIVE IMPRESSIONS AND EXAMPLES

Some teachers had trouble accepting the notion of a bully who picks on weaker victims without legitimate provocation. In explaining why they would reserve judgment about what happened between Ron and Phil, many teachers mentioned that boys who frequently get in fights are often baited by their peers or blamed for things that they did not do. Those who were willing to reserve judgment about Tom also tended to mention that once students get a bad reputation, they are likely to be blamed for things that they did not do.

Among teachers who suggested the generally sound notion of holding conferences to investigate and try to resolve aggressive incidents, some appeared unlikely to be very effective because of misguided notions about what to do during such conferences or vulnerability to manipulation by aggressive students. For example, the empathy approach ("How would you feel if someone did that to you?") may be wasted following incidents of unprovoked bullying or extortion, because the aggressor already knows that the behavior is wrong (although there may be some positive effect if the teacher helps the aggressor see the extent to which his behavior hurts the victim and makes most onlookers see him as an evil person). Similarly, when one-way bullying gets interpreted as two-way fighting, asking the bully why he did what he did and encouraging him to discuss his motivations at length may invite rationalizations (e.g., false claims of provocation by the victim).

When appeals to empathy or invitations to the aggressive student to express his feelings or motivations might be counterproductive, it might be worth saying something like, "I can't let you hurt anyone else in the room, just like I can't let anyone else hurt you. It's part of my job to make sure that the class is a safe place for everyone." This is an authoritative rather than an authoritarian way of restating limits on aggressive behavior, and it includes the aggressive student as a beneficiary of the policy. Even an aggressive student who lacks empathy for his victims might see the value in ensuring that the classroom is a safe environment for everyone (including him).

For some teachers, getting Tom or Ron to own up to his misbehavior was treated as an end in itself (sometimes the only one—the incident would be closed when this admission occurred). In Tom's case, such teachers would "keep the incident in class" if he admitted his guilt and appeared contrite, but would notify the principal or the parents otherwise.

Despite the wording of our vignette, some teachers viewed the Ron-Phil incident as a two-way fight and spoke of holding Phil just as responsible as Ron, such as by demanding that the boys reach agreement about what happened or prescribing equal punishment for both. Or the teacher might punish Ron more severely but still punish Phil, on the grounds that he was fighting too. In effect, such teachers substituted a rigid "no fighting" rule for a more responsible (but time-consuming) strategy of finding out what happened before deciding what to do.

Attempts to resocialize hostile–aggressive students, if mentioned at all, often were too brief and focused on "we don't do that at school" rather than on trying to get the student to see where his life is headed if his aggressive behavior continues. Many teachers understood the potential value of talking about feelings and asking students why they behave as they do, but they did not distinguish between legitimate feelings (frustration, disappointment, justified anger) and illegitimate feelings (anger that is completely unjustified or is far out of proportion to the provocation). Such teachers' responses appeared more likely to reinforce aggressive students' tendencies to externalize blame and deny responsibility for their behavior rather than to help them develop more accurate, less defensive perceptions.

Similarly, although most teachers were clear about the distinction between acceptable and unacceptable ways of acting on legitimate feelings, few reported saying much to aggressive students about how aggression isolates them from their peers, makes them unpopular, and so forth, or about how society will not tolerate aggressive behavior and requires people to learn to solve conflicts nonviolently. Also, it appeared that many teachers would be easily distracted or confused by rationalizations such as "I was just playing with him," and that many would become so caught up in trying to get the facts that arguing about who did what to whom would take precedence over attempts to socialize the aggressor. Few teachers spoke of making strong, heartfelt attempts to get through to aggressive students by noting that their aggression is a serious symptom indicating the need for radical change in behavior and for examination of what is happening in their lives that predisposes them to act this way.

Many teachers spoke of trying to teach aggressive students ideas about other ways of handling conflict situations (walking away, taking out their anger on substitute objects), but few spoke of training them to solve the conflicts through verbal assertiveness and negotiation of mutually agreeable problem definitions and solutions. In effect, the hostile students often were being instructed to stifle their anger and remain frustrated rather than taught how to solve their problems.

Specific techniques mentioned uniquely by one teacher included:

1. Use of the filmstrip *The Boy in the Red Hat* (about a boy who comes to a new school wearing a red hat and thinks that everyone is laughing at him when in fact they are laughing at other things) as a stimulus for discussion of the need to avoid jumping to conclusions about the thoughts or intentions of others.

2. If poverty breeding resentment is part of the problem, work to see that the student gets good clothes, free lunch, or other things he might need.

3. Tell the student that you know there is a "good Tom" because you have seen it, and urge him to "get back to the good Tom."

4. Tell overly punitive parents who encourage the teacher to punish their child physically that you "intend to work on his head rather than his bottom," that physical punishment is ineffective, and that if you start it, you end up having to use it every day. Instead, you intend to establish control through firm expectations and determination.

DISCUSSION

The vignette data and especially the interview data support the value of behavior management, resocialization, and self-control training over less direct methods (e.g., nondirective therapy and environmental engineering strategies) that do not include confronting aggressive students about their behavior, requiring them to accept responsibility for it and take the consequences, or instructing them in better ways of coping with conflict and managing anger.

Lower rated teachers had limited and mostly vague ideas about how to respond to aggressive students. A few of them would try to deny any responsibility for coping with such students, but most would involve the principal or other professionals at the school because they lacked clear ideas about what to do beyond scolding, punishing, or informing the parents.

Almost all of the teachers would at least restate limits on aggressive behavior and warn against its repetition. For many lower rated teachers, this was confined to a brief "talking to." For some higher rated teachers, this meant a severe lecture designed to make it clear that aggression was inappropriate and would not be tolerated. More typically, higher rated teachers responded with equally determined but less emotionally intense socialization that included logical (i.e., not just moralistic) rationales for behavior change demands and attempts to counsel or instruct the student in more acceptable ways of dealing with frustration and conflict.

Given that aggression is not merely disruptive but involves physical harm to other students, it may be necessary for teachers to take coercive action to curb it (e.g., by informing the principal or parents or by threatening or applying punishment). Most teachers did mention one or more coercive strategies, especially in response to the vignettes, which confronted them with specific incidents of aggression. However, the vast majority stressed strategies for using threat of punishment to pressure aggressive students to behave more appropriately. They did not advocate physical punishment or other coercive responses that could be described more as revenge mechanisms or predispositions to inflict punishment for its own sake. Instead they used the threat of punishment as a strategy for controlling students who failed to control themselves. This was especially the case for the higher rated teachers, who tended to mention threat of punishment as part of a larger approach to curbing aggression and resocializing the aggressive student.

Thus, the key to the effectiveness of the *coercive aspects* of responses to aggression was not retribution or even "getting tough" for its own sake. Instead it was the construction of a response that would bring sufficient pressure on the aggressive student to cause him to curb his behavior. Effective teachers were credible in enforcing limits rather than punitive but ineffectual.

The key to the effectiveness of the *instructive aspects* of responses to aggressive students was instruction in more effective ways of handling frustration, controlling their temper, solving conflicts through communication and negotiation rather than aggression, and expressing anger verbally rather than physically.

These techniques will be applied most effectively by teachers who have cultivated productive personal relationships with their hostile–aggressive students. These students tend to have few if any positive relationships with adults or authority figures, and thus little motivation to try to please them. However, they may respond well to teachers who greet them with a friendly comment when they enter the classroom, provide them with positive attention, ask about their hobbies and interests, and seem to care about them and believe that they can be successful.

Finally, consider arranging for professional help for students whose hostility and aggression problems pervade their lives and do not seem to be getting any better. This may include students who are behaving better in your classroom but are still persistently involved in incidents of aggression or delinquency on the school grounds and in the neighborhood. It is important to try to turn such students around before a pathway toward criminality becomes well established. With situational problems, it will be important to determine the nature of the events that trigger the students' anger, discuss these situations with them in detail, and work with them to help them gain better self-control and develop better coping strategies.

9

Passive–Aggressive Students

Passive–aggressive students display the following characteristics: These children express opposition and resistance to the teacher, but indirectly. It is often hard to tell whether they are resisting deliberately or not. They:

1. Are subtly oppositional and stubborn
2. Try to control
3. Show borderline compliance with rules
4. Mar property rather than damage
5. Disrupt surreptitiously
6. Drag their feet

What special strategies might you use to minimize such problems and help these students to function more successfully in your classroom? Before reading further, take time to think about this and make notes about your ideas.

CSS INTERVIEW EXCERPTS

Here is what three of the CSS teachers had to say about teaching passive aggressive students.

A LOWER RATED TEACHER

"The first thing I would do with a youngster like this is let him know that I know what he's doing. He's not just doing it and I don't know about it. And I'd like to know why he's doing this. I'd tell him that I'm not going to put up with this: 'You're causing me to spend undue time making you stop these noises' or whatever he's doing. Let him know that it's not fair to the other children, and just explain to him how unfair he is to the others, wasting our time, and he's not sent to school to do that. Of course, he already knows that. He's pretty smart in trying to keep it concealed that he's doing all this. I'd say that's just a sneaky child, doing things and then trying to cover it up, but I definitely would let him know that I'm not going to put up with it, and he's just going to have to stop that. My strategy would be not to permit him to do something that the class is doing. For instance, if we're having game time, then he doesn't play games. He'll just have to sit and watch. Or any other privilege, you know, that we have, just keep those from him until he's ready to comply and do what he should be doing. That's the way I would handle it, and I think that after he found I knew what he was doing, then he'd know I am not going to put up with it. I think this would perhaps straighten some of that out anyway. Time just doesn't permit it. I'll omit him from doing things that are pleasurable."

Rather than give the student any benefit of the doubt, this teacher would assume that he is deliberately creating problems for her. Consequently, rather than use Gordon techniques ("I" messages followed by attempts to negotiate a solution), she would announce to the student that she was "on to him" and then rely on punishment in an attempt to suppress his misbehavior.

A HIGHER RATED TEACHER

"These children seem to resist your authority but in very subtle, indirect kinds of ways. Frequently it's most notable when you're trying to do a group activity. They're the ones who are the last to get their shoes tied, last when it's time to go to the gym or the library. When you have an art project, they're just taking forever to get their other things put away so you can get started. Frequently with children like this, I've said that if they can't get ready on time, then they can't do the activity. I've done it a couple of times this year when it's been time to line up to go down to gym. There are three or four people who are always kind of lagging behind. I said, 'Sorry, but you just can't go. You couldn't get ready, and you're punishing the whole class in your tardiness. You'll have to stay here in the room,' and I've gone without them. It's been a reasonably successful strategy because they don't want to miss the activities. They're just sort of lagging behind, and the teacher has to say something to them in particular, and they always have to be pulled along. I frequently find that if you exclude them from an activity a couple of times because they're dragging their feet, so to speak, they come around a little quicker the next time.

"I've also tried talking about the fact that when we're in the class-room situation, you're basically functioning as a large group and you owe it to the group not to be lagging behind because you're unfair and you're thinking only of yourself when you do those things. You have to broaden your scope and think of somebody else as well. Some kids are receptive to that sort of thing. When you're perhaps explain-ing a new skill up in front or giving directions for something, you have kids who may not talk out loud to the point where other people can hear them, but they're whispering back there, and they're whisper-ing enough so that they're not knowing what you're saying and neither is the person that they're talking to. I have done things like say, 'Would you like to tell the class the directions here? Would you like to tell me what I just said?' Put them on the spot a little bit. The strategies may seem a little unkind, but I find that they work. I think lots of times they're attention-getting devices, things that they're doing so they're singled out a little bit from the group.

"If these other approaches fail, you might try talking to the child and ask him just why he does these things. See if they can give you some kind of reason, depending on the age of the child. Really young children may not be able to give you a reason, but by the time they're in third or fourth grade, they probably could. . . . It's not really a seri-ous sort of problem, one that's gonna have you tearing your hair out. I just basically say, 'I'm sorry. You just can't do it today. It's too bad you couldn't do what was asked of you the first time.' And remain calm about it, because with kids like that, lots of times they're doing it just to see if they can get a rise out of you. I think you can keep your cool and keep it together and not let those things irritate you excessively, but just say, 'I'm sorry. You're left out this time.'"

This higher rated teacher responded in a way that was similar at a general level to the response of the lower rated teacher quoted above, but she was very different in the specifics of its implementation. Instead of being abrupt and punitive with the student, she would invoke conse-quences and explain her actions in ways intended to help the student un-derstand the need to accept and fulfill his classroom responsibilities. She would include natural consequences that might put the student on the spot in the classroom or cause him to miss going to the gym, but she would not add on additional punishments for good measure.

ANOTHER HIGHER RATED TEACHER

"A child who exhibits these behaviors usually is looking for attention. Perhaps a teacher has overlooked this child for a few months of school; perhaps at home he is one of these middle children in a big family who isn't getting the attention he feels he needs. A third possibility is that he is bored with the school curriculum, the classroom activities. He hasn't found anything to challenge him, to capture his interest. I think you have to go with all three of these possibilities and investigate them. Try to see why this student is acting as he or she does. I find a lot of this can be minimized, if not erased, if you will look for the cause first. I will always look for the cause and not deal with the behaviors, because there always is a reason. Students generally come excited the first day of school: anxious to learn, thrilled about this new classroom, new experience. If they start exhibiting very negative behaviors, then I think that you have to look at yourself as a teacher and your classroom strategies and say, 'What am I doing that is turning him off instead of on?' A one-to-one interview with this child, several interviews, usually will give you some inkling as to why he is exhibiting these behaviors, why he is feeling the way he is. As for strategies, I guess it would depend a lot on how often the child had repeated the same offense, whether there were particularly stressful circumstances that day for the child, the extent of the damages for whatever incident occurred, and the results of a private talk with the child. I do use witnesses a lot when there is something that someone says Andy did but no adult saw Andy do it. Until I am convinced that the witnesses actually did see this incident happen, I don't jump on Andy. You have to look at a period of months rather than hours and days. You will find that they will happen with less frequency, less intensity. This works beautifully in my own classroom. As far as dragging feet and this sort of thing, I guess I wouldn't be too concerned unless it got to the point that it was actually disrupting the whole classroom. Occasionally students are so hyperactive or whatever reason that they need to move about frequently, and if they do, I give them that freedom to the greatest extent possible because I think it is an actual need. It is not something they can control. . . . For a student like this, I would probably set up a contract situation. The first time that it came up would not be the time that you would start a contract, but after a number of incidents I would talk with the student with the idea that we would set a goal, not just me telling him or her what was wrong but also getting some feedback from the student as to the types of things that were expected in this room and that were not being met. The contract would probably go just 2 days at first, and then maybe 3 days, and then we'd stretch it to a week. There would be much positive feedback for meeting the terms of the contract. For those times when they weren't met, we would discuss that and end with 'OK, we'll try again next week on the same goals.' I think a student of this type, seeing progress coming slowly but steadily, would by Christmastime probably be over most of these needs to draw attention to himself. . . . I try to keep in close touch with parents if it is really becoming a daily problem. I like to find out if they notice this behavior at home. Almost always you will find that they do, if you have the parents' confidence, that is. Sometimes they will say, 'We have found that this is a successful way to deal with it.' Sometimes they will ask for your advice."

This teacher would analyze the situation and talk to the child and the parents to get a better idea of what was happening and perhaps generate suggestions about how to address the problem. If these discussions or the suggestions that resulted from them were not sufficient, she would use a behavioral contracting approach. Her response is noteworthy for her willingness to consider that she might have been contributing to the problem and for her nondefensive emphasis on finding solutions rather than assigning blame.

WHAT THE SCHOLARLY LITERATURE SAYS

Unlike the aggressive child, who defies authority and argues with the teacher's request, the passive–aggressive child employs an arsenal of tactics designed to drive the teacher crazy. These passive–aggressive tactics are as effective and painful as the infamous Chinese water torture. Drip by drip, the passive–aggressive child slowly breaks the teacher down. . . . (Berres & Long, 1979, p. 28)

Veteran teachers are likely to shudder in recognition of this characterization of the exasperation that passive–aggressive students cause. Berres and Long went on to describe the "tactics" used by these students:

1. *Selective Vision.* If you ask him to get something when he doesn't want to do it, he agrees but then can't seem to find it.
2. *Selective Hearing.* If you ask her to do something she would prefer not to do (such as put away her art project and get ready for a lesson), she doesn't seem to hear your instructions to the class, and maybe not even the initial follow-ups directed specifically at her.
3. *Slow-Down Tactics.* He is "coming" but still has to tie his shoe, put away books, etc. Meanwhile, you and the rest of the class wait.
4. *Losing Objects.* She continually leaves her possessions everywhere but in the right place. You find yourself always picking up after her or nagging her about irresponsibility.
5. *The Destructive Volunteer.* He agrees, perhaps even volunteers, to perform tasks, but in the process, he does more harm than good

(e.g., he volunteers to water the plants but knocks one off the window sill, then jabs a classmate with the broom while sweeping up the plant debris).
6. *Don't Ask Me for Help.* She asks you for help but then stares at the ceiling, hums, rocks in her chair, taps a pencil, or plays with a rubber band while you try to explain the work.

Berres and Long interpreted these behaviors as indirect expressions of anger by students who have a great deal of it bottled up inside of them but cannot accept it or express it directly. Instead, they create delay, disruption, or other exasperation to the teacher (and often to classmates as well), but seem to do so accidentally or obliviously. Furthermore, they are "proper, polite, sorry, and confused" if the teacher calls their behavior to their attention. Meanwhile, the teacher may drift into counterproductive modes of interacting—yelling at them when exasperation boils over, nagging them regularly, distancing them, treating them vindictively, or labeling them in ways that suggest that no change in their behavior is expected.

Although less colorfully, other authors also describe passive–aggressive students as angry children who are unable to accept their anger but have learned to express it indirectly in ways that exasperate parents, teachers, or other authority figures. Gordon's concept of problem ownership is useful for understanding the behavior of these students: They are masters at creating problems that are owned by teachers but not by themselves. For example, passive–aggressive tactics have been implicated as contributors to problems of underachievement (Morrison, 1969) and work inhibition (Bruns, 1992).

Bruns noted that passive–aggressive students are unlikely to refuse to follow directions. Instead, they agree politely but then "forget." Or they may delay the class from getting started on an assignment by requesting repetition of the directions or asking what to do if some unlikely scenario should develop. Morrison included the following symptoms on a scale for rating passive–aggressive tendencies: does what is asked to do but takes a long time, often argues a point for the sake of argument, often does the opposite of what is asked, does not follow directions closely, would rather say "I can't" than try to do it, often complains about rules, doesn't turn in homework on time, often requires you to repeat requests, and often offers implausible excuses for failure to do something.

Spaulding (1978) described passive–aggressive students more in terms of a strong need for autonomy than in terms of expressing anger indirectly. He viewed them as resistive to authority and structure, preferring to do things in their own way and at their own pace. He added that these students are often peer-oriented and talkative, especially when they are supposed to be working on assignments.

Psychologists and psychiatrists have described passive–aggressive personalities that include other traits besides resistance to authority and indirect expression of repressed anger (Parsons & Wicks, 1983). Millon (1981), for example, argued that the following traits should be included as secondary characteristics: frequently irritable or moody, easily frustrated and angered, feels misunderstood and unappreciated, pessimistic and disillusioned with life, and puts off other people by constantly complaining about the negative side of things. Millon believed that children who develop this personality pattern are routinely exposed to contradictory socialization messages because their parents are inconsistent or in conflict with each other. This makes the children feel confused about how to please their parents and thus ambivalent about how to respond in social situations.

So far, such attempts to develop a broader definition of and explanation for the development of a passive–aggressive personality type have not generated much support (Fine, Overholser, & Berkoff, 1992). However, there is good support for the more limited passive–aggressive syndrome characterized by resentment of and subtle resistance to external control.

Suggested Strategies for Coping with Passive–Aggressive Behavior

Unfortunately, few authors have offered advice to teachers about dealing with passive–aggressive students, and even fewer have conducted classroom research on the issue. One who has done both is Spaulding (1978), who developed the following suggestions based on classroom case studies:

1. Allow these students autonomy and choices concerning their assignments and the conditions under which they will work.
2. Assign them to work alone in a workstation or learning center (so that they will be less likely to socialize rather than work).
3. Use indirect teaching techniques, avoiding direct commands and confrontations.
4. Do not hover but remain nearby to reinforce appropriate behavior. Use material or activity rewards rather than praise, because the latter conveys submission to your authority and may threaten the autonomy that these students seek to maintain.
5. Where possible, ignore resistance, delay, and attempts to manipulate you. If necessary, use time-out or response–cost punishments, but do not convey exasperation with the student.

Berres and Long (1979) suggested the following strategies designed to break the conflict cycle that tends to develop between teachers and passive–aggressive students:

1. Understand that passive–aggressive tactics are expressions of repressed anger and that if you are not careful, they can create anger in you and make you begin to treat the student inappropriately.

2. Show passive–aggressive students that you are aware of their tactics, and help them to become more aware themselves, by interpreting the behavior along the lines suggested by Dreikurs: "Hmm, you seem to have perfectly good hearing when you talk with friends, so I wonder why you don't hear me when I ask you to start cleaning up. I wonder if you really don't want to hear me and are only pretending not to hear. Maybe you're angry at me for some reason." Berres and Long called this the Detective Columbo technique. Others have referred to it as using "Could it be?" questions.

3. Meet with the student to share your concerns. Perhaps arrange to use a personal signal, such as pointing to your ear, when the student is being passive–aggressive.

4. Talk to the student about how to handle angry feelings. Emphasize that it is more productive to talk about these feelings than to express them indirectly through provocative behaviors.

Millon (1981) suggested minimizing the degree to which you act as an authority figure making demands on passive–aggressive students, and being very consistent in articulating and enforcing the demands that you do make. He also suggested confronting these students with the obstructive and self-defeating character of their behavior, but in a way that communicates your interest in helping them.

Parsons (1983) suggested two ways to reduce these students' need to engage in passive–aggressive tactics. First, work to increase their assertiveness and communication skills, so that they can begin to express their feelings more directly. Second, adjust your curriculum and instructional methods where possible so as to provide these students with more autonomy and choice options (and thus less reason to resent your imposition of control over them).

My own advice underscores several of the key themes suggested by other authors. I also believe that it is important to let passive–aggressive students know that you are "on to them," but with a light touch and within a context of acceptance and support. Encourage them to communicate their frustrations and concerns verbally, noting that this will help you to understand them better and will make you want to help them, whereas provocative behavior has the opposite effect. Use "I" messages to describe the problems and resultant frustration that their behavior creates.

If these students do not respond to invitations to talk about their feelings, try asking directly if you have done something to upset them (or use less direct Dreikurs/Columbo/Could It Be? techniques). As the discussion proceeds, help the student begin to see you as a person and not just as an authority figure. Use Golden Rule appeals and related approaches to stimulate the student's thinking about issues of justice and morality (communicate that both you and the students have jobs to do in the classroom and deserve each other's support; that you do not deserve to be the target of their anger if you have not been the cause of their frustrations; and that if you have been the cause of their frustrations, solutions lie in communication and problem solving).

ANALYSIS OF INTERVIEW RESPONSES

Many teachers had difficulty accepting the notion of passive aggression directed against the teacher as a generalized syndrome that might include any of the behaviors mentioned in the description. Some responded as if the description were a list of unconnected behavior problems. The rest recognized the larger syndrome, but some said that they had rarely or never encountered it, either because they were caring teachers who did not engender such hostility or because they taught in the early grades and believed that young children do not respond to their teachers in this fashion.

Teachers also differed in their views on the seriousness of the problem. Some were clearly threatened by the notion that certain students might develop such abiding hostility toward them. Most, however, minimized the problem by viewing it as attention seeking or home problems spilling over into the classroom.

Almost half (46) of the teachers would confine their response to control or suppression strategies. Among those who suggested more positive strategies, the most popular were attempts to appeal, persuade, or change attitudes (18); to encourage, reassure, build self-concept, or provide a supportive environment (13); or to identify and treat external causes (12). Almost two-thirds (62) of the teachers mentioned long-term prevention or solution strategies.

Three specific problem-solving strategies were mentioned much more frequently than the others: proscribing against passive–aggressive misbehavior (57), threatening or punishing (46), and attempting to extinguish provocative behavior by ignoring it (42). Other specific strategies included praising appropriate behavior (22), minimal intervention (21), inhibiting through proximity or eye contact (19), involving the parents for support or problem solving (19), attempts to appeal or persuade (18), time-out used as an extinction or punishment tool (17), building a more positive relationship with the student (15), prescribing more desirable ways to behave (14), involving peers to pressure or punish (14), and involving the principal or school-based professionals to support or problem solve (13). These strategies, along with others mentioned less frequently, represent a mixture of positive/problem-solving strategies and punitive/control strategies. The strategies emphasized by individual teachers depended on how they viewed the problem.

As responses to particular situations (incidents of the behaviors listed in the problem-type description), 56 teachers would emphasize power assertion, 41 would ignore the problem or respond minimally to it, 13 would use proximity control or other subtle ways to discourage problem behavior, and 10 would use humor, teasing, or cajoling. Concerning longer term strategies, 66 teachers would confront the problem directly in a private discussion with the student, 37 would attempt to improve the student's attitudes or the quality of the teacher–student relationship, 36 would rely on threat or punishment, 19 would assign the student classroom responsibilities or leadership roles (in the belief that this would supply needed attention or in other ways respond to emotional needs, and thus reduce the frequency of provocative behavior), 14 would provide more personal attention (but with emphasis on reinforcing desirable behavior rather than responding to provocations), and 11 would take steps to see that the student did not gain anticipated satisfactions from provocative behavior.

Among teachers who would hold private discussions with passive–aggressive students, 28 would ask them to explain why they were behaving so provocatively or would allow them to ventilate their emotions, 25 would seek to intimidate by threatening punishment if the behavior is repeated, 25 would communicate their awareness of what the student is doing (often with the implication that they would punish further provocations), 11 would try to justify their demands by explaining teacher and student roles or reasons why the provocative behavior is inappropriate, 11 would make empathy or fairness appeals (by pointing out that the students would not like to be treated that way themselves and noting that the teacher does not treat them that way), and 10 would use "I" statements to explain the frustrations and angry feelings that passive–aggressive behavior creates for teachers.

Among teachers who mentioned power assertion, the majority (54) would use it simply to intimidate passive–aggressive students by convincing them that further provocations would be punished and that the negative consequences of their behavior would exceed whatever benefits they might anticipate deriving from it. In addition or instead, 14 would stress that these students are merely being asked to follow the same rules that other students are being asked to follow, 11 would emphasize being consistent in making demands and following through with promised consequences, 10 would watch these students closely so as to be prepared to follow through if they got out of line, and 9 would try to nip the problem in the bud early in the year before it became entrenched.

Among strategies listed as ineffective, the most frequently mentioned were lecturing, nagging, yelling, threatening, or punishing (30); overreacting emotionally by allowing yourself to be baited, to get angry, or to be drawn into a personal conflict with the student (21); and ignoring the problem or delaying response to it for too long (11).

Lower rated teachers were likely to confine their general approach to control or suppression strategies. In contrast, higher rated teachers were likely to mention problem solution attempts, particularly instruction or helping strategies, encouragement or support strategies, and attempts to identify and treat external causes. Among more specific strategies, lower rated teachers were more likely to suggest ignoring provocative behavior in an attempt to extinguish it, threatening punishment, using time-out punitively (as an extinction or removal device rather than an opportunity for the child to calm down and reflect), and appeal/persuasion techniques.

Higher rated teachers were more likely to suggest minimal intervention/redirection strategies, attempts to eliminate the source of the problem, provision of academic help, prescribing or instructing the student in more desirable ways to behave, getting input from the student as a way to help them understand the situation, and getting more information by observing the student in class, interviewing the student, or interviewing peers. Higher rated teachers mentioned more strategies for shaping improved behavior through successive approximations, more strategies for counseling or providing insight to the student, and more strategies for getting additional information. They were more likely to be coded for concern about the problem student as a motive underlying their interview responses and less likely to be coded for concern about self or survival.

Among teachers who mentioned extended discussions, higher rated teachers were much more likely to speak of inviting the students to explain the reasons for their behavior or allowing them to ventilate their feelings. Among teachers who mentioned control or power assertion strategies, lower rated teachers were more likely to speak of using them strictly for intimidation purposes rather than as part of a broader strategy for addressing the problem behavior.

In general, the data suggest that lower rated teachers would be more threatened by passive–aggressive behavior and more likely to respond punitively to it. In contrast, higher rated teachers would be more likely to find it puzzling, seek to find out more about it by talking with the student and getting information from other sources, and address it using a variety of problem-solving strategies in addition to or instead of imposing limits and suppressing misbehavior.

Vignette: Audrey

The class is about to begin a test. The room is quiet. Just as you are about to begin speaking, Audrey opens her desk. Her notebook slides off the desk, spilling loose papers on the floor. Audrey begins gathering up the papers, slowly and deliberately. All eyes are on her. Audrey stops, grins, and then slowly resumes gathering papers. Someone laughs. Others start talking.

Before reading further, take time to think about how you might respond to this incident. Make notes about your ideas.

CSS Vignette Response Excerpts

Here is what four of the CSS teachers had to say.

A LOWER RATED TEACHER

"The little girl, Audrey, who manages to make a big commotion just before a test is an attention getter. But among other things, she also breaks the concentration of the class right when I would have given the instructions for the test. I wouldn't let Audrey get her papers. I would make her leave them there. I'd make her sit down and start that test immediately and not get the papers until the rest of the class were done, because every minute that she delays getting her papers means a delay for the children who are concentrating on the instructions you have just given. She can mess up test scores. I would say also that Audrey is a class problem. That would not be the first time she tried something. [Would you treat her any differently after it had happened several times?] After the second time, I would tell Audrey that if anything happens, she is out of the room until that test is over. She may miss the gym period, whatever I thought would get her into a different behavior pattern. As I say, she is out to get attention. If I had her phone number, I would also contact her parents to see what they thought of it. Most parents don't like a child that messes up other children in a test situation. Also, she is not going to be ready for the test. She has just got herself on a nice high. She is not going to settle down and do what she is supposed to do."

A HIGHER RATED TEACHER

" 'Audrey, I'll come and help you pick up things, and let's get things picked up very quickly. We're ready for a test, and you have interrupted the other children who are ready to start and are very quiet. So let's get things picked up. Put them back into your desk, and you can get your test. Your test is right here with your pencil, and then you will be ready to start.' 'All right children, Audrey's things are put away now, so I guess we can start the test.' My goal would be to have her as quickly as possible get things put away and not to disrupt the class any further. That's why I would go over quickly and, without saying anything else, help her get things put away. This would cause, hopefully, the rest of the class to get back to concentrating on their work and be ready to start the test. I just feel that if you argue or reprimand a child at this particular time, the attention of the class goes to that, and it is very hard to get them settled down. I think the quicker you handle the situation, get it taken care of, then the faster you can go right on without delay to the test."

ANOTHER HIGHER RATED TEACHER

"From the paragraph it almost seems like Audrey did it on purpose, because she stops and grins, she slowly gathers it up, and she doesn't seem to be at all embarrassed about the whole thing but really carries on. If this is happening all the time, I'd say, 'Audrey, we were ready for a test, so when all those things are in your desk, I'm going to ask you to sit over at the table in the corner, and you may take the test after school or at lunchtime, because I don't think you are being fair to the other children.' And so I would quiet the others down, and we would go on. If I felt it was an accident— sometimes a child will stop and grin because it is their way of acting out if they are embarrassed— if I know this is an accident, I'd help her and I'd say, 'Audrey, let's get the things you need out of your desk and keep it closed.' Then quiet the children and go on. So it would depend on which kind of a child I have already assessed her to be."

ANOTHER HIGHER RATED TEACHER

"First I would quiet the classroom down by saying, 'All right, we are ready to take a test. We will have it quiet.' Then I would say to Audrey, 'I don't appreciate the fact that you think this is a menial thing.' Then I think I would ask the others to raise their hand and tell Audrey what they think about what she is doing. I would hope that they would not say that they think she is being funny and that they would want to laugh. I would hope that they would say, 'We don't like to have to wait for you,' 'We wish you would hurry up.' This kind of situation frustrates me because very often a child like Audrey can get the better of an adult, and they know it. I think perhaps the strong medicine for Audrey is the peer pressure. If she can begin to believe that other children are not happy with what she is doing, they don't think she is funny, then perhaps the group can help to modify her behavior.

I don't think this kind of child will modify behavior simply because an adult reacts in an angry manner, even though that is my first impulse. I think that after the test I would take Audrey aside and tell her how I felt, that it made me very angry when she decided to pick up the paper slowly and she thought it was very funny because she was having everyone wait. Then I would ask her why she did it. She may or may not know. If she doesn't know, I may say, 'I think you did it because you want to make me angry so that I have to pay attention to you.' Then I would tell her that I would rather pay attention to her if she had done something that was helpful to someone else and that I hoped to see her doing something helpful to another person in the rest of the day or the next day. Kind of give her a time limit. I think that by giving her an opportunity to get recognition for something positive, I would be giving her a way to begin to modify some of her behavior. I would characterize her as someone who feels that the only way they can get attention is by doing something negative. My feeling would be that this child probably is yelled at a lot at home and feels that this is the only way that she can get adults to pay attention to her."

The lower rated teacher made it clear that she would be quite angry with Audrey and would tend to treat her sharply, perhaps punitively. However, she didn't say anything about instructing or resocializing Audrey. The three higher rated teachers would respond differently. The first would move quickly to end the disruption and get on with the test, without expressing anger at Audrey but also without saying much to instruct or resocialize her. The other two higher rated teachers also would avoid expressing anger at Audrey but would attempt to make her understand the problems that she is causing. In addition, the last teacher would challenge her to find ways to draw attention to herself through positive behaviors.

Analysis of Responses to Audrey

Although we failed to state explicitly that the depicted incident was part of a larger passive–aggressive syndrome, more than two-thirds (66) of the teachers assumed that Audrey's behavior was intentional, and 63 believed that the problem was generalized.

A brief management response, such as telling Audrey to quickly pick up the dropped materials or else leave them there until after the test, was the most commonly mentioned strategy for responding to the depicted problem (52). Other responses included prescribing desired behavior (29), threatening or invoking punishment (28), proscribing against misbehavior (18), ignoring provocative behavior (14), seeking to eliminate the perceived source of the problem (10), seeking to develop Audrey's insight into what she has been doing (9), making tension release comments (8), changing Audrey's seat (7), and making no response at all or attempting to avoid dealing with the problem (7). Only 28 teachers mentioned long-term prevention or follow-up strategies, mostly socialization attempts (10) or attempts to shape improvement through attention to Audrey's desirable behavior (9).

Most (81) of the teachers would make demands on Audrey, but only 34 would accompany their demands with rationales. The rationales included citing classroom rules (17), logical analysis linking Audrey's behavior to undesired effects (13), attempting to induce empathy for the teacher by explaining the frustrations that Audrey's behavior causes (10), and making a personal (try to do better so as to please me) appeal (10).

The teachers' reactions to the depicted incident were coded for how they suggested dealing with Audrey's dropped papers, regaining the attention of the class, and responding to Audrey's provocative behavior. Concerning the dropped papers, 47 teachers would expect Audrey to pick up the papers by herself, 24 would help her do so, and 7 would ask classmates to help. In addition, 21 teachers would tell Audrey to leave the papers on the floor until after the test was completed.

To regain the attention and control of the class, 40 teachers would use some kind of signal, such as standing with arms folded and a stern expression, flipping the light switch off and on, praising students who were still attentive and ready for the test, or reminding the class about expectations for behavior during test situations. In addition, 25 teachers would publicly "diagnose," scold, or punish Audrey. Instead of making an issue of the inattention problem in this manner, 35 teachers would minimize attention to the disruption and refocus the class on the test as quickly as possible (by seeing that the papers were picked up quickly, or telling the student to leave them there, and then giving brief reminders about concentrating on taking the test).

The majority (60) of the teachers would treat the incident as a minor problem and focus on getting the class back to the test without addressing the provocative aspects of Audrey's behavior. However, 34 would respond critically or punitively (criticize Audrey, give her a "dirty look," isolate her from the class, require her to make up the test later at recess, etc.). In addition or instead, 13 would attempt to socialize Audrey by getting her to see that her behavior causes problems for the teacher, herself, or the class as a whole, and 12 would attempt to create peer pressure by labeling her behavior as unfair to her classmates or indicating that time lost due to her disruption would be subtracted from time available for the test or for recess. A total of 36 teachers spoke of confronting Audrey publicly in some way. Thirty-five teachers spoke of moving closer to

Audrey following the dropped papers. Of these, 22 would come to help her pick the papers up, but 13 would come to use physical proximity as a way to provide additional pressure on her to get the papers picked up quickly.

Most of the teachers made assumptions or speculations about Audrey's motives. A majority (70) viewed Audrey as acting deliberately, but 6 viewed the incident as purely an accident, and 18 said that it might have been an accident or it might have been deliberate. Teachers who speculated about Audrey's possible motives usually assumed that she was seeking attention from classmates (71). Motives suggested in addition or instead included attempts to bait the teacher or test the rules (24), to get attention from the teacher (18), or to avoid the test (13).

Higher rated teachers were more likely to say that the depicted incident was or might have been an accident, whereas lower rated teachers were more likely to view it as a deliberate provocation, part of a broader pattern. This is one of several findings indicating that higher rated teachers were more likely to give problem students the benefit of the doubt in ambiguous situations, whereas lower rated teachers were more likely to jump to conclusions and assume deliberate provocation.

Lower rated teachers' responses usually focused on dealing with the immediate incident, without describing a more systematic response to Audrey. These teachers were likely to suggest one of two contrasting approaches. The first was a negative overreaction, featuring public confrontation with Audrey and threat or imposition of punishment. The second was underreaction, in which the teacher would simply wait for Audrey to finish picking up the materials without saying or doing anything else, or would confine response to a minimal comment and an attempt to refocus the class on the test quickly. The latter response is widely recommended (and supported by research) as a way to respond to minor, fleeting misbehavior or to nip a potentially more serious problem in the bud without losing the momentum of an activity. In this case, however, the momentum already was lost, and Audrey's behavior was provocative enough to call for a more proactive response.

Even though higher rated teachers were more likely to note that the incident was or might have been an accident, they suggested more systematic responses to it. Some mentioned ignoring as a possible strategy, usually as part of a systematic attempt to shape improved behavior. In contrast, lower rated teachers who mentioned ignoring usually did so in the context of saying that they didn't consider this incident to be worth responding to and would simply wait until Audrey had completed picking up the papers and then resume the test.

Most of the higher rated teachers would do something more than wait for Audrey to get ready or make some minor comment encouraging her to do so. Some would move closer to her, using physical proximity to pressure her to get ready for the test more quickly. Others would try to socialize her by attempting to induce empathy or develop insight. That is, they would use "I" messages (usually later rather than on the spot) to help her understand that she causes frustrations to the teacher and her classmates when she makes them wait for her unnecessarily.

Vignette: Jack

The class has just been given instructions to line up quickly. The students comply, with the exception of Jack, who is always the last to follow directions. Jack remains at his desk, working on a drawing. He looks up, in the direction of the line, and then resumes his work on the drawing.

Before reading further, take time to think about how you might respond to this incident. Make notes about your ideas.

CSS Vignette Response Excerpts

Here is what four of the CSS teachers had to say.

A LOWER RATED TEACHER

"I would tell Jack to get up, in no uncertain terms, and get in line. He is holding up the whole class. And if he went back to work on his drawing, either I would yell or I would move the class out of the room, and I would go back and yell again. By this time, he would be moving too. . . . Sometimes you have to use peer pressure. You don't move the class until Jack gets in line. And if it is lavatory time and they are 10 minutes over and they have to go, they will put the pressure on Jack to move him out."

A HIGHER RATED TEACHER

"I would simply say to Jack, 'I am very pleased to see that you are so interested in your work, but we have to get to where we are going, so would you please join us in the line?' I think he would do so. This happens all along. [What if Jack did this every week?] I think over a period of time, he would begin to get the idea that when it is time to move from one class to the next, we must stop one activity to begin another. I would simply just remind him of this. No doubt it would take a number of times because he likes what he is doing and he wants to continue it, but we have to go on to something else. I would just remind him of this. If it took a period of time to get the concept to him, then that is what I would do."

"First I would say to Jack, 'Let's line up; that's what I asked you to do. Put away your drawing.' If he didn't do that, then I would walk to his desk, put away his drawing for him, and ask him to line up, or take his arm and lead him to the door to line up. If they have been asked to line up quickly, I would assume that there was something that they needed to do posthaste, and that it was important for Jack to join the class. Then at a later time I might talk to him about the fact that I am disturbed because he seems to be always the last one to do what I ask, and I would ask him why. Does he like being the last one, because it's more fun to be at the end of the line? Does he not like to follow my directions? Is it hard for him to change what he is doing? Does he like to finish what he is doing before he does something else? I would let him know that it bothers me that he is always the last one, and I would ask him if it would help in the future if I told him, ahead of the other children, when we were going to change activities, like telling him, 'In 5 minutes we're going to have to line up. I'm telling you now so that you can get ready and be ready with the rest of us.' This may be something that would work with him. If he is doing it just to be ornery, then I would probably make a point of being next to him when I gave directions and hurrying him along verbally at that time. Jack could be one of two types of kids, either the kid who is being stubborn or the child who actually has a hard time shifting gears and needs more preparation before he switches to another activity. If he is a child who is ornery, he needs to know that I am not going to ignore the behavior and that complying with my directions is something that is important to me and that I will wait for him to do that. Hopefully this will help him to know that he might as well comply because I am still going to wait for him. I would imagine that other children would say to him without my saying anything to them, 'Hurry up, Jack, we're waiting; we want to go outside,' or go to the library, or do what's coming next. If I were to carry that further, then I could say to the class, 'I want you to tell Jack how it makes you feel when you're ready and standing in line, and he is the only one who is making the whole class wait.' Maybe Jack would then realize that he is not winning acceptance, that the way he is getting attention and being the center of attraction is not the way he would like. If he is the child who has difficulties shifting gears, then probably warning him ahead of time would help him to stop one activity and get ready for the next. That may make him aware of how long it takes him to finish up, and it would give him a chance to save face in front of the class, if that is his problem."

"If this child is sitting at his desk working on a drawing, it is going to depend a little bit on whether I have an extra person in the room that I can depend on. If I have a college student or student teacher, I would say, 'Jack, we have called you for line, and since you are not ready to go, I am taking all of your things and I am going to ask you to sit here for 5 minutes and think about your need to come when we are going someplace. We have a certain time for (whatever we are doing), and you are holding everybody up. I don't think you are being fair to the group.' Many times I emphasize their responsibility to the group. Here I would be emphasizing his responsibility to our group and that he is not being fair at this point. So I would have him sit for 5 minutes and think about it. If this happened twice, I would go and get him every time, emphasizing, 'I said, "Come," come now.' I would take him by the hand and lead him for a while until he learned to come. Many times this is the kind of student who really hates to be interrupted in what they are doing. They have a great difficulty in changing from one activity to another, especially in the middle of it. Sometimes they do this deliberately too. Either they want to get a rise out of the teacher, or they just couldn't care less (he is more interested in what he is doing . . . regardless of the group). There again, we would start working on his responsibility to the class."

The lower rated teacher mentioned yelling at Jack or bringing peer pressure on him, but not attempting to give him information or resocialize his attitudes. The three higher rated teachers would respond more productively. The first would simply repeat instructions to Jack, assuming that she would gradually condition him to respond to directions more promptly. The second would adopt a similar response, backed by development of peer pressure on Jack, if necessary. The third would emphasize socialization, seeking to develop Jack's sense of responsibility to the group. Both of the latter teachers also considered the possibility that the problem was not a passive–aggressive provocation but a "difficulty in shifting gears" problem and suggested alternative strategies to be used in this case.

Analysis of Responses to Jack

Most teachers recognized Jack's problem behavior as stable (72) and generalized (71), but only 62 viewed his behavior as fully controllable by him, and only 43 viewed the depicted provocation as intentional.

Six teachers said that they would not respond at all to the depicted incident or would attempt to avoid dealing with it. The rest suggested one or more problem-solving strategies, most notably brief management responses (54), punishment (35), prescribing desired behavior (34), changing Jack's seat or social environment (16), proscribing against his misbehavior (13), or attempting to increase his insight (12). All but 7 would make behavioral change demands on Jack, although only 32 would provide rationales for their demands. Most would cite classroom rules (19) and/or attempt to induce empathy by explaining the problems that Jack's behavior causes (19).

In response to the immediate problem, 57 teachers said that they would place Jack in line physically or demand that he get in line in a manner that implied punishment if he refused. In addition or instead, 17 spoke of excluding Jack from the group (requiring him to remain in the room or go to the office and miss out on what the class was about to do), and 14 spoke of encouraging, or at least allowing, peers to pressure Jack by calling for him to line up or expressing their frustrations with him. Instead of using these direct pressuring strategies, 37 would simply repeat requests to Jack that he get in line or else attempt to persuade him to do so by pointing out that he is causing a problem for the teacher or the class, reminding him that the class needs to be somewhere else now, etc. Finally, 13 would arrange for Jack to continue working on his drawing, either by allowing him to stay in the room or by bringing it to where the class was going and allowing him to work on it there instead of doing what his classmates would be doing.

Most (75) teachers mentioned one or more strategies for addressing Jack's more general passive–aggressive syndrome. Of these, 48 mentioned power assertion (making firm demands on Jack, backed by threat or implication of punishment for noncompliance), 22 mentioned attempts to change his perceptions or attitudes during private conferences, 12 spoke of accommodating to his special needs or desires (to be the last student in line, to get advance warning about upcoming transitions, or to get more opportunities to draw), and 11 spoke of using instructional or shaping strategies to improve Jack's behavior.

Among teachers who would request or demand that Jack get in line, the majority would accompany their demand with some form of rationale, typically telling Jack that he is being unfair to the class by keeping them all waiting (30), stating that the class is now scheduled to go somewhere else and the teacher is not allowed to leave him in the room unsupervised (28), or attempting to cajole him by asking him politely, reasoning with him, reassuring him that he will get a chance to finish the drawing later, etc. (15). Fifty-two teachers mentioned moving closer to Jack, either to physically guide him into line or to use physical proximity to bring pressure on him. Twenty-two said that their response would depend on the reasons for Jack's behavior, and named two or more possible causes and related response strategies.

The few teachers who said that they would make no response to the situation or would attempt to avoid dealing with it tended to be lower rated teachers. Most lower rated teachers would respond, but their responses would tend to be restricted to brief managerial interventions (telling Jack to get in line), perhaps accompanied by threat of punishment for noncompliance. These teachers usually would not include a rationale with their behavioral demands or follow up with strategies designed to address the larger problem.

Higher rated teachers had the opposite pattern. Even though they were more likely to recognize that Jack's behavior was part of a larger passive–aggressive syndrome, they were more likely to suggest that he might not be fully able to control his actions and thus might not be fully responsible for them. Their goals and strategies usually went beyond exerting control in the immediate situation by mentioning training or shaping strategies, and their behavioral demands usually were accompanied by rationales. Thus, higher rated teachers were more likely to be coded for supportive instruction or counseling strategies: attempts to change Jack's attitudes or perceptions, explaining the problems that his behavior was causing, explaining about school schedules and rules, or attempting to induce empathy by making him more aware that he was keeping the teacher and the class waiting. In short, rather than only exerting situational control over Jack, higher rated teachers would try to make him understand why it was important for him to follow directions and thus try to make him more likely to do so in the future.

COMPARISON OF RESPONSES TO AUDREY AND TO JACK

The general pattern of responses to these two vignettes was quite similar, as was the pattern of contrasts between higher rated and lower rated teachers. In each case, lower rated teachers were more likely to suggest doing nothing at all or (especially) emphasizing control/pressure strategies in the immediate situation, whereas higher rated teachers were more likely to mention socialization or insight building strategies designed to make Audrey and Jack more aware of the problems that their delaying tactics cause for the teacher and the class.

Higher rated teachers' attributional inferences were better matched to the specifics of the wording of the vignettes. They were more likely to recognize that Jack's behavior was part of a larger passive–aggressive syndrome but less likely to infer this about Audrey's behavior. Even so, in both cases their responses focused more on developing insight and using other strategies to induce larger changes in behavior patterns, not just on exerting control in the immediate situation.

QUALITATIVE IMPRESSIONS AND EXAMPLES

Some teachers viewed the passive–aggressive syndrome as a relatively minor problem and took a low-key approach in responding to it. These teachers were split between those who unrealistically denied the problem and failed to deal with it and those who recognized it accurately but believed that passive–aggressive students will come around if you just reach out to them. Most of the remaining teachers viewed passive aggression as a much more serious problem, tantamount to direct defiance. These teachers were split between those who would react very negatively by punishing these students or trying to embarrass them publicly and those who would get everything out on the table in a private conference, but within the context of a sincere attempt to find out what the problem is and come to some negotiated agreement. In each of these cases, the latter of the pair appears to be the better approach.

Teachers who had trouble accepting the notion of a child who would be deliberately passive–aggressive toward them tended to suggest that symptomatic behaviors were motivated by a desire for attention, were part of an attempt to establish dependable limits (by a child accustomed to inconsistent discipline at home), or represented indirect communication of home- or school-related concerns by a child who had not learned how to communicate more directly. These teachers emphasized reaching out to these students and establishing good relationships with them, such as by inviting them to stay after school to help clean the chalkboards and then using that private time to chat with them about their interests and concerns. Teachers who spoke of "winning over" these students often claimed consistent success, although several admitted that the students would start the whole testing or resistance routine all over again if a substitute teacher came to class. One teacher cynically commented that "the tougher the case, the more sweet talk they get in September, the more time they get chosen to do the little errands. You don't pick your goody-goodies to run your errands. You pick the kids who are going to give you a bad time."

Teachers who emphasized limit testing often spoke of trying to socialize these students to understand that now that they are in school and a member of a group, they have responsibilities to that group. One noted that a wise teacher can take advantage of the fact that these students often become scapegoats because classmates discover that they are always instigating something and thus tend to blame them. She developed improved relationships with these students by defending them when they were blamed unjustly, even though she was firm about her limits and prepared to hold these students responsible when their behavior warranted it.

Some teachers suggested that limit testers want to be caught, and they usually added that it is important to reassert your rules and invoke announced sanctions when you do catch them. Several said that you need to be direct and firm with them in stating the misbehavior you have observed, lest they persist in denying it and engaging you in a long but pointless debate about what happened. One teacher commented on the difficulty of remaining consistent in enforcing limits on these students and keeping yourself from responding counterproductively to their provocative behavior: "It's hard to determine whether these kids are resisting or not, and it's hard to modify their behaviors because you've got to modify your behavior."

In this regard, several teachers said that they let a lot of little things go with passive–aggressive students ("If they are always the last in line, let them be the last in line, so long as they are there"). Also, several mentioned the importance of voice tone and manner: Avoid potential power struggles by speaking in a soft or conversational voice, embed your demands within longer chatter, and don't issue direct orders to them. Where feasible, treat them as if they have created a problem inadvertently rather than deliberately.

Many teachers, but especially lower rated teachers, spoke of attempting to negate the value (to the child) of passive–aggressive behaviors by seeing that the student did not enjoy the anticipated rewards from them. Thus, they might keep a child in during recess or after school in response to foot dragging that caused a significant delay in making a transition between activities. Or they might create peer pressure, such as by observing publicly that the student is holding up the class. Other "frustrate the goal of the behavior" suggestions included the following: If they dawdle in the halls, take their hand and make them walk with you; if they make things to play with or throw, require them to stay after school and keep making these things until they are satiated; if they mar a book, require them to use that book thereafter; and if they mar other property, require them to clean up or repair the damage as much as possible and perhaps to do additional maintenance work.

A few teachers talked about going out of their way to find a punishment that would hit these students hard, such as leaving them home from a class trip or requiring them to spend some time in a classroom in a lower grade level. These teachers tended to say that they disliked passive–aggressive students even more than hostile–aggressive or defiant ones, because at least the latter students are open about their emotions and "you

can deal with them." One teacher admitted that she disliked these children so much that she made them an exception to her rule against tattling.
She told her class that the one time she wanted them to tattle was "if you
see somebody doing something that they and you know is really wrong,
and they are doing it in a sneaky way, in a way to get by with something."

More effective teachers favored private conferences featuring direct
confrontation about misbehavior, followed by negotiation of solutions.
They often spoke of working out a deal with the student, noting that they
were going to be together 5 hours each day and would have to get along.
They might suggest possible changes or invite the child to do so, being
prepared to go along with any that were feasible (such as instituting a
private signal to use when the child is behaving inappropriately or agreeing to be responsive when the child requests time-out or some other form
of support).

A few teachers said that passive–aggressive students are more likely
to be girls than boys, whom they viewed as more likely to be directly defiant. One spoke of using humor ("You're up to your old tricks again; I'll
have to put you in a cage") as a way to lighten her tone when intervening
with these students, saying that "if it is a kid who responds to it, he will
quit hassling you and straighten up just because he likes you — the game
might change into something else that is less damaging." Another suggested
that persistent passive aggression directed at her was a sign that she might
be treating the child inappropriately, so she would try to analyze her interactions with the child and seek to improve them.

One teacher's interview contained several interesting observations
about passive–aggressive students. First, although she asked them to run
errands and do other things to build up a relationship with them and communicate acceptance, she didn't want this to become obvious to the rest
of the class or to be seen by the student as a reward for passive–aggressive behavior. Therefore, she delayed the interval between the child's
provocation and her errand request, attempting to avoid letting the child
see any connection between them. Second, she was careful to be genuine
in reaching out to these children with praise or compliments, fearing that
they or others in the class would realize it when she was not genuine. Third,
although she projected positive affect toward these students, she was careful about touching them physically because many of them respond poorly to this approach.

Many teachers did not recognize Audrey's behavior as chronic and
provocative in intent, but even many of those who did said that the best
thing to do was ignore it and get on with the test. Some would just persist
with the test and have Audrey miss an item or two or be forced to catch
up (if it were just a weekly test). If it were a standardized test, they would
get her and the rest of the class settled down before proceeding. One
teacher would both pretend that she viewed Audrey's behavior as acciden-

tal and help her pick up the materials, not only as a way to get on with the test more quickly but also as a way to deprive Audrey of satisfaction in provoking her. Others spoke of taking punitive action against Audrey—requiring her to sit on the floor, writing a note to her mother about this and related incidents, or removing her from class and requiring her to take the test after school. Suggested verbal responses included "You've won your award, so sit down and get ready for the test," "Were you feeling neglected because we weren't paying enough attention to you today?" "Well, you've had a little attention now," and "When you finish, I'll start."

Many teachers who would ignore Audrey or respond minimally to her provocation nevertheless would make an issue of Jack's behavior. They viewed his failure to follow directions as a form of defiance, so they suggested such responses as warning him to get in line before they counted to five or ten, leaving him or sending him to the office if the class was headed toward something that he would like to do, tearing up his drawing and throwing it away if he didn't get in line, sending his drawing home with a note telling his parents that this is what he did instead of what he was supposed to be doing, or announcing to the class that time spent waiting for Jack would be lost from recess. Some teachers said that if the class was headed toward something important, they would make sure that Jack got into line quickly, but if the class was headed toward something less important, they might consider leaving him or arranging for him to continue working on his paper. Others said that they would cut Jack more slack earlier in the year or on a day when they were feeling good, but not later in the year when he knew better or on a day when their tolerance for such behavior was limited.

Finally, some teachers would respond neutrally or even supportively to Jack, suggesting that perhaps he hadn't heard the original directions or that he needed special consideration. Some would reassure him that he would be able to finish his paper later. Others would begin to give him advance warning of upcoming transitions, designate him to be the first or the last in line for a while, or tell him that they were pleased to see that he wanted to do his work but that right now he needed to join the line to leave the room. One teacher used a special humorous "hey ho" call in situations like this, both as shorthand and as a way to avoid issuing direct orders. Finally, one teacher would tell Jack "You miss a lot of good things if you don't listen" if he frequently told her that he hadn't heard a direction.

DISCUSSION

The response strategies recommended by higher rated teachers squared well with recommendations from the research literature, although each set of recommendations contained several ideas that the other did not.

Our findings suggest that the keys to successful coping with passive–aggressive students are first to recognize their passive–aggressive syndrome accurately and then to follow up with appropriate problem-investigation and problem-solving strategies.

Accurate recognition of the passive–aggressive syndrome is not always easy, because passive–aggressive students express their anger in subtle and indirect ways. You may be aware of having various problems with them but fail to see that these seemingly separate problems are symptoms of a core syndrome. Also, even if you notice the connections, you may find it threatening to think that passive–aggressive students might be angry with you and are expressing this anger in subtle ways, so you may interpret the syndrome inaccurately (e.g., as immaturity or attention seeking). Thus, the passive–aggressive syndrome is worth keeping in mind as a possible explanation behind the behavior of students who consistently create problems for you that are miscellaneous in form but exasperating in effect.

Once the syndrome is recognized, it is important to respond to it by using instruction and support strategies. This was emphasized by higher rated teachers, who recognized the need for socialization and problem-solving efforts with passive–aggressive students. They avoided the mistakes of, on the one hand, failing to recognize and address the angry or resentful feelings behind various passive–aggressive symptoms and thus not taking them seriously and, on the other hand, overreacting to them with inappropriately resentful or punitive responses.

Thus, an effective response to passive–aggressive students depends on recognizing the anger underlying their behavior but not letting this make you become angry yourself. Instead, observe and talk to these students to determine more specifically what is bothering them, communicate your interest in seeing them enjoy school and helping them to succeed there, help them to gain insight into their behavior, solicit their suggestions for change and follow through on those that are feasible, and encourage them to come and tell you if something is bothering them. If you do these things consistently, passive–aggressive students will begin to relate to you more as a trusted and valued resource person and less as a resented authority figure.

10

Defiant Students

Defiant students display the following characteristics: These children resist authority and carry on a power struggle with the teacher. They want to have their way and not be told what to do. They resist verbally by:

1. Saying, "You can't make me"
2. Saying, "You can't tell me what to do"
3. Making derogatory comments about the teacher to others

They resist nonverbally by:

1. Frowning, grimacing, and mimicking the teacher
2. Posturing with arms folded, hands on hips, foot stomping
3. Looking away when being spoken to
4. Laughing at inappropriate times
5. Sometimes being physically violent toward the teacher
6. Deliberately doing what the teacher says not to do

What special strategies might you use to minimize such problems and help these students to function more successfully in your classroom? Before reading further, take time to think about this and make notes about your ideas.

CSS INTERVIEW EXCERPTS

Here is what three of the CSS teachers had to say about teaching defiant students.

A LOWER RATED TEACHER

"There aren't too many that will resist verbally, although I've had some that did. It just depends on what degree it would be. I think I'd get hold of the parents, first of all, and then of course the principal or the assistant. They wouldn't want that sort of thing, because it wouldn't be long before the teacher wouldn't have any control over the class. Lots of times I think I'm tougher on something like that, or I take time on it because I figure it saves more time than letting some others, who are just kind of watching and would like to be nuisances but didn't quite dare, see somebody else get away with it. I've had some that mimic me and did things like that. Well, of course, there aren't too many things a person can do. All you can do is try to appeal to the child, and if that doesn't work, isolate them from the rest. Of course, we're not supposed to even put them outside the door. We put them in the corner once in a while or something like that. I don't believe in putting them outside for very long, but sometimes I think the shock of being put out there, with some children, will help. And then with others, well, they like to see what's going on out in the hall, and it doesn't do much good. So I think in most cases in our school we have to have the parent over. I call lots of times on the phone. I write down exactly what the child did, and then I call the parents. If I can get them over here, usually the parents will work on them and say that they had no idea they'd been doing those things. In fact, there are some parents that are so strict with those children, and some of them would beat them with belts. I've had some children that caused problems and were impolite and quite a few other things, but I wouldn't report it to the home. I just made the best of it and tried to ignore it as much as I could and tried to go on from there because I figured that the punishment was out of proportion to what the offense was. Of course, little kids don't do these things much. I mean, it's older kids, and I know they do it a lot of times because of their peer relationships and showing what they can get away with. It's a whole different setup that I'm glad I'm not involved in."

This response was much better than those of many other lower rated teachers because it was not replete with authoritarian language and strategies, power struggles, or teacher loss of control. This teacher intuitively understood that emotional overreactions and authoritarian responses are counterproductive, and that it helps to appeal to these students and try to minimize conflict with them. However, she lacked the confidence and strategic knowledge that would have allowed her to implement these strategies more systematically, so she often found herself appealing to the principal or the parents for help. However, she hesitated to do this when she thought it might lead to brutal treatment of the student by his parents, and apparently it had not occurred to her to try to make the parents understand that this reaction is counterproductive.

A HIGHER RATED TEACHER

"Children who resist authority and constantly carry on a power struggle, with not just the teacher but probably most adults in a position of authority, have had inconsistent discipline. Perhaps they have not had an adult model, or the significant adults in their life have not been consistent in how they deal with that child, have not presented a model the child can look up to. I think a lot of this comes from the home situation. If the child behaves that way, the parent might ignore it and say very little about it and, perhaps the next time around, might be very physical, very punitive, so that these children have inconsistent treatment. I think with children like this the first thing you have to do is, if at all possible, remain calm because when they're saying things like 'You can't make me. I'm not gonna do what you told me to do,' if you come back emotional, then they're more likely to think, 'Hey, I've got you going. You're in the exact position where I want you.' I'm sure that these children by making statements like this have frequently gotten their own way when perhaps they really didn't want to. Rather than the adult putting their foot down and saying, 'I'm sorry but that's the way it is, and you're gonna have to accept it and deal with it,' they have given in to the demands. So I think first of all you must be consistent with them, very consistent in the way you deal with their misbehavior. By being consistent, by staying in control of yourself, I think it's a starting point and perhaps the child can begin to have some respect for you. Once that has begun, your chances of controlling their behavior increase. I think a lot of it is just lack of respect, lack of being taught to respect adults in general. In terms of resisting nonverbally, frowning, making fun, I think that with some of those behaviors — like laughing at inappropriate times, looking away when spoken to, making faces — if you don't make a big deal of it, the frequency of those actions drops off. A lot of kids will take any kind of attention they can get, negative or positive, and if they're frowning, maybe mocking what you're saying, mimicking you, and you're getting all upset about it, you're only reinforcing that behavior. You're giving them the kind of response that they want, so I have found for myself that frequently you can just ignore that kind of thing. If you can encourage the other children to ignore it, to not reinforce it at all, that sort of thing drops. In terms of being physically violent toward a teacher, I've never really had to deal with that. I've never had a child hit or kick me. I guess the first thing to do would be just to restrain them. Obviously I don't think you should hit them back because then you're doing exactly what you're getting after them about. I think that's one of the biggest reasons not to punish children physically. It sets a bad example, a bad model for them to follow. In terms of children who deliberately do what the teacher tells them not to do, I guess maybe as firmly as possible insist that they do it, and if they do not, deprive them of privileges, take something away. . . . I definitely feel that these children would need counseling to see just where the problem came from, why they feel such a need to resist authority. If you can pinpoint where the problem originated, then you might have a better chance of working and solving it. It's definitely a kind of problem where I think that the teacher, child, counselor, and the parents, and perhaps even the principal, would have to work on it together. I think if the child is that openly rebellious, it's pretty serious. I have never taken this sort of thing lightly when I've had children like this. I have usually looked for counseling help for the child, and I've also tried to enlist the help of the parents. If you can get the parents to be open about what the parent–child relationship is in the home, you can start to get a handle on it. I think problems like this originate in the home rather than the classroom. [Are you talking about mental health counseling or a counselor in the building?] I would start with a counselor in the building. If she felt there was a need for mental health counseling, we would go that route as well. I know that sometimes children of this nature are referred to emotionally impaired rooms if they're really out of hand, but I think that unless the child is so disruptive that he or she is taking all your time, they should stay in the normal classroom. They need to be around normal healthy children."

This teacher was aware of the difficulties involved in working with defiant students, but she possessed the confidence and knowledge to enable her to apply consistent pressure on these students without allowing herself to be drawn into public power conflicts with them. Also, she spoke about not merely reacting to their behavior or handling particular incidents of defiance but rather engaging in longer term efforts to work on the more general pattern of oppositional and defiant behavior, in cooperation with the parents and a mental health professional.

ANOTHER HIGHER RATED TEACHER

"The child who openly resists and is really verbal about it is the hardest to deal with because not only are you dealing with a discipline problem but you are dealing with a classroom environment. They can disrupt the whole class; they can disrupt me, emotionally, for the whole day. When I have a severe discipline problem that I have to handle, I find that after it is all over with, I am exhausted. Even if there is no blow up and I handle it very quietly, it drains me totally because I try so hard to avoid a scene. I don't think I have ever lost my temper with a severe problem. To lose your temper is to lose the battle. This type of child usually comes from a home where there is just no consistency. The rules vary from day to day, bedtime, meal-time. Yes might mean yes today, and no might mean yes tomorrow, and so on. Usually there is too much freedom in the home. The kid has never been made to know specific limits, so they go as their mood pushes them to try to get as much as they can. If somebody frustrates or crosses them, they are going to fight to get what they want because they are used to getting what they want, one way or another. The way of handling it, first of all, is to meet them at their level. Know what their academic level is so that you don't start them too simple or too difficult, which is frustrating. When the academic level is set and you have them working and you see the looks and the sulking and so on beginning, sometimes you have to just ignore some of those things. Make sure that they understand what they are supposed to do, un-derstand the room regulations, but also make sure that what they are doing is really bugging you. If it isn't, overlook it. Second, walk over to them and talk to them individually. Find out if there is a question. Find out if there is anything they want to talk about. Sometimes if they just have a chance to talk for a couple of minutes, that will settle it. Find something mutual to talk about—a mutual interest. I have a whole lot of faith in this idea of friendly little visits. Just a couple of minutes, whatever. Just a little conversation. Another tactic is to be especially friendly outside of class. . . . Also, you have to be extreme-ly consistent with these kids. They know every single word you ever said. Always try to remove them from the room, remove them from the audience so that you avoid that power struggle. My goal is to get them to have some self-respect and self-control, to have a little con-cern for my way of feeling and not always think of themselves as be-ing punished or picked on all the time. They have to see the other side of the coin. They have to realize that their mother at home or their father at home is getting all of this hassle from them too. They feel just as frustrated as the child does. They have got to learn to see the other person's point of view. By these methods, I am trying to make them realize that life isn't made up of give me, give me, give me. It is made up of cooperation and respect and things of this sort. Physical violence is not a solution and self-control has got to come first before anything else. If they can't control themselves, there is nothing I can do. I have got to teach them somehow. There has got to be another way to control themselves. This is what I am trying to do by talking, ignoring, organizing their time, scheduling their time, being consistent and things of this sort. I have selected these strategies because over the years this is what I have discovered works. Force, screaming, and threats do not work. The only thing that works with this kid is removal, repeating and talking about the limits, and I guess the main thing is to say, 'OK, school is a small sample of life, community life. If you can't operate within a classroom, you can't operate within society. If you can't operate within society, you will be dealing with authority in society. You will be dealing with the courts. Violence is going to lead you to nothing but trouble.' I always use examples when I talk to them like 'How would it be if every person reacted violently to every little thing that happened?' They have got to be made to sit down and see the stupidity of their behavior, and they don't see it easily. They fall back. These kids are used to being beaten. They are used to being belted around. They are used to being shut in the room and not let out. They are used to being grounded—no TV, no running around, or whatever. They react to the violent method of dealing with them by being violent themselves. I just think that the quieter approach, the commonsense approach for me, works a lot easier than any other. I don't believe in being violent or physical with them. By the time a kid is in the sixth grade, if you can't sit down and talk him out of a type of behavior, you are never going to beat it out of him."

This teacher was unusually eloquent in explaining why power conflicts with defiant students need to be avoided and power assertion is unlikely to be effective as a strategy for coping with them. She also had valuable suggestions to offer about ways to establish and maintain positive personal relationships with these students and to begin to socialize them toward recognizing their responsibilities and developing a more mature moral sense.

WHAT THE SCHOLARLY LITERATURE SAYS

Like aggression directed against peers, defiance of teachers is often part of a larger conduct disorder that includes various forms of hostility and aggression in childhood and develops into juvenile delinquency and criminality later. However, some children are not so much generally hostile and aggressive but rather resistant to attempts to impose control over them. They display what the American Psychiatric Association (1987) described as oppositional defiant disorder:

A pattern of negativistic, hostile, and defiant behavior without the more serious violations of the basic rights of others that are seen in Conduct Disorder. . . . Children with this disorder commonly are argumentative with adults, frequently lose their temper, swear, and are often angry, resentful, and easily annoyed by others. They frequently actively defy adult requests or rules and deliberately annoy other people. They tend to blame others for their own mistakes or difficulties. (p. 56)

Reeves, Werry, Elkind, and Zametkin (1987) found that conduct disorders and oppositional defiant disorders were common among children referred for assessment due to behavior problems, and that these two syndromes often occurred together or in combination with other syndromes such as attention-deficit/hyperactivity disorder. Of 108 children assessed, only 4 displayed a conduct disorder alone and only 2 displayed an oppositional defiant disorder alone. Horne and Sayger (1990) reported similar findings.

Patterns of oppositional and defiant behavior typically begin as reactions to ineffective parenting (Frick, 1994; Horne & Sayger, 1990; Patterson, 1982; Schaefer & Millman, 1981). The parents may either fail to articulate clear expectations and impose needed limits or else impose limits in ways that are authoritarian and punitive rather than instructive. Even more likely, the parents vacillate unpredictably between these extremes or else cannot agree and frequently come into conflict over expectations for the child. Vague and inconsistent expectations leave children unclear about how to please their parents, and to the extent that the parents are authoritarian, they erode their children's motivation to attempt to please them. The children begin to ignore parental wishes, to exploit parental inconsistencies, and to wear down the parents through oppositional behavior. This pattern of resistance to parents then generalizes to other adult authority figures, notably teachers.

Suggested Strategies for Coping with Defiance in the Classroom

Treatments developed for working with oppositional and defiant children have focused more on parents than on teachers. Typically they involve either or both of two strategies: teaching the parents to be more authoritative and less authoritarian or laissez-faire in their general socialization and discipline practices, and teaching them to use behavior modification methods that feature clear expectations and limits backed by contingent rewards and punishments. These approaches have achieved some success in changing both parents and children. They often feature a home–school collaboration component calling for the teacher to send home daily or weekly reports on the child's behavior at school, which the parents follow up by delivering or withholding reinforcements (Horne & Sayger, 1990).

Advice to teachers also typically features authoritative socialization practices backed by sanctions as needed. Good and Brophy (1997) emphasized the importance of remaining calm in conflict situations and resisting the natural tendency to get angry and strike back at defiant students with a show of force designed to indicate that they "can't get away with it." By pausing a moment before responding to defiance, you gain time to control your temper and think about what to do before acting, and during this time the mood of the defiant student may change from anger and bravado to fear and contrition. Good and Brophy went on to suggest that when you do act, act decisively but in a calm and quiet manner. If possible, remove the defiant student for a private conference or schedule one for later in the day. Perhaps say something such as, "I can see that something is very wrong here and that we'd better do something about it before it gets worse." Stating that the matter will be dealt with in a private conference tells the class that you will handle the situation yet does not humiliate the defiant student or incite further defiance. You can even afford to let the student "get in the last word," because you will take up the matter again later.

Defiant acts usually culminate a buildup of anger and frustration in the student, so it is a good idea to begin conferences with defiant students by inviting them to express their concerns and then hearing them out before you attempt to respond to the points they raise or move on to your own agenda. This will allow you to get the full picture, to gain time to think about what you are hearing, and, if feasible, to make a good start on improving the overall situation by agreeing to accommodate legitimate concerns. Then go on to deal with the conflict situation and perhaps to clarify other things as well (e.g., for students who wrongly complain of being picked on, point out that you are merely asking them to follow the same rules that all of your students are expected to follow). Make it clear that certain expectations are nonnegotiable and that related limits will be enforced, but also express concern for these students and a desire to treat them fairly. Incidents of defiance can be blessings in disguise because they bring smoldering problems out into the open. Well-managed conferences following these incidents should leave defiant students receptive to developing a more constructive relationship with you.

Advice about minimizing incidents of defiance typically boils down to consistent use of the principles for effective classroom management described in Chapter 1, and advice about responding effectively to those incidents that do occur typically boils down to consistent use of the socialization and conflict resolution principles described in Chapter 2. Swift and Spivack (1975) suggested that defiant students need (1) structure and clarity about expectations, (2) an improved personal relationship with the teacher, (3) opportunities to air their feelings about school demands,

(4) instruction in alternative ways of thinking and behaving, and (5) instruction in ways of handling emotional pressures and heading off loss of control. These authors also suggested inviting and, where feasible, accepting defiant students' suggestions about alternative ways for them to accomplish goals or for you to make their school experience more rewarding; making it clear that you are trying to help them succeed and not to embarrass or invoke sanctions against them; speaking of "our" rules rather than "my" rules or the school's rules; ignoring minor negativistic behaviors; reinforcing positive behaviors and accomplishments; holding periodic conferences in which you note their progress in addition to citing areas in need of improvement; and arranging for them to come to you and request a private conference or a calming time-out if they should begin to become upset and fear loss of control.

Along with emphasizing these same general principles, other authors have contributed additional comments (Blanco & Bogacki, 1988). Thompson and Rudolph (1992) suggested interpreting the goal of defiant behavior to the student ("Could it be that you would like to show me that you are boss?"). When asked during a helping-oriented conference (not during or immediately following serious conflict), such questions open the door for nonjudgmental discussion of the student's motives and for planning better ways of meeting needs. Also, look for patterns: If defiant incidents are concentrated in particular situations (e.g., when you publicly warn the student to finish an assignment quickly or you will impose some punishment), you might be able to change your behavior and help the student to handle these situations more effectively (e.g., by privately delivering a friendly reminder that time is running out).

Drawing from assertive discipline and other sources, McIntyre (1989) suggested ways to bring pressure on defiant students: Make it clear that assignments must be completed before the student will be allowed to do other things or go home, make a show of writing notations in your grade book when the student is uncooperative, tape-record the student during defiant incidents and discuss the tape later, ask the student to write a letter explaining his behavior to you and to his parents, and isolate him or send him to the office if necessary. However, McIntyre also cautioned against making threats that you do not intend to follow through on, and he emphasized various preventive and problem-solving strategies: Use private messages or prearranged signals to minimize public confrontations; during time-outs, have the student list or role play more appropriate responses to the situation and prepare to discuss these with you later; discuss with the student which forms of expression of anger are acceptable and which are not; make a special effort to get the student settled down each morning by greeting him positively and overlooking minor misbehaviors; avoid imposing sanctions without prior warning; and become aware of the student's personal values so that you can appeal to them in seeking to socialize him.

In summary, the literature is remarkably consistent concerning the reasons why children develop oppositional behavior patterns and the strategies that teachers might use for coping with them in the classroom. It recommends authoritative socialization practices and the kinds of crisis intervention and conflict resolution strategies emphasized in the first two chapters of this book. In addition, authors typically advise teachers to build good personal relationships with these students, avoid power struggles, and accommodate their needs to a degree by ignoring minor provocations and helping them to learn better ways of handling their feelings, while at the same time being clear in stating limits and consistent in enforcing them.

ANALYSIS OF INTERVIEW RESPONSES

A majority (59) of the teachers would confine their general approach to attempts to control or suppress misbehavior. The remaining teachers suggested one or more of the following approaches: appeal or persuasion (15), treating external causes (13), suggesting or training the student in ways of coping with (11) or solving (10) the problem, or providing a more encouraging and supportive environment (8). Of the 12 problem-student types studied, this was the only one for which more than half of the teachers mentioned only control or suppression approaches.

The most frequently mentioned specific strategies were threatening or invoking punishment (61) and proscribing against misbehavior (59). Other frequently mentioned strategies included attempts to inhibit through physical proximity, voice control, or eye contact (33); time-out for extinction or removal purposes (29); involving the principal or other school authorities to pressure or punish (28); involving the parents to pressure or punish (27); involving the principal or other school-based professionals to support or problem solve (25); and attempting to extinguish provocative behavior by ignoring it (25). Other strategies included prescribing desirable behavior (20), offering rewards for improvement (18), praising desirable behavior (15), involving the parents for support or problem solving (15), time-out to allow the student to calm down or reflect (14), appeal or persuasion attempts (14), minimal interventions (12), attempts to build self-concept (12), attempts to eliminate a perceived source of the problem (9), and involving peers to pressure or punish (8).

Concerning how they might interact with defiant students during conflict situations, 49 teachers would demand or force compliance using threat or physical manipulation, whereas 44 would try to avoid or minimize direct conflict. In addition or instead, 32 would communicate understanding of the students' angry feelings and willingness to allow them to ventilate those feelings; 24 would put the students on the spot by acting insulted or hurt, asking them to explain inappropriate laughter or back up unjustified statements, or waiting for an anticipated negative peer reaction or for the defiant student's bravado to give way to fear, confusion, or guilt; 18 would model calmness and self-control, such as by speaking in a controlled or soft voice; 8 would establish and maintain eye contact; and 6 would make polite requests rather than assert power more directly.

Most teachers mentioned strategies for preventing the frequency of conflict situations or for following up on them to minimize the damage that they produce. A majority (51) would make sure that defiant students knew what was expected of them and what the consequences would be if they did not comply (so that they would be less likely to feel picked on later if they failed to comply). In addition or instead, 27 would attempt to reduce conflict by ignoring minor provocations; 12 would schedule role playing group discussion, or other group activities relating to defiance; and 6 would clarify the rationales underlying their expectations in the hope that defiant students would begin to see them as reasonable and necessary.

Coding of the apparent motives underlying the responses indicated that 61 teachers expressed survival/self-concerns. In addition or instead, 48 focused on group functioning or safety, 30 on the welfare of the defiant student, 23 on the disruption of their instructional programs, 22 on personal irritation or anger, 9 on upholding school rules, and 7 on preparing the student for a better future life.

Concerning strategies rejected as ineffective, 45 teachers mentioned arguing, yelling, nagging, emotional outbursts, or physical force. In addition or instead, 29 mentioned ignoring or giving in, and 16 mentioned causing the student humiliation or loss of face.

Two lines of response were common among lower rated teachers. The first was notable for its lack of ideas about how to cope with defiant students except by bringing increased pressure to bear on them, especially by involving the principal. The second was associated with the notion that defiance is due to a desire for attention, particularly from peers, so it called for using minimal intervention or redirection strategies and attempts to reinforce more desirable behavior by praising defiant students when they were compliant or otherwise "good."

Higher rated teachers were unlikely to interpret defiance as mere attention seeking, and they had more ideas both about how to cope with defiant students and about strategies that would not be effective with them. Almost all of these teachers (as well as many lower rated teachers) mentioned clarifying rules, expectations, and consequences as a prevention or follow-up measure. In addition to or instead of "laying down the law" in this way, higher rated teachers were more likely to speak of attempting to help defiant students by appealing to their sense of fairness or making them see that they were not being picked on when asked to follow the same rules that applied to all students; by providing suggestions, indirect modeling, or training in better ways of handling conflict; or by involving classmates to provide support or assistance. Higher rated teachers also were more likely to be motivated by concern about preparing defiant students for a better future life, along with more commonly mentioned survival and control motives. Finally, higher rated teachers were likely to say that it is ineffective to be drawn into arguments or power struggles with defiant students, to nag them constantly, or to "lose your cool" and respond with emotional tirades or punitive overreactions.

Vignette: Roger

Roger has been fooling around instead of working on his seatwork for several days now. Finally, you tell him that he has to finish or stay in during recess and work on it then. He says, "I won't stay in!" and spends the rest of the period sulking. As the class begins to line up for recess, he quickly jumps up and heads for the door. You tell him that he has to stay inside and finish his assignment, but he just says, "No I don't!" and continues out the door to recess.

Before reading further, take time to think about how you might respond to this incident. Make notes about your ideas.

CSS Vignette Response Excerpts

Here is what four of the CSS teachers had to say.

A LOWER RATED TEACHER

"If they walk out my door, wherever they are going, when I say no, I have told them, 'Don't bother coming back. Just keep on going right to the office, because your records are coming right behind you.' I will not tolerate this type of behavior at all. Either you have set yourself up as the boss of your classroom or you are dead. The minute the kids get away with anything like walking out your door and not coming back when you tell them, you are dead. So this would go right down to the administration. My kids learn, very fast. They won't go to recess. I won't put up with them either; I have work to do. It is right to the office. You have to lay a strong line down, and they are going to test it. . . . Usually, first of all, they are chastised in the office, and then they will stay down there for the rest of the day. They will be back the next day, and they will know that they are going to miss whatever they were to miss before. They won't try it again. If they try it again, then the mother is called. There again, they are thrown right out to the office. Sometimes the fact that they are not allowed to come back to the group works out. There is nothing like sitting out your recess in the office. Or even worse than the office, put them in a second grade room . . . or, better, the kindergarten. Put them in the corner of the kindergarten to observe how kindergartners behave. They don't want to go back there again."

A HIGHER RATED TEACHER

"First of all, I would make sure that I am at the head of the line as the kids are marching out the door, which is a rule anyway. I would very quietly let the rest of the kids go out the door, and just as Roger came by me, I would take his arm, wouldn't squeeze it, no force, just take his arm and say, 'Roger, you and I have something to talk about.' I imagine he would be a little bit grumpy, and I would say, 'Let's just settle down. We'll discuss this sensibly, and when we have it discussed, we will decide whether you go outside or whether you sit down in your seat.' I would make sure the other kids were outdoors so I am not embarrassing him. Then I would take him back into the room that is now empty, sit down with him, and say, 'This paper has been done by everyone else in the class. You have to do this paper as well. I can't excuse you, because you don't have any special privileges around here. You are able to do it, or I wouldn't give it to you. I know that you might need some help, so I am right here. I will help you with it. We will get it finished, and if there is any remaining time, you can go out, and if not, then you just have to get your break time after school.' I would hope that would work. If it didn't work, if he said, 'I'm still not going to do it,' I would make sure that he stays in his seat even if he is not working on his paper, and I would say, 'The choice is yours. You can do it now, or you can do it after school.' If he didn't do it then, I would be a little bit aloof with him. After school, I wouldn't yell, and I wouldn't touch, but I would make sure that the paper is on his desk, pencil is on his desk, and say, 'Do you have every-thing you need to do the lesson? OK, I am going back to my desk to do my work. I'll check with you in about 15 minutes. If it is not finished at that time, then I guess we had better see either if the work is too hard for you or if we need to call your mom and talk about the work or the behavior.' In other words . . . I'd give him an out. I always do that. Give him the choice, are you going to let me help you solve your problem, or do we have to go to an outside source? Usual-ly, if you give the child an out, they will choose to do it on their own without bringing the outsider in . . . as long as they see you are not going to lose your temper and scream at them. I've discovered, with the type of kid we have here, you just can't use a whole lot of force because they are used to it. They are used to the belt. They are used to the beatings. They need a quiet, firm 'This is the way we do it. You have to do it. This is your responsibility, and I expect you to because you are the student that you are.' That usually works better than anything."

ANOTHER HIGHER RATED TEACHER

" 'Roger, hold it right there. You have two choices. If you walk out that door, you're not coming back in that door, or you're going to sit back down and do your work. We'll call your parents, and we'll send you to the office, whatever, but if you walk out, you don't walk back in. Either you sit right back and do your work or you're out. Good, you've got 10 problems, and we'll be back in 20 minutes.' I think that for kids who get very negative with you, you have to give them a choice. Never get yourself into a battle situation. As soon as they have you in a battle situation, they're in control. You've got to stay on top, and if you always give them two choices and neither involves you manhandling them or touching them, they then have control of their destiny. What they do is what they decided, and they can't turn around and say, 'Well, it was your fault.' Kids like this have a tendency to feel that they really didn't do anything, that it's all you. It begins to narrow their choices, and they see that the choice they make is their destiny."

ANOTHER HIGHER RATED TEACHER

"I would go out the door after him and say, 'Roger, come back here.' If he wouldn't come back, I would go get him. I would say, 'Roger, I am sorry but you cannot go outside today. You haven't been using your time wisely, and you're way behind in getting your assignments finished. Like it or not, you are going to have to stay in. If you and I cannot deal with the situation, then I am going to have to talk to your mother about it. If need be, I'll have to send the work home, and you'll have to do it at home. I'll simply ask that you give up things like TV to get it done.' [What would your rationale and goal be?] To try to help him understand that he needs to get serious about what he is doing at school and that unless the work is taken care of, then he really doesn't deserve (in a sense) the privilege or the free time to go outside, because he has already used up his work time by fooling around. He needs to understand that it's his responsibility. He needs to learn that he has the responsibility to himself, to me, to his parents, to do what he has to do in terms of his schoolwork."

The lower rated teacher was obsessed with winning a power conflict with Roger and thus responded in a purely authoritarian and punitive manner. In contrast, the three higher rated teachers all would attempt to avoid or minimize power conflict. They would insist that Roger fulfill his responsibilities and would be prepared to see that he suffered the consequences if he failed to do so, but they would communicate this to Roger in an authoritative rather than an authoritarian manner. They would emphasize to Roger that his behavior involves making choices, so that whatever happens as a result of the incident will happen because he forced it, not because the teacher was picking on him or initiated some action against him. Also, two of the three higher rated teachers would emphasize the importance of schoolwork and attempt to socialize Roger in addition to reestablishing control over his behavior in the situation.

Analysis of Responses to Roger

Only two teachers mentioned offering rewards to Roger, and surprisingly to us, none mentioned contracts. In contrast, all but four mentioned threatening or invoking some form of punishment. This usually involved reporting his behavior to the principal and/or the parents (63), although teachers frequently mentioned withdrawal of privileges, especially recess (46), keeping him after school (20), punitive isolation (17), or physical punishment (10).

By far the most commonly mentioned specific strategy for responding to Roger's behavior was threatening or invoking punishment (73). Other strategies included brief management responses (28), prescribing desired behavior (28), proscribing against misbehavior (19), delegating the problem to the principal or another school-based authority figure (18), attempting to develop Roger's insight (12), postponing dealing with the incident until later (10), and attempting to eliminate a perceived source of the problem (10).

All but 8 of the teachers would make behavioral change demands on Roger, but 58 of these would not accompany their demands with rationales. Among those who would include rationales, 18 would cite classroom or school rules, 12 would offer logical analysis linking Roger's behavior to its consequences, 8 would moralize, and 7 would make personal ("Do it for me") appeals.

In response to the immediate conflict portrayed in the vignette, 77 teachers would demand or force compliance by physically restraining Roger, demanding that he obey using a tone that implied punishment for noncompliance, or directly threatening serious consequences. In addition or instead, 34 would call for help from the principal or some other adult, 15 would require him to go to the office or to another classroom where he could be supervised while he worked on the assignment, and 12 would let him go out to recess rather than try to detain him forcibly, but follow up later concerning his defiant behavior or unfinished work.

Almost three-fourths of the teachers mentioned some form of follow-up socialization or problem solving. Of these, 37 would remind Roger that he has duties and responsibilities as a student — obeying the teacher, completing his assignments, putting work before play, etc.; 21 would explain that their responsibilities include giving Roger assignments and seeing that they are completed, or they would indicate that Roger's behavior is frustrating their attempts to instruct him successfully and thus cannot be tolerated; 21 would assume that Roger's defiant behavior is a symptom of some problem that is bothering him and would try to get him to talk about it and then follow up with problem-solving efforts; and 12 would make a point of showing Roger that he is being treated the same as everyone else.

Sixty teachers spoke of using physical force if necessary (and feasible), and 41 viewed the incident as a win–lose conflict. A majority spoke of involving Roger's parents, primarily to report his behavior in the expectation that they would pressure or punish him (53). Twenty-nine mentioned strategies for depersonalizing conflict by pointing out to Roger that they were merely trying to fulfill their job responsibilities, by apologizing for having to exert authority or expressing sympathy for his feelings, or by indicating that the rules applying to Roger apply to all of the students.

Almost half (46) of the teachers suggested that Roger's behavior represented a deliberate testing of limits to see how far he could go. Other suggested explanations included the notions that Roger is a generally negative person — trouble maker, bad apple, etc. (22); that he has an interpersonal problem in the home or peer group that is spilling over into the classroom (15); that he is immature or emotionally disturbed (14); that he has been exposed to inconsistent or otherwise ineffective discipline at home and thus has a problem dealing with authority figures (11); or that he is reacting because the work is inappropriate for him (7).

The responses of lower rated teachers tended to be confined to negative and controlling strategies. The only responses that were coded more frequently for these teachers than for higher rated teachers involved stating that Roger acts as he does simply because he is a generally bad person and suggesting unusual punishments in addition to or instead of more conventional ones.

Higher rated teachers were more confident that they would be able to elicit improvement in Roger's behavior, and they suggested more strategies for doing so. They recognized that Roger's pattern of defiant behavior was serious and needed to be changed, although they tended to attribute it to a bad disciplinary history or troubled interpersonal experiences rather than simply labeling him as an all-around bad person. In addition, the few teachers who suggested that inappropriate work might have been contributing to the problem tended to be higher rated teachers.

Along with exerting control over Roger, the responses of higher rated teachers tended to include positive elements such as improving his mental health or coping skills as a goal and suggesting or teaching better ways of handling conflict as a strategy. These teachers were more likely to accompany their behavioral change demands with rationales and justifications, particularly personal appeals or logical analyses. They also were more likely to include follow-up socialization or problem-solving efforts, most notably appealing to Roger's own self-interest in trying to make him understand why he needs to change his behavior. In the process, they would be more likely to point out to him that he is being treated the same as everyone else or take other steps to depersonalize conflict.

Vignette: Scott

Squirt guns are not permitted in the school. Scott has been squirting other students with his squirt gun. You tell him to bring it to you. He refuses, saying that it is his and you have no right to it. You insist, but he remains defiant and starts to become upset. Judging from his past and present behavior, he is not going to surrender the squirt gun voluntarily.

Before reading further, take time to think about how you might respond to this incident. Make notes about your ideas.

CSS Vignette Response Excerpts

Here is what four of the CSS teachers had to say.

A LOWER RATED TEACHER

"When Scott refuses and won't bring me the squirt gun, first I would tell him to put it in his desk, and if he did it one more time, I would take it, making sure he understands what I'm saying. *Once* or it is mine. If he does it again and he won't put it on my desk, I would probably cause a scene. I would go over and, if possible, get it out of his desk and take him with it and have him sit by my desk until I could get back to him and talk to him about it. I wouldn't give the squirt gun back once I had it unless we'd work something out where he could get it back or if he took it home and never brought it back to school again. [What would you say to him?] I'd talk to him about why he's squirting people and find out why he brought the gun to school, go over the school rules, no squirt guns and things like that. If squirt guns aren't permitted in school, he shouldn't have it there, so he should have it in his desk or he shouldn't be using it. I guess I wouldn't mind him having it in school as long as he didn't use it and if it didn't have water in it, but I'd just try to make it clear that he has to follow the rules of the school."

A HIGHER RATED TEACHER

" 'Scott, you know the rules of the school. There are no squirt guns permitted. So I would like your squirt gun right now. If it is impossible for you to give it up, which you know that you should, you'll have to go down to the office. The principal will explain the discipline code to you and that squirt guns are not permitted here. When your teacher asks you to give something up, it is necessary for you to do it right then.' My goal would be to get Scott to give up the gun as quickly and easily as possible and to try to keep him from becoming too upset. I would not struggle with him for it. If he refused without my having to take it by force, then I would simply remove him from the classroom and send him to the principal's office. The principal would probably at that point call his parents to tell them the situation. My rationale would be that I wouldn't want to have to use force because this would be more upsetting to him. I would try to remain very calm so as to try to keep him as calm as possible, but have him know that this is something he just cannot do and that he has to abide by the rules."

ANOTHER HIGHER RATED TEACHER

" 'Scott, would you bring the gun to me please? Either bring the gun to me or I'll go down to the principal and he can come in. You are going to be dealing with either me or the principal. You can choose to stay in here now and hand me the squirt gun, or you can step outside and take it to the principal, or the principal can come in here. I'm not going to fight with you for it. Those are your two choices.' I do confiscate all materials like that and will surrender it only to a parent. [What is your goal and rationale?] That depends on whether this is a one-time thing and he's just using a toy to give him some attention for that day. If he's a real serious problem, I would try charting him, try working with a counselor, and try working with his parents. If it was a one-time thing, my goal would be getting the squirt gun away from him so that everybody else wouldn't be getting wet. If it's a more long-range thing, if this is an attention-seeking behavior, my goal would be to give him positive attention, eliminate the negative attention, so that he would be feeling more positive and good about himself."

ANOTHER HIGHER RATED TEACHER

"First of all, I wouldn't tell him to bring the squirt gun to me. He is squirting the gun, and he knows he is not supposed to. I would go back by his desk and quietly take it out of his hands. I would never call out, 'You aren't allowed squirt guns in school. You bring it up to me right now!' I never would do that. You never put the kid on the spot. Never. No matter how bad they are. No matter what they are playing with. Make sure the other kids are involved in what they are doing in their lesson or whatever. Get back to the kid, and don't create a scene. If a scene starts, if he is defiant and he says, 'No, you can't take that,' I just say, 'You come with me. You bring the squirt gun with you, and we will go right out in the hall.' It always works. I had the most defiant kid in the world last year, and we never had a scene. I'd stand by his desk, and I would say, 'Let's go to the hall.' I never raised my voice. I eventually said, 'I am going to walk out there. If you don't come behind me, I am going to go straight down and get on the phone and call your mom, and she can come down. Now, do you want to see me and your mom or just me?' [And what would your goal and rationale be?] By going back and saying, 'I will take the gun or come with me to the hall,' I am eventually going to get the gun. My goal is to instill in him the idea that 'these are school rules, and you are going to have to abide by them. You are disturbing other people, and you can't do that. This is a classroom. You owe it to me because I am trying to teach you something, and you owe it to the other kids because they are trying to learn. You are going to have to abide by what everybody else has to.' He has got to have responsibility."

Unfortunately, the response of the lower rated teacher exemplifies the kind of disciplinary inconsistency that contributes to the development of oppositional and defiant behavior patterns. This response included powerful threats that the teacher did not really intend to follow through on, vacillation between authoritarian reactions and friendly negotiation of some kind of agreement about what would be allowed, and other inconsistencies that would tend to invite oppositional students to test the limits regularly and to feel picked on when they didn't succeed in getting their way. In contrast, the three higher rated teachers would respond in ways that minimized the public power conflict aspects of the situation and yet brought strong pressures on Scott to surrender the squirt gun. As with the higher rated teachers' responses to Roger quoted earlier, these responses to Scott would clarify that it would be his choice and his responsibility if the situation became more serious than it already was. In addition, two of these teachers spoke of following up the incident in ways that would address the larger oppositional and defiant behavior pattern.

Analysis of Responses to Scott

No teacher suggested offering rewards or contracts to Scott, but 85 spoke of threatening or invoking punishment. A majority (61) would arrange for punishment by informing Scott's parents and/or the principal about his behavior. In addition or instead, 39 mentioned various "other" punishments (primarily confiscating his squirt gun), 15 mentioned punitive isolation, and 8 mentioned physical punishment.

Three-fourths (74) of the teachers included punishment among the problem-solving strategies they mentioned. Other commonly mentioned strategies included management responses (34), proscribing against misbehavior (30), delegating the problem to another authority (27), prescribing desired behavior (24), attempting to develop Scott's insight into his behavior and its consequences (10), and attempting to eliminate a perceived source of the problem (6).

All but one of the teachers would make behavioral change demands on Scott, and a majority of these would include rationales or justifications for these demands, at least to the extent of citing classroom or school rules (58). In addition or instead, a few teachers would make personal appeals to Scott (7) or attempt to make him more empathetic with his squirting victims (11).

In responding to the immediate conflict, 57 teachers would physically take away the gun from Scott or demand that he turn it over using a tone that implied serious consequences for noncompliance. In addition or instead, 32 would summon help from the principal or another adult, 21 would tell Scott that they would have to inform the principal and/or call his parents if he did not comply, and 17 would shift to some compromise action that did not follow through on the demand that Scott turn over the gun but would require him to put it away somewhere and stop squirting classmates with it.

A majority (68) of the teachers mentioned some form of follow-up socialization or problem solving. Most of these (62) spoke of reminding Scott that his responsibilities as a student include obeying direct orders from the teacher or school rules against squirt guns. A few teachers would point out to Scott that he is merely being asked to obey the same rules that apply to everyone else (8) or that his behavior is frustrating their attempts to maintain a proper learning environment in the classroom (6).

Among teachers who spoke of forcing Scott to comply, 27 would immediately take the gun away from him without any further attempt to persuade him to surrender it voluntarily; 20 would repeat their request for the gun at least once, hoping to avoid having to take it but being prepared to do so if necessary; and 33 would not attempt to take the gun but would threaten a trip to the principal's office, a call to his parents, or some other serious consequence. Eighteen teachers viewed the incident as a win–lose conflict, but 34 would depersonalize it by noting that they were merely trying to fulfill job expectations and enforce school rules, apologizing for having to exert authority, expressing sympathy for Scott's feelings about surrendering his squirt gun, stating that they did not even want the gun but were required to take it away, or pointing out that the rules apply to all students and Scott is not being singled out for punitive treatment.

Of teachers who mentioned some form of parent involvement, 49 would threaten to call the parents (or actually do so) with the expectation that they would pressure or punish Scott, 20 would inform the parents that they (but not Scott) could come and pick up the gun if they wanted to, and 4 would engage in information sharing and problem solving with the parents.

Thirty-nine teachers viewed Scott as deliberately testing limits to see how far he could go. Other suggested explanations for his behavior included the notions that he is a generally negative person (22), that his behavior represents concern about losing his squirt gun rather than more personal defiance of the teacher (21), and that the behavior stems from immaturity or emotional disturbance (18).

Of teachers who could be coded on the issue of the return of Scott's gun, 33 would return it the same day, 25 would either keep it for several days or require that Scott's parents pick it up at the school, 4 would return it only at the end of the school year, and 17 would not return it at all.

Finally, the teachers' overall responses were rated as authoritarian/impersonal or personalized/individualized. These ratings indicated that 57 teachers would deal with the incident impersonally, as a case of rule enforcement, but 39 would show some concern about Scott's individual perceptions or feelings, try to find out what is bothering him, make sure that he understands the reasons for rules rather than just enforcing the rules, or in some other way show a willingness to deal with him as an individual.

Lower rated teachers were more likely to attribute the problem behavior to factors solely within Scott and to suggest an impersonal, authoritarian approach that emphasized enforcing school rules against squirt guns but did not include supportive behaviors, follow-up socialization or problem-solving strategies, or involvement of Scott's parents. They also were more likely to speak of immediately taking the gun away from Scott using whatever force was necessary, as well as to say that they would keep the gun permanently or destroy it.

Higher rated teachers were more likely to mention home or school interpersonal problems that might be contributing to Scott's defiant behavior and to speak of identifying and eliminating these problems if possible, and they were more likely to suggest that Scott might not be fully in control of his behavior. Their responses were more likely to include personalized elements and mention of a greater number of strategies, particularly supportive strategies, behavior modification strategies, and parent involvement strategies.

Accompanying this familiar pattern of differences, however, were some unexpected correlations. First, the lower rated teachers were more likely to speak of responding to Scott in ways that involved making appeals rather than merely laying down the law to him. They also were more likely to mention attempts to depersonalize the conflict and to remind Scott of their responsibility for enforcing school rules. Just as unexpectedly, the higher rated teachers were more likely to mention the following things that are usually associated with lower rated teachers: summoning help from the principal or some other adult at the school, emphasizing behavior modification strategies (mostly punitive isolation as an attempt to suppress defiant behavior), brief management responses, and certain threat/pressure strategies (global personal criticism and involving the parents to pressure or punish). Finally, even though the higher rated teachers were more likely to speak of informing the parents of Scott's misbehavior in the expectation that they would pressure or punish him, it was also the case that all four of the teachers who spoke of initiating information sharing and problem solving with the parents were higher rated.

What are we to make of this seemingly contradictory set of findings? Inspection of the intercorrelations among the various response alternatives suggests certain parallels between these findings and findings reported in Chapter 8 concerning teachers' responses to hostile–aggressive students. First, the seemingly positive strategies mentioned more often by lower rated teachers (appealing to Scott rather than laying down the law, explaining the teacher's rule enforcement responsibility, attempting to depersonalize the conflict) often were mentioned by teachers whose overall responses to the vignette appeared weak, confused, or conflicted. Most lower rated teachers spoke either of removing the gun from Scott personally and following through with punitive actions or else contacting the principal or parents with this goal in mind. The lower rated teachers who did not suggest these courses of action, however, tended to suggest appeasement or compromise strategies. Often their responses did not seem assertive or powerful enough to make Scott understand that he would need to change his behavior.

The other part of the story is that the seemingly counterproductive responses suggested by the higher rated teachers were embedded within a larger context of systematic attempts to elicit improvement in Scott's behavior. Higher rated teachers who spoke of summoning help from the principal or another adult in the school did so in the context of talking about developing an effective response to the problem, not in terms of delegating the problem to someone else. Those who spoke of bringing various forms of pressure on Scott through threat or delivery of punishment tended to mention supportive or instructional strategies as well. Except for the few teachers who mentioned global personal criticism, the threatening and pressuring strategies suggested by higher rated teachers tended to be appropriate as coercive components of larger approaches to solving the problem, not inappropriate emotional reactions or vengeful retaliations.

In summary, the higher rated teachers were more likely to suggest systematic responses to Scott's defiance that combined supportive problem-solving efforts with use of pressure or threat to enforce limits. In contrast, the lower rated teachers' responses tended to be either conciliatory but ineffectual or punitive but not likely to reduce Scott's tendencies to behave defiantly in the future.

COMPARISON OF RESPONSES TO ROGER AND TO SCOTT

General patterns of response to the two vignettes were similar, indicating that most teachers found the depicted defiant behavior to be very serious, unacceptable, and cause for relatively drastic action, often involving the principal and/or the parents. Correlations indicated that the higher rated teachers suggested more strategies in general and more supportive and socializing strategies in particular. They also were more likely to speak of following up with prevention or problem-solving strategies in addition to asserting control in the conflict situation. For Scott, this common pattern was complicated by a subpattern indicating that some of the lower rated teachers were more likely to suggest certain strategies that ordinarily would be advisable but in this case appeared counterproductive because they amounted to ineffectual appeasement or compromise instead of a more systematic attack on the defiance problem.

QUALITATIVE IMPRESSIONS AND EXAMPLES

Many teachers talked about defiance symptoms in detail, even making distinctions between subtypes of defiant students or noting clues that tell them how a defiant student is likely to behave that day. Yet such teachers often lacked strategies for motivating or persuading defiant students to become more cooperative. The most impressive responses construed the problem in a way that suggested positive action: The student hasn't learned to trust adults, so he needs a combination of caring and consistent demands that will build trust; he is seeking attention but in the wrong ways, so give him lots of attention but focus on reinforcing his positive behavior and accomplishments; or he is constantly testing limits because parental discipline at home is inconsistent, so be very clear in articulating your demands and consistent in enforcing them.

Several teachers said that they had learned not to get into protracted arguments with defiant students, because they are skilled at rationalizing and stretching out arguments indefinitely. These teachers recommended avoiding public confrontations but making it clear, without much discussion let alone argument, that the student would have to do what must be done, either now or at some later time such as recess or after school. These experienced teachers cautioned new teachers against feeling that they have to "win" all the time. Some simply noted that you can afford to "lose" a few, but most went on to say that it is a mistake even to think in terms of winning and losing.

Several teachers suggested that it is important to handle defiant students in your classroom and not send them to the principal, except perhaps for backup or to deal with particularly bad situations. Several added that the payoff for such determination is that these students begin to view you as one of the few adults who seems to really care about them, and they stay in touch with you in later years.

Teachers who mentioned the value of ignoring provocative (but not intolerable) behavior from defiant students often noted that you may have to put a stop to the defiant behavior if it starts to become viewed positively by classmates. As extra insurance against this happening, a few teachers spoke of defining the defiant student to the class as one who is having a problem controlling himself properly and defining the classmates' role as helping this student learn to do so by reminding him when appropriate, discouraging his provocations, etc.

Teachers suggested various methods for avoiding or minimizing conflict with defiant students. Several would respond with a measured approach, first giving them a chance to explain the situation if they felt that they had been treated inappropriately. If this invitation yielded a credible response, they would take it seriously and seek to negotiate a mutually agreeable solution. If it yielded only sullenness or further defiance, however, they would call the parents or invoke other control/pressure strategies. One teacher would minimize public power struggles by giving the defiant student a privately arranged signal that meant "We will walk away from the situation now but discuss it later." Another teacher would walk away from confrontations by saying, "When you are ready to feel better about the situation and discuss it with me, I will be glad to talk to you." During the later talk, she would insist that unfinished work be finished before the student left school that day but would suggest some alternative ways in which this might be accomplished. Another would avoid responding to the issue of whether or not she could make the student obey by simply repeating polite requests ("Would you please sit down?") in response to "You can't make me" statements. Another would invite students to use a suggestion box or write notes to communicate concerns or explain claims of unfair treatment.

One teacher had developed techniques for avoiding responding to provocations and frustrating any desire to see her become upset. Even if she knew that a student had deliberately flouted her directions, she would ask, "Didn't you understand the directions?" In response to "You can't make me do it!" she would say, "I don't like being yelled at" and walk away. Other teachers would attack the "You can't tell me what to do" attitude more directly. They would first assure both the student and the parent that they would never ask the student to do anything inappropriate. Then they would elicit parental reinforcement of the notion that the teacher is in charge in the classroom and the student is supposed to do what the teacher tells him or her to do.

Several teachers viewed persistent defiance as an indication of something wrong at home or in the student's personal life, and they often spoke of involving school counselors or social workers to look into the situation and perhaps arrange for psychotherapy. Others would make forceful efforts to help these students see the seriousness of their behavior and its consequences. One would videotape them during defiant outbursts and then view the tape with them later, to help them realize how they sound and look to others during these episodes. Another would schedule social problem-solving lessons that included role play of defiant behavior, assigning nondefiant students to take those roles so that the defiant students could observe and perhaps begin to see how they look to others.

Other teachers described less productive socialization scenarios that depicted themselves undercutting their own efforts. For example, one would try to get defiant students to see that they are in school to learn and that doing so is in their best interests. She spoke of demanding that the student stay in his or her seat and be quiet, but explained her demand as follows: "I don't care if you don't put a thing on your paper, but don't you get out of your seat, and don't you open your mouth. Other people are here to learn, and if you don't want to learn, I don't care." Another would stress to such students that they were headed toward school failure and eventual dropping out, which would leave them unqualified for good jobs. However, she anticipated that the student might say, "I don't care" and that she would respond by saying, "Well, if you don't care, then I don't care either."

In Big City, teachers working in the later grades identified defiance as a common and serious problem. Many, especially the lower rated ones, spoke less about working with defiant students than about building a file documenting their offenses in preparation for invoking discipline code penalties and getting them removed from their classrooms. Others spoke of the need to document instances of serious misbehavior because they had found that many parents did not believe or accept what they were told about their children.

In general, teachers working in the upper grades in Big City gave the impression that incidents of defiance and out-of-control behavior were far more serious among their students, and the home problems that led to them were far worse. Several spoke of students who had been abused or neglected at home. When they weren't acting defiantly, these students often withdrew to some quiet, sheltered place in the room or even went to sleep. The teachers typically described these students as having severe psychological problems that made them qualitatively different from normal students. These teachers spoke much more of physically punishing defiant students or expelling them from the classroom, although some were aware that these students had already been exposed to too much brutal treatment and that it had not been effective. This was true, for example, of the less effective teacher whose interview is quoted earlier in the chapter. Although she lacked systematic strategies for coping with defiant students, she was not authoritarian or punitive, and she hesitated to report incidents to parents if she feared that they would respond by beating their child.

The vignettes elicited frequent "You have to nip this behavior in the bud" responses, even from teachers who didn't ordinarily emphasize force or punishment. Several said that they would try to underscore the seriousness of the misbehavior by taking unusual steps in dealing with it: Require the student to initiate the call to the parent and explain what he did in his own words before turning the phone over to the teacher; if he has a father, require him to call the father rather than the mother; call right now even if the parent is at work (when the teacher ordinarily would call later); or demand that the parent come to the school right now to deal with the situation.

Several teachers would delay any attempt to talk to the student until both they and the student had calmed down. Some would verbalize this to the student directly. Others spoke of snubbing the student — refusing to make eye contact or respond to his advances, acting as if he weren't there — in the hope that this would make him anxious and bring him around. This hope doesn't seem well founded, except perhaps with the youngest students.

Many teachers, especially in Big City, would tell Roger that they are responsible for his behavior and must have his obedience if he is to stay in the classroom. With Scott, they would emphasize that they cannot teach when someone is causing the kind of disruption that he causes. In each case the basic message would be that the behavior simply cannot be tolerated, so it will become a matter for the office to deal with if the student doesn't respond to this warning. Many teachers, especially lower rated ones, would cite school rules in the process of delivering such messages. Lacking the confidence to make significant disciplinary decisions on their own initiative, they were reassured by the extra legalistic backing that the rules provided.

A couple of teachers suggested unusual methods of applying pressure to Roger. One would offer a "People's Court" solution: The teacher and Roger would go to the principal, plead their case, and agree to do whatever the principal decided ought to be done after hearing both sides. This teacher noted that students who know they have no case will not accept this challenge and, in the process, will become less belligerent. Another teacher said that if Roger continued out to recess without responding to her demands that he return, she would arrange for him to be taken to the office and would not allow him back into the room until she had spoken to one of his parents and received an apology from him for his behavior.

Most of the unique comments concerning Scott dealt with the handling of the squirt gun. In constructing the vignette, we depicted Scott as having a squirt gun rather than a genuine weapon because school district rules usually require teachers to report weapons immediately and take the student to the principal. We wanted to depict a situation that teachers ordinarily would handle themselves rather than refer to the office. The squirt gun incident proved effective for this purpose, and it revealed enormous variation in teachers' levels of tolerance. Some teachers would tell Scott to keep it in his desk but would not confiscate it unless he repeatedly disobeyed them. Others would confiscate it but give it back after school. Still others would confiscate it permanently, without prior warning. Most of the latter teachers seemed more concerned about making a point to the class (forbidden items should not be brought to school) than about the problems Scott might cause with the squirt gun.

A couple of teachers had suggestions about things to say to Scott that might make him more willing to surrender the squirt gun. One would say, "Don't let the gun get *you* in trouble." Another would make it clear to Scott that he would have to turn over the gun one way or another but that what happened to it would depend on his behavior. If he turned over the gun immediately and behaved well for the rest of the day, he might get it back after school, but otherwise, he might have to wait awhile or perhaps never get it back.

Some teachers would return the gun this time but tell Scott that they would confiscate it permanently if he brought it to school again. Several indicated that they would inform the parents of this warning following the initial incident, so that if it did become necessary to confiscate the gun, the parents would understand that Scott had ignored fair warning and was not being treated capriciously.

Responses to these vignettes underscored the value of having an aide or another adult in the classroom. Many of the Small City teachers spoke of turning the class over to the aide while they dealt personally with the defiant student. A few even said that they weren't sure what they would do if they didn't have an aide.

DISCUSSION

The views expressed by the higher rated teachers reflect the consensus previously noted in the research literature. That is, these teachers agreed that defiant students need consistent application of authoritative socialization principles for managing the classroom so as to minimize the frequency with which they become defiant in the first place, along with consistent use of no-lose strategies for resolving conflict when responding to the incidents of defiance that do develop. It also helps to establish positive or at least functional working relationships with these students; to ignore or at least avoid overresponding to their less serious provocations; and to supply various forms of support, instruction, or counseling that might help them to achieve better insight into their behavior and its consequences and learn to handle frustration and conflicts with authority figures more productively.

Although easy to summarize, these guidelines will be difficult for some teachers to implement, even if they should receive significant training in strategies and techniques. I refer here to teachers who are prone to powerful emotional reactions to defiance, typically either because they have become conditioned to responding to defiance in an authoritarian manner or because they fear that they will lose control of their class unless they "win" any and all public power struggles. If you are prone to such reactions, you will need to get help in working through and getting past them if you want to become able to deal with defiant students effectively.

Fear of losing control of the class is likely to subside as you gain experience, especially if you consistently implement the classroom management and conflict resolution strategies described in the first two chapters of this book. Authoritarian predispositions can be harder to change, however. If you find that you become infuriated when students disobey or defy you, to the point that you focus more on "teaching them a lesson" or "showing them who is boss" than on engaging in more productive efforts to assess and resolve the immediate problem and help the student learn to cope with such situations more effectively in the future, you may have to learn new emotional responses as well as new coping skills.

The most effective teachers view defiant students as children in need of socialization and assistance with authority problems and self-control, not as threats to their personal dignity or classroom authority. Their approach focuses on providing assistance designed to meet these needs. To the extent necessary, it also includes setting limits on unacceptable behavior and enforcing them by imposing appropriate penalties when students fail to respond. However, these coercive elements are components in a systematic socialization and behavior change effort, not blindly emotional or pointlessly punitive reactions.

In order to change significantly, defiant students need to learn new ways of responding to authority figures. You can help these students to develop a better appreciation of the fact that society builds schools, and people choose to become teachers, in order to provide students with needed knowledge and skills, that there are important responsibilities built into the teacher and student roles, that you are there to help your students learn and develop as individuals, and that when you establish classroom rules and procedures or issue directions to students, you do so in an attempt to help them learn, not merely to boss them around. A related message is that people of all ages and walks of life have responsibilities and behavioral expectations to fulfill, so it is important for defiant students to learn to cope with these pressures productively; if they persist in patterns of hostile and defiant behavior, they will put people off, get themselves in trouble, and ultimately lead unhappy and marginal lives.

While working to help defiant students to appreciate some of these understandings and begin to behave more productively, you may find it useful to supplement personal relationship and socialization approaches with behavioral treatments, particularly negotiation of contracts. Common sense suggests that contracts would be well suited to defiant students, and the research literature indicates that they have proved useful as components of a treatment package for oppositional and defiant students, especially when made part of a home–school collaboration effort. Yet none of the teachers we interviewed mentioned contracts, even though most were familiar with them. Perhaps they found defiance so threatening and unacceptable that they couldn't think straight at the time. In any case, I believe that contracts would be a useful adjunct to treatment for defiant students, not only because they are a proven behavioral intervention but also because they help communicate in a concrete way to defiant students that you want to see them succeed and are willing to help them learn to do so.

Whatever strategies are tried, it is essential that you avoid falling into the vicious cycles of hostility and rejection that so often develop between teachers and their defiant students (Brophy & Evertson, 1981). The key here is to resist the temptation to adopt authoritarian formulations of the problem (the student cannot be allowed to get away with that, he needs to be taught a lesson, etc.) and the power struggles that they lead to. Instead, develop more benign formulations (e.g., the child has not known consistency and needs to develop trust that you mean what you say, the child reacts poorly to imposition of structure and needs your help in learning to handle this better, etc.). Unlike authoritarian formulations, these benign formulations of the problem suggest constructive problem-solving directions that you might undertake as a start toward genuine solutions.

IV

Student Role-Adjustment Problems

P art IV contains three chapters on types of students whose behavioral characteristics make it difficult for them to act as students are expected to act in most classrooms. Chapter 11 deals with motoric hyperactivity, and Chapter 12 deals with attentional distractibility. Hyperactivity and distractibility often occur together and are considered parts of the same syndrome—attention deficit disorder (ADD) or attention-deficit/hyperactivity disorder (ADHD). However, the terms refer to different patterns of behavior and may appear separately. In any case, they would seem to require separate coping strategies even when they appear in the same student.

Distractibility refers to difficulty in sustaining attention to lessons or assignments and thus describes students' mental responses to visual and auditory input. In contrast, hyperactivity refers to patterns of excessive physical movement. *Distractible* students have difficulty meeting the requirements for sustained concentration that are built into the student role, whereas *hyperactive* students have difficulty meeting the requirements for physical control and quiet.

A third syndrome indicating difficulty in adjusting to the student role is immaturity. *Immature* students have difficulty working independently, caring for themselves and their belongings, and "acting their age." They may be overly dependent on the teacher for help with things that other students handle on their own, and they may be considered socially immature by their peers. Immature students are the focus of Chapter 13.

11

Hyperactive Students

yperactive students display the following characteristics: These children show excessive and almost constant movement, even when sitting. Often their movements appear to be without purpose. They:

1. Squirm, wiggle, jiggle, scratch
2. Are easily excitable
3. Blurt out answers and comments
4. Are often out of their seats
5. Bother other children with noises and movements
6. Are energetic but poorly directed
7. Excessively touch objects or people

What special strategies might you use to minimize such problems and help these students to function more successfully in your classroom? Before reading further, take time to think about this and make notes about your ideas.

CSS INTERVIEW EXCERPTS

Here is what three of the CSS teachers had to say about teaching hyperactive students.

A LOWER RATED TEACHER

"I have quite a few of these children in my room. I first give them enough work to keep them busy, and then if they finish and begin to squirm and wiggle, have to bring them, most of the time, up to

my desk and let them sit right next to me. Then I reward them. I sometimes give them extra duty to do or give them a treat. That takes care
of some of the moving around and excitable behavior. Then sometimes if they blurt out answers or anything, I make them stand aside
and not participate in the class with the other children. That usually
quiets them down because they hate isolation and that's the only thing
that will keep them still."

This teacher had several useful ideas for keeping hyperactive students
occupied and using rewards to reinforce or isolation to punish their behavior. Although brief, her response was better than those of many lower
rated teachers who emphasized embarrassment and punishment. However,
her response did not include any ideas about instructing or socializing
these students to help them learn to cope with their problem more effectively.

A HIGHER RATED TEACHER

"I see these children as really not causing a severe discipline problem.
In a lot of cases they don't realize that they are in perpetual motion.
They have a hard time controlling themselves. And I think that sometimes it's physiological. Sometimes it's due to activities that are going
on in the classroom. For instance, you can tell when they're more wigg-
ly or squirmy or have outbursts and so on. But I think it's really that
these children don't see themselves as causing much problem at all,
that they're very unconscious of all the activity they do. They don't
really concern me a lot in a way. They need to try to gain some control over these behaviors, but they are usually fun kids to work with.
I like to work with these kids. But I think that with these types of children a teacher has to be extremely flexible. Now one of the strategies that I use is to find out if there are some physical reasons for
this, if this child, right from the beginning, has always been hyperactive. Have they matured any, have they settled down any, has it gotten worse, or is it just the same? And I have had children on Ritalin.
This is one thing that sometimes does work, if it's given in the right
amount and the right way. But getting back to the teacher being
flexible — you have got to be able to give these children breaks. They
can't work very long at one time; you need to pace them. You can
tell as you are working with them just about how long they can go.
I have often let them work on the floor. Sometimes they can't work
sitting at their desk, but if they can sit on the floor, fine, they can
work. [Do you have a certain place in the room where the kids can
work?] No. Sometimes it's under the table. Once in a while I let them
go out in the hall. Sometimes these children can be alone out in the

hall, and they can get a lot done. They can get up when they want to, they can walk around, come back, sit down, and I have found that this works very well. And we don't have any problem. But there are places in the room where they can go too. They wouldn't go and sit on the floor by somebody else's desk or anything, but at the back of the room or at the front of the room, farther away from other children. But at least this gives them the ability to move around a little bit more, and I think you have to. You just can't make these children stay in their seats for so long. But it is important for them to know that there are times when they do need to be in their seats, for instance, if you are teaching the entire class, if you're having a discussion, where they're not getting up and walking over and getting a drink or just walking to the wastepaper basket. These kinds of children like to do this type of thing. But to try to get them to keep quiet for a little longer, I think you can either write a contract or give some kind of reward if you say, 'Well, let's see if you can work for half an hour today.' Maybe you would start with 15 minutes. And have them keep track of their time; have them write down when they start a project or start an assignment and when they get up or leave the assignment (if it's not a bathroom type thing, or if it's just a 'wander' or 'I need to move'). And see how long they can work, and see if they can keep improving this. Some children start and it's hard for them to work 5 minutes without getting out of their seat. And this does bother other children, and I think you need to discuss with the child the rights of the other children, that there are boys and girls in the classroom who have the right to work without people disturbing them. If you are walking around the room or if you're going over to somebody else's seat and talking to them, this is disruptive. 'I know you enjoy talking to people, *but* someone else has the right to work, and if they need it quiet, then you should respect that right.' I think you need to make sure that these children are getting a change in activity so that they're not working too long, that you give them a choice of working on one particular thing for, say, 15 minutes, then going and playing a learning game for 15 minutes, and then coming back to their work. I have found that this works very well. This is something that would be short-term. And if they still need to do that, then it can go on for a longer time. [You can do this without repercussions from the other children?] Yes. Most children get their work done and then have some choices. So they don't have any problem because they're not able to do the other things that these children are doing. In most cases they realize that they would rather have the child do that than be bothersome. And I found that I might have one or two children complain, but I would explain to them why. And they usually are quite understanding. I haven't had any problems with that. Another thing that I have done, and this is when I have had an aide, is excuse some of those children if I can see that they're tired of working or that they just are really overactive that day. And they have days when they are really more so than at other times. Have the aide take them down to the gym if it's available or outside if this can be arranged and just let them run. Don't give them a free recess but really take them and say, 'OK, let's run three laps around the gym or three laps around the playground' and then come back in. And another thing that I do usually with a whole class, but this helps those children too, when I see that they're tired of sitting, is stop and play Simon Says in between or just play a short game where everyone is involved. But just be aware and not go beyond their point of endurance. I think you can really cause a lot of your own problems that way.... Another thing, too, is to let them be leaders. For instance, in a game like Simon Says, I don't usually lead it but I let a child do it. And I might let a child who is more active lead, so that they have a longer time to do it. And then I try to give breaks between classes. If we're working in groups moving around, then there's no need for that, but if there is a longer stretch of time, then I let them get up, have a break, talk, go to the bathroom, and do whatever for maybe 5 minutes. And that seems to help too. I'm not too concerned about a child if they can't sit in their desk (some of them want to sit up on their desk, and sometimes I let them do that). I don't usually stop what I am doing to control all of this wiggling; I think you could spend a lot of time stopping and talking to these children. One of the things that I think they have to work on is the blurting out — not waiting to be chosen to say something. They don't want to put their hands up; they just want to talk out and interrupt. One of the best ways that I've handled this is working on the whole class again about carrying on discussions, how we take turns, and so on. Sometimes we have to go back to specifically raising a hand. But I have found it best if you are positive about that, for instance, 'I really like the way the people with their hands up are waiting until they're called on to say something.' Usually you can work this out pretty well with the child. I think in a lot of cases it's a matter of maturity (just growing up and developing). I think it is an important thing as a teacher — you've got to know how a child grows and develops and what they do at certain ages and be aware of that — to determine whether it's really a problem or just a developmental stage, and not to curtail things that are natural and normal for the child. Kids have to move around, and I think it's important that you plan activities where they can be involved with other children and where they *can* be noisy sometimes.... There are times when they have to learn, and we try to develop this. There are times when we can't have as much moving around; this is a distraction for some children, and you have to teach that too. But just gear activities for these children so that they do have that flexibility of moving around, because it's just the way it is for some of them. And I think if you try to put too tight controls on it, you're going to have other kinds of problems — more severe problems. So I wouldn't require absolutely no talking, no moving around, you can't get out of your seat, this kind of thing, or tie a kid in their seat or tape their mouth, nothing that is going to hurt or humiliate the child. I just can't see that at all."

This teacher suggested a rich package of strategies that included medication, minimizing physical constrictions and demands for sustained quiet sitting, behavioral contracting, self-monitoring, and curricular variety. She also mentioned socialization and instruction designed to make these children more aware of their behavior and its effects on the teacher and their classmates and to help them begin to develop better self-control. She not only did not get angry at hyperactive students but had learned to enjoy working with them — an attitude that by itself probably went a long way toward helping her do so successfully.

ANOTHER HIGHER RATED TEACHER

"All children at one time or another need to move. A child's physical development is such that movement is a part of their whole daily life, whether they're sitting in a seat, studying something out of a book, or whatever. Many children just find it comforting to move a leg or wiggle a hand or tap a pencil top. If a child shows signs of extreme fidgeting, squirming, wiggling, or what have you, I will draw his attention to this. Then I would probably have him checked out to see if he wasn't a hyperkinetic child and if one of the services available to the school could help him out. Some of the things that I'll have a child do, when I do deal with it myself in the classroom, is if he is wiggling, I'll say, 'Wiggle 10 times for me and then stop for 5 minutes' or 'I want you to tap your pencil 20 times and then be quiet after that for a while.' I'll have him actually do the behavior, and then I'll see if he can stop doing it. Very often children don't realize what they're doing. I do think it's important if you have a hyperactive child to give him every opportunity possible to get out of his seat. I don't care if it's to go get a pack of papers for you down in the IMC [Instructional Materials Center], if it's 'Why don't you take and sharpen these 30 pencils for me?' but some activity that is going to direct his energy into something beneficial rather than just squirming. If he has a hand problem with fidgeting, I will have him clasp his hands together, or I may go over and hold his hands and say, 'Why don't you just hold my hands until you can calm down a bit?' If they are foot tappers, I might have them hold their feet flat on the floor for about 1 minute, just to see if they can hold it there. If they are a child who does something like blurting out answers or making comments continually, I'll say, 'Would you please raise your hand?' or 'Why don't you, if you're going to give an answer, give me some kind of indication rather than just blurting it out.' A child with a short attention span needs to be given activities that are broken up into very small segments and then gradually built on. His attention in a very short segment might be gotten by separating him from the rest of the room by putting up a room divider. This wouldn't be a punishment situation but would be explained to him like 'I want you to sit back here so that you can focus.' Study cubicles are very handy to have because they have wings on either side that keep a child from glancing about too much. Very often what I might do is just have a child who is having a tough time come up and work with me by my desk or wherever I happen to be working."

This teacher had developed informal diagnostic procedures to find out if her hyperactive students could control repetitive movements, and she would have them practice self-control exercises such as clasping their hands together and holding them still. In addition, she mentioned several other strategies for reducing stress on hyperactive students and helping them to develop greater control over their behavior.

WHAT THE SCHOLARLY LITERATURE SAYS

Teachers have always recognized motoric hyperactivity as a behavioral syndrome that impedes certain students' adjustment to the classroom. These students are commonly described as inattentive, easily distracted, impulsive, or hyperactive. Through the years, they also have been labeled with more technical terms such as minimal brain damage, minimal brain dysfunction, developmental hyperactivity, hyperkinetic impulse disorder, attention deficit disorder (ADD), and attention-deficit/hyperactivity disorder (ADHD). Evolution in terminology has reflected evolution in ideas about the underlying causes of the symptoms: physical damage to parts of the brain that mediate behavioral organization and self-control, failure of these brain structures to function normally even if not physically damaged, inefficient filtering of sensory input resulting in overstimulation of the cortex, developmental immaturity in maturation of control mechanisms, side effects of food additives such as dyes or preservatives, underarousal or underreactivity to stimulation, and inappropriate child rearing, among others. Even though hyperactivity has become the most heavily studied childhood behavior disorder, controversies continue concerning such issues as what its various manifestations should be called, whether these are all part of a single syndrome or are better considered as separate disorders, and what the causal mechanisms might be (Barkley, 1990; Fouse & Brians, 1993; Frick & Lahey,1991; Friedman & Doyal, 1992; Henker & Whalen, 1989; Lerner, Lowenthal, & Lerner, 1995; Pellegrini & Horvat, 1995).

It has long been known that attentional distractibility and motoric hyperactivity often go together, but opinions about the nature of this relationship have waxed and waned. Prior to the 1970s, attention focused on the more obvious and immediately troublesome hyperactivity problem, with distractibility treated as secondary. During the 1970s, however, evidence was developed to suggest that distractibility not only was part of the larger hyperactivity syndrome but was the key to it. In the third edition of the *Diagnostic and Statistical Manual of Mental Disorders* (DSM-III; American Psychiatric Association), the distractibility aspect was featured in the syndrome label and the diagnostic criteria for what was called attention deficit disorder. ADD was described as a disorder that might appear with or without associated hyperactivity, beginning before the age of 7 and peaking between 8 and 10. Three sets of primary symptoms were noted: *inattention* (often fails to finish things started, doesn't seem to listen, is easily distracted, has difficulty concentrating on school tasks or sticking with play activities), *impulsivity* (often acts before thinking, shifts excessively from one activity to another, has difficulty organizing work, needs a lot of supervision, frequently calls out in class, and has difficulty waiting turn in games or group situations), and *hyperactivity* (excessively runs about or climbs on things, has difficulty sitting still or staying seated, fidgets, moves about during sleep, is always "on the go" or acting as if "driven by a motor").

The ADD diagnosis was applied to quite different types of children. Those whose symptoms included hyperactivity (ADD + H) often displayed additional symptoms as well, most commonly achievement problems at school and hostile–aggressive social behaviors that caused them to be rejected by their peers. Distractible children whose symptoms did not include hyperactivity (ADD − H) often displayed the opposite pattern, being inactive, lethargic, or daydreamy.

Since 1980, researchers have sought to clarify definitions and produce more interpretable findings by making additional distinctions among students who fit the ADD diagnosis, such as by distinguishing the pervasiveness of the problem or the types of situations in which it is observed, the degree to which aggression or other associated symptoms are present, or the degree to which the problem responds to various medications. This work has clarified that more purely hyperactive children show problems with attention and overactivity that are associated with signs of developmental and neurological delay or immaturity, whereas more purely aggressive children show the behavior patterns and associated family background factors described in Chapter 8. It is now clear that some of the family dysfunction or ineffective child-rearing factors formerly thought to be causes of hyperactivity are actually associated with aggression and other conduct disorders. Such family backgrounds are commonly seen in ADD students who are also aggressive, but not in ADD students who are not.

The American Psychiatric Association published a revision of its manual (DSM-III-R) in 1987. At that time, the name for the disorder was changed from ADD to ADHD, the three separate lists of symptoms (for inattention, impulsivity, and hyperactivity) were replaced by a single list, and the subtype previously known as ADD − H was removed from the ADHD syndrome and placed in a separate category called undifferentiated ADD. ADHD was grouped with two other behavior disorders (oppositional defiant disorder and conduct disorder) within a larger category known as the disruptive behavior disorders, in view of their substantial overlap among clinic-referred children (Barkley, 1990).

DSM-III-R (American Psychiatric Association, 1987) called for an ADHD diagnosis if children exhibited at least eight of the following characteristics over a period of at least 6 months:

1. often fidgets with hands or feet or squirms in seat . . .
2. has difficulty remaining seated when required to do so
3. is easily distracted by extraneous stimuli
4. has difficulty awaiting turn in games or group situations
5. often blurts out answers to questions before they have been completed
6. has difficulty following through on instructions from others . . .
7. has difficulty sustaining attention in tasks . . .
8. often shifts from one uncompleted activity to another
9. has difficulty playing quietly
10. often talks excessively
11. often interrupts or intrudes on others . . .
12. often does not seem to listen to what is being said to him or her
13. often loses things necessary for tasks or activities at school or home . . .
14. often engages in physically dangerous activities without considering the possible consequences . . . (pp. 52–53)

This change in terms and definitions was controversial. Some researchers favored the 1980 DSM-III formulation that linked distractibility and hyperactivity within the single ADD syndrome and emphasized attention deficits in describing it. Others believed that the old ADD — H syndrome (renamed Undifferentiated ADD) should be considered a separate disorder and that the ADHD syndrome introduced in DSM-III-R in 1987 was helpful in emphasizing hyperactivity at least as much as attention deficits and in classifying ADHD with conduct disorders. The latter investigators usually acknowledged some neurological or maturational basis to hyperactivity but also emphasized motivational aspects. Some suggested that ADHD arises out of an insensitivity to the consequences of behavior—reinforcement, punishment, or both (Barkley, 1990). Others emphasized that the problem is at least in part socially defined: Whether a behavior pattern is called hyperactive and considered a problem depends not only on factors within the child but on the task performance demands or social expectations built into the situation.

The category labels were changed once again in the fourth edition (DSM-IV) of the American Psychiatric Association's diagnostic manual (1994). To provide continuity with DSM-III-R, DSM-IV has retained the ADHD label for the overall diagnostic category and continued to group it with disruptive behavior disorders. However, it lists three subtypes of ADHD disorders: (1) a predominantly inattentive type that displays at least six of nine listed symptoms of inattention; (2) a predominantly hyperactive-impulsive type that displays six or more of nine listed criteria of hyperactivity and impulsivity; and (3) a combined type that meets the criteria for both of the first two types. Thus, the new manual acknowledges that the ADHD diagnosis may apply to children who display symptoms of inattention, hyperactive–impulsive behavior, or both. It acknowledges a connection between the two sets of symptoms but does not address issues concerning the nature of their relationship or suggest that one is more fundamental or important than the other.

DSM-IV (American Psychiatric Association, 1994) calls for an ADHD diagnosis if the following symptoms of hyperactivity–impulsivity have persisted for at least 6 months to a degree that is maladaptive and inconsistent with developmental level:

Hyperactivity
(a) often fidgets with hands or feet or squirms in seat
(b) often leaves seat in classroom or in other situations in which remaining seated is expected
(c) often runs about or climbs excessively in situations in which it is inappropriate (in adolescents or adults, may be limited to subjective feelings of restlessness)

(d) often has difficulty playing or engaging in leisure activities quietly
(e) is often "on the go" or often acts as if "driven by a motor"
(f) often talks excessively

Impulsivity
(g) often blurts out answers before questions have been completed
(h) often has difficulty awaiting turn
(i) often interrupts or intrudes on others (e.g., butts into conversations or games) (p. 84)

Whatever its official label, it is clear that hyperactivity has been diagnosed with increasing frequency in recent years. Sources published prior to 1980 usually indicated that 3 or 4 percent of the children received this diagnosis. Sources published in the mid-1990s suggested a figure of 6 percent: 9 percent for boys and 3 percent for girls.

Suggested Strategies for Coping with Hyperactive Students

Despite the diversity in points of view about the nature and causes of hyperactivity, recently published reviews show a great deal of agreement in summarizing the research on treatment approaches (Barkley, 1990; DuPaul & Stone, 1994; Fiore, Becker, & Nero, 1993; Friedman & Doyal, 1992; Gomez & Cole, 1991; Henker & Whalen, 1989; Loney, 1987; Matson, 1993; Rosenberg, Wilson, Maheady, & Sindelar, 1992; Whalen & Henker, 1991). The consensus is that three main approaches are commonly recommended: *medication,* which produces the most powerful and reliable effects; *behavioral treatments,* which have proved useful as a supplement to medication; and *cognitive-behavioral treatments,* which appear ideally suited to the needs of hyperactive students but so far have produced mostly disappointing results.

The most prevalent therapy for ADHD, and also the most efficacious and carefully studied, is stimulant medication—typically methylphenidate (Ritalin). A "review of reviews" (Swanson et al., 1993) indicated that although different reviewers emphasized different aspects of the findings and developed different conclusions, there is a common core of findings that turn up repeatedly. First, in about 75 percent of the cases, treatment with stimulant medication produces immediate and dramatic reductions in hyperactive behavior and improved performance on tasks requiring concentrated attention. These effects may be enhanced by changed expectations in the children themselves, their parents, and their teachers, but they are not explained by expectation effects. Careful double-blind studies have shown that teachers notice much more improvement in and respond much more positively to hyperactive students taking stimulant medication than to hyperactive students taking placebos.

The reviews also produced consensus on two important qualifications of these positive findings. First, it is not possible to predict in advance which children will respond positively to stimulant medications, so experimentation is required to determine which (if any) medication is ideally suited to a particular student, as well as to adjust dosage levels (not only to ensure sufficient dosage to achieve effectiveness but also to limit dosage to minimize sleep problems, loss of appetite, or other side effects). Second, whereas stimulant medication produces dramatic reductions in short-term hyperactive behavior in the classroom, it has only negligible effects on long-term academic achievement and prosocial behavior.

Reviewers who are physicians, psychologists, or educators often criticize the scare tactics used by authors writing for the general public to advance a particular policy agenda. In the opinion of the reviewers, these authors exaggerate the degree to which medication is prescribed for schoolchildren, invent or exaggerate side effect problems, and falsely suggest that medication is the only form of treatment emphasized by educational and mental health professionals. These reviewers defend medication as effective treatment and suggest that undesirable side effects can be minimized or avoided altogether. However, they also acknowledge that although stimulant medication will reduce impulsive and hyperactive behavior and increase potential for task concentration, it will not improve academic skills, motivation to learn, or general intellectual or moral functioning. Thus, they describe it as a component of comprehensive treatment for hyperactivity but not as the whole treatment.

Behavioral treatment is commonly recommended as a second component: Select behaviors that you want to change, and seek to shape improvement in them through contracting and related reinforcement-based methods. Certain qualifications on the usual behavioral approaches are commonly suggested for teachers working with hyperactive students. First, because of their attention deficits, you need to be unusually clear and specific in stating behavioral goals to these students, specifying the contingencies between behaviors and consequences, and reminding them of these contingencies when following through on them. Second, hyperactive students appear to require response cost approaches that include punishment for misbehavior in addition to reward for desired behavior. Within what is reasonable to expect of the child at the time, it appears necessary to state firm limits on hyperactive behavior in the classroom and punish misbehavior if necessary using time-out or withdrawal of privileges. You also may find it necessary to deliver consequences more immediately and frequently to hyperactive students, because they may not respond as well as their classmates to delayed rewards or partial reinforcement schedules. To the extent that you do use negative consequences, it is important to announce and apply them using what Rosén and colleagues (1984) called a "prudent" approach: Speak calmly, be concrete in stating behaviors and contingencies, and be consistent in following through. These authors found that an "imprudent" approach (loud, emotional, inconsistent) only made the problem worse.

The third widely discussed treatment for hyperactivity is the cognitive-behavioral approach (cognitive strategy training). This appears to be ideally suited to the needs of hyperactive students because it involves training them in skills such as coming to attention and settling into a task, concentrating on task-relevant stimuli, keeping aware of goals and strategies while engaging in the task, budgeting time, delaying gratification, and inhibiting inappropriate responses — in general, teaching them how to engage in cognitively demanding tasks by accessing needed motives, goals, and strategies.

Unfortunately, applications of cognitive strategy training with hyperactive students so far have produced only unsatisfactory or at best mixed results. Perhaps these students' attentional deficits do not enable them to learn cognitive strategies systematically enough to make the technique effective, or perhaps effective approaches have not been developed yet. The search continues because the relevance of strategy training to hyperactive students' needs suggests that these efforts may ultimately pay off. For information about cognitive-behavioral interventions with hyperactive students, see Goldstein and Goldstein (1990); Hughes (1988); Rosenberg and coworkers (1992); or Whalen, Henker, and Hinshaw (1985). For a particularly detailed treatment that includes a manual for planning and carrying out these interventions, see Braswell and Bloomquist (1991).

Popular books and articles on hyperactivity often recommend a fourth approach to treatment: avoiding or limiting the child's exposure to food additives, fluorescent lighting, bright colors, sugar, or other substances described as toxic to children in general or to hyperactive children in particular. Unfortunately (because it would be nice to see a complex problem have a simple solution for a change), research does not support these ideas. The consensus of current experts is that hyperactivity (ADHD) is a developmentally handicapping condition, generally chronic, with a propensity for hereditary predisposition but with degree of severity and presence of associated symptoms significantly affected by environmental factors, especially familial factors. Stimulant medication augmented by behavioral and possibly cognitive-behavioral treatment can be expected to produce notable improvements in behavioral symptoms and more modest improvements in academic performance in the short term, but as yet nothing has been discovered that will reliably produce significant improvements in long-term intellectual and social competence.

Advice written specifically for elementary teachers usually also begins with discussion of medication, behavioral treatment, and cognitive-behavioral strategy training. Concerning medication, you are usually ad-

vised to contact the parents of hyperactive students to assess their awareness of the hyperactivity problem and find out if their child is being treated
for it (if so, collaborate in seeing that the child takes his or her medicine
as prescribed; if not, suggest medical assessment if the problem is severe
enough to warrant it).

Collaboration with the home is also recommended if a behavioral
contract system is going to be used. This involves working out a plan with
the parents and the child, and then following up by sending home daily
or weekly progress reports and perhaps academic activities for the parents to do with the child as well. Recommended cognitive strategy training includes all of the commonly taught academic task engagement and
study skills, with emphasis on behavioral self-control, maintaining concentrated attention, and other skills that are poorly developed among
hyperactive students. These students may also need tutoring in reading
and other basic skills if their problem has impeded their academic achievement to the extent that they are unable to engage in independent learning at a level expected of students in their grade.

Several common themes appear in suggestions to teachers about instructing hyperactive students. One is "Don't let these kids turn you off
so that you begin to treat them inappropriately." The disruptions caused
by hyperactive students can be exasperating, making it difficult for you
to be welcoming and supportive with them (especially if, as often is the
case, they are also hostile–aggressive or defiant). Hyperactive students feel
less accepted by their teachers and feel that they are treated with nagging
demandingness (Peter, Allan, & Horvath, 1983). When interviewed as
adults, they remember feeling misunderstood and rejected by their
teachers and often by their classmates, constantly being criticized for doing things that they were not even aware of doing, let alone doing deliberately (Weiss & Hechtman, 1986).

Kirby and Kirby (1994) urged you to keep aware that ADHD children's
problems are rooted in neurological and physiological differences, that
they often do not know how to control or regulate their behavior and
are bewildered by it, and that the fact that they often display normal attention and self-regulation for short periods of time does not mean that
they could do it all the time "if they really wanted to." They also suggested
that you help these children understand their condition (i.e., they are just
as capable as other students, but their attention wanders and they sometimes miss things because of it, so that what they retain may resemble
memories of a television program that was interrupted several times by
transmission interference).

Karlin and Berger (1972) recommended that you help these students
to understand the undesirable effects that their behavior has on you and
their classmates. Without blaming them, make them realize that classroom

disruptions take away time from instruction and that hyperactive behavior (especially if aggressive) turns off peers and impedes the formation of friendships. Establish the understanding that you and the child will work on these problems together.

An ERIC digest put together by the Council for Exceptional Children (1989) summarized much of the advice commonly given to elementary teachers for working with hyperactive students. One set of suggestions focused on establishing the proper learning environment: Seat these students near your desk but include them as part of the regular class seating; place them in front with their backs to the rest of the class, so that other students are out of their view; surround them with good role models, and encourage peer tutoring and cooperative learning; don't place them near air conditioners, high traffic areas, heaters, doors, or windows if these are distracting to them; provide a predictable structure, and prepare them in advance for transitions or changes in schedule; create a stimuli-reduced study area that they can have access to when they need it; and encourage their parents to set up an appropriate study space at home, with set times and routines established for study, parental review of completed homework, and periodic notebook or book bag reorganization.

Suggestions for instructing hyperactive students included the following: Maintain eye contact during verbal instruction; use predictable instructional routines; make directions clear and concise; simplify complex directions and avoid multiple commands; make sure that they understand what to do before releasing them to begin the task; if need be, repeat the instructions in a calm, positive manner; help them to feel comfortable seeking assistance when they need it; shape them gradually toward more independent functioning, but bear in mind that they may progress more slowly and need more help for longer time than most students; and, if necessary, require them to keep a notebook in which they record daily assignments, and check them off as they complete them. Additional suggestions regarding giving assignments included these: Give only one task at a time; monitor their work frequently, but project a supportive attitude; modify their assignments if necessary to capitalize on their strengths and work on their weaknesses; make sure that your tests assess knowledge and not attention span; minimize their frustrations; and give them extra time to complete tasks if they need it.

Suggestions for modifying behavior and enhancing self-esteem involved both providing supervision and discipline and providing encouragement. To provide supervision and discipline, remain calm, state the rule infraction, and avoid debating or arguing with the student; have preestablished consequences for misbehavior; monitor behavior frequently and administer consequences immediately; enforce class rules consistently; make sure the discipline fits the crime; avoid ridicule and criticism; and avoid publicly reminding students on medication to "take their medicine." To provide encouragement, reward more than you punish, praise desirable behavior and accomplishments, change rewards if they are not effective in motivating behavioral change, find ways to encourage these children, and teach them to reinforce themselves and appreciate the progress they make.

Sandoval (1982) interviewed teachers and developed an overlapping list of suggestions: medication and behavioral treatments; increasing their opportunities for movement around the classroom or engaging them in substitute outlets such as physically demanding exercise; providing study carrels or other stimuli-reduced spaces for working; providing increased structure in the school day through a predictable schedule, shorter lessons that call for sustained concentration (at least initially), and periodic breaks where students can move around the room, go on errands, or take physical exercise; modeling and teaching self-control strategies using cognitive-behavioral methods; helping these students to realize that, despite their difficulties in attention and self-control, they have a responsibility to work on the problem and improve; setting and following through on clear limits on unacceptable behavior; and creating an emotionally supportive environment.

The same general lines of advice can be found in other sources on teaching hyperactive students (Blanco & Bogacki, 1988; DuPaul & Stoner, 1994; Fairchild, 1975; Fouse & Brians, 1993; Goldstein & Goldstein, 1990; Lerner, Lowenthal, & Lerner, 1995; McIntyre, 1989; Safer & Allen, 1976; Weaver, 1994). Along with the strategies already mentioned, these sources include the following suggestions: In setting behavioral goals, emphasize behaviors that support learning (be in class and in your seat on time, have your materials ready, pay attention to lessons, listen to and follow directions, keep at your work until it is finished), not just behaviors to avoid (e.g., don't yell or run around the class); use these students as messengers or assign them other helper roles that involve physical movement; allow them to "run it off" when it seems necessary, but see that they don't exhaust themselves on the playground during long recess periods; arrange some sort of signal to communicate quickly and privately to these students that they need to settle down or get to work; after getting the class as a whole started on an assignment, check with hyperactive students to make sure that they have understood the instructions; maintain proximity to these students much of the time, both as a subtle reminder to them of what they are supposed to be doing and as a way to increase your availability if they need help; if awareness is a problem, arrange to have some of your classes videotaped with (unpublicized) focus on hyperactive students, and then view the tapes with them to discuss their behavior and its effects on other people in class; schedule tasks that demand concentrated attention mostly in the morning, because hyperactivity problems tend to build during the day.

Pfiffner and Barkley (1990) reviewed the literature on removing distractions from the classroom and concluded that — while there is no need to remove colorful pictures, posters, clothing, etc. — it is a good idea to provide hyperactive students who seem to need it with minimally distractive work environments — send them to a study carrel or let them sit in a corner or facing a wall when they are working on assignments. Boyd and Hensley (1982) studied the effects of 20 minutes per day of running, calisthenics, or both on the ward behavior of institutionalized hyperactive children. They found large reductions in observed hyperactivity among students who ran, but not among those who engaged in calisthenics but did not run. This suggests that engaging in calisthenics within the classroom may not be sufficient and that hyperactive students may need to "run it off" literally in order to benefit from exercise breaks.

Finally, Reid and Borkowski (1987) found that hyperactive students who received cognitive-behavioral self-control training plus attribution training showed more reductions in hyperactive behavior and increases in self-control in the classroom than students who had received the self-control training but not the attribution training. The attribution training featured a "coping model" who made mistakes but then demonstrated (using think-aloud methods) how one maintains a goal-oriented focus and overcomes these mistakes to complete tasks successfully (see Chapter 4). Thus, if hyperactive students' problems have been compounded by learned helplessness or other failure syndrome symptoms, they may need attribution training in addition to more conventional cognitive strategy training.

ANALYSIS OF INTERVIEW RESPONSES

The teachers viewed hyperactivity as a problem that could be only partially controlled rather than completely eliminated. A minority favored or at least included control/suppression strategies that would involve pressuring or punishing hyperactive students, but most spoke of helping them control their problem by accommodating to their needs or by arranging for them to receive medication.

Commonly mentioned specific strategies included attempts to eliminate the source of the problem (42); minimal intervention or redirection (33); proscribing against undesired behavior (33); reward (31); inhibiting through physical proximity, voice control, or eye contact (30); prescribing desired behavior (25); changing the task (25); involving the parents for support or problem solving (23); changing the student's physical environment or using isolation techniques (20); involving outside medical or mental health professionals (19); threatening or punishing (18); involving school-based authority figures or professionals to support or problem solve (16); praise (14); appeal or persuasion (13); group work (10); time-out for extinction or removal reasons (10); attempts to extinguish by ignoring (9); providing support through physical proximity or voice control (8); time-out to calm down or reflect (7); and involving peers to provide support (7). Again, these strategies concentrated on supportive or neutral forms of intervention designed to help the hyperactive student become more aware of and gain more control over hyperactive behavior, rather than on threatening or pressuring.

Most teachers expressed minimal emotional reactions or resignation to hyperactivity, rather than exasperation or anger. The majority (62) believed that they could help the child achieve at least limited control over the problem. Minorities believed that little or nothing could be done and the teacher had to adapt to the problem (12) or that the child could learn to achieve full control and essentially eliminate the problem (19).

Forty-six teachers would allow hyperactive students to move around (do exercises or take a walk or run around the building) when they seemed to need to do so. Other strategies included making sure that the students had taken their medication or having them diagnosed for possible prescription (31), sitting them close by to make it easier to intervene when necessary (25), adjusting their assignments to minimize demands for sustained concentration (22), attempting to increase their awareness of their behavior and its consequences (21), arranging for isolated seating or a nondistracting environment to help them concentrate or reduce the degree to which they distracted classmates (20), instructing them in better ways to behave when feeling the need for activity (10), and keeping them occupied during lessons by calling on them frequently or giving them some role that required them to do something (9).

Some teachers spoke of changing the way that they taught the class as a whole, typically by minimizing activities and assignments that required students to sit and listen passively (17), teaching lessons on self-control (14), varying their activities to maintain interest (10), scheduling demanding activities at optimal times and preparing the students for them (9), or engaging the students in vigorous physical activity during transitions between lessons (7). Twenty teachers also mentioned strategies for involving classmates, mostly by inducing them to reinforce proscriptions against roaming the room and other hyperactive behaviors (9), seating hyperactive students amid peers who would not reinforce their hyperactivity and would help keep them calmed down and tuned in to lessons (7), and generally fostering peers' awareness of the problem in the hope that they would be helpful to the hyperactive students (6).

Thirty-two teachers mentioned some attempt to socialize hyperactive students regarding their behavior or its consequences. Most of them spoke of asking these students to be more considerate of the teacher and their classmates by avoiding disruptive behavior (22) or engaging in logical analysis emphasizing the undesired consequences that result from such behavior (17). Twenty teachers spoke of soliciting input from hyperactive students in trying to develop strategies for helping them to control their behavior; and more than half (50) spoke of getting more information by observing or interviewing these students, talking to their parents or to past teachers, or referring them for professional assessment (usually medical rather than psychological).

Among teachers who identified strategies that would be ineffective, the majority mentioned attempting to enforce unrealistically rigid expectations (29) or lecturing, nagging, threatening, or punishing (28). Most viewed hyperactive behavior as only partially controllable, reflective of inborn needs for activity and difficulty in remaining passive for very long, not as evidence of poor socialization at home or intentional disobedience at school.

Higher rated and lower rated teachers were similar in their general lines of approach. The major difference was that higher rated teachers mentioned more strategies and were less likely to speak of involving the parents or the principal in seeking to develop solutions. Higher rated teachers were more likely to speak of getting additional information by observing or talking to the hyperactive student, speaking with the family or with past teachers, or referring the student for medical diagnosis. They also were more likely to involve hyperactive students themselves in developing solutions, by questioning them to get information, soliciting their suggestions, or especially suggesting potential solution options and inviting them to express their preferences.

Higher rated teachers were more likely to speak of proscribing against disruptive behavior, making hyperactive students more aware that they were distracting classmates from their work and perhaps irritating them, and changing seating arrangements so that these students would be less distracted or less likely to distract their neighbors. Along with isolation in a corner of the room, this included construction of cubicles or "offices" that would minimize the potential for distraction by events occurring elsewhere in the room. Higher rated teachers also were represented more heavily among the few who spoke of involving peers to support hyperactive students or who stated that they might have been contributing to the problem by relying too heavily on passive learning activities or overly restrictive behavioral rules. Finally, higher rated teachers were more likely to state that attempting to enforce unrealistically rigid expectations is an ineffective way to respond to hyperactivity.

Vignette: Bill

Bill is an extremely active child. He seems to burst with energy, and today he is barely "keeping the lid on." This morning, the class is working on their art projects, and Bill has been in and out of his seat frequently. Suddenly, Roger lets out a yell, and you look up to see that Bill has knocked Roger's sculpture off his desk. Bill says he didn't mean to do it; he was just returning to his seat.

Before reading further, take time to think about how you might respond to this incident. Make notes about your ideas.

CSS Vignette Response Excerpts

Here is what four of the CSS teachers had to say.

A LOWER RATED TEACHER

"Well, before the project started I would have laid down some basic rules: Stay at your desk, watch your own work, raise your hand if you want something, and get permission to do it. Then I would call attention to the class to look at what has happened and talk about it as something that could have been avoided had this student listened to what had been said previously. I would classify him as a poor listener, not following directions. I wouldn't ask him why he did it, because if I say, 'You didn't follow directions' or 'You weren't listening,' this would be the reason. No explanation at this point would be good enough . . . students will offer to give an explanation, but I won't accept it. I just repeat what I had said previously. I would have him pick it up. [What would you say to him?] I would say, 'I'd like to have you go over and pick up his sculpture . . . if it's broken, maybe that student wants yours.' If he wants it, I'll make him give it up and let him take the broken one. If he wants to pout, I'd just have him sit down. . . . He's hyper, but at the same time I feel those kids listen well. I would say to him, 'I don't have time to stand and watch over you as if you were a first-grader or kindergartner. I have to get around to see how all the other students are doing,' and you know, talk about how it's all part of growing up and getting a hold of yourself . . . I think in terms of medication for hypers and sending them to the office. At any other time I probably would give him something extra to do, but at that time I would not. I would hope that he would be the lesson . . . an example to the class. I'm trying to prevent the same thing happening to someone else."

A HIGHER RATED TEACHER

"The first one I would get to is Roger. Roger has just had his sculpture knocked off, and I get the feeling that it really isn't so much Bill's fault. Bill is an active kid, he's having trouble keeping the lid on, and it's just not one of his days for calming down. Probably before this I would have done something to Bill as a preventive type thing. I would have talked to him quietly and simply said, 'Hey, we've got to try to cool our motor today.' This isn't an uncommon problem at all. Bill is going to have to be handled quietly. You don't have to go over there and chew on Bill. Bill is probably sincerely sorry that he did it. He knows that it's his fault, he knows it came off, but he may very likely be trying to control himself. He may be working his head off to do it. At this point, I would probably just settle Bill off to a corner or something. It could be up here at this table; it could be over in our corner. I would simply say, 'Hey just cool your motor until I get to you.' I see no indication here at any time where I'd be chewing Bill out for the broken sculpture, other than I believe that it will take an apology and that's it. That can be done the next day. [He apologizes?] Just for breaking the sculpture, even though it's something that just happened. I don't think it's the time. I don't think Roger is ready to accept an apology anyway. I think the first person that has to be dealt with is Roger. Can we get some extra time, can we get some new material for him to start over again, and can we make him aware that it was just an accident that happened? He's going to be aware of Bill's problem too, but I think Roger has to be dealt with first and get him started back on his project. Bill is going to need some time to cool down even before you talk to him. If he was excited before, after having this accident he's going to be more excited, and he's just going to have to cool down. With an extremely active kid, you've just got to be low key and you have to have a quiet talk. [When you get done with your talk, what's going to happen to Bill? Will he continue to work on his art project, or what?] Oh yes. Probably what I would do when I ended the talk with him is just say, 'Hey, do you want to go back into the room and work there, or do you want to sit over here and work with your art project, or do you just want to sit here and maybe read?' I'd leave it up to him. They make a good decision. Bill needs a place where he can just get away, and I've done that with kids too. They come here in the morning, and they're just superhyper; they're going. They just have to come and say, 'Hey, can I go work over there?' They mention a place to me. It's the same with the seating arrangements in here. If they say, 'Hey, I think I can work better if I sit over there,' that's fine with me. I say, 'Give me a couple of days, and I'll get it switched.' It puts responsibility on them. One of the things you have to get across to Bill is that he's not bad because he's active. He just has to try to control it. And if he's trying, nobody can ask for any more than that. There's no indication that Bill isn't trying. He's just got something to cope with. The overactivity."

ANOTHER HIGHER RATED TEACHER

" 'Bill, can we go over and help Roger pick up his sculpture now? I think that even though you didn't mean to do it, it is a shame something like this would happen. If you were in your seat working on your project, I don't believe this would happen.' 'Roger, is your sculpture all right? It looks like it is, so let's put it back on your desk.' 'Bill, would you like to help Roger work on his project, or would you like to do one of your own? I think it is very important that you work on the things that are assigned to you and let other people work on their things. It is very difficult when you have worked on something carefully and you are trying to do it well and someone comes along and, because they are careless, they cause you to either damage it or even ruin it. So let's go back to our seat now, and let me see if I can help you get started on yours, so that you can get something completed this afternoon.' Children really do have problems, a lot of them, staying in their seats, and it's often hard to say that they really do have to sit down. But I think you have to find something that keeps their interest so that they stay in their seats as much as possible and work there. Sometimes you have to go over and work on it with them for a little while to see that they get interested. My goal at that time would be to get him interested in his own particular work, to try to make him see how important it is to be working on his things and not interfering with what other people are doing, even if it is entirely accidental that he knocked the sculpture off."

ANOTHER HIGHER RATED TEACHER

"The first thing I would do is take Bill aside and ask him first what he was supposed to be doing. If he knows, I would then ask him, 'Why were you out of your seat when you were supposed to be working on your art?' and then get to what happened with Roger's sculpture. 'Why did it end up on the floor?' I would imagine that Bill would be able to tell me the answers to these questions. Then I would get Roger to join us, and I would like Roger to tell Bill how he felt about Bill knocking his sculpture off his desk. If any damage was done, I would imagine that Roger would be angry and would have a few things he would want to say to Bill. Bill may be very remorseful, but I think he needs to know that his actions, although well-meaning, ended up in something that hurt someone's feelings and perhaps damaged property. He needs to begin to think about how he is going to control his body in a situation that is less structured like an art lesson. I think Bill should be able to tell what he would try to do in the future or for the remainder of the lesson as far as staying at his seat and being more careful about other people's property. Perhaps he would be able to help Roger repair the sculpture, if that was possible. If Bill didn't suggest it, I might suggest that as something he might do. I wouldn't force him into it, but it might be a way to work out the problem. I think Bill probably is a well-meaning child who really is sorry about what he did, and it just seems to him that these things happen and he just can't help them. He needs to learn that he can help them. He just has to be more aware of his own situation, how his body reacts, and get tuned into himself. I would describe Bill as an enthusiastic, active child who just isn't aware of his own being."

The lower rated teacher stated that she not only wouldn't respond sympathetically to Bill in this situation but would attempt to use it as an object lesson for the class as a whole about what happens when you don't follow rules about staying in your seat. She apparently had not considered the damage to the teacher–student relationship that is likely to occur when a teacher publicly humiliates a student in this manner. In contrast, the three higher rated teachers all expressed empathy for Bill, confidence that he had knocked over the sculpture accidentally, and the presumption that he is sorry for having done so. All of these teachers wanted to make sure that Bill saw the connection between his out-of-seat behavior and the problem that he caused, but they would communicate this message in a manner that was primarily instructional rather than blaming or humiliating.

Analysis of Responses to Bill

A majority (58) of the teachers mentioned prescribing or instructing Bill in better coping strategies. Other commonly mentioned problem-solving approaches included attempting to increase Bill's insight into his behavior and its consequences (37), attempting to eliminate a perceived source of the problem (21), brief management responses (20), changing Bill's social environment (20), sending him on an errand or to engage in exercise as a way to "work off" his restlessness (20), changing his seat or physical environment (19), punishing him or threatening punishment for repeated misbehavior (17), and proscribing against misbehavior by reminding him of rules and limits (13). Thirteen teachers would gather more information before taking action, and 18 would get input from one or both students in developing solutions.

All but 10 of the teachers showed awareness that Roger might be upset or require assistance in cleaning up the mess or help in getting restarted on his sculpture. Of these teachers, 65 spoke of helping him get restarted, 54 spoke of making sure that he realized that the incident was an accident (either by explaining it to him or by having Bill apologize or explain), and 19 spoke of dealing with Roger's upset or angry feelings.

Of teachers who could be coded for whether or not they would attempt to help Bill understand what happened and why, 20 would not address this issue, 48 would lecture or chide Bill by pointing out that even though it was an accident, the incident would not have occurred if he had been in his seat where he belonged, and 16 would ask Bill to reflect on what he had done and talk about it. Of teachers who would take steps to see that Bill followed up the incident by interacting with Roger in some way, 55 would suggest to Bill that he help Roger clean up the mess or rebuild the sculpture, 44 would suggest that he apologize to Roger or reassure him that he didn't mean it and would not do it again, and 16 would raise the follow-up issue with Bill but leave it to him to decide what he might do to make amends to Roger. Among teachers who spoke of asking Bill to help Roger rebuild the sculpture, only 15 indicated awareness that Roger might not appreciate this or that it might lead to additional problems.

Only a minority of the teachers mentioned strategies for developing Bill's insight. Most spoke of attempting to increase his awareness of his behavior and its consequences (27) or helping him to realize that others do not appreciate the disruption or damage that he causes (15).

Higher rated teachers mentioned more strategies, especially for helping Bill avoid such incidents in the future. Lower rated teachers were more likely to confine their response to lecturing Bill about his out-of-seat behavior and telling him to make restitution to Roger in some way. Higher rated teachers usually included long-term prevention or problem-solving strategies along with responses to the immediate situation. They were more likely to be coded for goals of improving Bill's coping skills in addition to exerting control and providing for restitution in the situation, to include instructive elements along with power assertive elements in their response, and to express confidence that the improvements they could elicit would generalize. The few teachers who suggested that part of the problem might lie in inappropriate activities or unrealistic behavioral expectations also tended to be higher rated teachers.

Higher rated teachers were more likely to indicate that they expected both students to be upset about the incident and to suggest strategies for dealing with them. They more often mentioned helping Roger get restarted on his sculpture and dealing with any upset or angry feelings he might have, as well as telling Bill to help Roger pick up the broken pieces and/or rebuild the sculpture, suggesting that he do so, or raising it as a possibility and leaving it for him to decide. Even so, they also were more likely to express recognition that Roger might not want Bill's involvement or that Bill might cause additional problems in his attempts to help.

As responses to Bill, the higher rated teachers were more likely to speak of eliminating a perceived source of the problem, involving the parents to provide support, providing Bill with instruction or help in learning better ways of coping with his restlessness, and developing his insight into his behavior and its consequences. The latter differences were especially pronounced. Higher rated teachers were notably more likely to talk about helping Bill to recognize and counteract his tendencies toward hyperactivity, to become more aware of the forms of hyperactive behavior that he displays and the undesired consequences that they produce, and to realize that his classmates often find such behaviors irritating. Finally, higher rated teachers more often spoke of seeking input from one or both students in developing solutions, as well as trying to elicit insights from Bill by asking him questions (rather than confining themselves to more prescriptive telling or "lecturing").

Vignette: Paul

Paul can't seem to keep his hands off the things and people in the room. He also seems to want to inspect or play with whatever is at hand. When he is not physically manipulating someone or something else, he hums, whistles, grimaces, drums his fingers, taps his feet, or makes other noises through physical activity. Just now he has discovered that one of the screws holding the back of his chair to its frame is loose, and he is pushing and pulling at the loose piece. In the process, he is further loosening the connection and at the same time distracting the class with the noise he is making.

Before reading further, take time to think about how you might respond to this incident. Make notes about your ideas.

CSS Vignette Response Excerpts

Here is what four of the CSS teachers had to say.

A LOWER RATED TEACHER

"First of all, he has to be stopped from pulling his desk apart. Then I think I would call him in during lunchtime, after school, or whatever, and talk to him about his behavior and tell him exactly what is expected of him in school. There are certain things we do in school and certain things we don't do in school. And then, if that doesn't help, I'd probably give him a punishment and again call home and tell the parent that he isn't taking care of himself. Sometimes making them write, such as 'I will not talk in class,' will keep him quiet long enough so that the others can continue without being distracted. If he can't do his work, then this is something he can sit and do quietly because he knows, for instance, that he cannot go out for lunch unless this is done. Most of them don't want to write; they know it's punishment. And hopefully the next time they'll think twice about whether to do it again. If this doesn't help, I think it has to be worked on. Talk to the boy, whenever you can (preferably when the other kids aren't around), and find out what the problem is, why he isn't working, why he's bothering other people or humming and whistling, whatever he's not supposed to be doing. Again, too, if they are motivated, if they can do their work, a lot of this doesn't happen. It's just making them, finding the right thing that they can do that they like to do. Get them interested in it so that these types of things don't happen, maybe drawing their attention to the fact that if he's interested in TV, how does he like it if someone comes in and turns the television off or walks in front of him or sits down and talks? Does he like that? And it's the same thing in school when they're trying to do their work and they don't want to be distracted. Maybe this might make some sense to him."

A HIGHER RATED TEACHER

"First I would tell Paul to stop and look at what he was doing, and ask him to tell me exactly what it is. He should be able to tell me that one of the screws in his chair is loose, and he is pulling on it or pulling on the loose piece on his chair and it is getting looser. I would then ask him 'What can you do to fix the chair?' He may not know, and at that point I might suggest that he find the custodian and tell him that his chair needed to be fixed. That would give Paul a chance to solve the problem of the chair. However, he seems to have more problems than just that. Perhaps after the problem with the chair was solved, I would talk with Paul and say, 'Paul, you seem to have to keep your hands or your feet or your body making noises all the time. Do you know how other people feel about that?' He might know, and he might not know. If he doesn't know that he was bothering other people, I would tell him that it bothers me, and I might ask someone who sits near Paul who may have complained to me about his making noise to come and tell Paul about the fact that they can't work because he is making these noises. He should begin to realize at that time that his behavior is bothering other people and that Paul and I need to decide what I can do to help him get better control of his body. Perhaps I could tape a note to his desk saying, 'Do you know what your hands and feet are doing?' Or perhaps he could choose a buddy in the room who would remind him quietly by whispering in his ear: 'Hey Paul, you're drumming your pencil, and you may not know it but it is bugging me' or 'Paul, I think you're bothering someone else.' I think the main problem is that Paul is unaware of what he is doing. He may be very nervous, and he could be doing this when he is daydreaming. I think he just needs to become more aware of what he is doing. I guess I would call him a misdirected nervous person."

ANOTHER HIGHER RATED TEACHER

"I would go over to Paul and quietly whisper in his ear, 'Paul, would you please stop playing with the screw? Let's see if we can tighten the screw back up so that your chair doesn't fall apart.' I would let him screw it back in as much as possible so that he could get back to work. Then I would quietly ask him, rather than make a big deal about it, 'Let's see if you can be quiet and help the class out.' Be positive, and try to encourage him by saying, 'I really need you to be quiet so we can get ahead with what we are doing,' rather than jumping all over him, because that sort of reaction often gets the opposite results than what you want. Lots of times teachers encourage negative behavior by yelling about it. Some kids want attention and don't care what kind of attention they get. So just kind of quietly go over and say something to the child, something that is just between the two of you that doesn't involve the rest of the class. Ask for some help. You would really appreciate it, and it would mean a lot to you if he wouldn't do that. . . . I guess my goal would be to help Paul to see that when he does things like that, he is taking other children's attention away from things they are doing, and as a favor to them and to me and to himself, I would really appreciate it if he wouldn't do it."

ANOTHER HIGHER RATED TEACHER

"I would probably approach it by saying, 'Paul, would you like to be in charge of making sure that that loose piece gets fastened?' If this is the morning, I'd say, 'Hey, at noontime would you please go down and get the janitor and bring him back here and see that he tightens that up for us? In the meantime, we'll just have to try to ignore it. Would you like to sit up here so that it doesn't bother you?' That would probably solve the problem."

The lower rated teacher ignored the hyperactivity aspects of this vignette and responded to it simply as a case of a student who frequently
does things in school that he is not supposed to be doing. Although at
one point she suggested talking to Paul to try to find out what underlies
his behavior, most of her response emphasized "lecturing" Paul and
threatening or invoking punishment if he did not do what he was told.
It appears that this teacher's efforts to help Paul would be hampered by
her distant, impersonal approach that did not include developing and
working within a close personal relationship with him. In contrast, the
three higher rated teachers suggested diverse but more positive responses.
The first would try to make Paul more aware of his behavior and its effects on the teacher and his classmates, and would employ strategies to
help him increase his awareness in the future. The second would inform
him of the problems that his behavior causes and would make a personal
appeal to him to try to improve in order to please her. The third would
not make an issue of this particular incident, choosing instead to change
Paul's seat and get on with the lesson.

Analysis of Responses to Paul

Problem-solving strategies were spread over many categories: sending Paul
on an errand or telling him to perform exercises as a way to "work off"
hyperactive tendencies (36), eliminating a perceived source of the problem
(34), brief management responses (32), threatening or invoking punishment (32), proscribing against misbehavior (31), attempting to increase
Paul's insight into his behavior and its consequences (26), changing his
seat or physical environment (24), prescribing desirable behavior (19), and
isolation or removal from the classroom (15).

   Among teachers who spoke of making Paul aware of the noise he was
causing, 37 would take time to make sure that he understood what he was
doing or its effects on the teacher or the class, whereas 30 would confine
themselves to a brief verbal or nonverbal signal telling him to stop. A
majority would do something beyond stopping the noisemaking, such as
taking a break or switching to a more interesting or less demanding activity (19), changing Paul's seat or working conditions (19), or sending him
to a time-out area or on an errand to settle him down (16). Only a minority mentioned fixing the chair. Of these, 19 would invite or order Paul
to fix it himself, perhaps with help from the teacher or the custodian, and
12 would refer the problem to the custodian.

   More than two-thirds included long-term prevention or follow-up
strategies, typically giving Paul shorter assignments, more physically active assignments or duties, or more frequent opportunities to move around
the room (33); threatening punishment (26); or referring him for psycho-

logical (not medical) diagnosis or treatment (18). Only 8 teachers spoke of setting up a contract system, and only 7 spoke of referring Paul for medical diagnosis. The majority considered the incident relatively minor, but 36 considered it a more serious problem that required intensive and perhaps sustained intervention.

Concerning Paul's degree of responsibility, 17 teachers would consider his behavior normal or view it as governed by forces that Paul could not control, 57 would consider him thoughtless or inconsiderate, and 26 would blame him or treat him as if he were acting deliberately. The majority showed no apparent emotion or only minor irritation in response to Paul's behavior, but 28 found it exasperating (saying that they couldn't stand such behavior or that it drives them crazy), and 2 found it insulting or anger-provoking.

Overall, 34 teachers would confine their response to attempts to suppress Paul's hyperactivity or move him away from the chair so that he couldn't continue making noise, 26 would allow him some freedom of movement so that he could "work off" his hyperactivity, 23 would try to keep his hands busy doing something else (ask him to sit on his hands, or give him something specific to do with his hands), and 12 would try to teach him how to cope with his hyperactivity more constructively (such as by monitoring his behavior better).

Response patterns were more similar than different, although higher rated teachers responded less emotionally and more constructively. Lower rated teachers were more likely to view the depicted incident as a major exasperating problem, to view Paul as blameworthy for misbehavior (making noise, harming the chair, or both), to confine their response to reaction to the immediate situation without mentioning longer term preventive or problem-solving strategies, to confine their response to control or suppression strategies without mentioning shaping or instructional strategies, and to include criticism or punishment. Higher rated teachers had the opposite pattern. They tended to viewed the problem as a relatively minor one, to assume that Paul was not aware of what he was doing or was engaging in habitual hyperactive behavior without deliberate intention to disrupt the lesson, and to respond with instruction or help rather than just minimal interventions or criticism/punishment reactions. In particular, higher rated teachers were more likely to mention prescribing or teaching Paul better ways of coping with his hyperactive urges, proscribing by clarifying rules or limits, changing his seat or working conditions to make it easier for him to work without getting into trouble, and seeking to discover and solve the root problem causing his hyperactive behavior. Finally, the higher rated teachers were more confident that they could elicit stable improvements in Paul's behavior.

COMPARISON OF RESPONSES TO BILL AND TO PAUL

Although complicated by the need to deal with Roger's broken sculpture and Paul's broken chair, responses to these two vignettes were similar both in general trends and in patterns of correlation with effectiveness ratings. The majority of teachers recognized the depicted problems as due to chronic hyperactivity rather than intentional misbehavior. Immediate responses focused on settling down the hyperactive student and repairing the damage. Longer term responses emphasized such strategies as reducing concentration demands, or providing more frequent physical movement breaks for hyperactive students; arranging for them to work in isolated or sheltered areas; and attempting to increase their awareness of their hyperactivity, the problems that it causes, and their responsibility to learn to control it more effectively. Lower rated teachers were more likely to confine themselves to situational interventions and limit setting, whereas higher rated teachers were more likely to mention longer term prevention or solution strategies.

QUALITATIVE IMPRESSIONS AND EXAMPLES

Although many teachers spoke of exasperation with hyperactive students, most also expressed empathy with them and willingness to extend them special consideration. A common theme among the more impressive responses was that you have to walk a fine line between making demands on these students and allowing them leeway: Don't make school any harder for them than you must, but at the same time impress on them that there are times when they are going to have to control themselves and concentrate on learning. Most teachers suggested some of the more popular ideas (active learning methods, frequent activity breaks, reward or contract systems, using physical closeness or touching as a way to calm these students down and provide reassurance and support). The more impressive responses emphasized helping these students stay tuned in to lessons, not just getting them to sit quietly.

Several teachers mentioned the importance of a good repertoire of subtle, nondisruptive ways to regain these students' attention or reengage them in work on assignments. Often this repertoire included special signals arranged with these students privately. These teachers emphasized that this not only avoids disrupting the lesson but also avoids constant nagging of hyperactive students about their behavior.

Several teachers also emphasized the value of conferencing with these students to brainstorm with them and agree on what might be done to help (seat them separately from classmates all the time or at certain times, use a verbal or physical signal when they need to be reminded to settle down, involve peers as helpers or reminders, etc.). Along with enlisting peers to help settle down or provide reminders to hyperactive students, several teachers emphasized the importance of making peers understand that these students have a problem controlling their behavior and do not mean anything by it when they interrupt you or accidentally jostle you. One teacher underscored this by asking hyperactive students to apologize for class interruptions and personal jostling incidents, intending this not as punishment but as a way to make these students more aware of the effects of their behavior. Another teacher would make special efforts to develop such awareness in hyperactive students who were beginning to bother their classmates, having found that once classmates start disliking these students and not wanting to sit next to them in class, this tendency to reject them spreads to the playground as well. She would rotate their seating assignments, try to keep them away from classmates who already have made it clear that they don't like them, and, if necessary, physically separate them from all classmates until they achieved better self-control. For similar reasons, and also to make it easier to intervene when necessary, another teacher sat hyperactive students near her desk and separated from peers. She reported that some of these students who were aware of their problem actually preferred this, and that those who did not were given the opportunity to earn their way back to regular seating through improved behavior.

Teachers who used reward approaches often included charts or other methods to help keep hyperactive students aware of their behavior. One placed masking tape along the sides of their desks to remind them to stay in their seats, claiming that the students were "almost relieved that something is helping them" because they get tired of being nagged by the teacher.

Several teachers spoke of checking to see if hyperactive students known to be on medication had taken their medication on days when they seemed unduly hyperactive. Many also spoke of having students assessed for possible medication treatment, although they usually were aware of the controversies regarding Ritalin and spoke of using it only when necessary. Two teachers suggested using coffee, cocoa, or other stimulant liquids with hyperactive students. One said that she had gotten this idea from her school nurse.

Several teachers admitted that their reaction to hyperactivity varied with how they were feeling at the moment, with exasperation or sending the student out into the hall being more likely at times when they were stressed and more helpful responses being more likely at other times. A couple of teachers reported that hyperactivity problems seem to increase when the weather changes.

One teacher reported that she had worked to slow down her speech because she thought that she was overstimulating her hyperactive students. She also tried to keep a neat, routinized class to help keep herself and her students under emotional control. She found that touching hyperactive students or putting her arm around them during reading group helped to keep them calm. Another teacher also spoke of the value of closeness and touching "to let them know that I know they must be having some kind of problems within."

One teacher's unique method of providing an exercise break involved telling the student, "Here, take this stick and run around the school three times and then come back in and sit down." When asked why he included the stick, he said, "I have just always given it to them. I'm sure there is a good reason someplace, but I don't know where it is."

One teacher ran a classroom that featured individualized learning centers. She claimed that this minimizes hyperactivity problems because the students aren't expected to sit still for lessons except in small groups, and they get to work actively in the centers. However, she did say that a few students couldn't handle all of the variety and activity in her class and needed to be moved to a more conventional one. Another teacher reported using sustained silent reading immediately after lunch as a way to settle down the class in general and hyperactive students in particular.

Finally, one teacher reported that she makes a note when she observes hyperactive students engrossed in something, so that she can build on this interest in future learning activities.

The vignettes did not yield many noteworthy or unusual responses, perhaps because they seemed straightforward, at least for teachers who interpreted them as we intended. Some teachers responded to Paul more as a mechanically curious student than a hyperactive one. In this regard, one teacher said that she would keep old broken appliances around in a corner of the classroom where students like Paul could work on taking them apart or trying to fix them.

Compared to the interviews, the vignettes elicited less mention of rewards or contracts and more mention of threats or punishment for repeated misbehavior. The interview allowed the teachers to be analytic and communicate empathy with hyperactive students' difficulties in controlling themselves, but the vignettes featured the problems that these students present for the teacher.

Many vignette responses emphasized the point that even though it is hard for hyperactive students to control themselves, you need to train them to do so and impress them with the need to do so for their own good. Such teachers would acknowledge to Bill that they understood that he didn't harm the sculpture deliberately but, at the same time, would make it clear to him that the accident would not have happened if he had been in his seat where he belonged. With Paul, they would emphasize that he was making noise at a particularly bad time and place. More generally, these teachers spoke of the need to find a golden mean balancing the degree to which we expect hyperactive students to control themselves in class and the degree to which we adjust to their needs by providing them with more opportunities to be active. One teacher suggested that these students gradually learn ways to get relief when they need it, such as by asking to go to the bathroom.

Many Big City teachers showed little tolerance for Bill or Paul. Some immediately mentioned having them tested, either to get them on medication or to get them out of regular education. Others suggested punitive responses such as excluding them from the class, publicly embarrassing them, or calling their parents to tell them that they were making things impossible in the classroom.

One teacher would tell Bill, "You're really flying" and ask him to put his head down and try to get himself under control and think about why he was feeling that way and how he could control it. Another would talk to Bill's previous teacher to get a better sense of whether such behavior was truly accidental or whether it might be motivated by a desire for attention or some other cause. Another would tell Bill, "If you had been in the *right* place, this wouldn't have happened in the *first* place."

Among teachers who would require Bill to help Roger rebuild his sculpture, one said that Bill shouldn't be allowed to get away with a quick "I'm sorry," that he needed an object lesson to help him see how his behavior affects others. However, she didn't take into account that Roger might not appreciate being required to work together with Bill.

One teacher suggested several techniques to help Paul keep his fidgety hands under control: Hold them in his lap and press hard to grip them tightly, put his palms flat on the desk for 1 minute without making any sounds at all, sit on both hands until he settled down, make faces in a corner of the room until satiated. Another teacher said that she would ask Paul if he had the money to pay for the chair if he broke it, claiming that this question always stops students who are endangering property.

DISCUSSION

The responses of the teachers in general, and of the higher rated teachers in particular, reflected most of the expert advice suggested to teachers about coping with hyperactive students. That is, the teachers spoke of the need to increase these students' awareness of their behavior and its effects on the teacher and their classmates; to impress upon them the need to develop better self-control; and to help them do so by giving them cues and reminders, shaping improvements through successive approximations, praising and rewarding such improvements, reducing distractions during work times, allowing these students more frequent opportunities to move about, or providing other forms of assistance or support. A minority would respond punitively or seek to remove these students from their classrooms, but most would strive to avoid becoming exasperated with them and instead provide them with the help they needed.

The teachers' responses were actually more supportive and less rejecting of hyperactive students than we had expected, probably because our problem–type description and vignettes featured motoric hyperactivity uncomplicated by hostility, aggression, or defiance of the teacher. Studies of hyperactive students referred for clinical assessment and treatment indicate that most of these students also display aggression, underachievement, conduct disorders, or other problems in addition to motoric hyperactivity. The classroom implications of these base rates were evident in data reported by Brophy and Evertson (1981) in their study of teachers' perceptions of and patterns of interaction with different types of students in their classrooms. Those teachers described their "restless" students not only as motorically hyperactive but also as ill-behaved, unmotivated, underachieving, irresponsible, untrustworthy, and aggressive. Thus, they associated hyperactivity with a cluster of undesirable personal attributes. Classroom observation data supported these descriptions. Restless students not only were more active in the classroom than their classmates but were more likely to misbehave; to do so in a way that involved disrupting the class; to project a sullen attitude when corrected; and to gripe, sass, or defy the teacher. Furthermore, the teachers were especially likely to express negative affect toward the restless students, to respond to their misbehavior with rejection or punishment, to hold them up as bad examples to the rest of the class, and to refuse their requests for help or permission. In general, the teachers' interactions with students labeled as restless were almost as bad as their interactions with students labeled as defiant, revealing attitudes of mutual dislike and vicious cycles of counterproductive behavioral actions and reactions.

In combination, the findings from the Brophy and Evertson (1981) study and the present study suggest that the primary challenge you will face in coping with hyperactive students will not be figuring out what kind of treatment they need but rather persisting in your determination to consistently provide them with the needed treatment and not become so exasperated that you distance yourself from them and begin to treat them negatively. This will be easier to do with students who are hyperactive but not hostile or defiant. However, in dealing with hyperactive students who are hostile or defiant, bear in mind that they will need the same kinds of support and assistance in developing better self-control that other hyperactive students need, as well as appropriate response to their hostility and defiance problems.

12

Distractible Students

D istractible students display the following characteristics: These children have short attention spans. They seem unable to sustain attention and concentration, and are easily distracted by sounds, sights, or speech. They:

1. Have difficulty adjusting to changes
2. Rarely complete tasks
3. Are easily distracted

What special strategies might you use to minimize such problems and help these students to function more successfully in your classroom? Before reading further, take time to think about this and make notes about your ideas.

CSS INTERVIEW EXCERPTS

Here is what three of the CSS teachers had to say about teaching distractible students.

A Lower Rated Teacher

"I don't know what causes it. I really don't. I thought and thought about this. I said that the one thing that came out of this whole thing for me was that it really made me stop and think about these things that you just go in every day and deal with, but you really don't give much thought to it. I don't know what causes it. I think maybe teachers, and I think I'm guilty of this, that I demand too much of these kids sometimes. I have to stop and remind myself that these kids really are only fourth-graders, and maybe I'm trying to treat them like sixth-graders. So maybe part of the cause is that the teacher expects too much, maybe expects a greater task than many of them are capable of tackling at the time. . . . How I deal with it is I spend a lot of time reminding, not booming loud but 'Gee, Mike, I haven't seen you doing any of your work. I've been watching you on and off for maybe 5 minutes, and I haven't seen you do anything that you're really supposed to be doing. Pretty soon our time is going to be up, and you're going to be in a real bind because you haven't got that done.' These kids need to be reminded, not yelling and screaming kind of reminding but 'Did you forget you have to have this done in 5 or 10 minutes?' or however long the class time is going to be. If they're distracted by something else that's going on around them I might say something like 'You don't seem to be getting your work done sitting there. Would you like to go sit somewhere else where it's quieter or where you wouldn't be paying so much attention to other things that are going on?' Of course, with this kid they'll probably go somewhere else and start looking at, or fiddling with, something else anyway. But sometimes if they have that choice, then they'll get down to work if you kind of leave it up to them to make the decision about what they should do. I want to point out to them that the work still needs to be done, and 'I hope you won't have to come in after school or take it home. It's really kind of silly when you've had time here.' Appeal to them again. You have to be positive about it. 'Well, you did get it done after all. See there, I knew you could do it!' The kid that's not paying attention while you're talking or while something is going on in the class sometimes is a little harder to deal with, but if you don't think they're paying attention, you might ask them a question and it brings them back into focus. It's kind of hard to deal with."

This lower rated teacher did not have much confidence in her knowledge. She did suggest several strategies that appear likely to be helpful, although much of her response appears more suited to simple dawdling than to distractibility related to the ADHD syndrome or to preoccupation with personal problems.

A HIGHER RATED TEACHER

"I see these children as having possibly a physical problem, maybe being hyperkinetic, children who just have a very short attention span and need to be in an environment where things are quite structured and where there will be as few distractions as possible. The first thing I would do would be to try to find out the cause, to look at the background, to look in their file, to do observations of them and see if

I can tell if there is some physical problem that should be discussed with their parents or perhaps discussed with a doctor. I've had children of this sort before that have gone to a doctor and been put on Ritalin and have been able to focus on their work and then eventually been taken off and been able to have a longer attention span and keep to their work. But if it were just a matter of trying to control the environment in the classroom, one thing that I would certainly do would be to give them short assignments and try to break them up into smaller segments so that they wouldn't have to sit so long. I might put a timer and/or have them time themselves with a clock and maybe work for a period of 15 minutes and then be given a break and have them move to another assignment, maybe go to the center and play a game, this type of thing, so that they are able to move and they would not get so restless sitting in one place. I have two study carrels in the room, and I use those quite often for children with this type of problem, so that they can sit at the study carrel and have a lot less distraction. Another thing I've also tried is just to have them put on headsets without having them listening to anything but just so that if they're really having trouble concentrating, they will not have the sounds of the room around them. Another thing is I've had them work very often with the headsets and have work recorded in that way, so they're doing some activity that they're actually listening to. When they have the headsets on, it seems like they really don't pay much attention to things that are going on around them. In the room I would try to have them sit where there would be the least distraction, so they would be sitting either at the front of the room or over to one side, preferably away from windows so that they wouldn't be distracted by that. I also think that they need a structure, and they need to know what their schedule is. I often make out assignment schedules so that they know exactly how much they have to do and that they can check those assignments off as they do them. Very often, too, these children, when there are other things going on in the room, are able to go out in the hall. They seem to be able to work better there, so I let them have their choice. Sometimes the child feels they could work better out in the hall and get more accomplished, that there is a lot of distraction, and a lot of children do come up and say, 'I can't work because someone is using the back table and they have to be talking.' So I give them the choice of working out in the hall. Sometimes I also let my aide take them into another room that's available. This often helps, where there are just fewer things going on around them, because very often you can't keep the room quiet. [What would you say was the success of the various strategies?] Well, I think with this type of child I usually haven't seen very much change as far as attention span. There is some growth sometimes with some of these that takes place within a year that you have them in the classroom, where they just begin maturing, and sometimes I think it is just a matter of maturation, that as they grow up and mature they become able to lengthen their attention span, be able not to be distracted as much. But with those that just don't show that, I find that it's more a short-term thing, that you do things for that particular time. I think the Ritalin, when they have been put on it, certainly is longer term, but it's very important that the teacher work closely with the doctor and with the parents and keep track of how the child functions with the medication, so that you know you're getting the exact amount that should be for that child to function as well as they can. . . . If I tried all these other things but still saw no improvement at all, no growth, then I would have the parents take them to the doctor and see if medication would help or if there was something else physical, possibly if they weren't hearing or if they weren't able to see. This very often makes a child distracted, if they're bored or they aren't really with what's going on. Then also I would rather have them work within the classroom confinement, so a backup strategy would be using an aide and taking the child out of the room or going and working in the hall, that type of thing. Another thing I might mention too with the backup strategy might be a contract here to see if they can get so much work done in a particular amount of time, so that they feel that they are using their time for short periods and then trying to lengthen it to a longer period, maybe working 15-minute segments and trying to lengthen it up to a half an hour where they can keep at one task."

This teacher suggested an impressive variety of strategies, although they all were premised on the assumption that the distractibility reflected an ADHD syndrome rather than preoccupation with personal problems. She thought in terms of achieving gradual improvement over an extended time period.

ANOTHER HIGHER RATED TEACHER

"These children are inattentive, restless, easily distracted, easily frustrated, and immature. The strategy that has worked best with these children is first to establish eye contact; second, give individual and group praise, verbal praise, for sitting through explanations or directions; third, reward them for sitting still for short and long time periods. An alternative to working with these children would be eye contact and maybe just to touch the child. Some of them are so restless, you might sometimes just put your hand on their shoulder, look right in their eyes, and speak very calmly to the fact that they are going to have to settle down. Sometimes proximity helps too. You might have this child sit next to you, maybe be my helper for a few minutes and turn the page in this book or be my assistant while I'm giving this direction, to bring them back as to just what is going on now. Another alternative is to rant and rave and shout, but this does absolutely no good whatsoever. The poor kid is confused. He's been doing this all his life. Maybe no one has tried to give him some kind of cue as to how you do settle down and how you do listen, because listening itself is an art, and these type of children initially have a difficult time listening because they never have. One thing you might want to do is have his hearing tested. I would even go beyond just the school test. Maybe recommend to the parents that they go to a specialist to have their hearing tested to see if there is really something wrong where they cannot hear when they're asked to be still or listen. . . . You might have a counselor maybe work with the child on an individual basis and the school social worker work with the parents. If it gets progressively worse or there is no improvement whatsoever, maybe consider psychological testing, but a lot of times this is a maturation thing, and a lot of the children who are very immature at the end of kindergarten, by first grade—I don't know what happens over the summer—a lot of them really mature."

This teacher also implied that the distractibility was part of an ADHD syndrome, and she assumed that it would include hyperactivity as well. Along with various strategies for reducing distractions and for regaining attention that were mentioned by the other teachers, she spoke of instructing distractible students in listening skills.

WHAT THE SCHOLARLY LITERATURE SAYS

Most students have at least occasional problems maintaining concentration on lessons and assignments, but for certain students inattentiveness is a chronic problem. In the primary grades it typically takes the form of short attention span or distractibility. In later grades it often is manifested more as daydreaming or difficulty in sustaining concentration on work.

As noted in the introduction to Chapter 11, many students display both distractibility and hyperactivity, and this linkage was recognized by the American Psychiatric Association in its diagnostic categories of attention deficit disorder (DSM-III; 1980) and attention-deficit/hyperactivity disorder (DSM-III-R, DSM-IV; 1987, 1994). The ADD designation was based on the notion that the attention deficit problem is primary and may or may not be compounded by hyperactivity (as indicated in the more elaborated designations ADD + H and ADD − H). The newer ADHD designation reflects a different way of viewing these disorders. Attention deficit is still linked with hyperactivity but is no longer treated as the primary symptom, and the hyperactive students carrying the ADHD designation have been grouped with children displaying conduct disorders within a larger category that emphasizes behavioral conduct problems rather than attention deficits. The formerly designated ADD − H students who display attention deficits but not hyperactivity were designated undifferentiated attention deficit disorder (UADD) in the 1987 DSM-III-R (American Psychiatric Association, 1987).

Summarizing relevant research, Barkley (1990) suggested that UADD constitutes a different type of attention deficit than ADHD—one that probably involves focused attention and cognitive processing speed, rather than sustained attention and impulse control. Children with UADD appear somewhat sluggish in responding to tasks, often have their awareness focused on internal events rather than external demands, and are typically much slower than other children in completing pencil-and-paper tasks. They also have considerably greater inconsistency in memory recall, particularly on verbal tasks. In their behavioral presentation, they are often viewed as daydreamy, inactive, lethargic, and learning disabled in academic achievement. They are substantially less aggressive and less rejected by their peers than ADHD students.

DSM-IV (American Psychiatric Association, 1994) eliminated the UADD category in favor of a classification similar to the ADD − H category introduced in the 1980 manual. DSM-IV uses the designation ADHD rather than ADD, but it notes that within the ADHD classification there are three subtypes: a predominantly inattentive type, a predominantly hyperactive–impulsive type, and a combined type that shows both sets of symptoms.

DSM-IV (American Psychiatric Association, 1994) calls for an ADHD diagnosis when 6 or more of the following symptoms of inattention have persisted for at least 6 months to a degree that is maladaptive and inconsistent with developmental level:

(a) often fails to give close attention to details or makes careless mistakes in schoolwork or other activities
(b) often has difficulty sustaining attention in tasks or play activities
(c) often does not seem to listen when spoken to directly
(d) often does not follow through on instructions and fails to finish schoolwork, chores, or duties in the workplace (not due to oppositional behavior or failure to understand instructions)
(e) often has difficulty organizing tasks and activities
(f) often avoids, dislikes, or is reluctant to engage in tasks that require sustained mental effort (such as schoolwork or homework)
(g) often loses things necessary for tasks or activities (e.g., toys, school assignments, pencils, books, or tools)

(h) is often easily distracted by extraneous stimuli

(i) is often forgetful in daily activities (pp. 83–84)

Research continues concerning the causes and possible linkages between attention deficits and hyperactivity. For our purposes, however, all of the forms of inattentiveness that have been classified as ADD, UADD, or ADHD are included among the distractibility problems that make it difficult for some children to fulfill their student-role responsibilities. Also included are distractibility problems that may arise from other causes, such as boredom with content or tasks that are overly familiar or uninteresting, fatigue due to sleep or nourishment deprivation, or preoccupation with home or personal problems (Swift & Spivack, 1975). This chapter focuses on students who display limited attention span or distractibility, whatever the causes of this problem and whether or not it is accompanied by other symptoms.

Suggested Strategies for Teaching Distractible Students

Much of the research literature has focused on children diagnosed with the ADD or ADHD syndromes, which makes it difficult to distinguish treatment elements aimed specifically at attention deficit problems from treatment elements aimed at hyperactivity or associated symptoms such as aggressiveness. Review of research on treatments for ADD and ADHD generally repeats the same three main conclusions noted in Chapter 11: Stimulant medication provides dramatic short-term symptom relief in most (but not all) cases, behavioral treatments produce less immediate and dramatic results but are useful adjuncts to medication, and cognitive strategy training appears to be ideally suited to the nature of the disorder but has yet to prove itself as a reliably effective treatment.

Cognitive strategy training aimed at the attention deficit aspects of the ADD or ADHD syndromes tends to focus on teaching students to maintain concentration on tasks, rather than on teaching them to inhibit tendencies toward behavioral movements. Braswell and Bloomquist (1991) noted that the literature on behavioral self-control training with ADHD children is interesting because it contains findings that conflict with findings for other behavior problems. Research on other problems usually indicates that self-monitoring alone produces only weak and transient improvements, so it must be combined with self-evaluation and self-reinforcement. With children whose primary problem is attention deficit, however, attention itself is the target behavior to be changed, and teaching them to self-monitor their on-task behavior or work productivity tends to improve their task attention and work completion rates. In other words, many children with attention deficits are not very aware of the degree to which they tune out from lessons or assignments, so that simply increasing their awareness may increase their attentiveness and productivity.

These authors also suggested that the student's developmental level needs to be taken into account in selecting treatment approaches. Interventions for younger students may have to be more environmentally focused because these students do not yet have the cognitive sophistication needed to benefit from more direct cognitive interventions. Thus, younger students might require study carrels or frequent teacher proximity or intervention to help keep them on task, whereas older students may be able to learn to monitor and control their attention primarily on their own.

Some classroom treatments have used mechanical devices to support cognitive strategy training. For example, Hallahan and Sapona (1983) placed a tape recorder near the desk of an 8-year-old boy who was being taught to monitor his attention. Periodically, the tape would emit an audible tone. Every time the boy heard the tone, he was to ask himself, "Was I paying attention?" Then he was to record his answer by checking yes or no on a self-recording sheet on his desk. Findings from this and other studies indicated that self-monitoring of attention during academic work led to increased attention and academic productivity. Use of the cueing and recording procedures proved necessary initially, but students could be weaned from reliance on these supports as they became more accustomed to monitoring their attention. Other investigators have reported similar success using light flashers or other mechanical devices to self-monitor, using a variety of self-recording methods, and requiring students to record either their attention to lessons or assignments or their work productivity (how much they have accomplished in a given time period) (Barkley, 1990; Braswell & Bloomquist, 1991).

Teaching implications emerging from the ADD and ADHD literatures were reviewed in Chapter 11. Many of these suggestions apply to the teaching of distractible students as well as hyperactive students. In addition, various authors have made the following suggestions when focused specifically on attention deficits or distractibility.

Laub and Braswell (1991) collected suggestions from teachers. Concerning physical arrangement of the room, these teachers suggested seating distractible students away from both the hallway and the windows, near the teacher, and facing the teacher during lessons, as well as creating study carrels or other distraction-reduced environments for them to use when working on assignments. They also recommended standing near these students when presenting lessons or giving instructions, using the student's worksheet as an example, seating the student among good peer models, and using individual headphones to play white noise or soft music to block out other auditory distractions when appropriate. Concerning lesson presentations, these teachers recommended increasing the pace and variety of lessons and actively involving distractible students by asking them to hold up props or write key ideas on the board; encouraging them to develop mental images of the information being presented and asking them about these images; using their names or calling on them frequently during the lesson; and making frequent use of computerized learning, cooperative learning, or other formats that allow for more active participation by students.

Concerning worksheets and tests, these teachers recommended using large type; keeping the page format simple; writing clear directions with key words underlined; using borders, colors, or other highlighting elements to help structure the page; giving frequent short quizzes rather than infrequent longer tests; and minimizing distractions during seatwork or testing times. They also recommended a general classroom organization that featured an established daily routine and schedule, periodic times for reorganizing desks and folders, providing these students with checklists or other supports to help them self-monitor, and using goal setting and contracting approaches.

Apter and Conoley (1984) suggested the following ideas for attracting and keeping the attention of distractible students: Cause and create suspense by looking around before asking questions; be unpredictable in calling on students to respond to questions; when you see distractible students' attention beginning to wander, mention their name or call on them; use physical proximity or touch to help keep the student focused on you; decrease the length and increase the interest value of activities; incorporate the students' interests into lesson plans; give directions in a soft voice that compels attention; and arrange for tutoring of these students to help them keep up with the class.

Swift and Spivack (1975) recommended many of these same strategies, as well as pausing after answering a question to look at different students before calling on someone to answer, moving around the room during whole-class activities in order to require more active attention and enable yourself to use physical proximity or subtle touch or signal interventions with distracted students, asking students what they think will happen next or how a story will end during reading lessons, beginning with short work sessions and increasing length and level of demand only gradually, and avoiding suggesting that daydreaming is unnatural or bad.

Thompson and Rudolph (1992) suggested that teachers begin by noting whether distraction problems occur at particular times or may reflect some home or classroom factor that can be adjusted and then follow up accordingly. They also recommended teaching distractible students to "stop, look, and listen," by teaching reflective strategies and using games that require sustained concentration and impulse control. Concerning daydreaming, they recommended frequent eye contact, reinforced if necessary by occasional touching or calling the child's name; questioning the child about the content of the daydreaming to determine if it reflects home or personal problems that need attention; and if it does not, a combination of increasing the variation and interest value of activities, reestablishing attention through brief and subtle interventions, calling or mentioning the student's name periodically, and contracting and reward approaches (that focus on rewarding attention and academic productivity, not attempting to suppress daydreaming).

Finally, McIntyre (1989) suggested most of the strategies described previously as well as the following: Explain to distractible students the reasons why they need to pay better attention in the classroom, and reward them for doing so; teach them how to attend by squaring their shoulders toward the task, leaning forward, and keeping their eyes focused on the work; ask them for suggestions about how to help them keep focused, and follow through on those that are feasible; try to inoculate them against distractions by providing them with training in maintaining focused concentration and developing resistance plans to implement when they encounter tempting distractions; provide them with a straightedged object or a piece of cardboard with a narrow window cut out of it to use as a place keeper when reading; avoid standing in front of windows or open doors when speaking to the class; videotape the class, and then review the tape with the student to increase awareness of off-task behavior; set a purpose that will help focus the student's attention during listening tasks; and enlist peers to cue these students when they notice their attention wandering.

ANALYSIS OF INTERVIEW RESPONSES

No single general approach dominated the responses. The most frequently mentioned strategies were changing the task (44); providing academic help (33); eliminating the perceived source of the problem (32); minimal intervention or redirection (32); and proscribing by citing rules, limits, or expectations (30). Other strategies mentioned by more than five teachers included offering rewards for improvement (21); praising desirable behavior (19); threatening punishment (19); prescribing desired behavior (14); providing support through physical proximity or voice control (13); inhibiting through physical proximity, voice control, or eye contact (12); involving peers (10), the parents (10), or school-based authority figures or professionals (9) for support or problem solving; projecting encouragement or positive expectations (7); changing the social environment (7); and attempting to build the student's self-concept (6).

The coding distinguished between specific strategies for responding to particular incidents of distraction and more general prevention or follow-up strategies. Specific strategies included calling for attention directly or eliciting it by calling on or moving closer to the student (44), seating the student in isolation from classmates (32), using study carrels or other distraction-reduced work areas (23), helping the student get started on assignments (15), warning the student about upcoming time deadlines or transitions (15), and repeating or rephrasing questions that the student did not hear (6). More general prevention or follow-up strategies included modifying the classroom environment, rules, or routines to provide greater structure (54); providing the student with shorter tasks or more frequent monitoring (48); various strategies for keeping the student more attentive or accountable (23); modifying the curriculum to appeal more to the student's interests (18); enlisting classmates to help the student stay on task (16); picking up the pace of lessons or changing activities more frequently (12); working on the student's listening skills (7); and promoting involvement in lessons by asking the student to hold up a prop, point to something, etc. (6).

The majority of teachers spoke of taking steps to elicit or prod better attention from the student and/or to reduce distractions, whereas smaller numbers spoke of working with the student on time management, getting started on assignments, or completing assignments.

Strategies rejected as ineffective included being unrealistic in developing expectations or making demands on the student (23), punishing/scolding the student (22), and failing to intervene to address the problem (16).

The pattern of correlates with effectiveness ratings suggested that many of the teachers were confused by our description of distractible students. Higher rated teachers were more likely to talk about getting more information concerning the problem and then following up accordingly, rather than to describe detailed strategies for coping with distractibility problems. Lower rated teachers' responses often were confined to minimal interventions that would not be sufficient to address the problem or strategies that are not directly relevant to it.

Lower rated teachers were more likely to mention minimal intervention or redirection strategies, seating distractible students in isolation from their classmates, or threatening them with punishment if their attention didn't improve. They also were more likely to be among the majority of teachers who spoke of modifying the classroom environment, rules, or procedures in order to provide distractible students with more structure. The "more structure" notion is commonly recommended and is probably a useful response to distractibility problems, at least when included as part of a larger package of strategies designed to help the student cope more effectively. Here, however, many of the "more structure" responses involved making demands, threatening punishments, or changing the student's seat or working arrangements in ways that emphasized pressuring more than helping the student cope with classroom demands.

Higher rated teachers were more likely to suggest general approaches involving attempts to identify and treat the cause of the problem or to solve the problem by instructing or training the student in more effective coping strategies. These teachers also were more likely to speak of getting more information (especially by interviewing the student or by consulting school records, past teachers, or the principal). They were more likely to suggest different strategies for different subtypes of the problem and to suggest that preoccupation with home or peer group problems might be one reason for student distractibility. Finally, higher rated teachers were more likely to be among the few teachers who mentioned the specific techniques of repeating questions that the distractible student hadn't heard or physically involving these students in lessons by having them hold a prop or point to something.

In summary, higher rated teachers' responses included some specific ideas for managing or helping distractible students, but mostly emphasized the need to get more information about what was behind the distractibility problem and then follow up accordingly. The lower rated teachers' responses tended either to focus on strategies that did not directly address the distractibility problem or to speak of addressing it through minimal situational responses or control/pressure strategies rather than through more ambitious problem-solving strategies.

Vignette: George

George's attention wanders easily. Today it has been divided between the discussion and various distractions. You ask him a question, but he is distracted and doesn't hear you.

Before reading further, take time to think about how you might respond to this incident. Make notes about your ideas.

CSS Vignette Response Excerpts

Here is what four of the CSS teachers had to say.

A LOWER RATED TEACHER

"I would stop, call his attention again, repeat the question, and say, 'George, please pay attention. George, you're not listening,' and stop and . . . tell him, 'Put your eyes up here. I'm talking to you.' Then ask him a question, and they'll answer, if you are very plain about it. [Is there any way that you can see to make him pay attention more in general?] Just by motivation. They have to be motivated, and they have to know that they're learning something. They have to be interested in what they're doing. This is the only way you're going to keep their attention. It doesn't always work, but keeping your classes as interesting as possible is the only way that I can think of to keep their attention all the time. You can punish, but that's a negative thing instead of a positive. A class is really motivated if the teacher is motivated. Usually you have their attention. Or perhaps the child is very slow. Then I would do something else. But in my room, because I don't have an aide or anything, I can't take the time out for one or two people, unless we are having written work. Then I can send someone out and maybe have another child help them. The only thing I can do to keep their attention is to find things that they know about and keep them interested that way and hope that they will generally become interested in other things."

A HIGHER RATED TEACHER

"One way that I sometimes try to bring a child back when their attention does kind of waver is to ask them questions . . . but he is distracted and doesn't hear me . . . while I am talking. Then even before I ask him a question, I would maybe mention his name: 'Isn't this right, George?' or 'How do you feel about this?' Not a question type of thing, but include him in the discussion as much as I could before I would ask him a question, because if you ask a child a question and you know he is not paying attention, what you are doing is putting him on the spot. I know that teachers do that a lot, and I've done it myself, but I think I would work with him in that I would include him in the discussion, and as I see him wandering off, I would call him back. I would keep drawing him back so as to tune him in to what was going on, before I would stop and ask him a question and possibly embarrass him. [If he didn't hear you when you asked him, what would you do? Would you go on to another student, would you reprimand? . . .] No, I would usually say, 'I'll be back to you' so that gives him the option of listening because he knows that I am going to come back and ask him a question, and I always do. [How would you characterize him?] I guess as a daydreamer, but you know with a child like this there could be problems that are not related to school that are on his mind that are so heavy with him at the time that he can't clue into anything else but those problems, so it is kind of hard. If he does it on a consistent basis, I would say that he is just a daydreamer."

ANOTHER HIGHER RATED TEACHER

" 'George, is it possible that you were thinking about something else and didn't hear the question? I would be glad to repeat it again, but I would like you to look at me and listen so that I know I have your attention. I'll ask you the question again, and hopefully you will be able to answer it. You know, it's very important when we are discussing things together in class that you try to listen carefully to what we are discussing and to think about it, so that you can enter into a part of the discussion. I'm sure that what you have to offer the class is very important, and we would like to hear what your thoughts are.' My goal is to get his attention back to the discussion. Try to have him think about his contributions to the class, that they are worthwhile too and that he should become an attentive listener so that he can enter into the discussion. I feel that it does no good to get angry at this point or start an argument, because you lose the attention of the rest of the class. Just state the question again, and encourage him to listen more carefully."

ANOTHER HIGHER RATED TEACHER

"George is probably a child who needs attention. If you've had him very long, you know that his attention wanders easily, and when you ask him a question and he doesn't hear you, I would go on up to him and stand near him to keep his attention if it is a whole-group activity, to bring him back to where we are and make it my business that I am near him so that he will be following me. If I see his attention being distracted, I might go up and put my hand on his shoulder to bring him back to us. Now if it is a small group and his attention is wandering and he hasn't been sitting beside me, I would change his seat to sit beside me and from then on I would make sure, if he was always doing this, that he would sit beside me, where I would have physical control of George. You can't always tell what his problem is because usually if they're easily distracted, there is a problem of one kind or another. He may be a young child, if it is a first-grader. Many of those children are easily distracted. If you are working on a one-to-one and he is easily distracted, then you would put something between you and the other children or whatever is going on. If he can't work in a classroom, he would be like my little Andy. We have his quiet place in the hallway where he works, because that is the only place that he can work. He is very happy to work there because he seems to realize that he cannot work with other children around him. They distract him too much. With George, what you really try to do is find out why his attention wanders that easily. Is he an immature child? Is he one that has a hearing problem? Maybe he has a vision problem? You start delving into all the reasons why he could have a problem and his attention wanders, until you find out what's wrong. If necessary you have him tested to see what the problem is. But if it was just right then and there, I would go over to him, and

I may repeat it the first time, repeat it to him. If it is continuing, then I'd try to get near him so that I could keep his attention by putting my hands on him. If it is continuous, I'll say, 'Let's listen. You aren't listening to me. You need to listen to me.' Or many times at this level too you ask a question and they say, 'What' or 'Huh' or something and you say, 'Well, what did I say?' and many times they will say it back to you. It's quite amazing. They'll say they didn't hear you, but if you ask them, 'What did I say?' they'll say it as sort of a question. It's also an attention gimmick, or maybe they're not sure in their own minds what you are asking and want to be reassured. . . . You just don't let these things keep happening over and over. You try to find out why and what you can do about them. So it can't be an isolated situation. It has to be one of the whole child in the environment, what's gone on before, what you think might happen."

The lower rated teacher responded to the vignette as if it depicted a simple fatigue or boredom problem. The higher rated teachers more clearly recognized the incident as part of a continuing distractibility syndrome and responded accordingly. Still, only the last teacher spoke of following up by trying to get more information about the problem.

Analysis of Responses to George

Only a minority (40) of the teachers believed that George could control his distractibility, and only 6 viewed him as intentionally ignoring the lesson. Only 4 teachers mentioned offering rewards to George, and only 12 mentioned threatening punishments. A majority mentioned supportive behaviors, mostly kid gloves treatment (23) or instructional help (20). Only 25 teachers mentioned threatening or pressuring behaviors, mostly criticism of George's failure to pay attention (14) or sarcasm or ridicule in commenting on it (8).

A majority (53) included brief management responses among their problem-solving strategies. Other commonly mentioned approaches included attempting to eliminate the perceived source of the problem (36), prescribing desired behavior (33), changing George's seat or physical environment (23), threatening or invoking punishment (15), changing George's social environment (12), attempting to develop his insight (11), tension release efforts (6), and proscribing against inattentiveness (6).

Responses were coded for what the teachers said about getting George's attention, getting an answer to the question, and dealing with his inattentiveness problem. To get George's attention, 66 teachers said that they would call George by name, speak louder or more directly to him, or otherwise catch his attention and repeat the question; 16 would move near George and touch him or speak to him from close range; and 7 would try to minimize his embarrassment through humor or a tension release comment. To get an answer to the question, 46 teachers would simply repeat it, and 11 would ask George if he heard it. The teachers would address George's more general inattentiveness problem by frequently looking at him or calling on him, speaking louder or more directly to him, or taking other action designed to keep him alert and accountable (33); by reminding George that he could follow the lesson better if he kept his eyes and ears on the teacher, that it is important to learn the material, etc. (28); by moving closer to George (26); by scolding or warning him to pay better attention (21); by attempting to identify and remove whatever might be distracting George (8); or by bringing George up to date by reviewing the lesson to make sure that he heard the material he had missed (6).

A majority mentioned prevention or follow-up strategies. These included calling on George more frequently or taking other actions to see that he remained alert and accountable during lessons (23); adjusting the curriculum to try to appeal better to his interests (15); attempting to stay close to George or to move near to him during lessons (14); assuming that his distractibility stemmed from some personal problem and probing for information by talking to him or his parents (12); using seat location, partitions, or other manipulations of George's physical environment to minimize distractions (11); attempting to motivate him to pay better attention by explaining the value of participating in school activities (9); threatening him with punishment for continued inattentiveness (9); praising or rewarding improved attentiveness (6); or teaching him listening skills (6).

Most teachers cited at least one possible reason for George's inattentiveness. Reasons mentioned included blanket statements that George is distractible, has not learned listening skills, is immature, or cannot concentrate for long on anything (48); as well as the notions that George is tired or daydreaming (27), lacks interest in the content of the lesson (20), is preoccupied with some personal problem (19), is momentarily distracted by something going on at the time (15), has heard the question but is not responding because he is not sure about what is being asked or is hesitant to respond unless certain (14), or has a vision or hearing problem (10).

Higher rated teachers mostly understood the vignette accurately and responded with appropriate strategies, but many lower rated teachers misread the vignette and responded with irrelevant or inappropriate approaches. Lower rated teachers were more likely to see George's behavior as controllable or even intentional, to attribute it to lack of interest in the content, and to include threat of punishment in their response. Rather than speak of pursuing the original question with George, they tended to speak of switching their focus to his inattentiveness and pressuring him to pay better attention, especially by moving closer to him or moving him closer to them.

Higher rated teachers were more likely to speak of getting George's attention and then repeating the question to him in the immediate situation, and then to mention various prevention and problem-solving strategies for dealing with his larger inattentiveness problem (in particular, calling on him more frequently or taking other actions to keep him more alert and accountable, involving peers to provide help with assignments or other forms of support, and trying to socialize or motivate George to pay better attention by helping him to see the value of the learning he would gain by participating in classroom activities). Higher rated teachers also were more likely to assume that George's distractibility stemmed from a personal problem and thus to speak of talking to him or his parents to probe for more information about it.

Vignette: Sarah

Sarah never seems to finish an assignment. She is easily distracted and then isn't able to recapture what she had been thinking about before the interruption. You distribute a worksheet to the class, and the students, including Sarah, begin their work. After a couple of minutes you see that Sarah is looking out the window, distracted again.

Before reading further, take time to think about how you might respond to this incident. Make notes about your ideas.

CSS Vignette Response Excerpts

Here is what four of the CSS teachers had to say.

A LOWER RATED TEACHER

"Is Sarah distracted, or is Sarah just plain daydreaming? She doesn't want to face the reality of the assignment. It is much nicer to look outside at the pretty blue sky and dream about playing outside. This type of child, you have to go after. This is very difficult in a large classroom. After the assignment has been given, say you know it is going to take roughly 15 minutes, you have to walk over and see what she has put on her paper, if anything. If nothing, you have to say, 'Get going on the assignment,' sometimes two or three times. Sometimes you get a Sarah who isn't going to do it. So what you do is keep your mouth quiet, and after she has not done it, you pick it up. You may have corrected the assignment in class, but you have her paper, and after the children are on the next assignment, you hand it back to

her and say, 'Don't try doing it in class. You have homework tonight.'
And call Sarah's mother and inform her why she has homework, that
she hasn't completed the assignment. [How would you describe
Sarah?] Daydreamer. She can be smart, and she can be very dumb.
That is not the problem here. The problem is that she doesn't want
to be part of the class at that time. In fact, she doesn't even want to
be there. Her touch with reality is very poor. Sometimes there are
problems at home. That's about all I can say on this one."

A HIGHER RATED TEACHER

"Sarah never finishes her work and is easily distracted and appears
at the moment to be daydreaming out the window when she has an
assignment to finish. I would casually go by and drop a little note
on her desk saying, 'I would appreciate your getting busy' or 'This
is due today, not next year.' Or I might put on a smile and say, 'Gee,
I know that you are about ready to start, aren't you?' something that
would fire her up a little bit and let her know that I wasn't too happy
with the fact that she was daydreaming and that I was hoping that
she would speed up and get busy so that she could get out of here
on time with the rest of us. If it looked like she just wasn't, I might
take her aside and say, 'What's the problem? Is this something that
is too hard for you? Don't you understand the directions?' I would
try to find out if there was some reason other than the fact that she
is just kind of spaced out a little bit. Then, if this was a recurring kind
of thing, I would have to talk to her and let her realize and know
why it is that I want her to do these things on time. While it is current and fresh in her mind and while we are all doing it, it would
be easier to get help and assistance, plus she could be doing it on
assigned time rather than ending up doing it on recess time or after
school, which would be extra time. My goal for her would be to be
more responsible for her actions, to center in and focus on a task
so that she can get it over with. Then she can daydream a little bit
and enjoy taking a break. Just mainly that. Just center in on what she
is supposed to be doing and not let her mind wander so."

ANOTHER HIGHER RATED TEACHER

"In Sarah's case, I would probably say to everyone that 'we only have
15 minutes to complete this assignment, so instead of talking or being distracted, we had better get back to work.' If that didn't do it,
I might take a walk around the room, not starting specifically at her
table, but through the tables, commenting on how the boys and girls
were working. When I got to her table, I would whisper in her ear,
'You are going to have to come on, Sarah. You know that you want
to do art with us, or go outside with us, so you need to finish that

assignment.' There evidently is something that is on her mind so that she needs to be called back. This would be a way of calling her back to the group without embarrassing her or disrupting those who are working quietly."

ANOTHER HIGHER RATED TEACHER

" 'Sarah, you seem to be having some difficulty getting your work completed at your seat. So I want you to come up now to the study carrel and bring your materials and your assignment and work on them there. It might be easier for you to do it there because there is less going on around you. If this is a problem for you in the study carrel, then after school when the other children are gone, you would probably be able to complete your work without any interruptions.' My goal is to get Sarah's attention back on her work and to have her complete it. It is difficult for many children to work with distractions going on. So I would try to get them in a better position. If there were study carrels or some area in the room where there would be fewer distractions, I'd put them there."

Although she alluded to possible problems at home, the lower rated teacher responded to the vignette as if it depicted the actions of an alienated underachiever who simply did not care about school, rather than inadvertent inattentiveness by a chronically distractible student. Consequently, her suggested response was authoritarian and punitive. In contrast, the three higher rated teachers all recognized that the incident was part of a continuing distractibility problem and responded accordingly. Along with providing various forms of help, they would remind or even pressure Sarah to finish her assignment, but in an authoritative rather than an authoritarian manner.

Analysis of Responses to Sarah

Most (78) teachers attributed Sarah's distractibility problem to internal causes, although only 22 of them viewed her attention as fully controllable, and only 5 suggested that she was intentionally disregarding the assignment. Only 9 teachers mentioned rewards, and only 19 mentioned punishment, primarily loss of privileges (12). Most (75) mentioned supportive behaviors, primarily instruction in better ways of coping with assignments (33); supportive isolation during work times (21); kid gloves treatment if Sarah appeared to be embarrassed or upset (13); and involving peers (6), the parents (7), or other adults (9) to provide support. Only 13 teachers mentioned threatening or pressuring behaviors, particularly specific criticism of her failure to stay on task (6).

Commonly mentioned problem-solving strategies included prescribing better ways of handling assignments (41), brief management responses (39), changing Sarah's seat or working environment (32), attempting to eliminate a perceived source of her problem (29), reminding her of consequences or threatening her with punishment for failure to complete assignments (20), offering rewards for improvement or completed assignments (16), proscribing against distraction from work (12), and attempting to increase her insight into her behavior and its consequences (11).

Responses were coded for what the teachers said about getting Sarah engaged in the assignment in the immediate situation and about prevention or follow-up strategies for dealing with her larger distractibility problem. Strategies for engaging her in the assignment included brief reminders or focusing comments (36), dividing the task into shorter segments and/or monitoring Sarah periodically to keep her on task and provide any needed assistance (34), helping her get started on the task (24), removing anything that might be distracting her (24), reminding her of time deadlines (20), threatening negative consequences for failure to complete the task (17), encouraging effort and reinforcing progress or accomplishments (13), and trying to make Sarah understand the importance of doing her work (8).

Long-term prevention and follow-up strategies included reminding her of negative consequences or threatening her with punishment for failure to work persistently and complete assignments on time (23), praising or rewarding progress or accomplishments (15), minimizing distractions during her work times (15), involving her parents (11), providing her with more structure in making and following up on assignments (11), talking to Sarah or her parents to determine if some personal problem might be causing the distractibility (8), calling on her frequently or taking other steps to keep her alert or accountable (8), teaching her task completion skills (7), and seating her close by or moving close to her frequently to exert proximity control (6).

About half (47) cited general immaturity or distractibility as the explanation for Sarah's symptoms. In addition or instead, 31 suggested that she was tired or daydreaming, 25 said that she was confused about the assignment and unsure of what to do, 19 thought that she was preoccupied with personal problems, 13 indicated that she was not interested in the assignment, and 9 concluded that she was distracted by something occurring in the situation.

Once again, higher rated teachers read the vignette more accurately and responded more appropriately. They were more likely to recognize Sarah's symptoms as part of a generalized distractibility problem, whereas some lower rated teachers suggested that the problem might be situational or caused by preoccupation with a personal problem. Lower rated teachers were much more likely to be coded for adopting a tough-minded general approach and suggesting control/pressure/threat strategies. Otherwise, they were more likely to be coded for brief management responses and for involving the parents.

In contrast, higher rated teachers were more likely to suggest strategies that went beyond brief management responses but did not include threatening Sarah with punishment. They tended to adopt a neutral, problem-solving approach that featured prescribing desired behavior in the depicted situation and following up with preventive or problem-solving strategies such as eliminating or reducing potential distractors from Sarah's work area, providing more structure in giving and following through on assignments, or teaching her task completion skills.

COMPARISON OF RESPONSES TO GEORGE AND TO SARAH

General lines of response to the two vignettes were similar, although there was a tendency for the teachers to emphasize situational aspects of George's behavior but to focus on longer term responses to Sarah's behavior. There was concern about avoiding embarrassment to George and about helping him stay involved in the lesson, but with Sarah, the focus was more on teaching or pressuring her to stay focused on her assignments during work periods and complete them in a timely fashion. There was more emphasis on shaping improvement in Sarah through successive approximations and greater confidence that elicited improvements would be stable.

For both vignettes, higher rated teachers were more likely to perceive the problem accurately and respond with a variety of assistance and support strategies, whereas lower rated teachers were more likely to limit their response to brief management strategies or to attribute the behavior to lack of interest and emphasize control or pressuring strategies.

QUALITATIVE IMPRESSIONS AND EXAMPLES

Most of the Small City teachers emphasized providing accommodation and help to distractible students and avoiding expecting too much too soon from them or being too negative with them. Teachers who focused on these students' difficulty in adjusting to change talked about keeping a predictable schedule and forewarning them of upcoming changes. Teachers who focused on their distractibility talked about using shorter activities and tasks, frequent monitoring, providing a quiet place for them to work, using headphones, and praising increased attentiveness and work output. Small City teachers working in the lower grades emphasized maturational lags as the primary reason for distractibility and talked about keeping distractible students close to them, using touch and signals as well as verbalizations to regain their attention, and providing them with sheltered work spaces. Teachers working in the upper grades tended to attribute the problem more to lack of interest and spoke of the need to have an interesting curriculum and to be entertaining in their teaching.

One teacher talked about having these students tested not only for sensory acuity problems but for ear wax blockage. Another said that she would avoid giving these students work that contained a lot of small printing or else would attempt to spread out sections or cover up parts of the page if necessary. Another teacher spoke of the need to provide these children with a lot of tutoring, claiming that they remain attentive in one-to-one situations.

Many of the Big City teachers immediately spoke of having these children tested. Many also mentioned sending them to special education rooms or reading or math resource rooms, partly because in these rooms children were taught in small groups and often with earphones or other audiovisual aids.

For both the interviews and especially the vignettes, the vast majority of responses were limited to variations on the strategies included in the coding systems. One teacher said that she would let Sarah daydream if she knew that Sarah was preoccupied with home or personal problems, believing that such daydreaming helps the student to work through such problems. Another teacher mentioned several techniques for encouraging better attention from George, including telling him that she would ask him to summarize the lesson for her later.

Several teachers talked about using listening exercises or other activities supposedly designed to build concentration skills. However, these tended to be less impressive teachers and the suggested activities often didn't seem very credible as treatments for distractibility.

DISCUSSION

The responses of the teachers we interviewed reflected the scholarly literature on distractibility problems, suggesting a combination of environmental engineering and instructional support designed to reduce the frequencies with which these students become distracted, reduce the demands on them for sustained concentration (at least temporarily), and help them learn to monitor and control their attention more successfully. Correlations with effectiveness ratings indicated the importance of recognizing distractibility syndromes accurately—not mistaking them for mere boredom, alienation from school, or other conditions that reflect problems in motivation more than problems in focusing attention and sustaining concentration. These correlations also suggest the need to investigate such problems in order to characterize them more specifically, determine what might be causing them, and follow up accordingly. A first-grader's difficulty in sustaining attention to lessons is quite different, for example, from a fifth-grader's impaired concentration due to preoccupation with home or personal problems.

As you work with distractible students on whatever longer term problems need to be addressed, use environmental engineering and minimal interventions to sustain or regain their attention in particular situations. Where feasible, seat them near you and place them so most potential distractions are outside of their vision lines. Make frequent eye contact, use their names, and call on them frequently during lessons; and use physical proximity and frequent monitoring and assistance (if necessary) during work times. If organization is a problem, help them learn to keep track of things better by making schedules, keeping assignment notes and checklists, and periodically taking stock of their accomplishments and reorganizing their folders and work areas. Provide them with special consideration to the extent that they seem to need it, but move them by degrees toward more acceptable and independent functioning.

13

Immature Students

Immature students display the following characteristics: These children have poorly developed emotional stability, self-control, self-care abilities, social skills, and/or responsibility. They:

1. Often exhibit behavior normal for younger children
2. May cry easily
3. Lose their belongings
4. Frequently appear helpless, incompetent, and/or dependent

What special strategies might you use to minimize such problems and help these students to function more successfully in your classroom? Before reading further, take time to think about this and make notes about your ideas.

CSS INTERVIEW EXCERPTS

Here is what three of the CSS teachers had to say about teaching immature students.

A LOWER RATED TEACHER

"I probably do everything wrong with this kid, as far as helping him mature. I'm very impatient with an immature kid who cries easily, loses belongings, is helpless and incompetent. I just go bananas. I probably belittle that kid more than I should, prod him in that way. The kid obviously needs help, and I am not a very helping person in that situation. When he's lost something, I probably tell him, 'What

in the world are you going to do? Is your mother going to be hanging on to your hand all your life? You're going to have to start taking
on responsibilities yourself,' and 'Hey I'm sorry, but I don't accept
that you got your work done but you left it at home. You're breaking
my heart. You can redo it.' 'I don't care that your hat is out on the
playground. You left it there all this week. It will stay there. It will
be lost.' 'I don't care that you forgot to sign up in the safety room
for your lunch, and now you need to go out of the room and go down
and sign up again.' 'You can't find your book in your desk? Somebody's taken it? Just tough, kid. If that was a candy bar, you'd probably keep track of it, so if it's not important enough to you, it's not
important enough for me to feel sorry for you. Don't look to me for
any sympathy, because I don't have any.' He's just going to have to
deal with a little pain and either grow up or cry. I don't really care
which. I don't baby this kid, and I sure don't have much patience with
him. Success rate is probably low. I'm not going to reward this kid
probably at all. If anything I'm probably going to punish him in the
way of put-downs and stuff, and probably verbally hassle him a lot,
or her. I don't know if these strategies work, and I don't know if I
really care. I don't feel sorry for the kid. I don't have any backup strategies either that I know of. I'm not going to feel sorry for them. They're
going to have to fly someday; it might as well be today, at least in
here, or you're going to break his wings. He's on his own. Sympathiz-
ing with him I don't think works at all, or agreeing with him. Or saying, 'Gee, yes, you should go get your hat. I'm sure your mom and
dad will be worried about that.' Or 'Is Brian picking on you? Brian,
get up here. I'll have a word with you.' "

This teacher openly admitted that she had no empathy for immature
students and was not willing to provide them with support and assistance
in developing more mature levels of functioning. She implicitly recognized that her approach was counterproductive, but she said that she didn't
care. At least in this regard, her professionalism left much to be desired.

A HIGHER RATED TEACHER

"I feel that these children sometimes may be the youngest child in
the family, that they had been catered to, had been babied and gotten their own way and therefore are a little more dependent or haven't
grown up as easily. Sometimes I've found, too, that they are an only
child, where they've been given very few responsibilities at home, and
the mother or father, either one, but very often mother, is very pro-
tective of these particular children. They might be small for their age,
and that usually is the type that I see them as. Very often I would

talk to the parent as soon as I could about some of the problems that they were having, probably not till the first conference because this would give a longer time to really see them and see if there would be any change. If this was a consistent pattern of behavior, then I would talk about how the child acts at home and how they gain attention, if this is the way that they gain attention from the adults at home or if this is the way they act in order to get their own way. . . . I really have had very few of this type of child, but I have had children that seem to desire playing with younger children and maybe trying to be a little more dependent on the teacher, always wanting to hang on to the teacher or be close to the teacher, rather than being with the group. I've talked to parents about giving these kinds of children more responsibility at home and letting them become more independent. I can remember one mother I talked to felt it was much easier for her to pick up after the child. This was an only child. They would just come in and throw things down, and I said yes, I knew that it's easier when you had one, but the child wasn't learning to be independent and wasn't learning responsibility. So with the parent, often we've made up a responsibility chart, maybe starting off with two jobs that they could do at home. Then give them a responsibility here at school that they follow through on their own. I've found that giving reassurance helps, that I don't totally ignore these things. Sometimes it's just an attention-gaining device, and some of the attention seeking can be ignored. If they know they're going to get a reaction every time, it often continues, but I think sometimes if you do ignore it, then it does stop. I've found this to be true. But also with some of these children, you need to give reassurance and support and just give less and less (over time) but so that they know you are there if they do need you. But you want to let them do things for themselves, too, and not just always be catering to their needs. In the room I would give them small jobs that they would do. Sometimes I've had them work with another child who is also not as independent. I think it's better to let them work with somebody who is a little less independent than somebody who is very strong, because there again, they'll just take over, and they would be apt to rely more on them and become dependent on the other child. If I have two that are not so strong in being independent, working together they can sometimes gain a little more independency. They also sometimes find a friend their own age and begin mixing more with their peers. Another thing that might help too, and in talking to the parent, is trying to get them involved in groups with other children their own age. Perhaps if there's a Scout troop in the building or in the area, they could join it. I often find that this has been a big help to these children because there are projects within those groups that they have to do independently, and they begin finding some interests of their own and branching out. I think it's so important that they learn that they're each an individual person and become themselves, and this is a good way to do it. Also, working with the Y groups is good, and I think a camp experience is very good for these children too if they can get an experience in the summer or even going with the school camp. This helps them. They're with children their own age, and they begin to develop more responsibility. [Have you found that these various strategies have been pretty successful with the children you've had?] I've never had a child that's really stayed this way. If they've been a little immature, I've found it's been kind of a natural growth thing, and they've really grown out of it. I've never had ones that, as far as self-care abilities and self-control, stayed this way. I really think that they feel a part of the room and comfortable with the children in the group, just through everything I do as far as teaching."

This teacher would work not only with immature students but with their parents as well, seeking to gradually build up a readiness to accept and fulfill age-appropriate responsibilities. Her suggested techniques included ignoring immature behavior when possible, challenging these students to accept more responsibility, encouraging and supporting them as they begin to do so, and reinforcing her classroom efforts by engineering improvements in their home and peer group experiences.

ANOTHER HIGHER RATED TEACHER

"These children are immature. Probably the thing they need most is to get a little self-confidence in what they are actually able to do. So I would compliment them when they complete a task very well, or when they manage themselves in a social situation better than usual, like if they get out of an argument by discussion rather than hitting or crying and running away from it. They need to know that I expect appropriate behavior. If a child cries easily, I would say, 'You know, I think it would be better if you didn't always cry when things are bothering you. If you are hurt, I will understand why you cry, but when you are simply mad at someone, or if somebody calls you a name, they are going to tease you more if you cry rather than if you just say "Well, that's not going to bother me" and walk away.' And I would tell them that I know that it does hurt their feelings, or they do feel upset enough to cry, but you try not to cry. Then if the occasion arose that I saw the immature child looking like they were going to cry, I would put a hand on their shoulder and whisper in their ear, 'I think you can come through this without crying' or maybe just give them a comforting look. They would feel like 'It's going to be all right; I don't need to cry.' With the child that loses things, I would talk with them about the fact that the things that belong to them are their responsibility, and I expect them to take care of them. I would help them find lost belongings the first one or two times. After that, maybe the next two or three times, they could have another person in the class help them find lost belongings. After that, they would be responsible for their own things. Dependent or helpless behavior I try to deal with by first saying to the child, 'I think you can do this. I'll help you get started, and then I want you to try it on your own. You can check back with me after you have completed _____' (I would state how much). I would specify more than one thing, otherwise they would be running to me or another adult after each task completion. Then reassure them as they complete things: 'See, I told you that you could do this. This is hard, but I think you're learning. Tomorrow, maybe you can finish these five and then check with me, and then we'll see how you're doing.' The immature child usually shows improvement in behavior after 4 or 5 months and probably will need continued support all during the year. The key word for them is support, so that they gain confidence in themselves and develop the skills that they need to work with children their own age."

This teacher would act as a socializer and coach to immature students, providing them with suggestions and encouragement to help them begin to act more maturely in troublesome situations. She would cultivate close relationships with these students and initially reinforce their dependency on her but then gradually encourage them toward more autonomous functioning. By taking time to build trust and avoiding pushing the students too abruptly, she likely maximized their willingness to accept her suggestions.

WHAT THE SCHOLARLY LITERATURE SAYS

Immature students have difficulty fulfilling the student role because they do not "act their age." They cannot seem to remember where they are supposed to be or what they are supposed to be doing, have difficulty keeping track of their possessions, tend to whine or become upset over minor disappointments, or display immature social behavior that may cause them to become teased or rejected by their classmates. Some elicit empathy and nurturance from teachers despite their persistent dependency; others "turn off" teachers because they come across as overly self-centered, whiny, or demanding.

Schaefer and Millman (1981) described these children as overdependent: seeking excessive help, affection, or attention from the teacher. Overdependent students show signs of immaturity such as whining, crying, and dependency behaviors. They often interrupt to request teachers to do things that they could do for themselves, and they often ask for help quickly rather than show initiative in persisting with problem solving on their own. They may persistently seek attention or attempt to stay physically close to the teacher. Schaefer and Millman traced the origins of these symptoms to children's experiences in the home: Some children learn to manipulate adults and get their way by playing the baby role, or they get attention by acting cute or by crying or whining. In other cases, parental guilt or other causes lead to an overly permissive child-rearing approach in which the parent has difficulty setting limits and the child learns to whine and manipulate until the parent gives in. Some parents view this behavior as normal and are not particularly concerned about it, although it creates problems for teachers at school.

Hyde (1976) studied what maturity meant to elementary teachers by polling 51 of them for descriptions of behavior that indicated maturity in their students. Many of the most commonly mentioned responses reflected students' abilities to listen to and follow directions, work independently without unnecessarily seeking teacher help, keep track of assignments, and complete them on time. Others focused on social traits: is well liked by classmates, listens to and communicates successfully with peers, does not blindly "follow the crowd," readily helps classmates in a noncondescending manner and without showing off, can take teasing, settles conflicts verbally without fighting, is able to "wait his turn" without always having to be first or be the center of attention, is able to mind her own business without bothering or pestering classmates, and is considerate of others' feelings and concerned with their rights and with fairness. Other commonly mentioned traits included the following: maintains constructive work even when the teacher is out of the room, can handle frustrations or criticism constructively without pouting or crying, is not easily distractible or hyperactive, does not tattle excessively, has a realistic appraisal of his or her own strengths and weaknesses, and asks appropriate "why" questions.

In follow-up work that involved asking 33 elementary teachers to rate their students on maturity behaviors, Hyde found that girls typically were rated as more mature than boys and that maturity ratings were associated with intelligence and achievement test scores and with grades. Teachers throughout the K through 6 range considered immaturity to be a problem with some of their students, although the particular patterns of immature behavior that students manifested varied by grade level.

Teachers' responses to immaturity symptoms apparently depend on individual differences and situational factors. Algozzine, Ysseldyke, and Christenson (1983) found that such responses were related to individual differences in teachers' tolerance for immature behavior. Teachers who were not bothered by immature behavior held higher expectations for a student who evidenced such behavior than teachers who were less tolerant of immaturity problems. Presumably the former teachers would be more oriented toward and more confident in working with immature students than the latter teachers. Smith (1981) found that teachers' reactions also depended on individual differences in students. Teachers were more likely to use supportive and instructional strategies with mildly or sporadically dependent students, but to use controlling and pressuring strategies with more persistently dependent students.

Brophy and Evertson (1981) found that elementary teachers viewed immature students as low achievers and poor workers and as likely to be hyperactive, temperamental, dependent on the teacher, or above average in frequency of medical problems. However, the teachers did not hold these students responsible for their behavior or describe them with unflattering adjectives indicating deliberate misbehavior or faulty character traits. Behavioral data indicated that students rated as immature, like students rated as hyperactive, were especially likely to come to the teacher in attempts to tattle on peers, to misbehave frequently, and to respond sullenly when disciplined. Furthermore, the misbehavior of these students was often disruptive. However, unlike the hyperactive students, the immature students did not project hostility toward the teacher by griping, sassing, or defying them. In fact, they had notably pleasant social contacts with teachers. Thus, blame or rejection was not a factor in the teacher–student relationships involving immature students, even though these students presented frequent and often serious problems to the teachers.

Teachers did criticize the poor work of immature students and either criticized or punished their misbehavior. However, they also frequently praised these students' good work and were likely to give them physical affection. These patterns of interaction indicate that teachers can tolerate frequent and even disruptive violations of student-role expectations and still maintain a basically positive stance toward students if the students do not project hostility toward them personally and if the teachers are able to attribute the students' inappropriate behavior to limited ability, immaturity, or other factors suggesting that the students are not responsible for the problems they present.

Suggested Strategies for Teaching Immature Students

Schaefer and Millman (1981) suggested weaning immature children from overdependence on you by using a combination of encouragement of their autonomous efforts and discouragement of their attempts to get you to do things for them that they should be doing for themselves. They advocated providing these students with opportunities to make choices and operate somewhat independently, supporting their efforts to do so, reinforcing their progress or accomplishments, and criticizing their failures in ways that do not discourage further efforts. They also advocated being firm in making reasonable demands on these children, gradually increasing what is expected from them as they become more able to meet these expectations, and ignoring or discouraging whining.

Rimm (1986) emphasized that you will need to learn to discriminate between students' bids for help that reflect genuine need for assistance and bids for help that reflect unnecessary dependency. She suggested that overly dependent students ask for explanations regularly instead of only with regard to subjects with which they have special difficulty; appear to ask questions mainly to gain your attention rather than to clarify confusions and then get on with their work; appear to be working below their capabilities; and tend to exhibit "poor me" body language (tears, helplessness, pouting, copying) whenever new work is presented, apparently as a bid for your sympathy and attention. Rimm recommended that you redirect your attention to such children from their dependency bids to their achievement striving and accomplishments; that you teach them how to set goals, plan and organize their work, and monitor and adjust it if necessary; and that you teach them to organize and keep track of their assignments, supplies, and belongings. With those who are public whiners or otherwise socially immature, she also recommended socialization designed to make them more aware of how their behavior is perceived by others and to teach them more mature ways of coping with frustration or stress.

Rational–emotive education techniques and stress inoculation have been recommended for helping students learn to replace "catastrophic" emotional reactions to stress ("Oh no, I've lost my hat! It's gone!") with more mature responses that support effective problem-solving efforts ("My hat's not here. Let's see, when was I wearing it last, and where might I have left it?"). Similarly, social and cognitive skills training programs have been recommended for teaching immature students such skills as listening carefully to instructions, persisting in attempts to carry out these instructions and asking for help only when it is really needed, monitoring and adjusting strategy usage, assessing and self-reinforcing progress, setting goals and developing plans, and solving social problems.

McIntyre (1989) compiled a lengthy list of suggestions for responding to immaturity in general and to several of its particular manifestations. He suggested that teachers attend to and praise immature students when they behave maturely and attempt to avoid reinforcing their immature behavior, socialize these students about behavioral expectations and about how you and their classmates view immature behavior, provide special consideration if needed to students who are physically immature or going through emotional difficulties, assign these students classroom housekeeping tasks or other roles that may help them develop responsibility, provide them with training in any needed cognitive or social skills, encourage their involvement in scouting or other youth organizations that build social maturity and responsibility, and do not respond to whining or sulking except to reassert to these students that they will need to meet appropriate expectations or suffer the consequences.

Thompson and Rudolph (1992) also recommended allowing immature students to suffer the natural consequences of their problem behavior, especially chronic forgetfulness or carelessness (failure to turn in an assignment on time leads to a reduction in grade, while failure to keep track of belongings leads to temporary or even permanent loss of the item). For more general immature or dependent behavior, these authors recommended meeting with students to identify areas in which they would like to become more independent, setting goals, and helping them to make and follow through on plans for change; assigning them responsibilities to build confidence; having them observe a peer model whom they admire, and then discussing with them the mature ways in which the peer behaves; having them tutor a peer or younger student in areas in which they are knowledgeable; and using active listening to allow them to ventilate their fears or concerns, but then engaging them in constructive problem-solving efforts.

Other sources (Apter & Conoley, 1984; Blanco & Bogacki, 1988) also have suggested similar strategies, along with several others: Use role-playing situations to allow immature students to practice what you teach them about more mature behavior; talk with them periodically to point out and praise evidence of progress; reassure them that they are capable of meeting reasonable expectations, and provide attribution retraining if necessary; tape generic instructions, assignment schedules, or other reminders to their desks, or in some other way provide them with an easily accessible visual reference; keep extra supplies (such as stubby eraserless pencils) available for loan to forgetful students, but collect them at the end of the day; and disparage immature behavior as babyish while praising mature behavior as more grown up or sophisticated.

Most of this advice is structured around a few key principles: Communicate empathy with the concerns of immature students, and provide them with any special consideration they might really need, but at the same time, make it clear to them that they will have to meet reasonable expectations or suffer the consequences. Meanwhile, help them to do so by providing any needed socialization to increase their awareness of their behavior and its consequences, as well as any needed instruction or op-portunities to learn cognitive and social problem-solving skills. To the ex-tent that immature students also display failure syndrome or underachievement problems, you also may need to use some of the strate-gies described in Chapters 5 and 7.

ANALYSIS OF INTERVIEW RESPONSES

The most commonly mentioned problem-solving strategies were proscrib-ing by restating rules or limits (43) and prescribing by instructing the stu-dent in desired behavior (42). Other strategies mentioned by more than 5 teachers included praising progress or accomplishments (26), involv-ing the parents for support or problem solving (25), projecting encourage-ment or positive expectations (22), self-concept support (22), attempting to extinguish unnecessary bids for teacher attention or help by ignoring them (22), providing academic help (18), involving classmates to provide support (15), threatening punishment for continued misbehavior (14), providing support through physical proximity or voice control (13), ap-peal and persuasion efforts (12), changing the task (10), changing the so-cial environment (10), group work (9), offering or delivering rewards (9), criticizing (9), minimal intervention or redirection strategies (8), direct modeling (8), involving school-based authority figures or professionals to support or problem solve (8), providing comfort or reassurance (7), and attempting to eliminate a perceived source of the problem (7). This is an unusually broad collection of strategies, reflecting the variety of problems that immature students may present.

The teachers' responses were coded for what they said about inter-acting with immature students during particular situations and about longer term prevention or follow-up strategies. Immediate responses to particular situations included confronting immature students about the inappropriateness of their behavior and demanding or suggesting desired alternatives (38); providing extra attention or support to compensate for a perceived problem with self-concept (33); helping students who have lost belongings by asking them questions or making suggestions, but stop-ping short of actually helping them search (26); assigning or requesting classmates to help search (14); and joining in the search themselves (12). Thirteen teachers said that they would react to the problems presented by students but not to the students' emotionality. Thus, they would help students find lost objects but not respond to their crying, or they would explain why the schedule has been changed but would not respond to their upset feelings.

Among teachers who mentioned prevention or follow-up strategies,

34 would try to minimize problems by building more structure into class routines or providing advance warning of changes; 24 would give immature students classroom responsibilities or leadership roles; 20 would provide encouragement and reinforce independent functioning by pointing out these students' progress in learning to tie their shoes, remembering to bring their folders, etc.; and 9 would ease the demands on them by reducing the number of goals or task segments that they needed to address at one time.

Among teachers who mentioned socialization efforts, 28 would seek to make these students more aware of their immature behavior (believing that they may not realize what they are saying or doing), 17 would provide explicit instruction about how these students might cope more effectively, and 15 would let them know that they were responsible for their actions and would have to accept the consequences if they failed to meet their responsibilities. Among teachers who spoke of a conference with parents, 12 would urge the parents to expect the child to undertake more responsibility at home, 11 would make the parents aware of the problem and discuss possible solutions, 9 would suggest that the parents hold back the student from school for another year or remove the student from the school, and 7 would urge the parents to discourage clinging or dependent behavior and reinforce independent behavior.

Concerning reasons for immature behavior, 39 teachers suggested that immature students have not been adequately socialized, have not had important experiences, or are not aware of their problems; 21 said that they seek attention and have been reinforced for acting immaturely; 16 noted that they are younger than their classmates; 15 remarked that they act immaturely because they have poor self-concepts; 12 observed that they are the oldest or the youngest in the family (and thus babied by the parents); and 9 thought that they might act immaturely because they are tired, sick, or suffering from some chronic physical problem.

Concerning ineffective responses to immature students, 18 teachers mentioned scolding, punishing, threatening, demanding, or attempting to push them to behave more maturely; 18 mentioned being overly sympathetic, attentive, or helpful to them; 12 mentioned confronting them about immature behavior in ways that would cause humiliation or loss of face; and 7 mentioned ignoring or failing to respond to their inappropriate behavior.

Relatively few of the interview coding categories correlated significantly with effectiveness ratings, probably because so many different kinds of behavior problems are included under student immaturity that it is difficult to identify general strategies that apply to all or even most of them. The main pattern in the significant correlations that did appear reflected the tendency of higher rated teachers to mention more strategies than lower rated teachers, as well as to identify different strategies to be used with different subtypes of immaturity.

Higher rated teachers tended to identify inadequate socialization at home and lack of awareness of the inappropriateness of immature behavior in the child as major causal factors, so their strategies focused on socialization and instruction. They were more likely to speak of proscribing against immature behavior by reminding the student of rules and expectations and of the consequences of failing to fulfill responsibilities, as well as providing encouragement and projecting positive expectations. In addition, they were more likely to speak of helping immature students by building more predictability and structure into classroom routines and by providing advance warning when changes in routine were about to take place. Finally, higher rated teachers were more likely to be among the 12 who would personally help immature students look for lost belongings and the 7 who would urge parents to discourage clinging and immature behavior and to reinforce independent behavior at home.

Vignette: Betty

Betty seems younger than the other students in your class. She has difficulty getting along with them and is quick to tattle. She has just told you that she heard some of the boys use "bad words" during recess today.

Before reading further, take time to think about how you might respond to this incident. Make notes about your ideas.

CSS Vignette Response Excerpts

Here is what four of the CSS teachers had to say.

A LOWER RATED TEACHER

"I just don't listen to them. I tell them frankly, 'Don't tell me those things,' The first time this happened I would say, 'I understand that, that they're doing that.' I really discourage tattling unless somebody is getting physically beaten to a pulp, or something that's really, really serious. Because as soon as kids think that you're going to listen to all of this, then this same Betty will be here the next day with another story, and two or three other kids will see that you're listening to her, so they'll be there with more stories. I just frankly don't pay any more attention to that kind of thing than I have to. I brush it off and say, 'I really don't want to hear about that right now.' [How do you characterize this behavior?] Well, she certainly is immature and looking for attention. Most kids that are habitual tattlers are lookng for your attention when they're telling you these stories. I just don't like to give them the idea that that's the way to get it. 'You could come up and talk to me about something else, but don't tell me about all these other kids. In the first place, I know most of this stuff goes on anyway, and if it's anything really serious, I'll try to take care of it, but you don't need to tell me about it.'"

A Higher Rated Teacher

"Betty has just told me she has heard someone using bad words at recess and I would approach her, first of all, by saying that I would talk to the boys about it, but that often things will come up like that—not only bad words, but other things—but I was glad she reported it. She has to be careful, though, not to report every little thing that she picks up from someone or every little mistake someone makes, that she doesn't run and tell the teacher all the time. That gets to be a habit. But we will deal with it, and she will have to be a big girl and try to be a little more mature and try to discern when to come to me with things. She needs to learn what are really legitimate complaints and what are just busy, wasting-time kinds of things. Try to help her see the difference as to when it is crucial. My goal would be to help her realize that this does exist. There are going to always be people doing things that they shouldn't be doing, but we can't always be on someone constantly. We have to try and decide in our own values how bad the offense is, if it really does need our attention, or if it is something that we can ignore. Sometimes I try to help her understand that a student might do that just to upset her, knowing that it upsets her, knowing that she couldn't cope and that she would tattle, just to make her feel bad, and that she would have to learn to ignore certain amounts of things so that she didn't get upset and tattle. She is immature and has not had much exposure to the world and around people so that she doesn't realize that it isn't kosher to tattle on everything. Maybe she's just a little naive, doesn't know much yet about what is going on and what school can really be like. She is going to have to face reality."

Another Higher Rated Teacher

"'Betty, it's possible that some of the boys were using bad words. I know this has happened before, and it's not something that I like to have happen at all. I will speak to those boys, but you know there is a problem with you always telling on other children. People don't like that. Unless you're doing as you should be all the time, I don't think you should be looking for things that other boys are girls are doing. You seem to have some problems because of this. The boys and girls are not very happy with your tattling and therefore are not becoming your friends the way you would like them to be. Why don't you just try to stay away from these boys, if they have been using bad words, and join in some games with the other children? Then, I don't think you will have the difficulties, and if you learn to become their friends, I don't think that you will see things that are so bad that they are doing.' The goal would be to get Betty involved in some other activity with other boys and girls where she would become part of it and not be so concerned with watching for things that she could tell about. This is a real problem with some children, just to get them to be aware and responsible for their own activities and not be looking for other children and what they are doing. If it's something that I feel really endangers them or something that is very serious that I need to know about, then I certainly do want to know. But it's hard to solve the problems if they are always looking for things to tattle back to the teacher."

ANOTHER HIGHER RATED TEACHER

"Betty, who is either younger than her classmates or immature, is about to get herself into trouble if she doesn't learn about the undesirable habit of tattling. I would caution her that she should not tell every small thing that her classmates do; they would not like it. I might ask her how she would feel if someone was telling all these things on her every few minutes, that there are some things that should be told and some things that should not be told. Then I might ask her what kinds of things should someone tell. Some situation in which someone might hurt themselves or someone else would be my main concern. See if she knows what those things are. If she doesn't, inform her of the important things you might tell someone to prevent someone from hurting themselves or someone else. From this, I believe we could get an understanding as to what things she would tell and what things she would not tell, to save her a lot of heartache, because she is on the road to making herself very unpopular. Get her to see that if she did this, her relationships with peers would improve."

The lower rated teacher was more concerned about discouraging tattling than about developing relationships with students like Betty and providing them with the kinds of socialization that they need. Consequently, she would not likely be successful with immature students. In contrast, the three higher rated teachers suggested responses that seem more likely to be successful in helping Betty advance to more mature forms of behavior. They would help her distinguish between things that ought to be reported to the teacher and things that they viewed as nuisance tattling.

They would also help her to understand that her tattling is resented by peers and is interfering with her opportunities to develop friendships.

Analysis of Responses to Betty

Almost all of the teachers recognized Betty's tattling as part of a larger immaturity syndrome, and most viewed it as both controllable (82) and intentional (76). None of the teachers mentioned rewards, and only 7 mentioned punishments. Sixty mentioned supportive behaviors, mostly instruction in better coping skills (37), kid gloves treatment when Betty became upset (23), and involving peers in supportive roles (10). Threatening/pressuring behaviors were mentioned by 34 teachers, although these were mostly confined to specific (27) or global personal (6) criticism.

A majority (57) included proscribing against inappropriate tattling as part of their response. Other specific problem-solving strategies included prescribing or modeling desired alternatives (32), attempting to develop Betty's insight into her behavior or its consequences (29), brief management responses (19), changing her social environment (13), and attempting to extinguish her tattling by ignoring it (12). Most (85) teachers would make behavioral change demands on Betty, although 27 would not accompany these demands with rationales. Rationales mentioned by the remaining teachers included logical analysis linking Betty's behavior to its consequences or explaining why suggested alternatives would result in better outcomes (24), making a personal appeal by explaining to Betty that her tattling is irritating (20), citing rules forbidding tattling or regulating when and why students should report something (14), appealing to Betty's pride or self-concept by suggesting that she is too old to behave in this manner (12), or attempting to induce empathy by asking Betty how she would like to be tattled on or explaining the problems that such tattling causes the teacher (6).

Teachers' responses were coded for what they said about their immediate response to Betty's tattle and about any attempts they might make to socialize Betty or shape her behavior. Three-fourths (75) of the teachers said that they would listen to the tattle and then follow up by giving suggestions to Betty (that she shouldn't be tattling, in general or in this instance, or that she should ignore such comments, stay away from the boys who made them, or handle such incidents herself). In addition or instead, 27 would follow up on the tattle by talking to the boys who used the "bad words" or by discussing the problem with the whole class, 16 would ignore Betty or refuse to listen by cutting her off or walking away from her, and 12 would give the appearance of a sympathetic response in order to satisfy Betty in the immediate situation but would not follow up on the tattle. These teachers might cut Betty off and ask her to come back and tell them about the problem later (hoping that she would forget in the meantime) or else listen briefly and reassure Betty that they would deal with the situation (but not actually do anything about it).

All but 9 of the teachers would attempt to socialize Betty or shape her behavior. Forty would criticize her tattling and tell her that tattling is prohibited in all or at least most situations; 35 would provide guidelines indicating when tattling is appropriate and when it is not; 34 would tell Betty to avoid the problem in the future by staying away from peers who use bad words, tuning the words out, or not being so quick to look for things to tattle about; 20 would use Golden Rule reasoning by trying to get Betty to see that tattling makes peers angry and likely to reject her; 14 would offer suggestions about how Betty could handle such incidents in the future (by avoiding the problem or responding to it in some way other than tattling); 12 would attribute Betty's tattling to poor peer relations and thus attempt to promote friendships between Betty and selected peers or to make Betty more acceptable to the class as a whole; and 6 would see that Betty is continuously involved in work or ongoing activities so that she doesn't have time to worry about what peers are doing.

Thirty-seven teachers said that what they might do would depend on the situation, particularly their perceptions of Betty (her reasons for tattling, her beliefs about "bad words" and children who use them, etc.) or their perceptions of the seriousness of the incident that Betty reported. A majority (51) exhibited a relatively neutral attitude toward Betty; whereas 24 responded positively by showing concern for Betty and a desire to help her; and 24 responded with frustration, anger, or disgust with Betty and spoke of pressuring her to change her behavior.

In attempting to explain Betty's tattling, a majority (53) attributed it to immaturity, a developmental stage, or being younger than her classmates. In addition or instead, 32 suggested that it was just a symptom of a need for attention from the teacher, 16 suspected that she is ignored or rejected by classmates and will stop tattling if her social relationships improve, and 15 thought that her tattling is part of a generally flawed personality (Betty is a busybody, a negative person, etc.).

We were not surprised to find that many teachers responded quite negatively to tattling. Brophy and Evertson (1981) found that tattling was more frequent in the early grades than in the later grades and more frequent among students labeled immature than among those seen as more mature. However, the highest rates of tattling were not found among "goody-two-shoes" students who were overly teacher-oriented and morally offended by essentially minor misbehavior. Instead, tattling was most frequent among students viewed by their teachers as restless, careless, low in persistence, or uncooperative. For these students, frequent tattling appeared to constitute a "misery seeks company" defense against frequent teacher criticism and punishment on the part of students who frequently misbehave. These tattlers approach their teachers not so much with immature shock and outrage but with implicit messages of "You punished me, so punish him too!" or "I'm not so bad — she does it, too!" Such attempts to pull down peers to one's own level by pointing out their faults did not characterize all of the students who tattled frequently. Some may have been confused about what the teacher expected and used tattling as a way to test the rules. Others may have tattled for no better reason than to take a break from work or provide themselves with something to do. In any case, Brophy and Evertson found high rates of tattling to be associated with undesirable student attributes, and the teachers they studied were frequently curt or rejecting in response to their students' tattling initiatives.

Pittman (1985) described interesting differentiated responses to tattling in a case study of a first-grade teacher's approach to classroom management. If this teacher believed that the tattler spoke out of genuine concern about the observed problem, she would respond positively and look into the matter if the tattler reported stealing, cheating, fighting, or illness; but she would give a brief, mild admonition about minding one's own business if the tattler reported something minor that shouldn't have been brought to her attention. If she perceived the tattling as an attempt by the student to manipulate her or to cause harm to another student, however, she would give a much more curt verbal admonition accompanied by glaring, "go away" hand motions, and other nonverbal indicators of disapproval. Many of the teachers interviewed for the Classroom Strategy Study appeared to follow similar rules in their responses to tattling.

In contrast to the interview findings, the data for the vignette included a large number of significant correlations with effectiveness ratings. Lower rated teachers were more likely to attribute Betty's tattling to general immaturity related to age or developmental stage. Yet they also were more likely to view her tattling as fully controllable and intentional and to emphasize controlling (i.e., eliminating or restricting within prescribed limits) the tattling as the primary or even the only thrust of their intervention suggestions. In contrast, higher rated teachers were more likely to suggest that Betty might not be in full control of this behavior and to emphasize teaching her better means of coping.

The correlations for specific strategies indicated that lower rated teachers would rely on behavior modification techniques and their personal relationship with Betty in their attempts to change her behavior, but higher rated teachers would use a broader range of methods that featured instruction, counseling, and socialization techniques. Lower rated teachers were more likely to speak of ignoring Betty's tattling approaches in an attempt to extinguish them. More typically, they spoke of making behavior change demands on Betty without including rationales beyond a personal appeal and without mentioning attempts to increase her insight or socialize her attitudes or beliefs. A minority of lower rated teachers appeared to empathize with Betty and were heavily represented among the teachers who spoke of kid gloves treatment at times when Betty was upset about something or who spoke of making a personal appeal to Betty to reduce her tattling. A majority of lower rated teachers, however, displayed a more neutral or even negative response to Betty that emphasized proscribing against tattling and making behavioral change demands. These teachers were heavily represented among those who spoke of ignoring her approaches or putting her off for the moment in the hope that she would forget to come back later or else hearing her out briefly and promising to follow up later without actually intending to do so.

Higher rated teachers were more likely to respond positively to Betty, to provide her with help as well as improvement demands, and to indicate that their response to particular tattling situations would vary according to their perceptions of Betty or the seriousness of the incident she reported. These teachers were more likely to speak of instructing Betty in better means of coping, particularly by avoiding upsetting situations or by exercising better judgment about when and why the activities of other students should be reported. Higher rated teachers also were more likely to proscribe against tattling, although their proscriptions tended to take the form of guidelines about appropriate versus inappropriate tattling rather than more global "I don't like tattling, and I don't want you to do it" responses.

Besides providing Betty with more guidance about when and why tattling might be appropriate, higher rated teachers were more likely to speak of attempts to improve Betty's insight into her behavior and its effects, particularly by making her aware that peers resent tattling and might reject Betty socially because of it. Finally, along with these attempts to build Betty's understanding about tattling, higher rated teachers were more likely to speak of attempting to improve Betty's social adjustment by enlisting peers in supportive roles or by taking steps to stimulate the development of friendships between Betty and selected classmates.

The responses of higher rated teachers reflect the advice on handling tattling that has been offered in the scholarly literature. McIntyre (1989) collected the following suggestions: Tell tattlers that you do not wish to hear tattling, and ignore them when they attempt to tattle; have them monitor the frequency of their tattling and discuss the results; refuse to listen to hearsay or rumors; accept tattling only in written form, and tell the tattlers that you will review their notes later; thank them for their information, but then return them to task, if necessary asking them what they should be doing now; and provide them (or the class as a whole) with guidance about which kinds of observations should be reported to you and which should not.

Charney (1992) suggested that you use "Could it be?" questions to determine the motivation behind the tattling (testing the rules, desiring to see classmates get into trouble, seeking teacher help because the classmates have not responded to the tattler's requests that they stop doing what they are doing, or genuine concern that what they are doing needs to be stopped immediately). She suggested that 5-year-olds are apt to tattle in order to affirm their own law-abiding status, 6-year-olds to make trouble for classmates or test the punitive possibilities of various forms of misbehavior, and 7-year-olds to express their concern about disobedience to rules. She recommended helping students distinguish between "tattling" to get others into trouble and "telling" when you need help from the teacher because of an emergency, a conflict that you can't solve on your own or with classmates, or a problem that needs adult attention (such as an injury or fight). The teacher can later refer to this distinction when children come to her to report something, by asking them if this is "tattling" or "telling." She also noted that widespread tattling is indicative of problems in the classroom, such as too much competition or pressure or unclear expectations that students feel the need to clarify. Frequent tattling by particular individuals suggests peer adjustment problems and may call for help in forming friendships in addition to socialization about tattling.

Thompson and Rudolph (1992) noted that like gossipers, tattlers often attempt to gain attention and favor with adult authority figures, but they are hard to ignore because they often bring needed information. Also, they are usually lonely and rejected by peers, so they need help. They suggested meeting privately with tattlers to interpret their behavior as a cry for help in gaining acceptance and recognition in the group, to discuss alternatives to tattling, and to help them plan better ways of gaining acceptance (especially through their recreational interests and abilities). They also advocated cutting off tattlers when it becomes clear that their message is not needed ("Rather than discussing that now, perhaps we should _____"), helping them to understand that tattling is self-defeating because peers view it with contempt, and helping them to distinguish between tattling and more appropriate reporting of information to you. Finally, Love and Baer (1991), two first-grade teachers, described how they successfully taught their students assertiveness techniques for expressing themselves in social situations and negotiating resolution to conflicts, so that the students no longer needed to come to them and tattle as a way to get the teachers to solve their problems for them.

Vignette: Greg

Greg often loses his belongings, becomes upset, whines, and badgers you to help him. Now he has misplaced his hat, and he is pestering you again. Other students smirk and make remarks about this, and Greg becomes upset.

Before reading further, take time to think about how you might respond to this incident. Make notes about your ideas.

CSS Vignette Response Excerpts

Here is what four of the CSS teachers had to say.

A LOWER RATED TEACHER

"I wouldn't go and try to help this little boy find anything. If I did it for one, I'd have the whole class to deal with. I'd ask one or two of his peers to help him find his clothes or his things, and I'd ask his mother to be sure and put his name on all of his things and pin his gloves, and things that he can lose, onto him. But I would never help him look for anything. I would let the children do it. Because if I did it for one, I'd be always helping and dressing and so on with the children. [How would you characterize somebody like this?] Immaturity."

A HIGHER RATED TEACHER

"To immediately deal with the situation, I guess I would say, 'Greg appears to have lost his hat. Are there a couple of children in the classroom who would be willing to help him look? Perhaps its on the playground or in the hallway, or check in the lost and found to see if it's there first.' In this way, perhaps the other children will stop smirking. A lot of times when you ask the other children to help out, you get a really good response, rather than getting down on them. Later on, I think I would take Greg aside and try to set up some kind of system with him where each little belonging has a specific place where it is supposed to be. Since he seems to be disorganized and is consistently losing things and the whining is getting on my nerves, I guess I would try and find some kind of a situation or set up something where 'Your hat and coat go here. This is the only place you are to put them. Your books, etc., go here.' I would probably check with him at the beginning of each day to make sure that he puts the things exactly where they belong. [What would your goals with Greg be?] To help him realize that keeping track of your belongings and having a place where they should be would cut down on the fact that he is always misplacing things. I guess I would also tell him—I would just flat outright tell him that the whining, etc., just doesn't help at all, that I don't like listening to whining, and by getting upset he is not helping himself. I would help him get just a little bit more organized and take on a little more responsibility about his things, because obviously the fact that he misplaces so many things shows that he is not really looking after them the way he should."

ANOTHER HIGHER RATED TEACHER

"I would ignore the other boys and girls at that point and say, 'Greg, have you checked all the lockers?' because usually their things are out in the lockers. 'OK, you go ahead out and check all the lockers.' And when he is out, I would say to the other children, 'Your behavior is not very polite, and you're not making Greg feel happy.' Usually that will take care of it. If Greg still cannot find his hat, I would assign some child that was empathetic to him to go to the lost and found. Also, I would try to catch Greg at another time and say, 'Greg, let's think about what you are doing with your belongings, because you are responsible for them. You have a locker; now you be sure your things are in your locker, or if you have it in your desk, it is your job to take care of it. You are responsible.' I would keep hammering it in all year, and it does take several years with this kind of child. I suppose it's a child who does not have to do this at home. The children just come in and throw their things, and that is it. He's often the child who doesn't come to school, and you call up and say, 'Where is he?' and they say, 'Oh, he couldn't find his shoes today.' I would say this is the child who has never been taught responsibility for his possessions."

ANOTHER HIGHER RATED TEACHER

" 'Greg, I'm concerned about the many times that you are having difficulty being responsible for your belongings. We need to be sure that you put things in the correct place in the locker, that your hat, gloves, and coat are all hung together. I know that you are upset right now, but I'm going to have Tom help you. I think that if you go out in the hall and work together, possibly you can find your hat. Then after you have looked for it, come back here and we'll talk about ways in which you can maybe become more responsible and not lose your things as you have.' My goal would be to get Greg to try and find a solution to this by having one of the other children help him. Then they might stop making remarks about him and show more concern about Greg and the problems he has. But the immediate goal is to try to get him to find his hat and become less upset."

Here again, the lower rated teacher was more concerned about discouraging dependency initiatives by immature students than about meeting these students' needs. She did suggest strategies that would reduce the frequency of clothing loss problems and enlist assistance from classmates at times when clothing had been misplaced. However, she did not mention anything about providing these students with the kind of supportive coaching that would speed their development of more mature levels of functioning. In contrast, the higher rated teachers would work with Greg to help him learn to keep better track of his possessions. Two of them also would work with Greg's classmates to reduce their tendencies to ridicule or reject him because of his immature behavior.

Analysis of Responses to Greg

Compared to their perceptions of Betty, notably fewer of the teachers attributed Greg's behavior solely to causes residing within him (66) or interpreted his behavior as controllable (40) or intentional (12).

Only 3 teachers mentioned rewards, and only 7 mentioned punishments. All but 16 mentioned supportive behaviors, mostly instructing Greg in better ways of coping (51), involving classmates (38) or parents (11) in supportive roles, or providing kid gloves treatment at times when Greg was upset (8). Only 20 teachers mentioned threatening or pressuring behaviors, mostly specific criticism of Greg's immature actions (12).

Prescribing or modeling desired behavior was by far the most common problem-solving strategy, mentioned by 74 teachers. Other strategies included attempts to change Greg's social environment (23), proscribing against undesired behavior (17), eliminating a perceived source of the problem (14), developing Greg's insight (12), brief management responses (11), punishment (8), attempting to extinguish his behavior by ignoring it (6), and involving his parents (6).

All but 11 of the teachers mentioned behavioral change demands, but 36 did not include accompanying rationales. Those who did include rationales mostly emphasized logical analyses linking Greg's problems to their causes (e.g., he lost his hat because he didn't put it where it belonged) or explaining why the behavioral changes they were suggesting would be helpful, or else they appealed to his sense of pride or positive self-concept (e.g., indicating that he is too big or smart a boy to be losing his belongings all the time).

Responses were coded for what teachers said about responding to Greg's concern about his lost hat, responding to smirking classmates, and implementing longer term prevention or socialization strategies. In responding to the immediate problem of Greg's lost hat, 32 teachers would confine themselves to verbal help (asking questions to help him remember where he left it or making suggestions about where he might look for it); 32 would assign or request classmates to help; 22 would assist in the search personally; 19 would reassure Greg that the hat will turn up, that he could look for it later, or that he will get help if he needs it; and

89 would promise to help Greg search but only after the other students leave (either as a delaying tactic to avoid reinforcing Greg's dependency or allowing him to avoid work, or else merely because it will be easier to find the hat when the other students have left the room, along with their belongings).

Only a minority mentioned responding to the smirking classmates. Of these teachers, 17 would scold or punish these students or demand that they apologize to Greg; 15 would defend Greg by telling the peers that he may have good reasons for being concerned about his hat, that they would be concerned too if they were in his place, or that his problem deserves sympathy or help rather than ridicule; and 15 would enlist their help in the search.

The most common prevention or socialization strategy reported was stating rules or expectations (59) — informing or reminding Greg that he is responsible for his possessions and will be expected to fulfill this responsibility in the future. Strategies mentioned in addition or instead included emphasizing to Greg that he would not lose his belongings if he put them in the cubbyhole or locker assigned to him (or, if no such place is assigned, providing a specific place for Greg to use in the future) (33); proscribing against whining, or at least avoiding reinforcing such whining in the future (21); beginning to monitor Greg more carefully and to provide reminders when he enters the room or begins to put his belongings away (14); teaching Greg how to organize his belongings and remember where he puts things (12); and asking a peer or the class as a whole to keep an eye out for his belongings and return them to him or to a lost and found if they should find them (9).

Almost half (46) of the teachers attributed Greg's behavior to general immaturity, although 28 suggested that he had not been taught responsibility at home or in previous grades, and 16 thought that his behavior might have been part of a general pattern of attention seeking. A heavy majority (79) showed concern about locating Greg's hat, but 58 would seek to avoid reinforcing Greg's dependency and his expectations that he should be helped rather than taking responsibility for his belongings, and 19 would warn him that they would help this time but not if he lost his hat again. About half (49) adopted a neutral attitude toward Greg, whereas 20 responded primarily with concern for his welfare, and 29 responded primarily with annoyance or irritation.

Although less extensive in number, the pattern of significant correlations with effectiveness ratings for this vignette was similar to the one found for the previous vignette. Once again, higher rated teachers were primarily neutral or slightly positive in their attitudes toward Greg and tended to emphasize instruction or socialization in their responses. In contrast, one subset of lower rated teachers were primarily negative in their attitude and tended to emphasize threat/pressure strategies, whereas another subset were primarily sympathetic to Greg and spoke of providing him with emotional support and reassurance (as well as assistance in finding his hat), but not necessarily longer term prevention or socialization.

Higher rated teachers were more likely to respond to the depicted incident as a minor one, perhaps only calling for a brief management response or reminder to Greg about storing his belongings properly. However, these teachers were much more likely to speak of extensive preventive or socialization efforts as follow-up to the incident: emphasizing to Greg the importance of storing his belongings in assigned cubbyholes or closet areas, helping him to appreciate the connection between following prescribed storage rules and keeping track of his belongings, or beginning to monitor him more closely and provide cues or reminders to follow up on these socialization efforts. Finally, although they were unlikely to suggest scolding or threat/ pressure strategies with Greg, higher rated teachers were more heavily represented among the 17 who spoke of scolding or threatening to punish classmates who teased or ridiculed him.

COMPARISON OF RESPONSES TO BETTY AND TO GREG

Patterns of response were similar for the two vignettes in that the teachers emphasized brief verbal instructions as situational responses to the depicted incidents. A majority viewed the incidents as minor and adopted a relatively neutral attitude toward the student, but one minority emphasized sympathy and kid gloves treatment, while another minority expressed irritation and emphasized scolding. In each case, lower rated teachers were more likely to respond negatively and to emphasize controlling or pressuring strategies, whereas higher rated teachers were more likely to respond neutrally or positively and to emphasize instruction and socialization strategies.

There were some differences connected with the fact that Betty's tattling represented a problem of behavioral excess (taking positive actions that are inappropriate or that are sometimes appropriate but not to the extent or in the manner that Betty implemented them), whereas Greg's lost hat was part of a problem of behavioral deficit (failure to keep track of or store his belongings properly). As a result, the teachers were much more likely to view Betty's behavior as controllable and intentional, to criticize or proscribe against it, and in general to emphasize control or suppression strategies. With Greg, their verbal responses were more likely to emphasize prescription (suggesting places that he might search for his hat or ways to keep track of his belongings more successfully) rather than proscription or criticism. In short, the teachers concentrated on telling Betty what *not* to do (stop tattling, or at least, stop tattling when the situation isn't serious and doesn't call for it), whereas they concentrated on telling Greg what *to* do (undertake specific actions to find his hat or keep better track of his belongings).

QUALITATIVE IMPRESSIONS AND EXAMPLES

The most impressive responses generally followed the same basic model: Be patient and supportive with immature students, encourage them to function more independently while reassuring them that they can do so, and gradually increase expectations but continue to help them be able to meet those expectations if needed. Many teachers suggested the value of helping these students or showing them what they need to do the first few times they express a given problem, but they also made it clear that you expect them to learn how to handle the problem and assume more independent responsibility.

As the students begin to catch on, you can start to fade out your assistance and cueing. Help them when they really need help, but mostly give them a little personal attention, communicate positive expectations, and give them enough direction to get them started. Don't preach, but help them to see that they can do more things on their own and that minor problems are not a big deal.

In this regard, several teachers mentioned the value of getting these students to calm down, stop, and think about what would be promising strategies for addressing their problem. This is better than solving the problem for them or telling them what to do because it socializes them toward relying on themselves more to generate possible solutions. In the process, you can communicate positive expectations and reality definitions ("I know that you are smart and can figure this out if you take the time to do it"). One teacher emphasized the value of giving these students several choices to select from rather than just telling them what to do or, even better, responding to their statement of a problem by asking, "What are you going to do about it?"

Several teachers said that the best response to whining or crying is to tell the child directly that you don't like to see that behavior and that it isn't an effective way to communicate needs. They stated that students who are prone to whining or crying are accustomed to doing this at home and often believe that it is expected as a natural response to frustration, so they need to be taught a different way of thinking about how to respond when you have a problem. These teachers often would incorporate age or stage expectations into these explanations ("You're in first grade now"; "You can't be acting like a baby anymore"; etc.). One teacher noted that it is tempting but not wise to whine back at these students as a form of sarcasm. However, several suggested using benign humor as a way to calm down or redirect students who are upset. For example, in response to students who overreact to minor injuries, one teacher might say, "Do you want the ambulance now, or can you wait an hour?" or "Shall we call the doctor, the nurse, or the lady with the alligator purse?"

Many teachers mentioned the value of structure and sameness for disorganized students. They would assign them to the same seat and cubbyhole throughout the year, use a standard schedule and warn the students about any upcoming deviations from it, and so on.

Upper-grade teachers often emphasized attempts to increase immature students' insights into their behavior and its consequences. One tried to impress on these students that junior high teachers would be much less responsive to their needs if they failed to keep track of their materials or assignments, and that junior high students would be less accepting of childish social behavior. Another sixth-grade teacher used the fact that her students were the oldest in the school to appeal to their sense of being grown up ("You are a sixth-grader now, and we expect you not to act like those little kids in the earlier grades"). She also used formalities such as referring to the students as Mr. or Miss in an attempt to reinforce the grown-up notion. Finally, she used books by Judy Blume and other adolescent fiction authors who have written about problems in personal and social development in ways that can help enhance these students' insights or coping skills.

Many upper-grade teachers expressed exasperation with immature students and said that they had difficulty being patient with them. Also, some kindergarten and first-grade teachers expressed the belief that students do not belong in school yet if they aren't ready to handle basic self-care responsibilities. Some favored raising the age for beginning school or making it easier to delay school entrance for students who couldn't yet button their coats, etc. These teachers did not seem prepared to provide immature students with the acceptance and support that they need (along with instruction and socialization). It appears that these teachers would have been better placed in higher grades.

Several teachers in Big City talked about maturity being biologically based and not open to much effect of the teacher. Big City teachers also frequently spoke of insisting that students (or their parents) label their clothing and belongings, thus making it easier to identify and reclaim lost items.

Among common types of immature students, teachers frequently mentioned twins, only children, youngest children, and children who had been babied by their parents or grandparents. If the latter problem included bringing the children to school and picking them up after school, these teachers would suggest to the parents or grandparents that they stop doing so. One teacher had stock lines that she used in recurring situations with immature students. When habitual tattletales came up to her and began relating something, she would stop them and ask, "Is this going to be important?" With students who habitually lost their belongings, she might say, "Hey, I'm only a teacher, not Sherlock Holmes." Humorous or other stock lines need to be treated with care, however, because as many teachers noted, immature students need praise and reassurance of their capabilities, not shaming or nagging for being babyish.

Concerning the vignettes, the most noteworthy responses unfortunately tended to be negative ones. Many teachers not only didn't show much concern for the needs of immature students but seemed notably uninterested in their problems or, in the case of Betty, eager to avoid any responsibility on the grounds that the problem happened out on the playground rather than in their classroom. Some of these teachers flatly stated that tattling or whining irritated them, and they wouldn't tolerate even a little of it. A few said that they discouraged tattling by threatening draconian punishments, such as making tattlers wear a special tattletale hat or bull's tail or making them stand at the blackboard with their nose in a chalked circle and their hands behind their back.

The best responses to Betty included socialization attempts designed to help her become less sensitive to the behaviors she observes, to distinguish better between when and when not to tattle, and to understand how her peers view tattling. The best responses to Greg included instruction in better ways to keep track of his belongings.

One teacher kept a box of hats, mittens, scarves, etc., that she would lend to students until they found what they had lost. Several teachers in the early grades talked about having Greg or his parents label his clothes, attach his mittens to his coat, and so on. A few teachers in the upper grades would mention the possibility of taking such actions as a threat to Greg ("If you don't stop losing your hat, we're going to have to tie it to your coat like they do with little kids").

Finally, one teacher reported that when she had a problem with students losing things, she would read them the story *One Mitten Louis*, about a boy who was always losing his mittens. This teacher also had strung up a clothesline in a corner of the room for her students to use to hang any lost items that they found, so that they would be easily visible. She said that she never had to go and find things for her students because of this.

DISCUSSION

Immaturity problems embody key issues involved in choosing your role as a teacher (see Chapter 1). In the early grades, immature students need not only the usual instruction and support but often a great deal of nurturance and physical assistance, as well as tolerance and patience with their whining, crying, or displays of helplessness. In the later grades, they need not only the usual instruction and support but also sympathetic assistance in learning to handle frustrations and problems more competently, help in developing better peer relationships, and often protection from malicious teasing, scapegoating, or other victimization by classmates. It may be true that these children "should act their age" or that their behavior is exasperating, but it is certainly true that they need their teachers to reach out and help them, not distance themselves from them with disparaging criticism. If you believe that you are not capable of providing these students with what they need, you probably should avoid the elementary grades or else undertake resocialization of your own attitudes and beliefs, to enable you to become more understanding of these students and emotionally prepared to help them.

Assuming that the teacher has a productive attitude toward these students and has clear definitions of their problems and needs, the key to successful treatment of them is probably gradual improvement through successive approximations. They are unlikely to be prepared to handle a drastic shift from adult dependency to mostly independent functioning, even if they already possess the knowledge and skills needed to cope successfully on their own. They will need the security of knowing that you value and support them and remain available as a helper and resource person when they need you.

Along with this basic emotional support, they may need a great deal of assistance provided through environmental engineering, situational cues and reminders, socialization and insight development, and instruction in self-management and problem-solving skills.

You may find it helpful to think of immaturity problems as problems of behavioral deficit rather than behavior excess. That is, instead of thinking of these students as deliberately engaging in inappropriate behavior, learn to think of them as children who have not yet learned all they need to know about behavioral expectations for students of their age and grade level or about the self-management and problem-solving strategies needed to fulfill these expectations. Defining immaturity problems in this manner will help you respond to them effectively, initially by analyzing the problem to determine what forms of support, socialization, or instructional help the student might need, and then by following through. This approach will also help you to be patient and supportive with these students, because it will suggest goals and plans to follow in working with them and thus help you avoid unproductive (nagging, expressing frustration) or counterproductive (belittling, rejecting) responses.

Finally, keep in mind that immature students often fail to fulfill not only the student-role responsibilities expected by their teachers but also the social maturity expectations of peers. As a result, they are often lonely or socially rejected children who would like to make friends and be more accepted in the peer group but whose efforts in these directions are ineffectual or counterproductive. Consequently, along with assistance in meeting their student-role responsibilities more capably, immature students may need your help in developing better social relationships. In this regard, they may need some of the forms of assistance emphasized in the next two chapters.

V

Students with Social Relationship Problems

P art V contains two chapters on students whose problems lie primarily in their social interactions with peers. Chapter 14 focuses on students who are *rejected by their peers:* They desire and seek friendships but are not accepted, either because they display negative personal qualities or simply because they are new to the school or different in some way that shouldn't matter but does. In extreme cases, these students may become objects of malicious teasing or bullying by classmates.

Chapter 15 focuses on students who are *shy or withdrawn*—students who are not actively rejected by their peers but are socially isolated because they seldom initiate social interactions or respond effectively to the overtures of peers. These are not well-adjusted students who simply prefer to operate independently most of the time; rather they are extremely shy or withdrawn students whose social unresponsiveness worries their teachers.

14

Students Rejected by Their Peers

Peer rejected students display the following characteristics: These children seek peer interaction but are rejected, ignored, or excluded. They:

1. Are forced to work and play alone
2. Lack social skills
3. Are often picked on or teased

What special strategies might you use to minimize such problems and help these students to function more successfully in your classroom? Before reading further, take time to think about this and make notes about your ideas.

CSS INTERVIEW EXCERPTS

Here is what three of the CSS teachers had to say about teaching students who are rejected by their peers.

A LOWER RATED TEACHER

"This is what I call the isolate in the class. You cannot force other children to accept him. You give him a task such as passing out papers, and they'll go, 'Yechhhhh . . . he's touching my paper.' So I tell them, 'OK, you don't want your paper? Every paper you refuse, he is to throw in the wastebasket.' Or you have him pass out books. I've got him under control, and now I have to get the class under control in their actions toward him. They never will accept him completely, but if he hands them a textbook and they throw it on the floor, it stays on the floor. He is not allowed to pick it up, and they don't get another one until they pick it up. If they don't do the lesson, they get a failing grade. As I say, this child is picked on, is teased, and usually these are the Charlie Browns in the classroom too. They bring it on themselves quite a bit. There is not much you can do as a teacher. You can try to bolster the child's own self-image, but it is very difficult to get a class to accept them. He has to make them accept himself. And sometimes it is a real job. And a small child is really not up to this type of thing."

This teacher's potential for helping peer rejected students was severely impaired by negative expectations and an orientation toward trying to force the rejected student on the peer group rather than instructing the rejected student in social skills and socializing the peer group to create a positive classroom climate. From some of the things that the teacher said in passing, it appears that a very negative climate had developed in her classroom.

A Higher Rated Teacher

"I see these children as not being able to relate well to other children. Possibly they have tried in the past and have been rejected. Now this says that they seek peer interaction, and I think some of them really do continue to, but others don't after a while because they have been rejected. I find that this is a really pathetic child and one that I try very hard to have good things happen for. Sometimes they're a very dirty child, or sometimes they smell. Sometimes they might not have nice things. There are various reasons why. Maybe they can't play games as well, or they're very clumsy, but I see all kinds of different reasons where an individual might fall into this classification. Sometimes it's interesting to see how children feel about their peers by doing a sociometric study. I often do this to just see if the child is being rejected. I'd like to find out if it is a total group rejection or if I can spot one child that might be able to work with this student in some capacity. You could ask a number of things on the sociogram. You might say, if you chose a child you would sit beside, for instance, what would be your three choices? Or if you would choose a child to work with in math, or to be your team captain, what child would it be? Hopefully this child might show up as chosen in some area by someone else, and if there was another child that did accept this particular student in some way, I would try to get them together. It might be in an art activity, or it might be on the same team. Select them to be on the same team for a game, but somehow get them started with someone who is accepting of them. I think you need a lot of background work with the total class for this. *The Hundred Dresses* by Eleanor Estes (1974) is especially good for this one because it is about a child who was rejected by a whole class, and by three girls in particular who were not nice to her at all. Yet she was quite an artist, and when they found out her talent, they wished they had been nicer to her. But I think you can try to find somewhere where this child does excel and in some way point that out to the group. Perhaps it's a picture you might put up as a special picture of the week, or if they have a special hobby or something they can bring from home, they can share it with the class, just to get other children interested in them. I've often used the humanities series or some of these 'Inside/Outside' films that might point out how you react to the other children or how other children feel when they are rejected. We talked about friends today. We were just doing a little thing where they answer, how are you as a friend? what do you like about other people? what can you do with a friend? I think if you do these kinds of things with the class, it helps them to see these children that are rejected, and there will be some children that might become their friends. I think you as the teacher have to show them acceptance. Sometimes they're also rejected by teachers, and this is a very sad thing. I think it's very necessary, first of all, for a teacher to accept this child no matter what they are. And then very often, if you find the reason why they're rejected, if they're a dirty child for instance, then talk with the school nurse. If you feel comfortable talking to the children themselves or with their parents, say that there are some problems and maybe if the child would take a bath or see that they're careful about their cleanliness, this might help. I've had children that are rejected because of smell, and I've gone to the school nurse for help or the community helper who sometimes works closer with the families and feels comfortable talking with them. I think at this age, which is fourth-graders, very often you can talk with the child because lots of times they are responsible. There isn't anybody that really is looking after them. So I try to find the reason, and if there's some way that I could eliminate that reason, first of all, that would be a help. Here again, you might give them a special assignment like being helper for the week, where they would be mixing in more with the children. They would be passing out papers; they would be running errands and working closely with the teacher. They would be able to choose children to help them with a particular task. Very often other children are eager to do that, and even if the child is rejected, they would still volunteer to help them do a particular thing. [Have you felt that these strategies have been fairly successful in the short run or in the long run? Some of those sound like they are short-run strategies.] I think they're short-run if they work. Having them work with another child who accepts them would be short-run as long as that would continue. That friendship and other friendships would build, but usually I've found that with this type of child, it really takes quite a long time for them to become completely accepted. I've found very few instances where a child will be totally rejected. Usually you can find at least a small group that will accept them, and I think the thing is to really get them to understand how it feels to be rejected. You might even do this type of lesson when the child is absent or if you sent the child possibly to help in another room for that time. Another thing too is getting these children involved in after-school activities. Then they become part of a group, like the Girl Scouts or Boy Scouts, where the whole idea is working together."

This teacher expressed interesting ideas about using sociometric techniques to identify classmates who did not share the more general tendency to reject this student and thus were good starting places for developing friendships and social acceptance. She also had interesting ideas about working with the class as a whole to develop a positive and accepting climate, in addition to working with the rejected student. Finally, she would model acceptance of that student herself, work on the student's negative attributes that cause or contribute to peer rejection, and take a variety of steps to broaden and improve the student's network of social relationships.

ANOTHER HIGHER RATED TEACHER

"Sometimes it's difficult to pinpoint why a child who seeks interaction with other children is rejected by them or ignored or excluded, because lots of times the child seems perfectly OK to me, and I don't understand it. Sometimes it's very obvious, because the child may have some habit that grinds on the other kids. Sometimes just being different gets children excluded. They want to interact, they want to be accepted, but there's something within them that makes them a little bit different, a little bit odd to the other children. I have tried several techniques in this situation. First of all, the child that's being rejected is probably feeling awful, and I usually try to be as warm with them as possible. Even if the child is not particularly attractive to me, I usually go out of my way to put my arm around them, give them physical contact, give them smiles, and have a few extra words for them, because at least they'll feel accepted by me, and that's a start ing point. The kids see that the teacher has accepted that child, and they may be more likely to come around. I've found that one of the best ways to include them, if you have a free period in the classroom or free time outside at recess, is to organize some kind of small-group activity and include that child and ask other children to play with us. I will just gradually withdraw myself from whatever that particular activity is. A play situation is a good place to have it start. Another thing that might help is if that child has a particular skill or is particularly strong in one academic area, he or she might be able to help somebody else who isn't as strong. That puts them in the situation of being on top, so they're the ones that are giving forth and the other child has to look to them, kind of turning the tables a little bit. Sometimes if you can find some strength or talent in that child and let them be a little bit of a shining light, then they'll come around. . . . If the child is often picked on or teased, it has to be handled in the total group. There has to be some kind of awareness lesson, perhaps role-playing situations where maybe the prime person who does the picking on or the teasing is the person in the role-playing situation who is picked on and teased, depending on the age. Really young children are still so self-centered. Sometimes they just don't realize what they're doing to another person, and if you can reverse the roles and let them for 5 minutes be the other person and know how it feels, perhaps there will be a little light dawning. In terms of talking with the parents, I would encourage the parents to have the child perhaps be in Scouts. Sometimes if they share an extracurricular activity, it forms a bond of some kind. You have something in common with that person that you might not have had before. I've had parents who were reluctant for their children to do after-school activities. The parents had to be encouraged. I think lots of times odd things in children's behaviors have come from their parents not letting go of the children enough to let them explore and get out in the world, so the parents have to loosen up a little."

This teacher also spoke of modeling acceptance of rejected students herself to pave the way for peer acceptance of them. She also would structure activities that brought the rejected student into social interaction with peers, but then gradually disengage herself once the activity began to take hold, to condition both the rejected student and the peers to become accustomed to interacting without her presence in the group. Finally, she suggested ideas about improving the rejected student's image in the peer group, involving this student in extracurricular activities, and working with the class as a whole to develop a positive classroom climate.

WHAT THE SCHOLARLY LITERATURE SAYS

Children's experiences with their peers provide them with opportunities to learn how to interact with others, control their social behavior, develop age-relevant skills and interests, and share problems and feelings (Berndt & Ladd, 1989; Hartup, 1989). Children who are popular with or at least well accepted by their peers tend to derive these and other benefits from their social relationships. However, many children are not so well accepted. Some are social isolates who are mostly ignored; others are actively disliked and socially rejected. A great deal has been learned about students who develop these contrasting peer relationships (Asher & Coie, 1990; Berndt & Ladd, 1989; Juvonen & Weiner, 1993; Kennedy, 1990; McCallum & Bracken, 1993; Newcomb, Bukowski, & Pattee, 1993; Parker & Asher, 1987; Wentzel & Erdley, 1993).

Children who become popular with their peers are often physically attractive and possess special skills or talents, especially athletic ability in boys and social skills in girls. However, as the children develop into adolescents, peer acceptance becomes more closely associated with personal characteristics that make them liked as individuals and valued as group members. Popular students tend to be cheerful and optimistic, open and empathetic toward others, and at ease in social situations. As children, they know how to enter ongoing games, how to share, how to be an enjoyable play partner, and how to inhibit aggressive and insulting behaviors. As adolescents they make others feel accepted and involved, are able to self-disclose when appropriate, are emotionally supportive of peers, and engage in dialogue assertively but tactfully.

Unpopular students tend to lack these positive qualities and also to possess certain negative qualities that impair their peer relationships. Socially isolated students who are generally neglected by their peers tend to be ill at ease and lacking in self-confidence in social situations. Unable to assert themselves effectively, they may react to conflict with timidity, nervousness, or withdrawal. To the extent that they also say embarrassing things, they may be teased or picked on instead of merely ignored. To the extent that neglected students tend to be shy or withdrawn, they will need treatment with the strategies described in Chapter 15 along with those described in this chapter.

Students who are actively rejected tend to be angry, argumentative, and prone to start fights as children, and to be self-centered, inconsiderate, and tactless as adolescents. They usually have distrustful or even paranoid social expectations, so that they may interpret accidents as deliberate provocations and become unreasonably angry and aggressive toward peers. Consequently, peers understandably dislike and avoid them. To the extent that socially rejected students present this hostile, aggressive pattern, they will need treatment using the strategies described in Chapter 8 in addition to those described in this chapter.

It is worth noting that children who are actively rejected by their peers usually are not rejected simply because they are aggressive. Some popular children and most "controversial" children (those who are liked in some respects but not others, or liked by some peers but disliked by others) behave aggressively at least occasionally, but these children possess positive social qualities to balance their aggressive behavior. Rejected students not only behave aggressively but lack the social cognitions and skills needed to interact successfully with peers, or if they possess them, they do not use them frequently. Thus, they show behavioral deficits along with their behavioral excesses.

Similarly, neglected children are not socially isolated merely because they are shy (if indeed they are shy). In addition to low rates of social initiation and participation, they often show deficits in their knowledge and skills for responding to peers' initiations in ways that lead to sustained and productive interactions. Some of them also reveal a form of learned helplessness in social situations, tending to interpret unsuccessful social interactions as personal rejections, to attribute these rejections to their own personal incompetence, and thus to withdraw rather than persist in pursuing the interaction or relationship (Goetz & Dweck, 1980).

Suggested Strategies for Improving the Social Adjustments of Rejected Students

Various sources recommend similar strategies for teachers to use for promoting prosocial attitudes and behavior among their students generally and for improving the social adjustments of neglected and rejected students (Erwin, 1993; Karlin & Berger, 1972; McIntyre, 1989; Mergendoller & Marchman, 1987; Nowicki & Duke, 1992; Siegel, Siegel, & Siegel, 1978). In the process of helping class members get to know one another as individuals and begin to function as a learning community, you can provide all students with opportunities to present themselves in a positive light and to display their unique talents and interests. You also can incorporate cooperative learning methods that bring peers together in pairs or small groups. Peers who collaborate in pursuit of common goals tend to get to know and value one another, so that well-structured, cooperative learning experiences can lead to the development of friendships. Socially awkward students might be paired or grouped with friendly and socially skillful students who can provide modeling as well as opportunities to develop friendships. You may need to help students learn to function productively in pairs or small groups, however; otherwise, the experience might lead to hostility or continued victimization.

You can help social isolates by arming them with better social understandings and skills. Although these students are usually painfully aware of their unpopularity, they are not always clear about the reasons for it. Consequently, they may benefit from sympathetically delivered feedback about the things they do that make their peers uncomfortable. Better yet, you can help these students to develop social skills such as introducing themselves to others, initiating conversations, listening and responding appropriately to what peers have to say, and joining ongoing group activities (Asher & Coie, 1990; Bierman & Furman, 1984; L'Abate & Milan, 1985; Ladd & Mize, 1983).

For example, Oden (1982) developed coaching procedures to help students learn to apply four principles of positive social interaction (participation, communication, cooperation, and supportiveness) to concrete social situations. The students might be asked, for example, how they would respond to a classmate who wanted to play with the same toy that they were playing with.

Oden's procedure involves leading students through five steps in applying conflict resolution and friendship skills to naturally occurring conflicts. First, ask the student to describe the problem or event that provoked conflict. Encourage the student to describe his or her feelings, actions related to the problem, and perspective on the dispute. Second, ask the student to take the perspective of the other party to the conflict and tell how that person feels. Third, keeping both perspectives in mind, ask the student to suggest the strategy for solving the problem. Fourth, ask the student to consider the impact of this suggested solution on both this student and the other party. Finally, if the projected outcomes appear equitable and satisfactory to all concerned, the solution would be accepted. If not, however, the student is asked to suggest an alternative solution and go through the evaluation process again.

Students who are actively rejected by their peers may be difficult to work with if they are hostile or aggressive. If so, you will need to make it clear to these students that aggressive behavior is not acceptable and will not be tolerated (see Chapter 8). Beyond this, you may be able to help aggressive students by listening to them sympathetically, trying to resocialize their beliefs and attitudes through modeling and persuasion, and teaching them more effective ways of interacting with peers and solving conflicts. These students may benefit from being made more aware of their own behavior, how it is perceived by peers, and the effects that it has on them (Patterson, Kupersmidt, & Griesler, 1990). Finally, these students will need counseling or instruction in more effective ways of handling frustration, controlling their tempers, solving conflicts through communication and negotiation rather than aggression, and expressing anger verbally rather than physically.

To help rejected and isolated students, you may need to work with the peer group as well as with the students themselves (Asher & Coie, 1990). Private conferences with peers might lead to better treatment of these students, especially those who are being neglected or victimized rather than rejected because of their own antisocial behavior.

In some cases, it may be helpful to engage the entire class in a discussion of the problem (Mergendoller & Marchman, 1987). This might be done without specific reference to a particular child or incident, by engaging students in discussion of topics such as what it must be like to be a newcomer to the classroom, to be excluded from groups or activities, or to be a victim of ridicule or malicious teasing. If it is not feasible to mask the identities of the students involved, or if it appears that little will be accomplished unless these students can be drawn into direct communication with one another, you might want to pose the problem for public discussion much more directly, although in a way likely to lead to problem solving rather than angry exchanges. For detailed suggestions and case study examples of how to do this, see Allan (1981).

Karlin and Berger (1972) discussed the option of having a talk with the rest of the class at a time when the rejected student is absent. They suggested describing the rejected child as lonely and in need of friendship and, in the process of appealing to the rest of the class to supply that friendship, describing these classmates as kind and compassionate individuals who will be eager to help. As an alternative to appealing publicly to the class as a whole, they suggested privately enlisting the help of one or more classmates who would be willing to extend friendship to rejected students by inviting them to participate in activities with them.

ANALYSIS OF INTERVIEW RESPONSES

A majority (51) of the teachers mentioned the general problem-solving approach of attempting to identify and treat external causes for the student's rejection. Other general approaches included providing instruction, training, modeling, or help in learning how to solve the problem (22); attempts to encourage, reassure, build self-concept, or provide a supportive environment (16); attempts to control or suppress undesirable behavior (13); and attempts to develop the rejected student's insight (10).

The most popularly mentioned specific problem-solving strategies were changing the rejected student's social environment (59) and group work focused on either increasing acceptance of this particular student or increasing the general level of peer acceptance and prosocial behavior in the classroom (57). Other strategies mentioned by more than 5 teachers included attempting to eliminate a perceived source of the problem (34), enlisting peers to provide support (30), instructing the student in better ways of interacting with peers or coping with peer rejection (29), indirect modeling of acceptance of the rejected student (23), involving the parents for support or problem solving (20), involving school-based authority figures or professionals for support or problem solving (20), attempting to build the student's self-concept (18), counseling or attempts to produce insight (16), attempts to minimize stress or embarrassment (10), and proscribing against undesirable behavior (10).

Responses were coded for strategies directed to the rejected student and for strategies directed to the class as a whole. Strategies directed to the rejected student included befriending the student (38), holding a conference with the student to address the general topic of peer adjustment and perhaps give advice or initiate change strategies (31), appealing to the student's sense of self-interest by pointing out the undesired natural consequences of behaviors that lead to peer rejection (29), involving the rejected student in special classroom roles or activities designed to increase peer contact and hopefully peer acceptance (28), holding a conference with the rejected student following a specific incident of rejection (24), and providing or arranging for the rejected student to receive public recognition for accomplishments (17).

Strategies directed to the class as a whole included enlisting peers to help with the problem (30); holding a group meeting to address the problem indirectly by noting the need for better peer acceptance and more prosocial behavior among the students, but not mentioning the rejected student specifically (28); placing direct pressure on particular peers to initiate social contacts with or extend friendship to the rejected student (27); holding a meeting to pressure the class to be more accepting toward the rejected student (26); requiring peers to share materials or work interdependently with the rejected student (23); placing indirect pressure on peers to interact with the rejected student (18); and attempting to improve the rejected student's peer adjustment through social engineering, typically by seating the student among friendly classmates (18).

Most of the teachers mentioned one or more reasons why a child might be rejected by peers. The most frequently mentioned reasons were an unattractive physical appearance (45) and immature social behavior that peers might find babyish or irritating (39). Other suggested reasons for rejection included the notions that the rejected student was a bully (21); came from a poor home (16); lacked awareness of the problem or of strategies for doing something about it (12); was shy or withdrawn (12); lacked athletic ability or physical skills (10); was hampered by some temporary problem, such as being new to the class (9); or was a slow learner (7).

A majority (69) of the teachers included long-term prevention or solution strategies in their responses, and 30 mentioned different strategies for different subtypes of the problem. A majority (60) of the teachers would get more information about the problem by interviewing the rejected student (31), observing the student interacting with peers (29), interviewing peers (16), or interviewing family members (10).

Concerning strategies that they viewed as ineffective for responding to peer rejection problems, 22 teachers mentioned singling out the rejected student by name when talking about peer rejection problems to the class; 18 mentioned attempting to force peers to interact with the rejected student; 12 mentioned ignoring the problem; and 7 mentioned lecturing, demanding, threatening, or punishing. In general, the teachers spoke of prescribing better ways of coping or attempting to increase insight when they envisioned rejected students as creating problems for themselves through inappropriate social behavior, but emphasized encouraging or pressuring peers to become more accepting when they envisioned rejected students as being rejected through no fault of their own.

Most teachers expressed the same basic principles for responding to rejected students, but higher rated teachers suggested a broader range of strategies and elaborated them in more detail. All of the significant relationships between coding categories and effectiveness ratings were for categories coded more frequently for higher rated teachers; no strategy was mentioned more often by lower rated teachers than by higher rated teachers.

Higher rated teachers were more likely to include long-term prevention or solution strategies in their responses and more likely to mention different strategies for different subtypes of the problem. They were especially more likely to mention attempts to build the self-concepts of and provide a supportive environment for rejected students. These teachers mentioned more specific strategies of all kinds, but especially more supportive strategies, particularly self-concept support, indirect modeling of acceptance of rejected students, and arranging for these students to receive public recognition for their positive accomplishments. Higher rated teachers were more likely to mention interviewing peers to get information about why rejected students were being rejected, but their follow-up problem-solving suggestions mostly featured strategies for working directly with rejected students rather than for working with the class as a whole. To the extent that they thought these students were bringing on rejection through their own counterproductive behavior, they would attempt to make these students see what they were doing or suggest more effective ways of interacting with peers in the future. For the most part, however, their interventions would emphasize providing these students with conspicuous public acceptance and various forms of personal support.

Higher rated teachers generally identified more reasons why students might be rejected by their peers. In particular, they were more likely to mention an unattractive physical appearance, a lack of athletic ability or physical skills, or a lack of awareness of their own behavior and its conse-quences (i.e., its effects on peers). Finally, higher rated teachers were more likely to be represented among the 12 teachers who stated that ignoring the problem is an ineffective response to peer rejection.

Vignette: Mark

Mark is not well accepted by his classmates. Today he has been trying to get some of the other boys to play a particular game with him. After much plead-ing the boys decide to play the game, but exclude Mark. Mark argues, saying that he should get to play because it was his idea in the first place, but the boys start without him. Finally, Mark gives up and slinks off, rejected again.

Before reading further, take time to think about how you might respond to this incident. Make notes about your ideas.

CSS Vignette Response Excerpts

Here is what four of the CSS teachers had to say.

A Lower Rated Teacher

"This particular problem is something that would have to be dealt with over a period of time because you don't want to discourage Mark and make him finally give up and never try this again. I think it would be best to have a little meeting or conference with some of the other classmates when Mark wasn't around and try to explain to the boys and girls the importance of being kind and considerate and friendly to their classmates even though sometimes they don't like them. Don't be so cruel, because it can really hurt, and possibly they could be a little more humane in their approach toward Mark."

A Higher Rated Teacher

"I frequently find that when you come up against a situation where you are getting really negative behavior, one child is be-ing mistreated and left out, it helps to explain and try to talk things out. Sometimes we underestimate how much children can understand or empathize with other people. Lots of times they don't really stop and think about what is happening to that other child whom they exclude or leave out. I know that when a child is really young, the world revolves just around him, and it's hard for him to comprehend. But by the time they are 7 or 8 years old, they can start to see where other people's feelings have to be taken into account, that the universe isn't just them and what they need and what they want. I guess I would go over to Mark and say, 'Hey, come on Mark. Let's see if we can work this problem out.' I would call the other boys over, and I would have a huddle with them and say, 'It was Mark's idea to play the game, and he is feeling really bad because you took up his idea of playing the game and you left him out. You are being really unfair.' I guess I would put it on the line and say that they were really being unfair to him, and I would ask how they would feel if a bunch of people were playing a game that you had suggested and said, 'Well, I'm sorry, but we don't want you in the game, and you can't be part of it.' Then I would say, 'Of course you would feel bad. I have had that sort of thing happen, and I feel bad. When people are left out, there is no other way they are going to feel — they are going to feel unhappy and rejected. I think that you should at least give Mark a chance.' I guess my rationale is to at least open the door. Let him get one foot in the door and give them a chance to see that he has something to offer, that he is fun to play with and that he is nice to be around and that they have probably not given him a fair chance to prove himself."

ANOTHER HIGHER RATED TEACHER

"I would approach Mark and say, 'What's wrong?' He might say, 'Nothing,' but I wouldn't accept that. I would pursue it, and then if he was able to tell me about a game that he wanted to play and no one would play with him, I would call over the other boys who were playing that game and we would talk all together, Mark telling his feelings first and then letting any or all of the others give their opinions about the situation. I would ask the other boys why they had excluded Mark and then give Mark a chance to give his feelings as far as their excluding him. I would ask them all to try to arrive at a solution to the problem. Hopefully, they would say, 'Well, Mark can play with us.' If they still wanted to exclude Mark, my first impulse would be to say, 'Then you're not going to play that game.' However, I am not sure that would be constructive as far as Mark is concerned. I would try to get the feelings out, so that they would perhaps give in a little to Mark, and maybe Mark would understand why they feel as they do toward him, in the hope that gradually they would begin to include Mark. There might be something about Mark that puts them off. Mark is perhaps a child who may not know how to get himself into a game. He may say, 'Let's play such and such, and I am going to be the captain,' and that puts someone off. Or he may allow other people to walk all over him. So I don't know. Either he is the child who is obnoxious in some way and is rejected for that reason or he is the class scapegoat, which is another possibility."

ANOTHER HIGHER RATED TEACHER

"After Mark was excluded from the group game, which he in fact in-itiated, I would probably talk to him about there being some reasons as to why he is not accepted and that we need to be aware of them so that we can correct them, if it is in fact something you need to be working on. We would examine what was happening and who didn't play with him and why. We would try to find out the root of the problem. Does he argue, is he a poor loser, whatever the facts might be. Then we would talk about dealing with it. I would set up some kind of behavior modification program later. Right then, I would try to get him calmed down. He is probably feeling cheated because the game was his idea. I would try to support him and build his self-confidence back up, because he looks like he feels put down, and he has slinked off to the end of the playground by himself or something. Then I would say, 'OK, it looks like we are going to have to try and get with the group, and we'll explain it.' Then, I would take Mark back to the group (first I would let Mark know that I was going to do it, and if he felt uncomfortable, I wouldn't follow through with this, but most of the time they will go along with it). I would go back, and I would stop the game. I would make the group stop, and I would confront them with the issue as far as 'Mark really feels rotten. Do you realize how you have made him feel?' I would say, 'Look, this per-son feels left out, and I expect to see him being part of this group, just like I would expect everyone to include you. We can't have this. People are important, and we need each other. You are going to have to learn to get along with people in many situations—play, work, or whatever. You might as well start now. Let's get it together.' I prob-ably wouldn't make a big federal case out of it, but I would make sure they knew that I disapproved of their action because it was wrong. They know it was wrong to make him feel bad. I would just level with them. This is poor on your part. Normally, they respond to that. Also, just let Mark tell them how he feels about it. That usually gets them every time. . . . My goal would be for Mark to be accepted by the other children, for others to see his worth, but also for him to realize that everybody isn't going to accept him all the time. That's true of every-one, and he can't go around with his feelings stuck out on his shoul-der, just waiting for someone to knock them off. He is going to have to be a little bit stronger and let some of it just roll off and not take it to heart, not take it personally every time."

The lower rated teacher's response was good as far as it went. However, it was limited to an attempt to get the classmates to treat Mark more kindly, without including attempts to develop Mark's insight into his problem or teach him social skills. Also, the teacher said nothing about helping Mark during the incident depicted in the vignette. In contrast, all three of the higher rated teachers would deal with the incident directly, both by speaking to Mark privately to try to develop his insight into the problem and by bringing Mark together with the boys who had rejected him in order to initiate an exchange of views and negotiate a satisfactory solution. These teachers were not burdened by the negative expectations expressed by the lower rated teacher; although they did not underestimate the problem of achieving peer acceptance of students who project negative social qualities, they were confident that they could improve the situation substantially by helping Mark to work on his negative qualities and by appealing to the classmates' sense of fairness.

Analysis of Responses to Mark

Only 3 teachers mentioned rewards, only 2 mentioned punishments, and none mentioned threatening/pressuring behaviors in responding to this vignette. However, all but 1 of the teachers mentioned supportive behaviors, typically involving peers to provide support to Mark (74) or instructing Mark in more productive ways of interacting with peers (53). Other supportive behaviors mentioned were modeling acceptance of Mark (33), defending him against ridicule or other inappropriate treatment (17), kid gloves treatment at times when he was upset (10), and providing comfort or reassurance when he seemed to need it (6).

A heavy majority (82) of the teachers included changing Mark's social environment among their problem-solving strategies. Other strategies mentioned by more than 5 teachers included developing his insight (32), building his self-concept (25), eliminating a perceived source of the problem (19), prescribing or modeling better ways of interacting with peers (15), and intervening to release tension when Mark came into conflict with peers (9). Among teachers who would seek to develop Mark's insight, 21 would help him to recognize his own behavior or its consequences, 16 would focus on the causes of his peers' behavior (i.e., why they were rejecting him), 7 would focus on Mark's feelings, and 6 would focus on his peers' feelings (i.e., how they react when Mark treats them inappropriately).

A majority (67) of the teachers would make behavioral change demands, typically on classmates rather than on Mark. Sixteen of these teachers would not accompany their demands with rationales. The others would attempt to induce Mark's empathy with classmates or classmates' empathy with Mark (36); provide logical analyses linking behaviors to their consequences (typically, linking Mark's counterproductive social behavior to peer rejection (12); cite rules calling for peer acceptance and prosocial behavior (10); moralize about treatment of peers (8); or make a personal appeal, typically in the process of asking one or more classmates to befriend Mark (6).

Responses to this vignette were coded for mention of strategies for involving Mark in play activity, for socializing Mark, or for socializing the group of boys who excluded him from the game. Concerning involving Mark in a play activity, 43 teachers would try to get Mark into the original game with the original group of peers; 25 would get him involved in a new game or activity with a different person or group; 11 would tell him to find something else to do, tell him to solve the problem himself, or make some other response indicating refusal to intervene with the group that has excluded him; 9 would arrange for Mark to play the original game but not with the original group; and 7 would ignore the problem, leaving Mark either to remain alone sulking or to get involved in a new activity on his own initiative.

About half of the teachers would attempt to socialize Mark in some way. Of these, 35 would try to get Mark to recognize and change interpersonal behaviors that make him unpopular with peers or would try to get Mark to understand better what being a friend involves. In addition or instead, 16 would offer Mark specific instruction about how to handle the depicted incident more effectively (how to play the game if he doesn't know how or doesn't play it right, or how to initiate the game more successfully with this particular group of classmates).

In response to the group of peers who froze Mark out of the game, 25 teachers would moralize or scold the group for their behavior or cite classroom rules stating that everyone who wants to play a game will be allowed to play, 21 would question the group to seek their reasons for rejecting Mark or allow them to ventilate their complaints against him, 20 would engage in Golden Rule or empathy reasoning by trying to get the group to see that they would not like to be treated the way they treated Mark and so they should not treat him that way, 19 would cite fairness or Mark's claim on the game by explaining that Mark has a right to be included in the game (this time) because it was his idea in the first place, and 12 would appeal to the group's desire to do good deeds or be thought well of by explaining to them that they could help Mark by including him and treating him with friendliness (implicitly, these teachers would recognize that the group may have good reasons for wanting to exclude Mark but would appeal for their help in dealing with him).

About two-thirds of the teachers mentioned follow-up prevention or solution strategies directed at Mark. Of these, 38 would talk to him or give him any necessary practice needed to help him understand his situation with regard to peers, learn social skills, or improve his personal appearance or habits; 19 would make it a point to initiate social activities with Mark frequently (thus acting as a model to the rest of the students); and 19 would enlist help from peers by asking them to initiate social activities with Mark frequently.

In addition, 41 teachers mentioned long-term prevention or follow-up strategies directed at the class as a whole. Of these, 21 would lay down new rules or expectations (or review old ones) about accepting one another and cooperating; 13 would hold a problem-solving meeting, at which Mark would be present, either to discuss the specific problem of the class's rejection of Mark or to articulate expectations about class members getting along well with one another; and 11 would conduct a problem-solving meeting but schedule it at a time when Mark was absent or sent out of the room on some pretext.

Concerning possible reasons for Mark's rejection, 27 teachers mentioned social immaturity (he always wants to be first, can't take turns properly, etc.), 24 suggested that Mark has an unattractive appearance or physical characteristics, 22 thought that he might be a bully or a hostile–aggressive student who gets into fights and arguments frequently, 14 suspected that Mark does not know how to play the game or lacks the skills to play it well, and 8 indicated that Mark is new to the group and has not made friends yet.

Once again, most teachers emphasized the same general principles, but higher rated teachers mentioned more specific strategies, especially more strategies that involved providing support to Mark. These teachers did not tend to assume that Mark was bringing rejection on himself through inappropriate social behavior. In contrast, lower rated teachers were more likely to attribute the problem to causes residing solely within Mark, to view him as at least partly responsible for his problem, and to suggest that social immaturity was the cause.

Higher rated teachers mentioned more short-term and long-term strategies for assisting Mark. In response to the depicted situation, they were more likely to speak of getting Mark into the original game with the original group of peers who rejected him, whereas lower rated teachers were more likely to speak of ignoring the problem, refusing to intervene with the original group, or getting Mark involved in a new activity with a different group. Concerning longer term prevention or problem-solving strategies, higher rated teachers were more likely to mention conspicuously initiating social or play activities with Mark or in other ways publicly modeling acceptance of him, changing his social environment in some fashion, making tension release comments to defuse conflict situations, or attempting to develop Mark's insight into his peers' feelings or to develop his peers' insight into Mark's feelings.

Vignette: Kathy

Kathy is a loner in the classroom and an onlooker on the playground. No one willingly sits with her or plays with her. You divided the class into groups to work on projects, and those in Kathy's group are making unkind remarks about her, loud enough for all to hear.

Before reading further, take time to think about how you might respond to this incident. Make notes about your ideas.

CSS Vignette Response Excerpts

Here is what four of the CSS teachers had to say.

A LOWER RATED TEACHER

" 'I think this group has something to say to Kathy. I would like for you to apologize please. I don't want to hear any more stuff like that, or this group will just quit working. If you cannot work together, then we will not work at all.' I would do this because Kathy is very much unliked by the other students in the class. My goal would be to get her to be well liked. Kathy is a loner."

A HIGHER RATED TEACHER

"When you have a child who is a loner, and they occur very frequently, I think the first thing I would be concerned about is whether the teacher is unconsciously or consciously perhaps adding to the rejection of this child. If she can honestly say no, then you have to look at why the students do not care for this person. My approach would be to treat this student, Kathy, with as much kindness and consideration as any other student and hope that my influence as a role model would encourage the students to follow along. I have done this in the past and found that it works. I would ask Kathy to do some special errands for me, to work her in any way I could. When someone is short a partner, be sure that Kathy gets that job so that she isn't left out, this sort of thing, without making Kathy into a so-called teacher's pet. As the year goes on with a child like this, usually you can work them into the situation quite nicely if you indeed are a proper role model. You have to be very careful in treating any child as special, so you don't incur the wrath of the peers because it becomes a teacher's pet situation, but there are many ways that this can be handled without getting into that rut. Kathy probably is a child who has some economic or social problems within her neighborhood, or possibly she has not had many opportunities to play with other students. I would guess that she probably has not had the right interaction with students of her own age from the time she was little to bring her to this situation."

ANOTHER HIGHER RATED TEACHER

"First, I would take Kathy's small group aside. I would give Kathy an errand or something that would take her out of the room for 5 or 10 minutes, and I would talk with her group, in a spot where other people would not overhear, about why they were making unkind remarks about her, what it was about Kathy that was bugging them. Then when Kathy returned, I would take her aside by herself and say, 'Kathy, I noticed that the people in your group were saying some things that weren't very nice. How did you feel about it?' Let her tell me, and then say, 'Kathy, I think that your group should hear how you feel about this. Would you like to talk to them?' Hopefully, with my support she would feel confident enough in talking with the rest of the group. I would call them all together again and first have Kathy tell how she felt when unkind remarks were made about her. Then, if the group had stated fairly concrete reasons for making remarks about Kathy, I would ask one or two of them to enumerate these reasons. Then I think the group as a whole, Kathy included, should decide how they are going to carry on with their project, how they are going to include Kathy and allow her to contribute. Perhaps there needs to be a definition of jobs, so that each person has something very specific to do. I would stay with the group and oversee for a few minutes and then keep my ears open for any other remarks as the period went on. I think that it is important to get Kathy away from the situation in talking with the group, so that she is not completely aware that I am talking with them to begin with, to see if there really is anything that is concrete. And I think it is very important that Kathy share her feelings with the group. The other people in the group may not realize that Kathy has feelings too and that they have been hurt. And I think it is important that the group work together, with each person contributing in a positive way to the project. I would characterize Kathy as an isolate."

ANOTHER HIGHER RATED TEACHER

"I would go over to Kathy's group and deal with it as a group problem since the other children are working in their groups and seem to be getting along just fine. 'What's going on over here? Do you think it is really necessary to make those remarks about Kathy?' I would do a little role playing with that group. They need a lesson in awareness, perhaps role playing and having some of those people that are being the most vocal and the most unkind about Kathy be excluded in a role-playing situation and having other people make remarks about them. I would also talk to them about how we need to try to include everybody and it's a matter of acceptance, that people throughout life are going to meet people that are a lot different than yourself. They may seem strange, odd, you don't like how they look, or whatever it is, but you need to be able to tolerate and accept them. Sometimes you find you are greatly surprised that those people you excluded before have something special to offer. [What would you say to Kathy?] I would try to tell Kathy that 'I don't know if they really realize what they are saying. Lots of times when people are making unkind remarks, they are not feeling very good about themselves. When I am feeling bad about myself, I am the cruelest to other people, and when I am feeling good about myself, I'm the nicest to other people. I think that some people in that group must not be feeling very good about themselves right now.' . . . I guess that after the role-playing situation, maybe we could go back and work in the group. I would probably take more of an effort to work with Kathy's group to make sure that she is included."

The lower rated teacher would admonish the group and demand an apology, without saying anything at all to Kathy and without attempting to make the group members see why their behavior has been inappropriate. This approach seems unlikely to help the situation and might even worsen it by giving the group members one more reason to reject Kathy. In contrast, two of the three higher rated teachers would work both with Kathy and with the group, seeking to develop Kathy's insight and social skills and to make group members more aware of their unkind treatment of Kathy and its effects on her feelings. The remaining higher rated teacher did not address the issue of how she would handle the depicted incident, but she did suggest several ideas for improving Kathy's social adjustment in the classroom.

Analysis of Responses to Kathy

Only 8 teachers mentioned rewards in responding to this vignette, only 3 mentioned punishments, and only 7 mentioned threatening or pressuring behaviors. However, all but 2 teachers mentioned supportive behaviors. Most of these (79) mentioned involving peers to provide support to Kathy.

In addition or instead, 45 mentioned instructing Kathy in more effective social behavior, 31 spoke of defending her against inappropriate treatment by peers, 15 spoke of modeling acceptance of Kathy, 8 mentioned kid gloves treatment, and 7 spoke of providing comfort or reassurance.

Changing Kathy's social environment was by far the most commonly mentioned problem-solving strategy (87). Others mentioned by more than 5 teachers included building Kathy's self-concept (19), eliminating a perceived source of the problem (15), developing her insight (15), and prescribing or modeling more effective behavior (7).

All but 9 of the teachers would make behavioral change demands (usually on peers rather than on Kathy). Of these, 17 made no mention of rationales, but 69 spoke of inducing empathy (typically through Golden Rule appeals taking the form of "How would you feel if . . . ?" questions), 22 spoke of moralizing about appropriate treatment of peers, 15 mentioned logical analyses linking behaviors to their consequences, 12 mentioned making personal appeals to students, and 10 spoke of appealing to students' pride or self-concept.

Responses were coded for what the teachers said about reasserting or changing Kathy's group assignment, socializing Kathy, or socializing the group in the immediate situation, as well as for what they said about longer term prevention or follow-up strategies. Noting that Kathy was not accepted by her work group, 60 teachers would leave Kathy in the group but try to improve cooperation by socializing her and/or the other group members, 13 would order the group to cooperate without attempting to investigate why Kathy is not accepted and without attempting to increase her acceptance level, and 10 would reassign Kathy to a different group. Among teachers who would leave Kathy with her original work group, the majority would demand that group members accept Kathy, with the implication that those who did not would be punished in some way, but a minority (33) would give a rationale for why Kathy should be accepted but phrase this as a suggestion. Presumably, the latter teachers would not foist Kathy on the group if they remained strenuous in their objections to her.

Among teachers who mentioned socializing, the majority would direct their efforts to the group: 51 would moralize or scold the group for their behavior or cite classroom rules calling for everyone to get along and speak well of one another; 50 would attempt Golden Rule or empathy appeals noting that group members would not like to be treated the way they treated Kathy; 22 would question the group to seek their reasons for rejecting Kathy or allow them to ventilate their complaints against her; 13 would appeal to group members' desires to do good deeds or be thought well of by explaining to them that they could help Kathy by including her and treating her with friendliness (implicitly recognizing that the group may have good reasons for wanting to exclude Kathy, but appealing for their help in dealing with her); and 10 would simply assert that Kathy has been assigned to this group and thus will be included in it, whether the group members like it or not. Among teachers who would direct socialization efforts at Kathy, 13 would offer general socialization indicating that she has irritating personal habits or interpersonal behaviors that make her unpopular with peers and would try to get her to recognize these and make changes, and 4 would offer specific instruction to Kathy about how to deal with her group mates in this particular situation.

A majority of the teachers mentioned longer term prevention or follow-up strategies with Kathy. Of these teachers, 30 would enlist the help of one or more peers to initiate social or play activities frequently with Kathy; 21 would place Kathy in monitor/helper/leader roles to give her visibility and hopefully improve her standing with peers; 15 would talk to Kathy or give her practice to help her understand her situation better, learn social skills, or improve her personal appearance or habits; and 11 would make it a point to initiate social or play activities with Kathy frequently, to act as a model for the rest of the students.

A majority of the teachers also mentioned longer term prevention or follow-up strategies directed at Kathy's work group or the class as a whole. Of these teachers, 24 would lay down new rules or expectations (or review old ones) calling for peer acceptance and cooperation; 16 would conduct a class meeting, at which Kathy would be present, to discuss either the specific problem of the group's rejection of Kathy or the more general problem of expectations about how class members are going to get along with one another; and 15 would conduct a problem-solving meeting but schedule it at a time when Kathy was absent or sent out of the room on some pretext.

Concerning possible reasons for Kathy's rejection, 20 teachers mentioned an unattractive appearance or physical characteristics, 17 mentioned social immaturity, and 8 suggested that her problem was temporary because she was new to the group and had not made friends yet.

Majorities of the teachers in both groups mentioned the more popular strategies, so that significant relationships appeared primarily for strategies mentioned by only small minorities of the teachers. Higher rated teachers were more likely to accompany behavior change demands with rationales, particularly logical analyses (when socializing Kathy and attempting to make her see that her behavior irritated peers) or appeals to students' pride or self-concept (when socializing the other members of Kathy's work group and attempting to shame them by indicating that they knew better than to behave as they had been). Higher rated teachers also were more likely to mention attempts to eliminate a perceived source of the problem and to speak of following up by talking to Kathy or giving her any needed practice to help her understand her situation better, learn social skills, or improve her general appearance or habits.

Most teachers in both groups would keep Kathy in her current work group but socialize her and/or the other group members in an attempt to raise her level of acceptance. However, higher rated teachers were more likely to be represented among the 10 teachers who would assign Kathy to a new group and among the 10 who would assert to group members that Kathy is a part of the group and they will need to accept that whether they like it or not. In contrast, lower rated teachers were more likely to speak of gathering information from group members about why they rejected Kathy and allowing them to ventilate their complaints against her. Lower rated teachers were also more likely to say that they would merely suggest, rather than demand, that the group members accept Kathy in the future. Overall, the main difference between the two groups was that a significant subset of the lower rated teachers believed that little or nothing could be done to change the other group members' negative views of Kathy, whereas a heavy majority of the higher rated teachers believed that the attitudes of these students could be resocialized, if not through persuasion and articulation of ideals then through insistence on more prosocial behavior.

COMPARISON OF RESPONSES TO MARK AND TO KATHY

The teachers generally responded to both vignettes by suggesting a combination of support and assistance to the rejected student with socialization of classmates (particularly those who had expressed rejection of these students) that featured new articulation or reemphasis of already articulated expectations concerning peer acceptance and prosocial behavior. For reasons that are not clear, the teachers, especially lower rated teachers, were less confident about their ability to effect significant improvements in Kathy's peer adjustment than they were with respect to Mark's peer adjustment.

More teachers spoke of modeling acceptance of Mark, whereas more spoke of defending Kathy against inappropriate treatment by peers. More teachers spoke of attempts to increase Mark's insight than Kathy's, and more spoke of using Golden Rule or empathy appeals when talking to Kathy's peers than when talking to Mark's peers, even though these two strategies would seem to be equally applicable to both vignettes.

Finally, the data for both vignettes indicate that higher rated teachers would be more willing to take a harder line with peers who rejected Mark or Kathy—demanding rather than merely suggesting behavioral change and not always feeling a need to accompany these demands with rationales or justifications. These teachers' basic message to the rejecting peers seemed to be "You know that your behavior is inappropriate (unkind, contrary to our rules, etc.), so stop it. From now on, I want you to treat Mark (Kathy) the way you know you should."

QUALITATIVE IMPRESSIONS AND EXAMPLES

Most of the teachers had more to say about rejected students than about most of the other problem-student types. Interview and vignette transcripts were notably longer than average. Also, the emphasis was on long-term problem prevention and solution strategies. None of the teachers spoke of blaming, threatening, or punishing peer rejected students, although some mentioned the possibility of directing such strategies at peers who engaged in malicious teasing or other mistreatment of these students.

Lower rated teachers suggested most of the same general strategies as higher rated teachers, but they were less systematic and detailed in doing so. Often they spoke at length about individual students in their classes or enumerated the characteristics of rejected students or the reasons why they might be rejected, but they did not say much about what to do concerning these problems. Many of them felt powerless to do much at all, especially those who emphasized that peers may have very good reasons for rejecting a classmate.

Even higher rated teachers often spoke of the difficulty of addressing this problem if the peers had good reason for rejecting a student. Many spoke of the difficult but necessary task of calling rejected students' attention to their obnoxious characteristics (where this is the case) and perhaps talking to parents as well, especially if the child's social unattractiveness is based in whole or part on body odor, poor personal hygiene, or other problems suggestive of parental neglect. Many teachers in Big City related attempts to get parents of badly neglected children to wash their clothes more frequently and send them to school better cleaned and groomed. Sometimes these attempts yielded no response or even a hostile reaction. Several teachers spoke of referring students with hygiene problems to the school nurse, with the idea that the nurse would take the responsibility for working with both the student and the parents on this problem. Among teachers who would talk to students personally about body odor and cleanliness problems, several suggested a way to appeal to their sense of pride or self-concept without damaging it: Suggest to these students that their personal hygiene habits were acceptable when they were younger, but now they are getting older and need to begin bathing more regularly, because social expectations are different for older children than for younger children.

Many teachers, especially in Small City, spoke of using Magic Circle or other activities in which a story or a role-playing situation is set up and the students are engaged in discussion about how the participants would feel in the situation. These teachers usually noted the value of such activities for raising students' consciousness of their behavior and its consequences. In setting up role-playing situations, several teachers recommended having the rejected child and the rejecting child switch roles.

Many teachers, especially in the early grades, said that it is easy to get rejected students engaged in recess or free-time activities with peers simply by beginning an activity with the rejected peer yourself. They went on to explain that other students invariably seek to join the activity when the teacher is involved, so that soon the group will have grown. As the activity takes hold and acquires a momentum of its own, you can disengage from it, leaving the students to play with one another.

Another teacher suggested getting rejected students involved with peers by giving them a toy to play with that has to be used in collaboration with one or more peers (e.g., a long jump rope). Another teacher said that rather than always play with the rejected child at recess, she will ask the rejected child to first approach a classmate and ask that child to play. If this doesn't work out, then she will play with the rejected child. However, most of the time it leads to a successful play situation. Another teacher spoke of bringing students together based on common hobbies and interests as a way to link rejected students with one or more peers.

Many teachers spoke of shaming peers who rejected a classmate for no good reason or for reasons beyond his or her control (poverty, etc.). These teachers would label the behavior of rejecting students as cruel and unfair, ask them how they would like to be in the rejected student's place, and perhaps mock their behavior by pretending to reject one of them because he or she had freckles, blue eyes, etc. In the case of malicious teasing or other public ridiculing, one teacher said that she would have the victim tell the other students how he or she feels when picked on in this way, if the victim was up to that task. She said that when she does this, the rejecting students "get silent," and it has a powerful impact on them.

Another teacher spoke of the need to get to know the rejected students and discover their positive qualities so that you can genuinely like them yourself, because if you don't, your negative attitudes will slip out even if you are trying to model acceptance. If peers might have good or at least understandable reasons for rejecting a student, this teacher would speak to the class at a time when the student was out of the room. She would tell the class that they do not have to become best friends with this student, but they do have to treat the student fairly and put an end to all forms of mistreatment. In this situation, another teacher would acknowledge that the rejected student has problems but would explain to the class that their behavior is only making these problems worse and appeal to them to become part of the solution by extending friendship to the rejected student or at least treating him or her with more tolerance and understanding.

One teacher would ask the rejected student to watch a popular student that he or she liked, noting how this student acted with classmates. She would coach the rejected student in what to look for, such as the fact that the popular student smiles frequently, treats others respectfully, etc. Several teachers spoke of ways to present rejected students in a positive light to their classmates: Let them bring hobby materials from home to show off and explain, have them read aloud an unusually good piece of creative writing, etc.

The vignette responses indicated a tendency to focus on Mark and assume that he was causing his own problems, but to focus on the peers who made unkind remarks to Kathy. Usually there are classroom rules against the kinds of remarks made about Kathy, and the vignette stated that these remarks were heard by everyone, so most teachers felt an immediate pressure to deal with that issue first. This vignette brought out more Golden Rule and empathy rationales than any of the others, probably because of the public nature of the remarks made about Kathy. Most teachers suggested a Golden Rule or empathy approach. However, some teachers would carry this too far, such as by creating a supposed object lesson by picking out negative features in one or more of the other students and asking how they would like it if the teacher rejected them because of this feature.

With many of the lower rated teachers, especially in Big City, the problem wasn't reliance on counterproductive strategies but low expectations. Often they said that there is not much you can do to make kids like one another or that "kids are cruel." In contrast, higher rated teachers often remarked that children can be very understanding and accepting if you explain things to them or ask them to be helpful.

Expectation differences were especially notable on the issue of whether or not you can force the rejected child on classmates. Some teachers hesitated to attempt this and even said that it would backfire and lead to further problems for the rejected student later, but many others, especially higher rated teachers, spoke of establishing and enforcing the expectation that students will treat one another appropriately. Often they did not even feel a need to give a rationale for their behavioral change demands because they felt that their students already knew better. So they would simply say, "We don't treat people like that." Even when they assumed that the rejected student was at fault, these teachers nevertheless would brace the rejecting peers with comments such as, "So are you helping Kathy with her problem by making unkind remarks to her?" or "If you can't speak well of somebody, don't say anything about them at all." Meanwhile, their message to rejected students who bring problems on themselves would be "In order to have a friend, you have to be a friend."

Many teachers, especially in the early grades, not only spoke of joining in play with Mark or working on a project with Kathy but added that this draws the attention of other students, who then want to come and get into the act. Many of these teachers preferred this method of engaging rejected students with their peers to the more direct alternative of confronting the group and trying to thrust the rejected student into it, at least with respect to the situations depicted in the vignettes. In general, lower-grade teachers spoke more often about publicly befriending and praising rejected students or arranging for them to look good in front of their peers, whereas upper-grade teachers more often emphasized speaking to the rejected student or to the peers in an attempt to identify and intervene in the problem.

One teacher said that she would speak to the other boys about their inappropriate treatment of Mark but also would work with Mark to try to help him become less susceptible to shattering in response to this kind of treatment. She would let him know that you can't expect everyone to like you, that you have to bounce back from disappointments and move on, and that you have to find friends that you are compatible with and focus on them. Another teacher mentioned the book *The Ugly Duckling* and the song "It's Not Easy Being Green" (from the Muppets) as two tools to use in helping rejected students. Finally, a few teachers spoke of ways to get one or more of the boys who had rejected Mark to go and invite Mark to rejoin the group, suggesting that this is preferable to thrusting Mark into the group themselves. Usually this would occur after the teacher had explained to the boys the inappropriateness of their behavior and enlisted their cooperation in treating Mark more appropriately.

DISCUSSION

Even though our problem-type description and two vignettes depicted rejected students as victims, most teachers expressed awareness that rejected students often are rejected for good reasons and assumed that their treatment efforts would need to focus on helping these students eliminate socially unattractive characteristics, not just on changing the behavior of the rejecting peers. Even so, most responses emphasized empathy for and attempts to help rejected students, although less so to the extent that the teacher assumed that rejection was due to antisocial behavior or other blameworthy characteristics rather than to factors beyond the rejected student's control.

The general trends in the teachers' responses, especially in the responses of the higher rated teachers, fit well with the teaching implications that emerged from our research review. The teachers were not specifically knowledgeable about cognitive strategy or social skills training, but they understood intuitively the need to make rejected students more aware of their socially unattractive qualities that make it difficult for them to be accepted by peers, and to work with these students on acquiring social skills and changing their social behavior. They also understood the need to socialize the class as a whole, and rejecting students in particular, toward prosocial values and related behavioral expectations. In fact, most teachers took it for granted that they would have done so already before the depicted vignette incidents occurred, so they would respond with "We don't treat people like that" reminders rather than with a more extensive socialization message or lesson of the kind that would be used when introducing the class to some new concept.

For most teachers, and especially the higher rated ones, dealing with the rejected student was a more daunting prospect than dealing with the rejecting classmates, especially if the rejection was due at least in part to body odor, dirty or tattered clothing, urine smell, unkempt grooming, or other hygiene factors suggestive of parental neglect. Many of them were uneasy at the prospect of talking about these problems with the child or, even worse, with the parents, who might prove to be uncooperative or even hostile. Some would attempt to avoid this problem by asking the school nurse or social worker to deal with it.

Many of the differences between higher rated and lower rated teachers were connected to differences in fundamental beliefs and expectations about the degree to which current peer group relationships can be changed through teacher interventions. Higher rated teachers tended to view these peer relationships as malleable, being confident that they could both help rejected students become more socially acceptable and resocialize the attitudes and behavior of rejecting classmates so as to make them part of the solution rather than continuing to be part of the problem. In stark contrast, many of the lower rated teachers believed there was very little that a teacher (or at least they themselves) could do. In order to learn to deal successfully with peer rejected students, these teachers would need to acquire not only larger repertoires of intervention skills but, more fundamentally, enhanced appreciation of the possibilities for intervening successfully. Without such an appreciation, it would be difficult for them to set higher goals with the serious expectation of being able to meet them.

Some teachers would also need to develop more empathy for rejected students, to motivate them to care about these students more deeply and make greater efforts to respond to their needs. Most teachers' responses displayed these qualities, but a few were remarkably unsympathetic. It was not clear whether these teachers once cared about their students but had become burned out or whether they never cared much in the first place, but they were unwilling to offer much more than a single brief intervention, often one that would avoid the problem rather than deal with it. In responding to the vignettes, for example, such teachers might commit themselves to engaging the rejected student in some alternative activity, without making any attempt to investigate the problem more thoroughly, to try to help the rejected student develop better peer relationships, or to get the rejecting peers to accept that student better or even to stop mistreating the student. In short, they would provide situational distraction from the problem but no serious attempt to confront the problem and solve it.

Some of the research literature, as well as the responses of the teachers in our study, contain a great many useful ideas about helping peer rejected students, and these ideas all fit well with and support one another. They imply that the best response to such problems is to minimize them in the first place by establishing your classroom as a learning community that features a "we" feeling or positive group identity, prosocial values, and norms of caring and empathy in the community members' treatment of one another. Socializing your students along these lines from the beginning of the school year will minimize the frequency with which peer rejection problems appear, as well as establish a set of ideals and expectations for interpersonal behavior that you can appeal to and reinforce when speaking to your students about any peer rejection or other antisocial behavioral problems that do develop.

15

Shy/Withdrawn Students

S hy/withdrawn students display the following characteristics: These hildren avoid personal interaction, are quiet and unobtrusive, and do not respond well to others. They:

1. Are quiet and sober
2. Do not initiate or volunteer
3. Do not call attention to themselves

What special strategies might you use to minimize such problems and help these students to function more successfully in your classroom? Before reading further, take time to think about this and make notes about your ideas.

CSS INTERVIEW EXCERPTS

Here is what three of the CSS teachers had to say about teaching shy/withdrawn students.

A Lower Rated Teacher

"I have one, and I don't know what to do with her. She won't talk to me from a distance, and in a reading group she doesn't read out. She came to me I think in November, and the mother brought her in, and the first thing that the mother said to me is, 'She doesn't talk very much.' . . . The son told me that she talked at home, but in school she didn't talk. She didn't do it at her other school. There were days that I tried to talk with her, and she just wouldn't say anything. I'm good at letting students alone, so I let her alone. Finally, one day I had had all I could take, and I said to her, 'One of these times you're going to want to do something real bad, and you're going to ask me if you can do it, and I'm going to act like you. I'm not going to answer.' It didn't even bother her. . . . Anyway, that was just a threat that I couldn't carry through. I'm just unable to reach her. . . . The other day during reading, I told her, 'You don't talk to me enough for me to know what you really can do, and you don't do your work as much as you should or as well as you should, so you have from now until May to open your mouth to start reading where I can hear, start talking where I can hear and understand, and start to do more work.' We went back to reading, and she read so that we could hear her, but she only did it twice. Today she was right back where she started. I didn't say anything to her except, 'There's a truck out there that's making a lot of noise, so you're going to have to read a little louder so I can hear you.' She upped her voice just a little bit but not much. . . . I can't talk to her to find out her reasons for being like this because she won't talk to me. The only reason she'll talk to me is to ask if she can go to the bathroom, or get a drink, etc., but other than that if I try to talk to her about why she isn't doing her work, I have to almost put my ear in her mouth. I can't cope with this, so I just let her be. I check on her when she's trying to do her work to see if she understands what she's doing. She's a helpless kid. I really feel sorry for her, but I don't know what to do to reach her."

Sadly, this teacher attempted to deal with a shy student in her classroom by criticizing her and implicitly threatening her, which is the opposite of the kind of treatment that such students need. The teacher was painfully aware that her approach was not working, but she did not seem to have better ideas.

A HIGHER RATED TEACHER

"The first action I would take is to find out why such a student is exhibiting these behaviors. A number of these students are afraid for one reason or another to call attention to themselves. They are shy, they are insecure, they have a poor self-image. . . . You just look for his reasons for becoming uninvolved. They probably will be rather serious problems within the student. My strategies would be to make the child feel as important and comfortable in the room as possible so that he would feel secure enough to become more outgoing, more involved. . . . Is the child happy within himself in his place in society and specifically within the classroom society? If I find unhappiness, uncomfortableness, I take any steps I can to alleviate it. If I find the child is quite comfortable with the situation, of course I leave it alone.

The child who doesn't volunteer is almost always the child who is very shy, who is very quiet, who perhaps hasn't been invited to a great deal of participation at home in family decisions, and so on. I think it has to be a long-term strategy rather than short-term, and it has to be a constant encouragement, a warmth in the classroom, a feeling of being relaxed or being free here. Almost always these students will make some measurable progress in interacting with their peers or perhaps even to the point of volunteering to get up in front of the group and present something, which is a major step.

"But I think it has to be brought along in a very easy, slow manner, in no way putting pressure on the student, such as saying, 'you must be able by next week to give a 5-minute report in front of the class. It's good for you.' That type of thing. That's going to drive them right back into the shell even further. Again, I guess I would have to say that the room atmosphere, the feeling of being relaxed and part of a group where you contribute, is very important, seeing your peers enjoying themselves while giving a play, talking in front of the class, seeing that the class is not going to make fun of them. Eventually, you will make some measurable progress. A student who is shy in first grade quite likely might still be shy in sixth grade. Maybe that is the nature of people, but you can modify it. You can make them feel that they have an important contribution for the class. . . . I have never yet had a student who hasn't been able to voluntarily make some contribution in front of his peers without feeling like the walls are going to cave in and that he will disappear forever. I guess I have some empathy because as an elementary student myself, I was very quiet and very shy and very unsure of myself. I can remember often having the right answer in my head but being afraid to raise my hand because 'what if it was the wrong answer?' So I have a lot of empathy for these types of students, and I want them to feel that if you make a mistake . . . so what? No one is going to censure you for it; no one is going to be angry about it. If they can indeed feel this sort of atmosphere and be free to make mistakes, these are the kind of students I think will make progress that you can certainly see and almost measure over the span of a school year.

"I try to include such students, when they are ready, just in being part of the large group and being free to contribute or not as they wish. Then I start working with them on a smaller group basis where they don't feel quite as threatened if there are four or five rather than a classroom of thirty. Almost always you can get them to contribute to some extent in that situation. Usually we have four or five plays a year within the classroom at the initiation of students. Quite often it comes from a reading group, and I have yet to have a student say,

'I'm afraid to be in the play. I don't want to appear in front of my classmates.' They get so wrapped up in the play that they don't even think about the fact that they are going to be appearing in front of a group of people. For those who have a particularly strong case of withdrawal, I often suggest a puppet show to a group that they are part of. You can hide behind a puppet, and you can talk but you don't have to actually appear in person. This is very successful. If they find success in having a puppet doing their acting and talking for them, often the next time they can come out and do it as a real live actor and find that indeed it was a fun experience rather than a threatening one."

Partly because she was shy as a child herself, this teacher had great empathy for her shy students and possessed a rich repertoire of strategies for helping them. These included developing and working within a close personal relationship with these students, bringing them along slowly from individual through small-group to whole-class situations, providing them with encouragement and showing interest in their class contributions, and engaging them in various social activities that would build their confidence and help them develop social skills. The contrast between this teacher and the previously quoted one is striking.

ANOTHER HIGHER RATED TEACHER

"If teachers aren't on their toes, they overlook these children. I think that excessive quietness and failure to assert yourself could be indicative of a serious problem. It may come from parents who say, 'Don't bother me, I'm too busy' to the point where the child feels that they should never bother anyone. The world is just too busy for them; others just don't have time for them. It's really hard to say where this sort of thing originates. The first thing I would try to do is establish rapport with this child, get the child talking to me and perhaps at the same time assign him a buddy in the room, somebody that he perhaps does quiet games with, who I would make sure was a very considerate, kindhearted child. I think children of this nature are probably pretty fragile and may have suffered a lot of rejection previously. They also might have a low self-concept, feeling like they're not going to bother someone since they won't like them anyway ('I'm not going to raise my hand to volunteer because I'd probably be wrong'). It's not that they cry about it, but they're resigned to it ('I don't know how to do this, but I don't want to bother the teacher because she's busy'). I think you should seek these children out, just to get them talking. If you start talking to the child, you can assign them a buddy who perhaps would make sure, if there's a free-time activity, that they play with that person or make sure that person's included in a group activity. They probably would do much better in a small-group situation where they don't feel as threatened, where you can give them more attention and perhaps help them feel that they have more self-worth than they've given themselves credit for. I might ask for some kind of counseling for this child. I would also talk to the parents and see what this child is like in the home. What are his social relationships outside of school, if indeed he has any with children his own age. I think that children like this should be encouraged to do things like extracurricular activities, things that almost force them to be a little more outgoing, to have to put forth a little bit, like Scouting or gymnastics or dancing."

This teacher showed good understanding of the fears and inhibitions of shy students. She also emphasized the importance of building and working within a close personal relationship with these students, as well as involving them in productive peer relationships in and out of the school setting. This included speaking to the parents about involving their children in extracurricular activities.

WHAT THE SCHOLARLY LITERATURE SAYS

Most problem students are readily identifiable because they behave in ways that are salient as well as undesirable. In contrast, shy/withdrawn students rarely call attention to themselves. Among students who are relatively inactive in the classroom, many are well adjusted academically and socially but are relatively quiet and content to work independently, some are problematically shy or withdrawn in varying degrees, and a few are headed toward schizophrenia. Our research focused on the middle range of such students, who are commonly described as shy (inhibited, lacking in confidence, socially anxious) or withdrawn (unresponsive, uncommunicative, daydreaming, spacey, out of it).

A degree of shyness is normal whenever social expectations are new or ambiguous. Shyness begins to emerge as a problem if it becomes not merely situational but dispositional, so that the child gets labeled as shy. Especially if the child internalizes this label, a generalized pattern of shyness may become established and begin to include such additional symptoms as diffidence about entering social situations, discomfort and inhibition in the presence of others, exaggerated self-concern, and increasingly negative social self-concepts (Honig, 1987; Thompson & Rudolph, 1992). Shyness patterns that become well established in childhood tend to persist throughout life, especially in men. Compared to their peers, shy boys show later entry into marriage and reduced occupational achievement and marital stability. Shy girls are more likely than their peers to follow a conventional pattern of marriage, childbearing, and homemaking, but are less likely to develop careers outside the home (Caspi, Elder, & Bem, 1988).

Zimbardo (1977) portrayed shy students as follows: They speak softly, are reluctant to volunteer, do not initiate interactions with the teacher, spend more time at their seats than other students, tend to obey and not get into trouble, and rarely are selected for special errands or duties. Their unwillingness to ask for help and their sensitivity to being evaluated may cause them to perform poorly even when they possess the skills needed to succeed.

Brophy and Evertson (1981) found that teachers usually reached out actively toward shy students by trying to involve them in lessons and discussions, responding positively when they did initiate contact, praising them when they did respond or do good work, minimizing criticism, and communicating positive affect. Nevertheless, these students generally persisted in avoiding teachers except when they needed help, and they reacted to the teachers' overtures with passivity rather than positive affect. In other words, they responded to teacher initiations in ways likely to extinguish such initiations. Thus, you face a dual problem in trying to reach shy or withdrawn students. First, these students seldom initiate interactions, so you have to make proactive efforts to reach out to them, get to know them, and involve them in activities. Second, you must be prepared to sustain these outreach efforts indefinitely without enjoying reciprocation or reinforcement in the form of gratitude, warmth, or other positive affect from the student.

Varieties and Causes of Shyness and Withdrawal in the Classroom

Symptoms of shyness or withdrawal may appear as part of a general personality trait or as situation-specific responses to particular stress factors. Buss (1980, 1984) developed a conception of shyness as a generalized personality trait. He defined shyness as discomfort, inhibition, and awkwardness in social situations. Shyness includes a behavioral component (withdrawal, reticence, and inhibition) and an emotional component (fear, self-consciousness, or both). When fear predominates, the person experiences panic in the immediate situation and worry about future social encounters. When self-consciousness predominates, the person feels naked, vulnerable, inept, and concerned about saying or doing something foolish. Different combinations of behavioral indicators, fear, and self-consciousness occur among different types of shy people.

Children are especially susceptible to self-consciousness in social situations that make them feel conspicuous and psychologically unprotected. Buss identified the following as potential immediate causes of such reactions: novelty of the situation (the child is not sure how to act), formality of the situation (the child realizes that particular behavior is expected and does not feel confident about producing it), either too little or too much attention (the child either is ignored or becomes the focus of attention), and breaches of privacy (the child becomes embarrassed because actions intended to be private become public). Other potential immediate causes include recognition that one is different from or occupies a status subordinate to others, awareness that one's behavior will be evaluated, and a prior history of failure and anxiety in similar situations (McCroskey, 1984).

Shy children have poor self-images and negative expectations. They feel less intelligent, attractive, or popular than their peers, and they feel that others will not like them if they get to know them (Strauss et al., 1986; Zimbardo, 1977). Their parents are likely to use authoritarian rather than inductive socialization techniques (Maccoby & Martin, 1983).

Several types of social unresponsiveness result from specific experiences or environmental causes. Some children have not developed effective conversational skills because their parents seldom converse with them or respond positively to their verbal initiations, and they have not had much opportunity to interact with peers. This may explain much of the shyness seen in kindergarten and first grade.

Social anxiety also can develop as a continued reaction to repeated failure or mistreatment in particular situations. Children who have come to expect rejection or abuse from peers may keep to themselves as a defense against such treatment. Children who have been abused at home may come to expect trouble from people in general and adults in particular.

Some students are unresponsive at school because they are preoccupied with anxiety stemming from trauma experienced at home. Such troubled students may also lapse into daydreaming as an escape from their anxieties (Koplow, 1983). This kind of withdrawal is different from the inattentiveness seen in distractible students. It involves sustained preoccupation with traumatic events occurring outside of the classroom, not just flitting attention.

Children starting school for the first time may exhibit school phobia (usually fear of the unknown or unwillingness to be separated from the parent rather than a specific negative reaction to the teacher or the school). Other students show good peer group adjustment and ability to interact socially with the teacher but display communication apprehension (Daly & McCroskey, 1984) or elective mutism (Friedman & Karagan, 1973) when asked to answer academic questions, perform in public, or engage in activity that they know will be evaluated. Finally, many students experience at least temporary social adjustment problems because they have changed schools, are repeating a grade, or have skipped a grade (Byrnes & Yamamoto, 1983).

Suggested Strategies for Coping with Shy or Withdrawn Students

Common sense suggests the following teacher strategies for coping with shy or withdrawn students: (1) Develop a supportive, trusting relationship so as to be seen primarily as a helper rather than an authority figure; (2) visit with these students often to monitor their work and speak privately with them; (3) talk to their parents to get information about what they are like at home and about outside interests that might be useful in drawing them out at school; (4) when calling on them in class, use a soft, invitational tone—do not shock or "bark" at them; (5) encourage and praise their contributions; (6) involve peers through buddy system assignments and small-group cooperative activities.

Johnson (1956) compiled the following list based on interviews with first- and second-grade teachers who were asked to describe ways to bring withdrawn students into the group:

1. *Enhance Self-Esteem and Confidence (55 percent of the suggestions).*
   a. Take every opportunity to praise such children.
   b. Give them recognition by talking "to" them during group sessions (looking directly at them from time to time). Perhaps use their names to designate groups ("Tom's group," etc.).
   c. Give them responsibility by assigning them important tasks.
   d. Find areas or activities in which they feel secure enough to participate (some may be drawn out through art activities, while others may feel comfortable talking about their families or pets, etc.).
   e. Ask their advice when this may be helpful (such as teacher–pupil planning).
   f. Give them objective descriptions of their progress in learning to do things that they were not able to do before.
   g. Help them when they need help to avoid traumatic failure.
2. *Encourage Contact with Peers (13 percent).* Place withdrawn children in group activities with friendly peers, encourage peers to play with them, or seat them near outgoing classmates.
3. *Gently Move Them toward Participation (10 percent).* Allow them to remain relatively quiet at first and yet to participate in the group. When they seem more ready for individual participation, encourage them to become more active.

4. *Other Methods.* Discuss with them the importance of participating in activities and sharing with peers; help them to feel secure and "at home" in the classroom; develop a climate of relaxed calmness (move at a moderate speed, speak in soft but clear voice tones).

Blanco and Bogacki (1988) collected recommendations from school psychologists. For coping with *general shyness or withdrawal,* they suggested encouraging the children to join volunteer groups or recreational and social organizations outside of school; involving them frequently in small-group, cooperative interaction with peers; using them as peer tutors; praising them frequently and minimizing criticism; waiting patiently for them to respond if they do not do so immediately; letting them practice answers beforehand; calling on them only when you believe that they know the answer; telling them ahead of time what you are going to ask questions about so that they can rehearse privately; involving them in games that require verbal responses; talking to them privately about things of interest to them; determining their peer preferences and seating them near preferred peers; leading but not forcing them to communicate; avoiding putting them in situations that would be embarrassing or frightening; assigning them to messenger roles or other tasks that require communication (e.g., storekeeper in an economics simulation); and encouraging expression through dolls, puppets, or stuffed animals.

For students whose withdrawal symptoms include *excessive daydreaming,* call on them frequently; stand near them or touch them to ensure attention; draw up contracts that allow them to earn rewards by completing a specified amount and quality of work within a specified time; at the beginning of work time, make sure that they get started successfully on their assignment; minimize their involvement in silent listening or reading activities that encourage daydreaming; do not scold them for daydreaming but stress the need for attention and participation; and assign partners to work with them and keep them involved.

Other syntheses of advice to teachers (Honig, 1987; McIntyre, 1989; Schaefer & Millman, 1981; Thompson & Rudolph, 1992) all contain suggestions similar to those offered in the sources already cited, along with the following ideas: Use inventories to determine the interests of shy or withdrawn students, and then follow up by using these interests as bases for conversations or learning activities; display their (good) artwork or assignments for others to see in the classroom; assign them as a partner to or promote their friendship with a classmate who is popular and engages in frequent contact with peers; check with these students frequently if they are prone to daydreaming, and use touch or a signal (clearing your throat, tapping your finger on their desks) to regain their attention subtly; help these children to set social development goals, and assist them by providing training in assertiveness, initiating interactions with peers, or other social skills; provide them with any information needed to develop social insight (e.g., explaining that new students often have trouble making friends at first or that kidding or teasing does not necessarily mean that peers do not like you, suggesting ways for them to initiate productive peer contacts or to respond more effectively to peer initiations); in social situations in which they might otherwise become shy and retreat to the fringes of the group, provide them with a designated role that will give them something to do and cause them to interact with others; teach them social door openers for greeting others and speaking to them in person or on the telephone, especially assertive requests ("Can I play too?"); make time to talk with them each day even if just for a few minutes, and listen carefully and respond specifically to what they tell you; and use bibliotherapy materials such as *The Very Little Girl,* a story by P. Krasilovsky (1992) about a sad and shy girl who becomes more outgoing.

Shy children may need direct instruction in social skills, such as those included in the various Goldstein programs (e.g., McGinnis & Goldstein, 1984): starting and sustaining conversations, asking and answering questions, introducing yourself, asking for help, joining a group, sharing and helping, responding to teasing. Other commercially available social skills training programs that have been used successfully with shy or withdrawn children include ACCEPTS (Walker et al., 1983); Getting Along with Others (Jackson, Jackson, & Monroe, 1983); and Procedures for Establishing Relationship Skills (PEERS; Hops, Walker, & Greenwood, 1979). These packages differ in the specific social skills taught, but they share the following common elements: They all use modeling to introduce the skills, provide ample practice opportunities via role playing and behavioral rehearsal, supply performance feedback, and require "homework" along with self-monitoring of performance in real-life situations (Rosenberg et al., 1992). See Cartledge and Milburn (1986) or Hughes (1988) for more information about social skills training programs with elementary students; and see Sheridan, Kratochwill, and Elliott (1990) for description of a program that included collaboration between teachers and parents.

Other sources of advice to teachers offer similar suggestions, although they differ in their relative emphasis on being purely supportive of shy or withdrawn children versus making performance demands on them.

General Advice

Koplow (1983), writing from a psychoanalytic perspective and primarily for early childhood educators, interpreted unresponsiveness as an attempt by an anxious child to exert control and avoid feared catastrophes. She urged that teachers "follow that child into his hiding place, to discover the source of his fears and then to make the world of the classroom a safer place for him" (p. 127). Cautioning against getting into power struggles by demanding responses, she advised teachers to build close relationships with these students, to encourage their development of good relationships with peers, and to prepare them ahead of time for situations that demand verbal response.

Writing from an applied behavior analysis perspective, Spaulding (1983) suggested that teachers (1) emphasize specific, concrete academic tasks and clear structuring of demands in making assignments for passive or withdrawn students; (2) assign them to work near supportive peers; (3) provide structure and support while they work on assignments; (4) reinforce all emerging active, prosocial, or productive behavior; and (5) minimize criticism or punishment.

Writing from a more general social learning perspective, Apter and Conoley (1984) suggested that teachers build personal relationships with shy students by talking with them privately each day; get them talking by scheduling sharing times, storytelling, or small-group projects for which they can be made the group reporters; be responsive and rewarding when they make contributions; gradually increase response demands as they begin to gain confidence; and train them in relevant social skills (initiating and sustaining conversations, making introductions, giving compliments, asking for help, giving help, joining in, and convincing others).

Unresponsiveness

Several authors have contributed suggestions about dealing with unresponsiveness (sometimes called "elective mutism"). Good and Brophy (1997) suggested developing supportive personal relationships with inhibited students but also subtly conditioning them to become more responsive: Use a friendly and informal tone, but ask questions directly (rather than preface them with stems such as, "Do you think you could . . . ?"). Then look at the students to communicate that you expect an answer. If they answer appropriately, praise or give feedback. If they answer too softly, praise and then ask them to repeat the answer louder. If they appear to be about to answer but hesitate, prompt by nodding your head or encouraging verbally. If waiting for several seconds does not yield a response, simplify the question through rephrasing or clues, or else give the answer and then ask the student to repeat it. Occasionally follow up by asking additional questions or asking the student to elaborate on the response. Instruct these students to say, "I don't know" rather than remain silent when they cannot respond. If necessary, temporarily avoid calling on them in whole-class situations while bringing them along slowly in individual and small-group settings.

Friedman and Karagan (1973) suggested the following guidelines for working with electively mute children: Do not use punishment or bribery to force speech, because this will only increase their insecurity; involve them in all regular group activities; whenever they seem to be at ease, encourage them to speak through such tasks as reading or storytelling; invite but do not force them to speak during class activities; begin with easy response demands (nonverbal responses or single-word answers), and proceed gradually toward more extended response demands; and begin with private interactions, and proceed through small-group interactions to whole-class settings.

Cognitive Restructuring

Most shy and withdrawn students are inhibited by unnecessary anxieties or unjustifiably low self-concepts (Biemer, 1983; Glass & Furlong, 1984), so they stand to benefit from cognitive restructuring treatments. Two of the better known approaches to cognitive restructuring are rational–emotive education and cognitive-behavior modification.

Rational–emotive education focuses on eliminating irrational beliefs that cause students to behave counterproductively (Knaus, 1974; Vernon, 1989). In the case of forms of shyness that focus on communication apprehension, for example, such beliefs might include "No one wants to listen to me" or "Whatever I say sounds stupid." Rational–emotive education helps students to replace these anxiety-provoking and inhibiting thoughts with more rational and adaptive ones that reaffirm their confidence in the value of their ideas and help them to concentrate on expressing those ideas effectively (Watson & Dodd, 1984).

Cognitive-behavior modification strategies focus less on analyzing irrational thoughts and more on developing effective coping responses to such thoughts. Meichenbaum (1977) used a three-stage process: (1) Teach students to become good observers of their own thoughts, feelings, and behaviors; (2) make the process of self-observation the occasion for generating adaptive cognitions and behaviors; and (3) alter the student's internal dialogues so that changes can be generalized. Problem situations are role played so that the student can practice using coping statements before, during, and after these situations.

Combining rational–emotive and cognitive-behavior modification approaches, Fremouw (1984) suggested four steps for treating communication apprehension in the classroom: (1) Introduce the concept (explain that communication apprehension is learned behavior that can be modified by learning new skills); (2) identify negative self-statements (provide examples of self-statements commonly made by shy or anxious people, and get the students to recognize their own negative self-statements and related social inhibitions); (3) teach adaptive coping statements that can replace the negative self-statements (I'm part of a small group of students who are just like me; speak slowly; so far so good; continue to speak slowly and ask questions); (4) practice (role play making these coping statements, discuss topics of increasing controversy, keep a diary describing stressful situations and coping statements used during them).

Harris and Brown (1982) developed a treatment involving several of these elements working with shy fourth-, fifth-, and sixth-graders. It began with cognitive restructuring. Through group discussions and modeled examples, students were helped to recognize any negative self-statements, images, and self-instructions that they produced before or during interpersonal or public speaking situations. Next, they were taught to replace these statements with task-relevant coping and self-reinforcing statements. Then, they were taught to counteract anxiety through deep muscle relaxation and systematic desensitization. While deeply relaxed, they would first imagine that a feared event was about to occur and would visualize responding to it with coping self-statements and behaviors. Then they would imagine that the situation was actually happening and that they were handling it successfully. Finally, they would produce self-reinforcing statements.

Peer-Oriented Strategies

Several authors have suggested treating shyness and withdrawal through peer involvement (see Rosenberg et al., 1992, for a review). Lazerson (1980) reported significant improvement among withdrawn students involved in a *cross-age tutoring* program (students from grades 5 through 8 tutored students from grades 2 through 4). Good results were obtained whether the students acted as tutors or as tutees, so long as the withdrawn students were paired with more outgoing or assertive students rather than with other withdrawn students.

Furman, Rahe, and Hartup (1979) reported that *opportunities to play in pairs with younger children* increased the sociability of withdrawn preschool children. Play sessions with same-aged peers produced less improvement. Apparently, the assertive behaviors of withdrawn students meet with greater success when they interact with younger children.

Strain, Shores, and Timm (1977) enlisted peers as confederates to draw out withdrawn children. These *increases in social initiations by peers* increased the target students' positive social behaviors.

Lew, Mesch, Johnson, and Johnson (1986) increased the social attractiveness of socially withdrawn students by involving them in *small-group, cooperative classroom activities*. Approaches that involve enlisting peers in drawing out withdrawn students may be of special interest to you because they are less time-consuming and easier to integrate into everyday activities than most of the approaches reviewed earlier.

Combining Strategies

Combinations of complementary strategies probably will be more effective than any single strategy, and remediation tactics should vary with the nature and causes of the symptoms. Systematic desensitization would be most useful where fearfulness predominates. Rational–emotive education would be indicated for students who lack insight into their own negative self-statements, cognitive restructuring for students who need to learn adaptive coping statements to replace self-deprecating statements, and peer-oriented strategies for students who lack friendships or social experience.

Few teachers have the time to implement cognitive restructuring treatments to the extent that they are implemented in shyness clinics. However, if you know the basic principles underlying these treatments, you can use them to some extent. In addition, you are in a strong position to use peer-oriented strategies, because you have continuing access not only to shy students themselves but to their peer groups. Finally, you can improve the school adjustment of shy and withdrawn students not only by helping them learn to cope more effectively with stressful situations but also by building personal relationships with them and establishing a supportive learning environment so as to minimize the stress that they encounter.

ANALYSIS OF INTERVIEW RESPONSES

A large majority (71) of the teachers mentioned providing some form of instruction, training, modeling, or help designed to enable shy students to become more participatory or responsive. In addition or instead, 48 mentioned attempts to encourage, reassure, build self-concept, or provide a supportive environment; and 31 mentioned attempts to shape increased responsiveness through successive approximations. Thus, instruction, support, and shaping strategies predominated in teachers' responses to shy/withdrawn students.

The most commonly mentioned specific strategies were changing the social environment (44); encouraging or shaping increased responsiveness (38); minimizing stress or embarrassment (33); building the student's self-concept (29); adapting instructional methods (27); praising (26); involving other professionals to help solve the problem (23); trying to ensure that shy students would enjoy positive experiences when they did participate (23); building a close relationship with them (20); communicating encouragement and positive expectations (19); and providing support through physical proximity, voice tone, or eye contact (18).

As methods for drawing out shy or withdrawn students, 43 teachers mentioned special activities, 39 advocated frequent private talks, and 31 favored supplying extra attention. Commonly mentioned methods of involving peers included working to develop peer understanding of and support for shy or withdrawn students (31), assigning these students to small groups where they would feel more comfortable participating overtly (20), scheduling special activities designed to work on the problem (15), environmental engineering (moving shy students closer to the teacher or seating them among friendly and outgoing peers) (11), and promoting an attitude of acceptance and friendliness (9).

Consideration of everything the teachers said indicated that 7 teachers would do nothing to try to make shy/withdrawn students more responsive, 11 would confine their efforts to providing indirect support, 55 would pressure these students to change but only through gentle and indirect means, 13 would encourage change directly but back off if they met resistance, and 4 would try to force change even if they met resistance.

Among strategies that the teachers rejected as ineffective, the most frequently mentioned were attempting to force or push shy students to become more responsive (34), calling on them in ways that would put them on the spot or cause embarrassment (28), ignoring the problem (12), and scolding (9).

Taken together, the data indicate that the teachers stressed applying gentle pressure for change but within a context of kid gloves treatment, support, and encouragement. Most would avoid direct confrontation or attempts to force change.

Most teachers stressed the same basic principles, but higher rated teachers suggested a broader range of strategies. In particular, they were more likely to go beyond indirect methods (building a relationship, providing support and encouragement, environmental engineering) to include direct methods of stimulating change: Provide extra attention to shy/withdrawn students; praise their efforts or progress; build up their self-concepts; or offer them specific instruction, special activities or small-group experiences, or helper or messenger roles that would require them to communicate with others. Higher rated teachers would take the problem of shyness/withdrawal seriously and attack it on several fronts simultaneously, but they would remain prepared to back off if their efforts produced significant anxiety or resistance.

There were differences between Small City and Big City in the degree to which shyness was considered a serious problem and addressed through personalized treatment. In Small City, higher rated teachers' suggestions for shy students were more direct and intensive, to the point of making special allowances for them (perhaps because Small City teachers had greater opportunity to engage in individualized interactions with their problem students). In Big City, higher rated teachers would not make special allowances for shy students, but they would go beyond minimal shaping attempts to provide personalized support and assign special messenger and helper roles.

Vignette: Linda

Linda is bright enough, but she is shy and withdrawn. She doesn't volunteer to participate in class, and when you call on her directly, she often does not respond. When she does, she usually whispers. Today, you are checking seatwork progress. When you question her, Linda keeps her eyes lowered and says nothing.

Before reading further, take time to think about how you might respond to this incident. Make notes about your ideas.

CSS Vignette Response Excerpts

Here is what four of the CSS teachers had to say.

A LOWER RATED TEACHER

"Since the child is bright, although she's shy and withdrawn, I would start off with a simple exercise, simple game, or some activity that she could do right off the bat with everyone to look, and say, 'This is great!' Something like that. I would just keep working on that until I got her to have some progress."

A HIGHER RATED TEACHER

"I would pull a small chair up to Linda's desk and ask her the question again about her work, and if she didn't answer, I would start reading through what she had done and ask her to read what she had done. If she still didn't do anything, I would ask her if she was afraid to answer the question. If that was not the case, I would try again calmly to read through what she had done with her, and hopefully she would read it for me, and then I could help her with the next problem. I feel that if she realizes that I am going to take the time to be with her for just a few minutes by herself, then maybe she would be willing to talk to me, if she knows I am not going to rush off to someone else and that she can feel safe in responding to me. I would try to reassure her so that she would not be as shy with me another time.... If her work was nearly correct, I would say, 'You have this much right. Let's see what we can do to fix this so that it answers the question.' If the work is correct, I could say, 'You have done this very well. Let's see what the answer would be for the next one, or how would you begin to work the next one.' I would characterize her as withdrawn, and I would hope that after a few weeks she would begin to feel more comfortable if the situation was consistent and supportive."

ANOTHER HIGHER RATED TEACHER

" 'Linda, is there some problem that you have today with your work? Apparently you have some difficulty. I don't know what it is at this point, and because I have to work with the other boys and girls and find out what they have done, I think that maybe tonight after school, if you wait a little while until the other boys and girls have gone, we'll sit down and talk about your work and if you are having some problems with it, and you can ask me about those problems at that time.' My goal would be to try not to put any more embarrassment on Linda. Apparently something is bothering her at that time, and she is shy anyway, so I don't want to have any more attention drawn to her from the other children in the class. I feel that if she worked with me after school, she would be able to respond and I would be able to find out what was wrong without involving her with any other children."

ANOTHER HIGHER RATED TEACHER

"I would say, 'Linda, you seem really quiet today.' I would probably just ask her something totally unrelated to work, like maybe 'What did you do at home last night?' or 'What's your favorite TV program?' or just something to get her to talk to me that has absolutely nothing to do with schoolwork. Just to try to bring her out so that she feels a little more comfortable about it. Then I would question her about her schoolwork once I had gotten her talking just in general. . . . I was like this when I was in elementary school. I was quiet as a mouse and terribly timid. I think sometimes before you can help a child academically, you have to touch them as a human being, to let them know that you care about them and that you are interested in them and that they can feel comfortable with you. I think you should try to establish a rapport where they just feel comfortable on a person-to-person level rather than a student-to-teacher level. For a child who is really shy and withdrawn and perhaps a little insecure (even though she probably knows she is right), just try to build her up and make her feel like "I care about what you have to say, and I would like to hear what you have to say." My goal is to make her feel comfortable with me first before I would even ask her to be comfortable in a small group, much less a large group. If she feels some kind of rapport, or friendship, between me and her, then she is more likely to be able to discuss her work with me."

The lower rated teacher suggested only one idea for helping Linda, and this involved the relatively indirect approach of calling peers' attention to something that she was doing. In the absence of any attempt to speak to Linda to learn more about her perceptions and begin to develop her social skills, this strategy seems unlikely to have much positive effect and might even do more harm than good (i.e., if Linda panicked when the teacher called everyone's attention to her). In contrast, the three higher rated teachers recognized the need to help Linda become more willing to respond to them in the context of talking about her work (not just to improve her relationships with peers). Furthermore, they emphasized building a personal relationship with her and bringing her along slowly in private situations, not suddenly thrusting her into the spotlight. These responses are much more attuned to shy students' perceptions and needs than that of the lower rated teacher.

Analysis of Responses to Linda

The vast majority of the teachers suggested support and encouragement for Linda, especially through kid gloves treatment (45), instruction (30), encouragement (23), or specific praise (21).

The most frequently mentioned strategies for responding to Linda were trying to build up her self-concept (53); prescribing or modeling better coping strategies (43); changing the social environment, typically by enlisting peer support (29); developing a close personal relationship (23); brief management responses (19); trying to identify and eliminate the source of her problem (17); and postponing action until a more opportune time (11). Only 7 teachers mentioned attempts to develop insight into Linda. Most believed that it would be unproductive to confront her with her problem directly.

In handling the depicted incident, 31 teachers would minimize their response or delay responding until a better time, 28 would reassure Linda or praise whatever success she had achieved so far, 27 would tell her to speak up, 17 would try to get eye contact, 17 would try to get her talking (about anything, not necessarily about the original question), 13 would invite her to whisper the answer or speak it privately, 13 would see that she got tutorial help, 7 would confront her directly by asking her why she had not responded, and 5 would simply repeat the question.

Most teachers mentioned at least one prevention or follow-up strategy. These included attempts to encourage or shape increased responsiveness (54), enlisting peers to provide support or draw her out (24), praising or rewarding her accomplishments (19), building a close relationship with her (17), trying to ensure success experiences and avoid putting her on the spot when called on (14), probing to discover an underlying emotional problem (11), and finding out about her interests and then building these into activities (7).

In summary, most teachers saw Linda as fearful, inhibited, and in need of being brought along slowly through encouragement, shaping of increased responsiveness, and kid gloves treatment. A minority saw her problem more as a bad habit that needed to be corrected, but even these teachers stressed relatively benign behavioral shaping and cueing rather than demands backed by threats of punishment.

The vast majority of the teachers interpreted Linda's behavior as inhibition due to anxiety and stated that they would respond by providing her with support, assistance, verbal and nonverbal communication designed to draw her out, reassurance of her abilities, praise for her successes, and so on. Higher rated teachers spoke with greater confidence of achieving significant improvements, and they more often mentioned strategies that went beyond general emotional support (such as calling Linda's attention to her accomplishments and providing tutorial help to enable her to achieve consistent success in her work).

Lower rated teachers were more likely to speak of involving peers to provide support or to help draw her out. Peer support strategies usually show positive relationships with effectiveness ratings. However, Linda's problem centered around confidence in her ability to handle work assignments or around her relationship with the teacher (i.e., not her peers). Apparently, many of the teachers who spoke of involving peers misinterpreted the problem or failed to mention other strategies that would be more specifically responsive to it.

Vignette: John

John often seems to be off in his own world, but today he is watching you as you lead a discussion. Pleased to see him attentive, you ask him what he thinks. However, you have to repeat his name, and he looks startled when he realizes that you have called on him. Meanwhile, you realize that he has been immersed in daydreams and only appeared to be paying attention.

Before reading further, take time to think about how you might respond to this incident. Make notes about your ideas.

CSS Vignette Response Excerpts

Here is what four of the CSS teachers had to say.

A LOWER RATED TEACHER

"I would try and draw him back into the discussion and maybe start with something little—what television program do you most enjoy, this sort of thing. Maybe he'd be able to tell me that and then what's the favorite character that you like. Maybe then he'd be more interested in discussion, and we could veer him back to what we're really thinking about."

A HIGHER RATED TEACHER

"I would remind John that we are discussing something very important: 'John, we're talking about this subject. I need you to listen and pay attention to me.' I might have someone repeat the last couple of things we have talked about. Then I would continue the discussion but ask him questions every so often to make sure that he is paying attention. I might even move him up close to the front so that I could have more eye contact with him. I could look directly at him and repeat things and remind him and keep the eye contact going. My goal would be for John to not only listen but participate in the discussion too. . . . He needs to learn to concentrate. It's important in school and whatever situation you might be in. He seems to have a lot of things on his mind. I'm not sure if he's bored with what we're talking about or if there are a lot of pressures. He might have some problems that he needs to sit down and talk with somebody about."

ANOTHER HIGHER RATED TEACHER

"I would first say, 'John, I'm sorry, you were looking at me, so I thought you were paying attention to what we were doing. I'm sorry you didn't hear.' Then I would ask other students what the discussion had been about and then go back to John and say, 'Do you think you can answer my question now?' If he says no, then I would simply drop it at that time. Later, I would talk with John and say, 'John, would it be easier for you if your desk was closer to me when I am talking to the whole class, so that I can tap you on the shoulder or speak your name quietly so you know that you need to pay attention?' I might even say that 'we will try that first and see if it works.' He needs to learn that he can attend to a discussion that is maybe 10 to 15 minutes in length, maybe with some reminders at first."

ANOTHER HIGHER RATED TEACHER

" 'John, it looked like you were really listening to what I was saying, and I thought you could add to the discussion. Let's go back and go over that last point, and then I am going to ask you another question about it, now that I know that your attention is on what the rest of the children have been listening to. I know that you can really give me a good answer when you are listening. Are you ready?' My goal would be to try to get him back into the class and thinking about what our discussion is, to have him concentrate on listening and be able to answer a question when he is asked, to get him to understand that you realize that sometimes he is distracted and his attention wanders, that this is natural for anybody. But I wouldn't embarrass him or have him feel badly or put him down because he wasn't listening again and I really thought he was. Get him to realize that this is something that is natural to most people, and he just needs to improve his listening skills."

The lower rated teacher's response is based on a general principle that applies in many situations: Get shy children talking comfortably about nonthreatening content before easing them toward content that might be threatening to them. However, this principle does not apply very well in the situation depicted in the vignette. The teacher is in the middle of a whole-class lesson, and this is no time to interrupt to engage John in a discussion of his favorite television programs and characters. In contrast, the responses of the three higher rated teachers are more suited to the situation. They advocated clarifying the situation for John in a way that makes it clear that they understand what has happened and are not angry with him, then resuming the lesson in a way that allows John to connect back into it, and finally calling on him shortly thereafter. All of these responses show awareness of the need to balance special consideration ("kid gloves treatment") for John with teaching him to pay better attention to lessons.

Analysis of Responses to John

The teachers' responses to John showed a less supportive, more demanding pattern than was observed with Linda, although the majority still stressed positive (support, shaping) methods over negative (demand, threat) methods. Most (79) teachers mentioned at least one supportive behavior, frequently kid gloves treatment (33), instruction (22), or involving other adults to provide support (12).

The most commonly mentioned specific approaches were brief management responses (46) and prescribing or modeling better coping strategies (42). To handle the immediate incident, 31 teachers would repeat or rephrase the question to John; 30 would question him frequently to keep him involved; 28 would tell him to pay better attention; 20 would use touch, physical proximity, or movement toward John to gain his attention; 14 would explain to him what had happened; 11 would use humor or tension release comments; 9 would ask him a new question; 9 would minimize or delay responding until a more opportune time; 8 would bring him up to date on what he had missed; and 7 would use some gimmick to maintain his attention (such as asking him to hold up a picture for the class to see). Thus, in contrast to the emphasis on building up Linda's self-concept, most responses to John were brief management responses or demands for better attention.

Fewer than two-thirds of the teachers mentioned prevention or follow-up strategies. These included probing for personal or emotional problems (28), trying to encourage or shape John's responsiveness (19), demanding or appealing for better attention (12), trying to make the work more interesting or to capitalize on John's interests (10), changing his seat (7), and teaching listening skills (6).

In summary, the majority of the teachers would deal with the incident through brief management responses designed to regain John's attention, then continue with the lesson, and finally follow up later by pressuring John to pay more careful attention in class or by probing to find out what might underlie his tendency to tune out.

Instead of just regaining John's attention at the time and perhaps urging him to pay better attention in the future, higher rated teachers would help him to maintain attention by moving his seat closer, providing instructive suggestions, or using nonverbal communication methods to help him focus on them when they were teaching. These teachers were more likely to demand improved attention from John but also less likely to threaten punishment for repeated inattention. Lower rated teachers tended not to speak of following up the incident at all or to speak vaguely of involving the parents or seeking an underlying cause of the problem.

COMPARISON OF RESPONSES TO LINDA AND TO JOHN

Most teachers responded to these two vignettes with similar (and apparently effective) approaches. Almost all of them mentioned strategies for handling the immediate problem (getting Linda to talk and restoring John's attention), and the majority (especially higher rated teachers) suggested follow-up strategies designed to prevent its recurrence.

The teachers were overwhelmingly sympathetic toward and willing to be supportive of Linda, and they stressed the need to build up her academic self-concept by praising her successes and providing encouragement. In contrast, they were more demanding of John. Some would remain essentially supportive, attempting to help him by changing his seat, directing nonverbal communications toward him, or providing helpful instruction or modeling (but not the encouragement or self-concept support provided to Linda). Others spoke of pressuring him by demanding improved attentiveness. These contrasts are part of a larger set of findings suggesting that shyness/inhibition problems call for relatively indirect and highly supportive treatment, whereas withdrawal/daydreaming problems call for more direct treatment that may (but not necessarily must) include direct appeals for improved attention.

QUALITATIVE IMPRESSIONS AND EXAMPLES

Many teachers stressed the value of opening up shy or withdrawn students by using their interests as conversation starters and activity topics. These teachers would assign shy students to do special projects in their areas of interest, especially projects that would require them to work together with other students or would culminate in a presentation to the class. They also would encourage these students to bring things from home for Show and Tell or to write about areas of interest in book reports or composition assignments. Another common theme was cautioning against trying to move too quickly. Many teachers mentioned the need to give shy students time to warm up to the teacher and to develop confidence in themselves. They often recommended strategies such as calling on shy students whenever they raised their hands but not often otherwise (except when sure that they could answer successfully).

Certain responses seemed unlikely to be effective. Some teachers favored the use of humor to get the student "off the spot" but suggested humorous comments that seemed likely to increase the student's embarrassment. Some spoke of creating special roles to encourage shy students to interact more in the classroom but mentioned roles ("police officer") or assignments (tell peers that the teacher wants them to quiet down) that might do such students more harm than good. Finally, some started with a basically sound idea (such as capitalizing on the student's interest in a cartoon superhero) but then spoke of carrying it to extremes when discussing implementation.

The following are noteworthy commonly mentioned strategies or unique suggestions made by individual teachers.

Advance preparation: Meet with shy students privately, and tell them that you want them to volunteer during an upcoming activity; prime them by asking questions today during private informal conversations that are similar to the ones you will ask during tomorrow's lesson (such as questions about a story read today that will be discussed tomorrow); have them practice speeches at home in front of a mirror, or better yet, use a tape recorder so that they will hear that they sound OK.

Special roles and assignments: Place them on committees or other groups that require interaction with others; let them choose a game to play and be captain; encourage them to share experiences with the class or a small group (when you know that the student has something to share and you can make a leading suggestion about it); allow (but not require) them to read to the class from a favorite book or story (reading is less stressful than speaking extemporaneously); assign them to work with younger students by tutoring them, leading them in games, or reading to them; give them jobs that require them to talk or to be in front of the class frequently (greeter of visitors, messenger, cleaning the boards).

Peer and recreational activities: Pair them with a peer for tutoring or cooperative learning activities; place them among peers who are outgoing but not too boisterous; assign a compatible classmate to act as a buddy; ask peers to invite them to play, giving them guidelines (one or two students ask quietly—don't mob the shy student); suggest to parents that they enroll the child in a group therapy situation with other shy children or in extracurricular activities such as choir, scouting, gymnastics, or dancing.

Medical tests or hypotheses: Check Linda's hearing; check John for possible epilepsy; consider that John could be on medication that would render him groggy; "put the earphones on" John to see how he does at listening skill diagnosis and development activities.

Humor: "A penny for your thoughts, John. They must be better than mine." "Was it a good sleep? That's the first time I've seen someone sleep with his eyes open."

Parents: Encourage the parents to talk more with their child and especially to draw out and *listen* to the child; find out if the parents have warned the child to be "good" (e.g., quiet) at school; ask them if the child has said anything about being afraid of the teacher (and, if so, why).

Miscellaneous: Model icebreakers and social initiation talk for shy students; be aware that certain African- or Native-American students may be taught at home to avoid eye contact and remain quiet around adults; reinforce participation in class activities (but through private expressions of appreciation rather than public overkill such as "Linda spoke up today! Let's all cheer!"); develop a relationship by corresponding with the student (using actual letters sent through the mail); if the class is reading, have John use his finger to keep track; otherwise, tell him to keep his eyes (not just his ears) trained on you at all times, and check to make sure that he does so; bend or stoop to get down to Linda's level to establish eye contact with her.

DISCUSSION

The data suggest that most teachers are familiar with the problems that shy/withdrawn students present and are able to respond to them using accessible strategies. This is understandable because such students primarily need support, encouragement, and personalized assistance—behaviors that mesh well with the nurturant, student-oriented attitudes that are common among elementary teachers. They also form part of a naturally occurring empathetic reaction to children who are seen as victims of forces beyond their control (see Brophy & Evertson, 1981). Even so, codes reflecting positive expectations and confidence in ability to respond effectively to shy/withdrawn students were among the most consistent correlates of effectiveness ratings.

Higher rated teachers often mentioned that different subtypes of shy/withdrawn students require different treatment, and the contrasts in the findings for the two vignettes illustrated this. Linda showed shyness/inhibition problems that yielded responses focusing on support, encouragement, and buildup of academic self-concept; whereas John showed withdrawal/daydreaming problems that yielded responses focusing on making it easier for him to sustain attention to lessons (changing his seat, improving the nonverbal communication directed at him, etc.) or appealing for increased concentration.

Many interview responses included strategies for involving peers to support or interact with shy students, but these strategies were rarely mentioned in response to the vignettes because the depicted situations did not lend themselves well to peer involvement. Similarly, many teachers mentioned teaching shy students in small groups in their interviews, but this did not come up in response to the vignettes (it probably would have if Linda's inhibition about responding to the teacher's question had been portrayed as occurring during a whole-class recitation rather than during seatwork time). A contrast in the opposite direction was seen with seating John closer to the teacher to make it easier for him to pay attention. This strategy was never mentioned during the interviews (which focused more on shyness/inhibition problems than on withdrawal/daydreaming problems).

The vignette data also illustrated the importance of several relatively subtle situational responses and seemingly minor environmental engineering and behavior modification strategies that were not highlighted in the interview responses (which focused on the big picture by addressing such topics as building up a student's academic self-concept). For example, the data from the first vignette indicate the value of tension release strategies for defusing situational anxiety or embarrassment and of praise/reward strategies for encouraging and calling attention to the successes of shy/inhibited students such as Linda. Similarly, the data from the second vignette indicate the value of brief management responses for refocusing the attention of withdrawn/daydreaming students such as John without causing them unnecessary embarrassment or breaking the flow of the lesson, as well as the value of relatively subtle nonverbal communication methods for gaining and maintaining the attention of such students.

In summary, the teachers' intuition-based responses to shy and withdrawn students meshed well not only with common sense but with expert recommendations based on previously developed theory and research. Both the literature review and the present data suggest that *shy students* should be brought along slowly but surely by making them feel comfortable and secure in the classroom, reassuring them of their ability to handle academic challenges (and providing special instruction or help if necessary), and applying consistent but gentle and largely indirect pressure for change (in the form of invitations and encouragement rather than demands or direct confrontations). They also suggest that *withdrawn students* need direct appeals for improved attention; cueing, shaping, environmental engineering, and other support or assistance in sustaining such attention; and work on the underlying problems that have led these students to become withdrawn in the first place.

Applying these strategies in the classroom can be difficult, however, because the passivity of shy and withdrawn students tends to render them relatively invisible. Also, some students are relatively unresponsive to their teacher's questions, not because they are shy or withdrawn but because they are alienated from the process of classroom learning and have discovered that unresponsiveness is one way to condition teachers to lower their expectations, minimize their demands, and gradually reduce the frequency with which they call on them or initiate individual contact with them (Brophy & Evertson, 1981). It is important for you to distinguish between shy or withdrawn students and these alienated students who require a different (more confrontational and demanding) response. When unsure, it is best to assume initially that the student has a genuine shyness or withdrawal problem and respond accordingly. This will produce less serious and more reversible consequences than beginning by mistakenly assuming that the student is faking such a problem. In any case, support, encouragement, and sincere communication of concern and willingness to provide any needed assistance are likely to be helpful in coping with almost any type of problem student.

You may be able to help shy and withdrawn students considerably using strategies that are relatively easy to implement and well matched to the teacher's basic role as a helpful instructor to students. These include providing self-concept support, encouragement, and opportunities to develop confidence and comfort in the classroom to shy and inhibited students, as well as closer monitoring, improved nonverbal communication, environmental engineering, and instructive suggestions or demands for improved concentration designed to maintain the attention of students prone to withdrawal or daydreaming. Most teachers apparently develop at least an intuitive understanding of the needs of shy or withdrawn students, but many could meet these needs more effectively by systematically applying the principles and strategies highlighted here.

VI

Conclusion

16

Looking Back—and Ahead

I n this final chapter, I do not attempt to summarize the considerable range of information presented in earlier chapters on the implications of the scholarly literature in general, and the findings of the Classroom Strategy Study in particular, about teaching problem students. The material addresses 12 different problem-student types, with each type presenting its own unique concerns and issues, so it cannot be synthesized within a brief summary. Consequently, instead of attempting such a summary, I will devote this final chapter to a look back at some of the main findings from the Classroom Strategy Study, consideration of events that have developed since the data were collected that might affect their relevance to today's teachers, and a revisiting of the teacher-role issues raised in Chapter 1.

TEACHERS' KNOWLEDGE ABOUT PROBLEM STUDENTS

The descriptive data from the Classroom Strategy Study provide information about experienced elementary teachers' perceptions of and strategies for coping with problem students, and the correlational data suggest hypotheses about the relative effectiveness of various problem-solving attitudes and strategies. In general, the teachers' responses were more similar than different. We did find statistically significant differences, including some patterns representing clusters of related differences, between subgroups of teachers who differed in teaching location, grade level, role definition, and effectiveness ratings. However, these differences usually were relatively minor variations on a major theme represented by a modal response to the vignette or interview question. Instead of representing fundamentally different approaches to a problem, the responses of different subgroups of teachers usually focused around the same strategies but differed in the coherence and elaboration with which these strategies were articulated. Thus, it appeared that elementary teachers who differed in formal preparation and who worked at different grade levels and in different teaching settings nevertheless developed and worked from generally similar ideas about chronic student behavior problems and how to cope with them.

Typically, these were loosely connected and often tacit ideas developed through experience, not well-articulated theories learned through formal education. Most of these experience-based ideas probably served the teachers well, in that they typically led to problem-solving strategies that were generally similar to, if less completely developed and explicit than, research-based strategies developed by psychologists or other mental health specialists.

Although a few teachers appeared burned out and a few others consistently suggested punitive or otherwise counterproductive responses to our vignettes and interviews, a heavy majority of the teachers displayed caring about and eagerness to help most if not all of the problem-student types addressed. Interview and vignette responses that appeared unimpressive, including most of those offered by the lowest rated teachers, usually did not suggest commitment to authoritarian or laissez-faire principles or involve detailed articulation of strategies that were not compatible with those suggested by the highest rated teachers. Instead, unimpressive responses typically took one of two common forms.

In the most common form, the teacher simply did not have much to say about how to deal with the problem student. These relatively uninformative responses were not necessarily brief: Sometimes the teacher spoke at length about the characteristics of the type of problem student being addressed, the home factors or other causes associated with it, or the classroom situations in which it is most likely to occur, often illustrated through stories about current or former students. Teachers who frequently made these kinds of responses usually were animated and detailed when talking about the nature of the problem but then became uncertain and vague when asked about their strategies for coping with it.

The other commonly observed form of unimpressive response to the interviews and vignettes came from teachers who apparently had not paid careful attention to the problem-type description or the depicted vignette incident. Some of these teachers misinterpreted the stimulus material in a significant way, either by missing the main point or by reading something important into it that wasn't intended and in fact wasn't supported by the content of the stimulus material as it had been written. In effect, these teachers imposed their own meaning on the stimulus material and began talking about a different kind of problem student than the one we had asked them to address. A related but less extreme version of this problem was seen in teachers who focused on some minor or side issue in responding to the vignette or interview, to the point that they gave little or no attention to the main issue. In responding to the vignette depicting perfectionistic Beth, for example, these teachers might get sidetracked into focusing on their rules about how much paper students can use or their different expectations concerning artwork versus assignments in basic skills subjects, without saying much if anything about how to address Beth's chronic perfectionism problem.

My impression is that, not surprisingly, teachers who frequently made these kinds of responses tended to be those who elicited conflicting effectiveness ratings from their principals and observers and whose interview and vignette responses were unusually variable from problem type to problem type. These teachers appeared to have much richer repertoires of strategies for dealing with problem students than the lowest rated teachers, but they probably did not use these resources to full advantage consistently because they were prone to lose the forest for the trees (i.e., they focused on a side issue instead of the more important main issue) or to jump to conclusions and begin acting on them instead of gathering information about problem students more carefully. These teachers needed to become less impulsive, more observant and reflective, in gathering information to use as a basis for making decisions about how to cope with their problem students.

It seemed clear from the study that elementary teachers could benefit from systematic instruction in diagnosing and responding to chronic behavior problems. This knowledge would make their responses more "planful" and systematic, and it would arm them with additional concepts and strategies that they are unlikely to develop on their own. Such teachers also could benefit from instruction concerning attributional thinking and related emotional responses and behavioral reaction tendencies. This would help "inoculate" them against counterproductive responses to irritating or threatening student behavior and prepare them to adopt more professional and effective responses to such behavior.

CLASSROOM MANAGEMENT: NOTEWORTHY EVENTS SINCE 1980

The fact that the Classroom Strategy Study data were collected in the period from 1977 to 1981 raises questions about their currency. There is at least the perception that the challenge of dealing with problem students has increased during the intervening years. Instead of being removed to special education settings, most problem students are now back in regular classrooms full-time or at least mainstreamed for part of the day.

Problems in inner cities seem to be as bad as ever, and problems there and elsewhere have been complicated by crack cocaine and other drugs.

Yet there are compensating factors. Research on classroom management has yielded replicated findings that have been translated into a coherent set of principles that form the basis for good preservice and in-service education on the topic. School restructuring efforts have produced better communication among school administrators, teachers, parents, and students concerning expected behavior at school and steps to be taken when these expectations are not met. There also has been an increased emphasis on involving parents in the school's agenda. Finally, teachers have become more familiar with cognitive modeling techniques, although more for application to instruction (e.g., in teaching predicting, summarizing, and other reading comprehension strategies) than for teaching prosocial behaviors or coping skills to problem students.

As noted in Chapter 2, recent years have seen the development of better textbooks on classroom management, including texts that cover student socialization and issues involved in dealing with chronic problem students. Some of these books are merely surveys of different theoretical approaches, but several of them cover eclectically derived yet systematic approaches similar to the one developed in the first two chapters of this book. Thus, much better material is available now for use in educating teachers about dealing with problem students. Whether teachers get exposed to it, however, is another matter. Educational scholarship and teacher education reform movements in recent years have focused much more heavily on subject-matter teaching and other cognitive issues than on classroom management and other affective issues, and there are pressures for increased course work in the academic disciplines (which often means reduced course work in general teacher education). As a result, even though better teacher education resources are available, preservice teachers usually do not get much training in classroom management, and what they do get often does not extend to include student socialization and coping with problem students.

Recent research reviewed by Jones (1996) indicates that teachers rank individual students who have serious and/or persistent behavior problems as their number one cause of stress. Also, many teachers question whether they have the skills to work effectively with students with special needs, and both regular and special education student teachers rate classroom management as an area in which they need additional training in order to work effectively with mainstreamed students. Similarly, surveys of in-service teachers indicate that instruction in behavior management strategies is a high-priority in-service training need and that many of these teachers want more assistance from special education personnel in dealing with students who present serious behavior problems.

Many elementary teachers have been influenced by the Assertive Discipline in-service program that has been disseminated widely in recent years. This approach can be helpful for teachers who are notably lacking in both confidence and viable strategies for dealing with problem students. It is an improvement on earlier developed behavior control methods that placed even more emphasis on reward and punishment and less emphasis on helping students to understand the rationales underlying rules in addition to the rules themselves. However, the program emphasizes establishing externally enforced control over problem behavior rather than diagnosis of causes and treatment through long-term change strategies. Thus, even though it may be useful for some teachers as a classroom management technique, I view it as unhelpful, and perhaps even counterproductive, as a basis for dealing with the kinds of problem students addressed here. The designers of the Assertive Discipline program have recently expanded its initial focus on controlling student behavior by adding materials on beginning the school year, working with parents, and helping students with homework (Canter & Canter, 1992). Even so, this program retains its primarily behavioral character and thus, in my view, is less helpful than more eclectically derived programs.

In summary, despite some noteworthy events relevant to classroom management that have occurred since 1980, I believe that the Classroom Strategy Study would yield the same findings if it were repeated today. Most teachers get somewhat better instruction in classroom management than they used to, but most still get little or no systematic instruction in strategies for diagnosing and coping with chronic problem students, so they still have to rely heavily on commonsense psychology leavened by experience. If they have been exposed to unusually thorough classroom management instruction, they will be better prepared to deal with problem students than most teachers in the past. However, they may be even less confident, because the proliferation of special education labels and referrals to treatment specialists has left many classroom teachers believing that they are not equipped to handle ADD or ADHD students, "emotionally disturbed" students, or other "special" students who "don't belong" in regular classrooms. Ironically, these are the same children who used to be considered merely problem students before they were given special labels and sent into special classrooms.

LOOKING TO THE FUTURE: YOUR ROLE

This returns us to the difficult question of how much regular classroom teachers should be expected to do with problem students. Let me begin by making it clear that one cannot directly infer policy guidelines from the Classroom Strategy Study findings or from any other empirical research data. This would be true even if the findings were experimental rather than correlational because one must consider teachers within the context of their interests and abilities in working with problem students, the school milieu, the quality and availability of school-based professionals who might be able to help, and so on.

For example, one could argue that teachers who possess only vague and poorly organized ideas for responding to particular problem-student types should always refer such students to the principal or to their school counselors or social workers rather than try to handle them personally. Thus, our findings should not be taken as evidence that the responsibility for handling problem students should rest primarily with regular classroom teachers. However, there is reason to believe that continuing problems that manifest themselves in the classroom must be dealt with at the classroom level, at least in part. To the extent that it is possible for you to divert time and energy from primary instructional goals to work on students' problems, I believe that you should do so. In order to develop genuine solutions to students' chronic personal and behavioral problems rather than merely inhibiting the frequency of misconduct by applying sanctions, you will need to use effective student socialization strategies if you possess them and to develop them if you do not.

Teachers who have a long way to go in this area may be daunted at the prospect of committing themselves to becoming more active and effective in socializing their problem students. This is understandable. The change process might take a long time and involve difficult adjustments in attitudes, beliefs, and expectations — maybe even self-concepts — along with acquisition of information and strategies. However, the potential payoffs for making such commitments are enormous.

The research literature paints a tragic picture of futility and frustration in the professional lives of teachers who have not learned to manage classrooms and students effectively. What they end up doing in the classroom is not what they envisioned when they decided to become teachers, and it rarely provides them with the rewards and satisfactions that they anticipated. Their instructional efforts are constantly interrupted and frequently negated by behavior problems, and instead of enjoying close and mutually rewarding relationships with students, they find themselves acting as a distant and often punitive authority figure most of the time. They constantly struggle to "put out fires," respond mostly to symptoms rather than causes, rely on psychological defense mechanisms such as avoiding or "not noticing" problems when they are just too depressed to try to deal with them, and abandon serious problem-solving attempts with the most difficult cases, instead settling for implicit "if you don't bother me, I won't bother you" bargains (Bush, 1985; Hargreaves et al., 1975; Wubbels & Levy,

1993). Such teachers are stressed, depressed, and headed toward burnout, if they are not there already, even though some of them are quite young.

This bleak picture changes dramatically when teachers make and follow through on commitments to become effective classroom managers and problem solvers. Instead of being authoritarian and often punitive, yet frustrated and ineffectual, they become authoritative leaders and socializers—in control but not "controlling," refusing to allow inappropriate behavior yet perceived as caring. They gain confidence, stop magnifying difficulties, and become better at observing and listening to students, more organized about problem solving, and more willing to take time to deal with students' personal and behavioral problems. Yet they spend more time teaching and praising, less time reprimanding and punishing. Their students like them better and respect them more, and they have better classroom climates. Their thinking about problem students shifts from an emphasis on blaming and attributing problems to causes that they can do little or nothing about to an emphasis on finding what kinds of help these students will need in order to begin to function more acceptably. Their response strategies correspondingly shift from an emphasis on discipline and punishment to an emphasis on assistance and problem solving (Adalbjarnardottir, 1994; Ashton & Webb, 1986; Dann, 1990; Hawkins et al., 1988; Millman et al., 1980; Soodak & Podell, 1994).

The first step on the road toward such satisfying, effective teaching may be the most difficult: committing yourself to making any needed changes. Ideally, you should do so in collaboration with other teachers at your school, working together to improve the affective climate and preparedness to deal with problem students effectively at the level of the school as a whole in addition to helping one another improve as individuals. However, this might not be possible, at least initially, if you work in a school that has become stultified by apathy, defeatist attitudes, or an authoritarian management style. You may even encounter administrative or collegial resistance to efforts to do things differently, so that you might have to work mostly on your own or with just one or two colleagues (Blase, 1985; Rosenholtz, 1989).

You may even have to overcome significant obstacles within yourself. If your current thinking about problem students is dominated by motives of survival, self-interest, or personal anger or irritation, you may need to take action (and, if necessary, get help) to shift your emphasis toward concern about meeting the current needs of your problem students and helping them to prepare for better lives in the future. If you grew up in a family that emphasized an authoritarian approach to socialization, you may need assistance in working through tendencies to think of classroom management as discipline, to overreact to provocative behavior and get into power struggles, or to generate other forms of authoritarian behavior that have become conditioned responses that tend to appear "automatically" in certain situations. Such reaction tendencies can inhibit progress toward concentrating on teaching students what to do and how to do it rather than on threatening them with punishment for failure to do so, toward recognizing that successful socialization involves developing inner controls in addition to imposing controls externally, toward learning to use punishment sparingly and only as part of a program for changing behavior rather than as a retribution mechanism, and toward appreciating the need to avoid and defuse power struggles rather than trying to "win" them.

Even if you are free of authoritarian tendencies, you still may have to work through some issues if you harbor overly idealistic notions of the teacher role or overly romanticized notions about human nature. Dedication to your job, a strong student orientation, and overall good intentions are important, but these alone will not allow you to succeed in socializing problem students. You cannot function strictly as a buddy or facilitator for your students; some students will not act responsibly unless pressured to do so. More generally, you have authority figure responsibilities to fulfill and instructional agendas to accomplish and therefore must make and enforce demands on your students, so you will need to be prepared to do so effectively.

As data from the Classroom Strategy Study show, all teachers need to learn to inhibit certain natural response tendencies and replace these with more professional behavior. When students misbehave, and especially when they present teacher-owned problems, the natural tendency is to attribute the behavior to internal, stable, and controllable causes; to become angry in response to this perceived intentional provocation; and to respond in an authoritarian or punitive fashion. However natural and understandable these reactions may be, they are not appropriate for teachers who have professional obligations toward their students, including students who are "undeserving." Acting on these natural response tendencies can lead to counterproductive expectations and behavior, resulting in deterioration of the teacher–student relationship and escalation of the behavior problems. Thus, it is necessary for teachers to learn to inhibit these natural reactions and replace them with more professional responses.

It would be difficult to overstress the importance of productive attitudes, beliefs, and expectations in establishing a foundation for developing skills for managing classrooms and students. Note the frequency with which teachers' feelings of self-efficacy or confidence were associated with their effectiveness ratings in the Classroom Strategy Study. Other research suggests similar conclusions.

In general, the same kinds of emotional dynamics that were discussed in Chapter 5 with respect to failure syndrome or learned helplessness problems among students lacking confidence in their academic learning abilities apply to teachers who lack confidence in their classroom management and student socialization abilities. Teachers who believe that they possess, or at least are in the process of developing, good management and socialization skills will be able to remain patient and focused on seeking solutions when confronted with difficult problems, whereas teachers who view management and socialization skills as talents in which they are lacking will tend to become frustrated and give up easily. Rather than persist in trying to solve a problem, they will seek to turn it over to someone else or begin to think in terms of finding ways to live with the problem rather than solve it.

Such beliefs about the self sometimes extend to include notions about the possibility of change, with predictable results. Butler-Por (1987) found that the relative success of an intervention program designed to increase teachers' managerial effectiveness depended on the teachers' initial expectations. The treatment was notably more successful with teachers who expected it to be successful than with teachers who did not.

An attitude of caring and student orientation is also crucial to success in managing classrooms and socializing students. Managing students is not like training animals. Students are people and need empathy. Teachers need to talk with them about their problems and try to socialize them, not just confine themselves to minor curricular adjustments or impersonal behavior modification methods. Certain teachers' responses to our interviews and vignettes were notably lacking in evidence of such empathy. These teachers appeared oblivious to or even uncaring about the emotional trauma suffered by the students depicted in many of our vignettes, and they sometimes suggested responding in ways that would make the target student, and perhaps the class as a whole, mistrust, fear, or even despise them from then on. Once you express contempt for students, ridicule them, or act hostilely or vengefully toward them, you cannot expect them to forget it and simply take what you tell them at face value when you try to socialize them in the future. You will have put yourself in the position of asking them to "do what I say, not what I do."

CONCLUSION

As Goldstein, Harootunian, and Conoley (1994) noted, a teacher cannot be "superman" or "superwoman." Certain students need more help than a teacher alone can provide, and some need more help than can be provided by resource teachers, school psychologists, social workers, or other professionals at the school.

Sometimes teachers are asked to cope with problems that cannot be solved, at least in the short run. If enough seriously disturbed students are in the room, the teacher cannot deal with all of them successfully and teach the curriculum too. When things get unbearable, something has to give; either the problem has to be reduced or the teacher needs help from professionals inside or outside the school. Busy caseloads sometimes delay access to some forms of help, and financial limitations sometimes prevent access to other kinds of assistance. Often this means that the student is unlikely to get much sustained help unless the teacher is willing to "bear the unbearable" by persisting in working with the student and seeking to find solutions.

When considering the degree to which you are willing to include this expectation as part of your definition of your role as a teacher, keep in mind your opportunities to make a significant difference. It is true that in the classroom you do not have conditions that would enable you to use reinforcement and other behavioral methods with the kind of precision and immediacy that is possible in a laboratory, and you do not have the luxury of time and privacy needed to sustain individual psychotherapy. You also must work within your institutional role as classroom authority figure, so that you cannot adopt the nonjudgmental and nondirective role favored by professional psychotherapists.

However, you do have certain advantages that are not enjoyed by treatment specialists. You interact with your students for several hours each day and see them in a variety of situations, so you are in a good position to judge the accuracy of their reality contact and the truthfulness of their statements. Also, as noted in the discussion of findings for failure syndrome and perfectionistic students, you sometimes are in a position to take direct action in assisting students to cope with their problems, rather than just coach them from afar. Even if you arrange to get certain of your problem students involved with treatment professionals, you will spend much more time with the students than these specialists do. Thus, whatever your current stage of development as a teacher, you have the potential to have significant positive impact on the lives of your problem students, if you are willing to make the commitment to do so.

The Classroom Strategy Study

C hapter 3 provided a brief overview of the Classroom Strategy Study and summarized a few of its general findings that cut across responses to the 12 interviews and the 24 vignettes. This appendix elaborates on Chapter 3 by providing more information about the study's design and data collection and analysis procedures, as well as more details about general findings that cut across problem types.

THE TEACHERS

The study was designed to draw on the wisdom accumulated through teaching experience, so our sample was limited to experienced teachers. All had at least 3 years of experience, and most had 10 years or more. All taught in regular classrooms in public schools located either in a small city or in the inner-city neighborhoods of a big city. The Small City schools included a good cross section of students, in terms of both socioeconomic status and ethnicity. However, Small City did not contain an extensive economically depressed area, so it did not have "inner-city schools." Yet the need for information about coping with problem students appeared to be greatest at such schools, and it was possible that the most effective strategies in the inner city would not be the same ones that worked best elsewhere.

These considerations led us to include the inner-city schools of Big City as a second site for data collection. The vast majority of students in the Big City schools were from African-American families, and most were poor. I refer to the Big City subsample for convenience when reporting the results, but bear in mind that this sample was confined to the inner-city schools in the larger Big City system.

There were 98 teachers in the sample, 54 in Small City and 44 in Big City. The Small City subsample included 28 teachers in grades K through 3 and 26 in grades 4 through 6. The Big City subsample included 22 teachers in grades K through 3 and 22 in grades 4 through 6.

One additional criterion was used in recruiting the sample: principals' ratings of teachers' success in coping with problem students. We wanted to look for differences between teachers rated as highly versus moderately effective, and discussions with teachers and school district personnel steered us toward principals as the best source of effectiveness ratings. Most teachers felt that they did not have enough information about their teaching colleagues to enable them to rate these colleagues validly. Principals were asked to nominate teachers by responding to the following questions:

1. *Outstanding Teacher(s).* Do you have a teacher whom you consider to be truly outstanding in handling difficult students—minimizing their problem behavior and responding to it effectively when it does occur? Please indicate the name of this teacher below. (Note another if you believe that more than one teacher at your school is truly outstanding in this regard, but bear in mind that we seek to identify the top 10 percent or so of these teachers.)

2. *Other Experienced Teacher(s).* For each "outstanding" teacher included in the study, we want to include another teacher with at least 3 years of experience who is not as outstanding in effectiveness in dealing with the 12 types of difficult students that we have identified for focus. We do not seek teachers who are overwhelmed with problems and cannot cope with difficult students. Instead, we seek the 80 percent or so of teachers who are neither outstandingly effective nor notably ineffective in this regard—teachers who maintain satisfactory classroom control and who usually can cope with the problems that difficult students present, even though they are not as outstanding as the teacher(s) named above. Teachers who teach at the same grade level as the teacher(s) named above are especially desirable.

Note that the principals nominated teachers according to their *general* effectiveness in dealing with problem students, rather than rating their effectiveness with each of the 12 problem types separately. This was because the principals did not feel that they could make separate ratings validly. Only a minority had direct observational knowledge of teachers' strategies for coping with problem students. Most appeared to nominate teachers according to impressions gleaned from personal interactions with them, the frequency and nature of their disciplinary referrals, and their general reputations.

We recruited teachers by first obtaining a commitment from an "outstanding" teacher and then recruiting a paired teacher for the comparison group. If possible, we paired the outstanding teacher with another teacher working at the same grade in the same school. Otherwise, the outstanding teacher was paired with a teacher working at an adjacent grade in the same school or at the same grade in a nearby school serving similar students.

Participation in the study involved three elements: (1) two half-day visits to the teachers' classrooms, to allow us to observe them in action and see what their students and daily routines were like; (2) lengthy open-ended interviewing to elicit their general strategies for dealing with the 12 problem-student types and their specific responses to vignettes depicting particular problem situations; and (3) brief checklist, questionnaire, and short-answer items on their background and training, their students, the resources available at their schools, and their experiences with problem students.

DATA COLLECTION

Each teacher was assigned to an observer/interviewer who collected all data on that teacher. These research assistants did not know how the teachers had been rated by their principals.

Observation

Data collection began with two half-day observations that allowed the observers to develop a context of reference within which to interpret later interview and vignette responses. They developed impressions of the teachers' styles and levels of success in managing their classes and dealing with problem students. After completing their observations but before interviewing the teachers, observers turned in a set of notes and ratings concerning the teacher's general style and level of success in managing the classroom. As a global assessment of their effectiveness at dealing with problem students, observers rated the teachers on a 5-point scale.

Administration of Vignettes

Teachers were interviewed at times and places of their convenience, although usually in their classrooms after school. Interviews averaged 3 to 4 hours each, spread over at least two sessions. They were audiotaped to preserve verbatim responses and eliminate the need to take notes. Interviewers allowed teachers to make an initial free response to each question in their own words and without interruption. Then they probed to clarify ambiguous points or address aspects that had been omitted or not fully explained.

Interviewing began with the vignettes, which are shown in Table A.1. They are labeled to identify the problem-student type and to indicate whether we viewed the depicted incident as a teacher-owned problem, a shared problem, or a student-owned problem. These labels were not included on the vignette cards shown to the teachers.

The vignettes were administered in the order shown in the table, so as to minimize the similarities between vignettes presented close together. This encouraged the teachers to address the specific information depicted in each vignette rather than to give responses such as, "That's just like the last one — I'd treat it the same way."

TABLE A.1. The 24 Vignettes

1. *Failure syndrome student, shared problem*
   Joe could be a capable student, but his self-concept is so poor that he actually describes himself as stupid. He makes no serious effort to learn, shrugging off responsibility by saying "that stuff" is too hard for him. Right now he is dawdling instead of getting started on an assignment that you know he can do. You know that if you approach him, he will begin to complain that the assignment is too hard and he can't do it.

2. *Hostile–aggressive student, teacher-owned problem*
   This morning, several students excitedly tell you that on the way to school they saw Tom beating up Sam and taking his lunch money. Tom is the class bully and has done things like this many times.

3. *Hyperactive student, shared problem*
   Bill is an extremely active child. He seems to burst with energy, and today he is barely "keeping the lid on." This morning, the class is working on their art projects, and Bill has been in and out of his seat frequently. Suddenly, Roger lets out a yell, and you look up to see that Bill has knocked Roger's sculpture off his desk. Bill says he didn't mean to do it; he was just returning to his seat.

4. *Student rejected by peers, student-owned problem*
   Mark is not well accepted by his classmates. Today he has been trying to get some of the other boys to play a particular game with him. After much pleading the boys decide to play the game, but exclude Mark. Mark argues, saying that he should get to play because it was his idea in the first place, but the boys start without him. Finally, Mark gives up and slinks off, rejected again.

5. *Perfectionistic student, student-owned problem*
   Beth has average ability for schoolwork, but she is so anxious about the quality of her work that she seldom finishes an assignment because of all her "start-overs." This morning you have asked the children to make pictures to decorate the room. The time allocated to art has almost run out, and Beth is far from finished with her picture. You ask her about it and find out that she has "made mistakes" on the other ones and that this is her third attempt at a "good picture."

6. *Passive–aggressive student, teacher-owned problem*
   The class is about to begin a test. The room is quiet. Just as you are about to begin speaking, Audrey opens her desk. Her notebook slides off the desk, spilling loose papers on the floor. Audrey begins gathering up the papers, slowly and deliberately. All eyes are on her. Audrey stops, grins, and then slowly resumes gathering papers. Someone laughs. Others start talking.

7. *Distractible student, shared problem*
   George's attention wanders easily. Today it has been divided between the discussion and various distractions. You ask him a question, but he is distracted and doesn't hear you.

8. *Shy/withdrawn student, shared problem*
   Linda is bright enough, but she is shy and withdrawn. She doesn't volunteer to participate in class, and when you call on her directly, she often does not respond. When she does, she usually whispers. Today, you are checking the seatwork progress. When you question her, Linda keeps her eyes lowered and says nothing.

(continued)

TABLE A.1. (cont.)

9. *Underachieving student, teacher-owned problem*

Carl can do good work, but he seldom does. He will try to get out of work. When you speak to him about this, he makes a show of looking serious and pledging reform, but his behavior doesn't change. Just now, you see a typical scene: Carl is making paper airplanes when he is supposed to be working.

10. *Defiant student, teacher-owned problem*

Roger has been fooling around instead of working on his seatwork for several days now. Finally, you tell him that he has to finish or stay in during recess and work on it then. He says, "I won't stay in!" and spends the rest of the period sulking. As the class begins to line up for recess, he quickly jumps up and heads for the door. You tell him that he has to stay inside and finish his assignment, but he just says, "No, I don't!" and continues out the door to recess.

11. *Immature student, shared problem*

Betty seems younger than the other students in your class. She has difficulty getting along with them and is quick to tattle. She has just told you that she heard some of the boys use "bad words" during recess today.

12. *Low-achieving student, student-owned problem*

Jeff tries hard but is the lowest achiever in the class. This week you taught an important sequence of lessons. You spent a lot of extra time with Jeff and thought he understood the material. Today you are reviewing. All the other students answer your questions with ease, but when you call on Jeff, he is obviously lost.

13. *Failure syndrome student, shared problem*

Mary has the intelligence to succeed, if she applied herself, but she is convinced that she can't handle it. She gets frustrated and disgusted very easily, and then she gives up. Instead of trying to solve the problem another way, or coming to you for help, she skips the problem and moves on. Today she brings you her assignment, claiming to be finished, but you see that she has skipped many items.

14. *Hostile–aggressive student, teacher-owned problem*

Class is disrupted by a scuffle. You look up to see that Ron has left his seat and gone to Phil's desk, where he is punching and shouting at Phil. Phil is not so much fighting back as trying to protect himself. You don't know how this started, but you do know that Phil gets along well with the other students and that Ron often starts fights and arguments without provocation.

15. *Hyperactive student, shared problem*

Paul can't seem to keep his hands off the things and people in the room. He also seems to want to inspect or play with whatever is at hand. When he is not physically manipulating someone or something else, he hums, whistles, grimaces, drums his fingers, taps his feet, or makes other noises through physical activity. Just now he has discovered that one of the screws holding the back of his chair to its frame is loose, and he is pushing and pulling at the loose piece. In the process, he is further loosening the connection and at the same time distracting the class with the noise he is making.

16. *Student rejected by peers, student-owned problem*

Kathy is a loner in the classroom and an onlooker on the playground. No one willingly sits with her or plays with her. You divided the class into groups

(continued)

TABLE A.1. *(cont.)*

to work on projects, and those in Kathy's group are making unkind remarks about her, loud enough for all to hear.

17. *Perfectionistic student, student-owned problem*
    Chris is a capable student who is exceptionally anxious about making mistakes. He doesn't contribute to class discussions or recitation unless he is absolutely sure he is right. You recognize his anxiety and try to call on him only when you are reasonably sure he can handle it. When you do this today, he blanches and stumbles through an incorrect answer. He is clearly upset.

18. *Passive–aggressive student, teacher-owned problem*
    The class has just been given instructions to line up quickly. The students comply, with the exception of Jack, who is always the last to follow directions. Jack remains at his desk, working on a drawing. He looks up, in the direction of the line, and then resumes work on his drawing.

19. *Distractible student, shared problem*
    Sarah never seems to finish an assignment. She is easily distracted and then isn't able to recapture what she had been thinking about before the interruption. You distribute a work sheet to the class, and the students, including Sarah, begin their work. After a couple of minutes you see that Sarah is looking out the window, distracted again.

20. *Shy/withdrawn, shared problem*
    John often seems to be off in his own world, but today he is watching you as you lead a discussion. Pleased to see him attentive, you ask him what he thinks. However, you have repeated his name, and he looks startled when he realizes that you have called on him. Meanwhile, you realize that he has been immersed in daydreams and only appeared to be paying attention.

21. *Underachieving student, teacher-owned problem*
    Nancy is oriented toward peers and social relationships, not schoolwork. She could be doing top-grade work, but instead she does just enough to get by. She is often chatting or writing notes when she is supposed to be paying attention or working. During today's lesson, she has repeatedly turned to students on each side of her to make remarks, and now she has a conversation going with several friends.

22. *Defiant student, teacher-owned problem*
    Squirt guns are not permitted in school. Scott has been squirting other students with his squirt gun. You tell him to bring it to you. He refuses, saying that it is his and you have no right to it. You insist, but he remains defiant and starts to become upset. Judging from his past and present behavior, he is not going to surrender the squirt gun voluntarily.

23. *Immature student, student-owned problem*
    Greg often loses his belongings, becomes upset, whines, and badgers you to help him. Now he has misplaced his hat, and he is pestering you again. Other students smirk and make remarks about this, and Greg becomes upset.

24. *Low-achieving student, student-owned problem*
    Tim is a poor student. He has a low potential for schoolwork and also lacks the basic experiences that help a child function in the classroom. You have just presented a new lesson to the class and have assigned related seatwork. You look over the class and see that Tim is upset. When you ask him if something is wrong, he tells you that he can't do it—it's too hard.

The vignettes were constructed to depict behaviors typical of the 12 problem-student types, described within contexts and in terms familiar to elementary teachers. They contained no references to student age, grade, geographic location, or other context factors that might apply to certain teachers but not to others. These features were designed to ensure that all of the teachers would understand each vignette as we intended (both the specific problem depicted and the implication that it was part of a larger chronic pattern) and yet could respond to it as if it had occurred in their own classroom. We were generally successful in this effort. The teachers found the depicted incidents familiar and realistic. They often commented that they encountered such situations frequently or mentioned students who did what was depicted. There were two partial exceptions to this, however. Many teachers working in Big City, especially in the upper grades, said that they had never encountered perfectionism problems like those depicted in Vignettes 5 and 17. Also, in Vignette 6, we neglected to state clearly that Audrey's delaying of the test was part of a chronic pattern of passive–aggressive behavior. Consequently, some teachers interpreted this vignette as an isolated incident or as part of a pattern involving something other than passive aggression (such as clumsiness or test anxiety).

The students depicted in the vignettes were given common names that identified them as male or female. This was not done in an attempt to study how teachers' responses differed according to student gender (which would have required many more vignettes). Instead, the names were included because pilot work suggested that they enhanced realism. Teachers found it easy and natural to talk about "Tom" or "Mary" but not about someone described only as "a student." Names were assigned according to the gender distribution of the problem behavior in the student population. Both defiant students, both hostile–aggressive students, both hyperactive students, and both low achievers were identified as boys because the majority of students given these labels are boys. The other problems are distributed more evenly across the two genders, so that vignettes representing these problems included one boy and one girl.

There were two vignettes for each problem type. The vignettes in each pair depicted the same general syndrome but illustrated different symptoms occurring in different contexts. We expected the responses generated by the vignettes to complement the responses generated by the subsequent interviews (i.e., general strategies for dealing with each problem type). The general strategies were mostly proactive (planned and initiated by the teachers themselves). In contrast, the vignettes elicited immediate, reactive teacher responses to events initiated by the problem students.

We administered the vignettes first because we wanted the teachers to respond to them "cold," without having had a chance to think about them beforehand. The teachers were asked to read the vignette and then "tell me what you would say and do in the immediate situation if you were the teacher. After telling me what you would say and do, you can elaborate by explaining your goals, the rationale for your goals and behavior, or any other details that you might wish to add."

Administering the General Strategies Interview

After completing the vignettes, teachers were given the 12 problem-type descriptions shown in Table 3.1. They were allowed to take these descriptions home and think about them in preparation for the interview. Their instructions were as follows:

> Attached is a list of 12 types of problem students that elementary teachers often identify as time-consuming, frustrating, and/or worrisome to teach. For the interview, you will be asked to draw on your knowledge and teaching experience in order to tell how to handle each of these 12 types of problem students.
>
> We are interested in whatever you have to say about each problem-student type, so we will schedule as many appointments as we need.
>
> For each problem-student type, first explain your general philosophy about dealing with this kind of student, indicating why you favor this approach over alternatives that you may be aware of. Then, list the specific strategies you would use. Try to be as richly descriptive as possible, including any step-by-step sequences that might be part of your larger strategy, as well as any backup strategies you would use if your preferred method did not work. Explain exactly what you mean, or give examples when you use terms like *reward* or *punishment*.
>
> In addition to describing your strategies, include an explanation of the rationale for each one (the assumptions on which it is based, the reasons why it should work). Also, evaluate the relative success of the various strategies you recommend. How likely are they to succeed, both in the short run and in the long run? Are certain strategies more successful than others? (We are also interested in strategies that do not work. Please let us know about any of these that you may be aware of, and tell us why they do not work or why your recommended strategies are better.) Include any important qualifications about particular strategies. (Are some especially successful or unsuccessful with certain kinds of students? Are some feasible only if certain conditions are present? Are some successful only if used as part of a broader approach?)

Teachers were given at least a week to prepare for the interview and were encouraged to make notes. However, they were reminded that we wanted their personal experience-based knowledge, so that they should not consult books, colleagues, or resource persons.

In contrast to the vignettes, where similar problem behaviors were separated, the general strategy interview grouped similar problem-student types together. The teachers now had full descriptions of all 12 types, so they could attend to nuances of difference between similar types and think about how they would respond to them. Consequently, grouping similar types sensitized the teachers to the differences between types and made it easier to note similarities and draw contrasts between their responses to, for example, failure syndrome students and perfectionists.

Data Preparation and Coding

The vignette and interview responses were transcribed and coded into categories describing the teachers' perceptions of and strategies for coping with problem students. This coding yielded scores indicating the teachers' reported beliefs, attitudes, expectations, and coping strategies. The scores were then subjected to statistical analyses that yielded two general types of information: (1) descriptive data indicating the relative frequency of each response in the sample of teachers as a whole and in various subsamples, and (2) correlational data indicating relationships between these responses and ratings of the teachers' effectiveness in coping with problem students. The technical aspects of the study are summarized only briefly here. For more details about the study's design, data collection procedures, and statistical analyses, see Brophy and McCaslin (1992) or Brophy (1995).

FINDINGS

The remainder of this Appendix summarizes general findings that cut across the 12 problem types and then describes contrasting findings for different subsets of problem types.

Teachers' Responses to the 12 Problem-Type Interviews

Interview and vignette transcripts were coded for presence or absence of various themes, concepts, and treatment strategies. The coding made distinctions between short- and long-term goals and between strategies designed merely to control immediate behavior and strategies designed to prevent problems from developing or to address underlying causes. In addition to the teachers' reported coping strategies, the coding addressed their associated perceptions, beliefs, attitudes, motives, goals, expectations, and causal inferences.

General Problem-Solving Approach

The teachers' reported general approaches to the problem-student types were coded into one or more of eight categories:

1. Controlling or suppressing problem behavior without doing any of the things described in categories 2 through 8.
2. Shaping improved behavior through successive approximations.
3. Providing instruction, training, modeling, or other help designed to enable the student to recognize and eliminate the problem.
4. Teaching the student strategies for coping with the problem (as opposed to eliminating it).

5. Identifying and eliminating the assumed underlying cause of the problem.
6. Counseling or other techniques for increasing the student's insight.
7. Trying to change the student's beliefs or attitudes (and thus behavior) through persuasion or appeal to reason.
8. Providing encouragement or other supportive treatment designed to develop greater confidence and a more positive self-concept.

The most common general approaches were attempts to encourage or support (mentioned by an average of 26 teachers) and attempts to control or suppress undesirable behavior (24). Thus, brief interventions involving talking to the student about the problem or attempting to manipulate the student's behavior through reward or punishment were mentioned more frequently than more extensive instruction or counseling designed to develop insight.

Specific Problem-Solving Strategies

Besides being coded for general problem-solving approaches, the responses were coded for mention of more specific problem-solving strategies:

0. Said that the behavior was not a problem, so they felt no need to do anything about it.
1. Recognized the behavior as a problem but believed that nothing could be done about it.
2. Would not deal with the problem personally but would refer the student to the principal or some other school authority figure.
3. Would deliberately ignore problem behavior in an attempt to extinguish it.
4. Would intervene in some minimal fashion, such as by redirecting the student to another activity.
5. Would break tension with a humorous or distracting remark.
6. Would take some action (such as sending the student on an errand out of the room) to reduce stress or spare the student from further embarrassment.
7. Would try to inhibit undesirable behavior through physical proximity, eye contact, or tone of voice.
8. Would communicate support to the student through physical proximity or tone of voice.
9. Would use time-out as a punishment, to deprive the student of some opportunity (sometimes credit toward reinforcement, but usually just the chance to be a part of the class).
10. Would use time-out as a form of help, to give the student a chance to escape pressure or embarrassment or to take time to calm down, reflect on the incident, and regain composure.

11. Would publicly "diagnose" the student's intentions and behavior, in an attempt to embarrass the student or to communicate the message that "you can't fool me; I know what you're doing."
12. Would deliver severe personal criticism or scolding.
13. Would punish or at least threaten to do so.
14. Would remind the student about limits, rules, expectations, or proscriptions against the problem behavior.
15. Would attempt to reason with or persuade the student to see the wisdom in a recommended course of action.
16. Would use formal performance contracts or at least try to get a commitment from the student to strive to meet agreed-upon goals.
17. Would prescribe, instruct, or otherwise make sure that the student knows what is expected, by either telling or eliciting this from the student (in contrast to category 14, where the emphasis is on what *not* to do, the emphasis in category 17 is on what *to* do).
18. Would model desired behavior directly as a way to instruct the student.
19. Would try to "reach" the student indirectly by modeling the behavior consistently but would not directly call attention to this modeling.
20. Would praise desirable behavior.
21. Would reward desirable behavior.
22. Would provide encouragement or communicate positive expectations to discouraged students who needed to see that they were improving, even though they had not yet eliminated their problems.
23. Would provide comfort or reassurance to students who had become anxious or upset.
24. Would provide at least temporary special consideration ("kid gloves" treatment) to students who had become upset or frustrated.
25. Assumed that the problem stemmed from some source in the student's home or school social life and stated that they would try to eliminate this cause.
26. Mentioned active listening, counseling, interpretation, or other insight techniques.
27. Mentioned strategies designed to build up the student's self-concept, such as praising accomplishments, calling attention to progress, or arranging for success experiences.
28. Stressed establishing a close personal relationship with the student and working within it to help solve the problem.
29. Would change the task (level or type of assignment).
30. Would change the student's seat, provide a study carrel, or make some other change in the physical environment.
31. Would change the student's social environment, such as by seating the student among peers who are easy to get along with or by moving the student away from a peer with whom he or she gets into trouble.

32. Would use classroom meetings to discuss the problem directly or schedule group social education activities with the problem student in mind (lessons on dealing with conflict aimed at hostile–aggressive students or lessons on social assertiveness aimed at shy students).
33. Would involve the class as a whole or particular peers in providing support (explaining to the class that the problem student needs their understanding and patience, appointing a peer to act as a buddy).
34. Would involve peers to pressure or punish the problem student (by actually encouraging them to do so or, more typically, by letting it be known that the class had lost some privilege because of the student's behavior).
35. Would contact the parents and use them as resources in helping to determine the nature of the problem, develop responses to it, or provide support to the student.
36. Would contact the parents primarily to ask them to pressure or punish the student.
37. Would involve school-based authority figures (typically the principal) or professionals (school psychologists, social workers, counselors) in an effort to be supportive or helpful.
38. Would involve these other adults primarily to pressure or punish.
39. Would refer the student to outside physicians or mental health professionals.
40. Not only would use the parents as resources and provide them with general suggestions but also would seek to work with the parents to improve their skills for coping with their child.
41. Would provide academic help (extra tutoring, etc.).

Trends in the teachers' reported specific strategies were similar to those noted in their reported general approaches. Proscribing undesirable behavior was mentioned most frequently, by an average of 32 teachers per problem-student type. This was followed by prescribing desirable behavior (24), threat or punishment (22), praise (22), reward (21), attempts to build self-concept (20), involving parents to support or help (19), changing the task (18), involving school authorities to support or help (17), attempts to persuade (16), attempts to eliminate the source of the problem (16), changing the social environment (16), and providing academic help (15). Among the least frequently reported strategies were denying that a problem existed (2); declaring that nothing could be done (2); delegating the problem to an authority figure (1); criticizing or blaming (3); using behavior contracts (4); providing prescriptive instruction that included modeling (4); providing comfort or reassurance (4); counseling in an attempt to improve insight (5); involving peers (5), the parents (6), or school authority figures (4) to pressure or punish; involving outside medical or mental health professionals (3); and counseling the parents (2).

In agreement with data reported by other investigators, these findings indicate that *teachers tend to rely on brief verbal responses that they can make on the spot* (possibly backed by a conference later) rather than on responses that are more time-consuming. *Also, they prefer methods that are neutral or positive/supportive to methods that are negative/punitive* (although, as we will see, this varies dramatically with the type of problem they are faced with). *Finally, their responses tend to be based on common sense and personal experience* rather than on expert advice or well-articulated theories of diagnosis and intervention.

For the most part, these averages are less meaningful than the variation observed across problem types. For example, the most frequently reported general approach (encourage/support) was mentioned often for failure syndrome, perfectionist, and shy/withdrawn students, but seldom for passive–aggressive or defiant students. In contrast, the second most frequently reported general approach (control/suppress) had the opposite pattern. Also, instruction, training, modeling, or help were mentioned frequently only for immature and shy/withdrawn students; helping the student cope with the problem, only for hyperactive students; treating external causes, only for hyperactive, distractible, and rejected students; and persuasion, only for perfectionists.

Long-Term Prevention/Solution Strategies

In 70 percent of the interviews, teachers mentioned at least one general strategy designed to prevent the problem from developing or to bring about a long-term solution to it. They were most likely to do so for shy/withdrawn students and least likely for underachievers and hostile–aggressive students.

Different Strategies for Different Subtypes

An average of 25 teachers mentioned different strategies to be used with different subtypes of the problem (e.g., work on resolving conflicts nonaggressively for students rejected due to argumentativeness, but work on hygiene and grooming for students rejected for being unkempt). Differentiated strategies were mentioned most often for students described as immature, shy/withdrawn, or rejected by their peers, and least often for perfectionists and underachievers.

Teachers' Motivation

We did not question teachers directly about the motives that lay behind their responses, but these motives often were stated or implied. Frequently, in fact, a response was coded in two or more of the following categories:

   0. No motive could be inferred.
   1. Spoke of acting out of concern about their own well-being or survival ("If I don't show who's boss in that situation, I'll lose the respect of the students for the rest of the year").

2. Emphasized instructional concerns ("I can't allow that sort of behavior because it disrupts the lesson; I'm here to teach and the students are here to learn").
3. Emphasized safety or smooth group functioning ("I can't allow an aggressive student to injure others or create an atmosphere of fear").
4. Expressed concern about the problem student, sometimes directly ("My heart goes out to such a child") but usually indirectly as part of their general responsibility to do whatever they could for any of their students.
5. Emphasized preparing the student for a better future life ("If I don't do something about this problem now, he's headed for a life of misery or criminality").
6. Placed more emphasis on the welfare of society than on the happiness of the problem student ("I have a responsibility not merely as a teacher but as a concerned citizen to do something about this problem; such individuals become an intolerable burden on society").
7. Took a Golden Rule morality approach ("I would try to make him see that his behavior is unjust — that it is wrong to treat other people that way").
8. Stressed their responsibility to uphold school rules.
9. Appeared to be motivated by anger or a desire for revenge.

Personal concern about the welfare of the problem student was the most frequently coded motive (48), followed by instructional concerns (34) and concerns about group functioning or safety (29). Survival concerns were likely to be mentioned with defiant or passive–aggressive students, concern about preparing the student for a better future life with underachievers, and personal irritation or anger in connection with defiant, immature, passive–aggressive, and hyperactive students.

GENERAL TRENDS IN THE TEACHERS' RESPONSES TO THE VIGNETTES

On average, 47 teachers confined their response to control through threat or punishment, 39 spoke of improving mental hygiene or coping skills, and 30 talked about shaping improved behavior. Responses were primarily controlling or punitive for underachieving, hostile–aggressive, passive–aggressive, defiant, hyperactive, and immature students; but primarily sympathetic and oriented toward helping failure syndrome, perfectionist, low-achieving, distractible, rejected, and shy/withdrawn students.

There were some interesting contrasts in relative emphasis on improving mental hygiene or coping skills as opposed to shaping improved behaviors. Both methods were mentioned frequently for failure syndrome and perfectionist students; counseling or instruction was mentioned more often for low achievers, hostile–aggressive, hyperactive, immature, and rejected students; shaping was indicated more often for underachieving, distractible, and shy/withdrawn students; and neither method was cited very often for passive–aggressive or defiant students.

The teachers usually believed that they could effect improvements in the depicted problems, although they were less confident that such improvements would be stable or generalized. They felt most confident with failure syndrome, perfectionist, passive–aggressive, distractible, immature, and shy/withdrawn students; and least confident with low-achieving, hostile–aggressive, and defiant students.

The teachers seldom mentioned rewards but usually cited one or more supportive behaviors, especially instruction (35), kid gloves treatment (18), or involving peers for support (16). Encouragement and other forms of support appeared less frequently, although teachers often suggested praise for failure syndrome, perfectionist, and shy/withdrawn students; comfort or reassurance for perfectionists; publicly defending or modeling acceptance of rejected students; supportive isolation for hyperactive and distractible students; and involving other adult professionals for low achievers. Few supportive behaviors were included among responses to disruptive, aggressive, or defiant behavior.

Typically, only about one-fourth of the teachers mentioned punishments or pressuring behaviors, but there was great variation across vignettes. Punishment was almost always mentioned for defiant students and usually for hostile–aggressive students and underachievers. Restitution was frequently prescribed for the hyperactive student who caused property damage and the hostile–aggressive student who stole money; punitive isolation for the underachiever who socialized instead of working on assignments; and referral to the principal for hostile–aggressive and especially defiant students. Occasionally, physical punishment was suggested for hostile–aggressive or defiant students, public "diagnosing" for passive–aggressive students, and "third degree" grilling for hostile–aggressive students. Once again, sympathetic and help-oriented strategies were emphasized with shy, anxious, rejected, and low-achieving students; but control-oriented or punitive responses were emphasized with disruptive, aggressive, and defiant students.

Rationales and Justifications

The rationales that teachers would offer when making demands were coded into the following categories:

0. No demands mentioned.
1. Mentioned making demands but not communicating rationales.
2. Justifying demands by citing rules.
3. Making a personal appeal ("Please do it for me").
4. Moralizing or appealing to norms or guidelines ("Good boys don't do that").
5. Appealing to the Golden Rule or trying to induce empathy for the victim ("How would you feel if someone did that to you?").

6. Appeals to reason geared to show the student that the behavior is self-defeating.
7. Appeals to the student's personal pride or positive self-concept ("I know that you're not the type of person who would do that again if you could help it").

When rationales were given, they usually incorporated the particulars of the problem situation. For example, citing rules was common in response to Vignette 5, in which the student was depicted as repeatedly using new sheets of paper (teachers often suggested that one piece of paper was the rule). Similarly, moralizing and attempts to induce empathy were common responses to vignettes that involved mistreating or frustrating someone else (Vignettes 2, 3, 4, 15, 16, 18, and 21).

Conclusions Regarding General Trends in the Teachers' Responses

The teachers showed little familiarity with theoretical concepts and treatment principles. Most of their responses were internally consistent and seemingly appropriate as far as they went, but relatively limited and unsystematic. Other than a few concepts and techniques picked up through brief in-service workshops or individual reading, responses were based on common sense and personal experience that was only partially examined and articulated; they did not indicate systematic and detailed knowledge. What the teachers said about controlling behavior through reward and punishment usually fell short of systematic knowledge about behavior modification, and what they said about using personal relationships and talking to students about their problems usually fell short of systematic knowledge about counseling and psychotherapy.

Given that few of these teachers had had courses in classroom management, let alone in methods of diagnosing and treating problem students, these trends are not surprising. However, they do verify that even teachers considered experts at dealing with problem students are usually working from rules of thumb developed through experience rather than from well-articulated knowledge developed through formal education.

DIFFERENT RESPONSES TO DIFFERENT CATEGORIES OF PROBLEM BEHAVIOR

The teachers tended to respond with concern and attempts to help when depicted problems were purely academic (low achievers) or confined to anxiety or difficulty in coping with the demands of school (failure syndrome, perfectionist, rejected by peers). However, they tended to respond with rejection and an orientation toward control or punishment when the depicted problems were disruptive or threatening to authority (defiant, hostile–aggressive). The same trends were observed in data reviewed by Brophy and Good (1974) and by Brophy and Evertson (1981) concerning teachers' attitudes toward and responses to different types of students, as well as in studies by Algozzine (1980); Brooks, Newbolt, and Archer (1985); Coleman and Gilliam (1983); Cundiff (1985); DeStefano, Gesten, and Cowen (1977); Hutton (1984); Lewin, Nelson, and Tollefson (1983); Medway (1979); Natriello and Dornbusch (1984); and Safran and Safran (1984). Similar trends appear in parents' responses to their children's problem behaviors (Brunk & Henggeler, 1984; Dix, 1993; Dix, Ruble, & Zambarano, 1989; Mills & Rubin, 1990). Thus, adults tend to respond with concern, assistance, and attempts at long-term solutions when children's problems do not threaten or irritate them; but they respond with anger, rejection, and emphasis on short-term control or punishment when they do.

Brophy and Evertson (1981) found that teachers were especially rejecting and punitive when misbehavior was threatening rather than merely irritating. Even frequent misconduct did not impair the teacher–student relationship if it was not disruptive or aggressive (i.e., if it was confined to hyperactivity, distractibility, excessive socializing, or forgetfulness) and if the student responded well to the teacher's interventions. However, teachers reacted quite negatively to hostile-aggressive and especially defiant students and to any students who displayed a surly or insolent attitude.

Another influence on teachers' interventions is the degree to which misbehavior threatens the teacher's ability to predict and control classroom events. Cooper (1979) has shown that teachers tend to minimize the frequency and length of their public interactions with students whose behavior is unpredictable or likely to become disruptive. They also tend to be more surveillant and controlling toward these students.

The Influence of Problem Ownership

Gordon (1970) emphasized the concept of problem ownership in categorizing conflicts between parents and children. Parents own a problem when their needs are being frustrated but the child's are not, children own the problem when their needs are being frustrated but the parents' are not, and a shared problem exists when each party is frustrating the other. Research on parents' responses to vignettes involving conflicts with children has shown that parents tend to be sympathetic and solution-oriented in response to problems owned by the children, but they are often unsympathetic and authoritarian when the children present parent-owned problems (Stollak, Scholom, Kallman, & Saturansky, 1973).

Teachers are ultimately responsible for their classrooms and therefore have some ownership in all problems that occur there. However, our vignettes ranged from primarily teacher-owned problems through more equally shared problems to primarily student-owned problems. Therefore, for purposes of analysis, we classified them into three types as follows: *teacher-owned problems* (Vignettes 2, 6, 9, 10, 14, 18, 21, and 22); *shared problems* (Vignettes 1, 3, 7, 8, 11, 13, 15, 19, and 20); and student-owned problems (Vignettes 4, 5, 12, 16, 17, 23, and 24). In vignettes depicting teacher-owned problems, the students' actions threatened the teacher's need for authority and control. In vignettes depicting shared problems, the students did not directly threaten the teacher's authority, but their failure to live up to the demands of the student role created management problems for the teacher. In vignettes depicting student-owned problems, the students' behavior did not directly thwart the need satisfaction of the teacher.

Analyses of responses to these three sets of vignettes indicated that the teachers saw students who presented teacher-owned problems as misbehaving intentionally, and thus as responsible and blameworthy for those problems. Responses to teacher-owned problems featured terse demands for behavioral change, often accompanied by threat or punishment but seldom by rationales, attempts to shape improved behavior, or attempts to work on the students' mental hygiene or coping skills. Most teachers were pessimistic about their chances for producing stable and generalized improvements in these problems.

In contrast, the teachers were the most confident about their prospects for solving student-owned problems. They viewed the students who presented these problems as victims of factors beyond their control. Even if they saw the problem behavior as controllable, they typically viewed it as unintentional (i.e., the students did not know any better or were prone to forget instructions). Responses to vignettes depicting student-owned problems featured extensive talk designed to provide support and instruction, with frequent stress on long-term goals such as improving students' self-evaluations or teaching them coping techniques.

Responses to shared problems yielded a third pattern. These responses featured long-term goals and related strategies for replacing current problem behavior with more appropriate behavior. However, the emphasis was on behavior modification strategies that rely less on language than on environmental engineering, modeling, or behavioral shaping. These strategy choices were consistent with the teachers' tendencies to view shared problems more as responses to particular situations than as general syndromes.

Gordon (1974) advised teachers to use empathy and active listening in response to student-owned problems and to use communication through "I" messages followed by negotiation of commitments for behavior change in responding to teacher-owned problems. The teachers we interviewed did respond sympathetically to student-owned problems, but usually with a combination of environmental manipulation and prescriptive advice rather than active listening. For teacher-owned problems, they were more likely to respond with power assertion than to engage in problem-solving negotiations. Thus, their responses followed the patterns seen previously in studies of parents' responses to vignettes involving conflicts with children, not the patterns suggested by Gordon.

Influence of Teachers' Attributional Inferences

Punitive, rejecting responses were associated with problem behaviors that the teachers perceived as controllable, especially if the student was perceived as misbehaving intentionally. In contrast, sympathy and attempts to help character-ized the teachers' responses when they viewed the problem students as victims of circumstances beyond their control. Other studies of teachers have produced similar findings (Medway, 1979; Tollefson & Chen, 1988). Such linkages between attributional inferences concerning the nature and causes of another person's behavior and one's own response to that behavior are not unique to teachers; they are part of a natural human process of making sense of the social environ-ment.

Psychologists have studied linkages between onlookers' thinking, emotional reactions, and behavior in helping situations (in which someone is suffering frus-tration or deprivation and the onlooker must decide whether or not to help). They find that the likelihood of helping depends on the onlooker's attributions con-cerning the causes of the problems and the degree of control that the person has over his or her plight. Sympathy and help are likely for people seen as victims of circumstances beyond their control, but anger and refusal to help are likely when people are seen as having gotten into trouble through poor decisions or failure to exercise self-control, especially if they are seen as causing problems in-tentionally (Graham, 1984; Maselli & Altrocchi, 1969; Shaver, 1985; Weiner, 1992).

RESPONSES BY DIFFERENT CATEGORIES OF TEACHERS

The previous discussion reviewed general trends in the findings as well as con-trasting patterns in the teachers' responses to different problem-student types. This Appendix concludes with a summary of contrasting patterns noted in subgroups of teachers who differed in role definition (instructor vs. socializer), teaching lo-cation (Small City vs. Big City), or grade level (K through 3 vs. 4 through 6).

Instructors versus Socializers

Good and Brophy (1995, 1997) have argued that differences in teachers' classroom behavior can be expected to flow from differences in their *role definitions* — their general beliefs about what they should accomplish as teachers and what tasks and functions they will need to perform in order to do so. *Instruction* and *socialization* are two key aspects of the teacher role. We asked teachers to characterize their relative emphasis on these aspects. Those who described themselves as placing more emphasis on instruction were characterized as "instructors." Those who said that they placed more emphasis on socialization were characterized as "socializer."

Of 84 teachers for whom data on role definition were available, 53 were instructors and 31 were socializers.

Instructors emphasized acting as a fair and consistent authority figure, establishing the classroom as a learning environment, and interacting with students primarily as learners. In contrast, socializers stressed patience and love for children as crucial to the teacher role, and they spoke of building personal relationships with students and using these to promote good personal adjustment and classroom conduct.

Group differences in interview responses were minor in degree but consistent in pattern with these role definitions. Instructors more often reported delivering brief verbal messages involving persuasion, criticism, or limit setting, while socializers more often mentioned extensive interventions involving behavior modification techniques or long-term prevention or solution strategies. Instructors focused more on helping distractible, immature, and shy/withdrawn students (who can be helped without deviating much from the instructor role except to provide extra attention and support). Socializers focused more on helping underachieving, hostile–aggressive, and defiant students (who present challenges to their motivating, socializing, and relationship-building skills).

There were extensive differences in vignette responses. Socializers more often mentioned mental hygiene goals, special time spent with the teacher as a reward, supportive isolation, "diagnosing" publicly, third-degree grilling, involving peers to pressure, tension-release techniques, changing the physical or social environment, counseling in an attempt to produce insight (especially concerning the teacher's feelings), and citing classroom rules as justification for change demands. In contrast, instructors more often mentioned making demands unaccompanied by attempts to teach better coping skills or to change attitudes or beliefs, and they were less likely to mention supportive behaviors, limit setting, criticizing, or punishing.

These differences suggest that socializers focused more on working with problem students but were not necessarily more effective in doing so (there was no group difference in the principals' or observers' ratings of effectiveness). Socializers were more likely to defuse blame for problem behavior by mentioning factors such as poor parenting or social environments, to acknowledge that some problems could have been caused at least in part by their own inappropriate behavior, and to try to help through supportive techniques. They also were less likely to speak of berating or punishing. Thus, the socializers showed greater tolerance of and willingness to work with problem students. However, they also presented themselves as more likely to "diagnose" problem students publicly, to discuss their behavior during class meetings as a way to minimize peer support, and to try to generate peer pressure against it.

These responses were consistent with socializers' expressed role definitions in that they indicated a willingness to go beyond academic concerns in order to get to know students as individuals and try to promote their personal adjustment and socialize their interpersonal behavior. Socializers apparently spent more time and effort trying to reach problem students than instructors, who usually concentrated on academics. However, good intentions are not enough. Teachers need to be willing and able not only to reach problem students through personalized individual counseling but also to articulate and enforce clear expectations and take action to curtail unacceptable behavior when necessary. The latter actions were mentioned more consistently by the instructors than by the socializers.

Small City versus Big City Teachers

Compared to Small City teachers, those working in inner-city Big City faced more difficult working conditions. Their schools were larger, police guards were assigned, entrance was restricted during school hours, and the buildings were cleared and locked 30 minutes after the students were dismissed in the afternoon. Class sizes also were larger, and observers often mentioned crowding as a problem complicating classroom management. Yet Big City teachers had less assistance from aides than Small City teachers.

These differences in working conditions suggest part of the reason for the differences in the teachers' responses to our interviews and vignettes. The two groups of teachers' responses were similar overall, but there were two contrasting patterns. The first, notable in the interviews, was that the responses of the Small City teachers generally were longer and mentioned more strategies, especially shaping, counseling, or providing support to the problem student. The Small City teachers had much more to say about strategies for dealing with problem students, and what they said was more in keeping with the advice offered by mental health professionals. Big City teachers' responses were generally similar in basic approach but briefer, less differentiated, and less elaborated. They mentioned more appeal, persuasion, and other "brief talking to" strategies and fewer extensive behavior modification or counseling strategies. They also showed more defeatism and low expectations, declaring that nothing significant could be done to improve the situation.

The second contrast, notable in the vignette responses, was that Small City teachers more often reported dealing with problem behavior on the spot, taking time to talk to the student privately and to implement long-term improvement strategies. In contrast, Big City teachers more often reported referring the problem to someone else or limiting themselves to controlling the student's behavior in the immediate situation. Big City teachers were more likely to mention rewards (especially special-privilege rewards) or punishments (particularly sending students to the principal). Nevertheless, Small City teachers were more likely to mention time spent with the teacher as a reward and to mention extra time or extra requirements as punishments. They also were more likely to mention keeping students after school. Moore and Cooper (1984) reported similarly contrasting patterns in groups of teachers who taught students from contrasting socioeconomic backgrounds.

Follow-up analyses yielded no indications that these contrasting patterns were associated with student race or ethnicity, teacher experience, or various aspects of school milieu. However, the second trend was associated with class size and availability of teacher aides. The teachers most likely to mention taking time to deal in depth with student problems as they occurred tended to have smaller classes and more help from aides. This made it more feasible to use strategies that required them to take time out from working with the class in order to interact individually and at length with a problem student. Several aspects of our findings indicated that such feasibility was an important predictor of teachers' mention of time-consuming problem-solving strategies. Compared to Big City teachers, Small City teachers more often were in a position to take time to deal at length with the problem on the spot rather than being forced to deal with it briefly and then try to follow up after class.

Early Grade (K through 3) versus Later Grade (4 through 6) Teachers

The few grade-level differences that appeared formed a general pattern: Upper-grade teachers were more brief/verbal and demanding/threatening, whereas lower-grade teachers mentioned more varied and intensive strategies and suggested a more sympathetic and supportive stance toward problem students. Upper-grade teachers were more likely to respond in authoritarian fashion, without much attempt to sympathize, encourage, or provide support. Their responses to particular incidents were more likely to be confined to a brief "talking to," perhaps combined with criticism, reasoning with the student, or threat or delivery of punishment. In contrast, lower-grade teachers were more likely to report personalized and time-consuming strategies that were sympathetic or supportive in tone and included long-term elements designed to identify and treat causes, shape desired behavior, or provide instruction in more effective coping techniques.

These differences may have occurred in part because the lower-grade teachers were slightly more experienced; worked in smaller schools; and taught in smaller, less crowded, and more homogeneous classes. However, the differences were not surprising, because grade-level comparisons usually reveal warmer and more nurturing forms of teacher–student interaction in the early grades but less personal and more academically focused interactions in the later grades (Brophy & Good, 1986). Brophy and Evertson (1981) reported reductions across grades 2 through 5 in teachers' use of praise, rewards, and various behavior modification techniques, as well as in time spent in nonacademic interactions with students. Also, DeFlaminis (1976) and Kearney (1987) reported that upper elementary and secondary teachers emphasized more power assertion and fewer methods involving offer of reward, negotiation of agreements, or other less coercive responses to student misconduct than lower elementary teachers.

Conclusion

Looking back across groups, we found that the inner-city Big City teachers, the upper-grade teachers, and the teachers who emphasized the instructor role were more likely to restrict their responses to brief, impersonal calls for behavior change backed by threat of punishment if necessary. In contrast, Small City teachers, lower-grade teachers, and teachers who emphasized the socializer role more often responded in personalized, extended, and supportive ways that called for a greater variety of problem-solving strategies.

CORRELATING THE TEACHERS' RESPONSES WITH THEIR EFFECTIVENESS RATINGS

The Classroom Strategy Study was not an experiment. Nor was it designed to assess directly the effectiveness of the teachers' reported strategies. However, we could address this issue indirectly by correlating the teachers' strategy codes with their effectiveness ratings. We eventually did so, after conducting preliminary analyses to decide which effectiveness ratings to include in the final analyses.

Correlations involving the principals' ratings formed more consistent patterns, made more theoretical sense, and more consistently reflected the feasibility limits imposed by the constraints within which teachers must work. This was not surprising, given that the principals' ratings were based on more directly relevant information about the teachers' handling of problem students than the observers' ratings. However, there were indications that some principals had put too much emphasis on teachers' ability to control students during conflict situations and not enough on their ability to help students develop more desirable attitudes and better coping skills. Also, the principals placed more emphasis on teachers' skills in handling disruptive and aggressive students than on their skills in assisting other problem-student types who require sympathy and encouragement more than control or discipline. In contrast, the observers appeared to have taken these teacher characteristics into account.

These considerations led us to use two criterion scores to represent teachers' effectiveness in dealing with problem students: the principals' ratings and an extreme groups score that took into account both the principals' ratings and the observers' ratings. Correlations involving the principals' ratings included the entire sample, with teachers scored either 0 (average) or 1 (outstanding). Correlations involving the extreme groups scores included only 45 of the teachers: 21 who were both classified as average by their principals and rated low by their observers (either 1 or 2 on the 5-point scale), and 24 who were both classified as outstanding by their principals and rated high by their observers (either 4 or 5 on the 5-point scale). For these analyses, the 21 lower rated teachers were scored 0 and the 24 higher rated teachers were scored 1. Analyses were then conducted to identify the teacher response codes that correlated significantly with either or both of these criterion effectiveness scores.

Findings from these analyses were presented in Chapters 4 through 15. The presentations focused on findings for the sample of 98 teachers as a whole. However, contrasting patterns for lower-grade teachers versus upper-grade teachers or for Big City teachers versus Small City teachers were noted in the rare instances in which the contrasts were statistically significant.

In general, the higher rated teachers showed more willingness to become personally involved in working with problem students, expressed more confidence in their ability to elicit significant improvement, and provided richer descriptions of long-term prevention or solution strategies (developing personal relationships, providing support and encouragement, teaching or modeling better coping skills, resocializing attitudes and beliefs). However, there were interesting qualifications and elaborations on these general patterns in the findings for each problem-student type. Also, there were interesting contrasts in findings within each pair of vignettes indicating how general strategies interact with situational factors when teachers respond to particular incidents.

References

Abbott, J. (1978). *Classroom strategies to aid the disabled learner.* Cambridge, MA: Educators Publishing Service.

Adalbjarnardottir, S. (1994). Understanding children and ourselves: Teachers' reflections on social development in the classroom. *Teaching and Teacher Education, 10,* 409–421.

Algozzine, B. (1980). The disturbing child: A matter of opinion. *Behavioral Disorders, 5,* 112–115.

Algozzine, B., Ysseldyke, J., & Christenson, S. (1983). The influence of teachers' tolerances for specific kinds of behaviors on their ratings of a third-grade student. *Alberta Journal of Educational Research, 29,* 89–97.

Allan, J. (1981). Resolution of scapegoating through classroom discussions. *Elementary School Guidance and Counseling, 16,* 121–132.

American Psychiatric Association. (1980). *Diagnostic and statistical manual of mental disorders* (3rd ed.). Washington, DC: Author.

American Psychiatric Association. (1987). *Diagnostic and statistical manual of mental disorders* (3rd ed., revised). Washington, DC: Author.

American Psychiatric Association. (1994). *Diagnostic and statistical manual of mental disorders* (4th ed.). Washington, DC: Author.

Ames, C. (1987). The enhancement of student motivation. In M. Maehr & D. Kleiber (Eds.), *Advances in motivation and achievement: Vol. 5. Enhancing motivation* (pp. 123–148). Greenwich, CT: JAI Press.

Anderson, C. (1985). The investigation of school climate. In G. Austin & H. Garber (Eds.), *Research on exemplary schools.* New York: Academic Press.

Andrews, G., & Debus, R. (1978). Persistence and the causal perception of failure: Modifying cognitive attributions. *Journal of Educational Psychology, 70,* 154–166.

Apter, S. J., & Conoley, J. C. (1984). *Childhood behavior disorders and emotional disturbance.* Englewood Cliffs, NJ: Prentice-Hall.

Asher, S., & Coie, J. (Eds.). (1990). *Peer rejection in childhood.* Cambridge: Cambridge University Press.

Ashton, P., & Webb, R. (1986). *Making a difference: Teachers' sense of efficacy and student achievement.* New York: Longman.

439

Bandura, A. (1982). Self-efficacy mechanism in human agency. *American Psychologist, 37,* 122–147.

Bandura, A. (1986). *Social foundations of thought and action: A social cognitive theory.* Englewood Cliffs, NJ: Prentice-Hall.

Bandura, A., & Schunk, D. (1981). Cultivating competence, self-efficacy, and intrinsic interest through proximal self-motivation. *Journal of Personality and Social Psychology, 41,* 586–598.

Barkley, R. (1990). *Attention-deficit hyperactivity disorder: A handbook for diagnosis and treatment.* New York: Guilford Press.

Barnes, D. (1963). An analysis of remedial activities used by elementary teachers in coping with classroom behavior problems. *Journal of Educational Research, 56,* 544–547.

Barrow, J., & Moore, C. (1983). Group interventions with perfectionistic thinking. *Personnel and Guidance Journal, 61,* 612–615.

Baumrind, D. (1971). Current patterns of parental authority. *Developmental Psychology Monographs, 4*(No.1, Part 2), 1–103.

Bellon, J., Bellon, E., & Blank, M. (1992). *Teaching from a research knowledge base: A development and renewal process.* New York: Macmillan.

Berkowitz, L. (1993). *Aggression: Its causes, consequences, and control.* Philadelphia: Temple University Press.

Berndt, T., & Ladd, G. (Eds.). (1989). *Peer relationships in child development.* New York: Wiley.

Berres, M., & Long, N. (1979). The passive–aggressive child. *Pointer, 24,* 27–31.

Besag, V. (1989). *Bullies and victims in schools: A guide to understanding and management.* Philadelphia: Open University Press.

Biemer, D. M. (1983). Shyness control: A systematic approach to social anxiety management in children. *School Counselor, 31,* 53–60.

Bierman, K., & Furman, W. (1984). The effects of social skills training and peer involvement on the social adjustment of preadolescents. *Child Development, 55,* 151–162.

Blanco, R., & Bogacki, D. (1988). *Prescriptions for children with learning and adjustment problems: A consultant's desk reference* (3rd ed.). Springfield, IL: Charles C Thomas.

Blase, J. (1985). The socialization of teachers: An ethnographic study of factors contributing to the rationalization of the teachers' instructional perspective. *Urban Education, 20,* 235–256.

Borkowski, J., Carr, M., Rellinger, E., & Pressley, M. (1990). Self-regulated cognition: Interdependence of metacognition, attributions, and self-esteem. In B. Jones & L. Idol (Eds.), *Dimensions of thinking* (pp. 53–92). Hillsdale, NJ: Erlbaum.

Boyd, J., & Hensley, J. H. (1982). *The use of physical exercise in the modification of ward behavior in institutionalized hyperactive boys: A preliminary investigation.* (ERIC Document Reproduction Service No. ED 213 183).

Braswell, L., & Bloomquist, M. (1991). *Cognitive-behavioral therapy with ADHD children: Child, family, and school interventions.* New York: Guilford Press.

Brookover, W., Beady, C., Flood, P., Schweitzer, J., & Wisenbaker, J. (1979). *School social systems and student achievement: Schools can make a difference.* New York: Praeger.

Brooks, D., Newbolt, P., & Archer, J. (1985, April). *Teacher perceptions and interventions to student-initiated discipline scenarios and episodes.* Paper presented at the annual meeting of the American Educational Research Association, Chicago.

Brophy, J. (1981). Teacher praise: A functional analysis. *Review of Educational Research, 51,* 5–32.

Brophy, J. (1983a). Classroom organization and management. *Elementary School Journal, 83,* 265–285.

Brophy, J. (1983b). Research on the self-fulfilling prophecy and teacher expectations. *Journal of Educational Psychology, 75,* 631–661.

Brophy, J. (1988). Educating teachers about managing classrooms and students. *Teaching and Teacher Education, 4,* 1–18.

Brophy, J. (1995). *Elementary teachers' perceptions of and reported strategies for coping with twelve types of problem students.* (ERIC Document Reproduction Service No. ED 389 390).

Brophy, J. (in press). *Motivating students to learn.* New York: McGraw-Hill.

Brophy, J., & Evertson, C. (1978). Context variables in teaching. *Educational Psychologist, 12,* 310–316.

Brophy, J., & Evertson, C. (1981). *Student characteristics and teaching.* New York: Longman.

Brophy, J., & Good, T. (1974). *Teacher–student relationships: Causes and consequences.* New York: Holt, Rinehart & Winston.

Brophy, J., & Good, T. L. (1986). Teacher behavior and student achievement. In M. C. Wittrock (Ed.), *Handbook of research on teaching* (3rd ed., pp. 328–375). New York: Macmillan.

Brophy, J., & McCaslin, M. (1992). Teachers' reports of how they perceive and cope with problem students. *Elementary School Journal, 93,* 3–68.

Brophy, J., & Rohrkemper, M. (1981). The influence of problem ownership on teachers' perceptions of and strategies for coping with problem students. *Journal of Educational Psychology, 73,* 295–311.

Brunk, M., & Henggeler, S. (1984). Child influences on adult controls: An experimental investigation. *Developmental Psychology, 20,* 1074–1081.

Bruns, J. (1992). *They can but they don't: Helping students overcome work inhibition.* New York: Viking.

Burns, D. (1980, November). The perfectionist's script for self-defeat. *Psychology Today,* pp. 34–52.

Bush, D. (1985, April). *Relationships among teacher personality, pupil control attitudes, and pupil control behavior.* Paper presented at the annual meeting of the American Educational Research Association, Chicago.

Buss, A. H. (1980). *Self-consciousness and social anxiety.* San Francisco: Freeman.

Buss, A. H. (1984). A conception of shyness. In J. A. Daly & J. C. McCroskey (Eds.), *Avoiding communication: Shyness, reticence, and communication apprehension* (pp. 39–49). Beverly Hills, CA: Sage.

Butkowsky, I. S., & Willows, D. M. (1980). Cognitive motivational characteristics of children varying in reading ability: Evidence for learned helplessness in poor readers. *Journal of Educational Psychology, 72,* 408–422.

Butler-Por, N. (1987). *Underachievers in school: Issues and intervention.* New York: Wiley.

Byrnes, D. A., & Yamamoto, K. (1983). Invisible children: A descriptive study of social isolates. *Journal of Research and Development in Education, 16,* 15–25.

Cameron, J., & Pierce, W. (1994). Reinforcement, reward, and intrinsic motivation: A meta-analysis. *Review of Educational Research, 64,* 353–423.

Camp, B., Blom, G., Herbert, F., & VanDoorninck, W. (1977). "Think Aloud": A program for developing self-control in young aggressive boys. *Journal of Abnormal Child Psychology, 5,* 157–168.

Canter, L. (1988). Let the educator beware: A response to Curwin and Mendler. *Educational Leadership, 46*(2), 71–73.

Canter, L., & Canter, M. (1992). *Assertive discipline: Positive behavior management for today's classroom* (2nd ed.). Santa Monica, CA: Lee Canter & Associates.

Cartledge, G., & Milburn, J. (Eds.). (1986). *Teaching social skills to children: Innovative approaches* (2nd ed.). New York: Pergamon.

Cartledge, G., & Milburn, J. (Eds.). (1995). *Teaching social skills to children and youth: Innovative approaches* (3rd ed.). New York: Pergamon.

Caspi, A., Elder, G., & Bem, D. (1988). Moving away from the world: Life-course patterns of shy children. *Developmental Psychology, 24,* 824–831.

Chance, P. (1993). Sticking up for rewards. *Phi Delta Kappan, 74,* 787–790.

Chapin, M., & Dyck, D. (1976). Persistence in children's reading behavior as a function of *N* length and attribution retraining. *Journal of Abnormal Psychology, 85,* 511–515.

Charney, R. (1992). *Teaching children to care: Management in the responsive classroom.* Greenfield, MA: Northeast Foundation for Children.

Chernow, F., & Chernow, C. (1981). *Classroom discipline and control: 101 practical techniques.* West Nyack, NY: Parker.

Christenson, S., & Conoley, J. (Eds.). (1992). *Home–school collaboration: Enhancing children's academic and social competence.* Silver Spring, MD: National Association of School Psychologists.

Clifford, M. (1984). Thoughts on a theory of constructive failure. *Educational Psychologist, 19,* 108–120.

Cohen, J., & Fish, M. (Eds.). (1993). *Handbook of school-based interventions.* San Francisco: Jossey-Bass.

Cohn, A. (1993). *Punished by rewards: The trouble with gold stars, incentive plans, A's, praise, and other bribes.* Boston: Houghton Mifflin.

Coie, J., Underwood, M., & Lochman, J. (1991). Programmatic intervention with aggressive children in the school setting. In D. Pepler & K. Rubin (Eds.), *The development and treatment of childhood aggression* (pp. 389–410). Hillsdale, NJ: Erlbaum.

Coleman, M., & Gilliam, J. (1983). Disturbing behaviors in the classroom: A survey of teacher attitudes. *Journal of Special Education, 17,* 121–129.

Comer, J. (1980). *School power: Implications of an intervention project.* New York: The Free Press.

Condry, J., & Chambers, J. (1978). Intrinsic motivation and the process of learning. In M. Lepper & D. Greene (Eds.), *The hidden costs of reward: New perspectives on the psychology of human motivation.* Hillsdale, NJ: Erlbaum.

Cooper, H. (1979). Pygmalion grows up: A model for teacher expectation communication and performance influence. *Review of Educational Research, 49,* 389–410.

Corno, L. (1989). Self-regulated learning: A volitional analysis. In B. Zimmerman & D. Schunk (Eds.), *Self-regulated learning and academic achievement* (pp. 111–142). New York: Springer-Verlag.

Council for Exceptional Children. (1989). *Teaching children with attention deficit disorder* (ERIC Digest No. 462). Reston, VA: ERIC Clearinghouse on Handicapped and Gifted Children.

Craske, M. (1985). Improving persistence through observational learning and attribution retraining. *British Journal of Educational Psychology, 55,* 138–147.

Cundiff, R. (1985, April). *Teacher tolerance and its relationship to disciplinary effectiveness.* Paper presented at the annual meeting of the American Educational Research Association, Chicago.

Cunningham, B., & Sugawara, A. (1988). Preservice teachers' perceptions of children's behavior problems. *Journal of Educational Research, 82,* 34–39.

Curwin, R., & Mendler, A. (1988). Packaged discipline programs: Let the buyer beware. *Educational Leadership, 46*(2), 68–71.

Daly, J., & McCroskey, J. (Eds.). (1984). *Avoiding communication: Shyness, reticence, and communication apprehension.* Beverly Hills, CA: Sage.

Dann, H. (1990). Subjective theories: A new approach to psychological research and educational practice. In G. Semin & K. Gergen (Eds.), *Everyday understanding: Social and scientific implications.* London: Sage.

Davis, S., Jr., & Boyar, J. (1990). *Yes I can: The story of Sammy Davis, Jr.* New York: Farrar, Straus, & Giroux.

Deci, E., & Ryan, R. (1985). *Intrinsic motivation and self-determination in human behavior.* New York: Plenum.

DeFlaminis, J. (1976, April). *Teacher responses to classroom misbehavior: Influence methods in a perilous equilibrium.* Paper presented at the annual meeting of the American Educational Research Association, San Francisco.

DeStefano, M., Gesten, E., & Cowen, E. (1977). Teachers' views of the treatability of children's school adjustment problems. *Journal of Special Education, 11,* 275–280.

Devine, T. (1987). *Teaching study skills: A guide for teachers* (2nd ed.). Boston: Allyn & Bacon.

Diener, C., & Dweck, C. (1978). An analysis of learned helplessness: Continuous changes in performance, strategy, and achievement cognitions following failure. *Journal of Personality and Social Psychology, 36,* 451–462.

Diener, C., & Dweck, C. (1980). An analysis of learned helplessness: II. The processing of success. *Journal of Personality and Social Psychology, 39,* 940–952.

Dix, T. (1993). Attributing dispositions to children: An interactional analysis of attribution in socialization. *Personality and Social Psychology Bulletin, 19,* 633–643.

Dix, T., Ruble, D., & Zambarano, R. (1989). Mothers' implicit theories of discipline: Child effects, parent effects, and the attribution process. *Child Development, 60,* 1373–1391.

Dodge, K. (1991). The structure and function of reactive and proactive aggression. In D. Pepler & K. Rubin (Eds.), *The development and treatment of childhood aggression* (pp. 201–218). Hillsdale, NJ: Erlbaum.

Dodge, K. (1993). Social-cognitive mechanisms in the development of conduct disorder and depression. In L. Porter & M. Rosenzweig (Eds.), *Annual review of psychology* (Vol. 44, pp. 559–584). Palo Alto, CA: Annual Reviews.

Dornbusch, S., Ritter, P., Leiderman, P., Roberts, D., & Fraleigh, M. (1987). The relation of parenting style to adolescent performance. *Child Development, 58,* 1244–1257.

Doyle, W. (1986). Classroom organization and management. In M. C. Wittrock (Ed.), *Handbook of research on teaching* (3rd ed., pp. 392–431). New York: Macmillan.

Dreikurs, R. (1968). *Psychology in the classroom* (2nd ed.). New York: Harper & Row.

Dreikurs, R., Grunwald, B., & Pepper, F. (1982). *Maintaining sanity in the classroom: Classroom management techniques* (2nd ed.). New York: Harper & Row.

Duffy, G., & Roehler, L. (1989). The tension between information-giving and mediation: Perspectives on instructional explanation and teacher change. In J. Brophy (Ed.), *Advances in research on teaching: Vol. 1. Teaching for meaningful understanding and self-regulated learning.* Greenwich, CT: JAI Press.

DuPaul, G., & Eckert, T. (1994). The effects of social skills curricula: Now you see them, now you don't. *School Psychology Quarterly, 9,* 113–132.

DuPaul, G., & Stoner, G. (1994). *ADHD in the schools: Assessment and intervention strategies.* New York: Guilford Press.

Durlak, J., Fuhrman, T., & Lampman, C. (1991). Effectiveness of cognitive-behavior therapy for maladapting children: A meta-analysis. *Psychological Bulletin, 110,* 202–214.

Dusek, J. (Ed.). (1985). *Teacher expectancies.* Hillsdale, NJ: Erlbaum.

Dush, D., Hirt, M., & Schroeder, H. (1989). Self-statement modification in the treatment of child behavior disorders: A meta-analysis. *Psychological Bulletin, 106,* 97–106.

Dweck, C., & Elliott, E. (1983). Achievement motivation. In P. Mussen (Ed.), *Handbook of child psychology: Vol. 4. Socialization, personality, and social development* (pp. 643–691). New York: Wiley.

Elias, M., & Clabby, J. (1989). *Social decision-making skills: A curriculum guide for the elementary grades.* Rockville, MD: Aspen.

Emmer, E., & Aussiker, A. (1990). School and classroom discipline programs: How well do they work? In O. C. Moles (Ed.), *Student discipline strategies: Research and practice* (pp. 129–165). Albany: State University of New York Press.

Entwisle, D., & Hayduk, L. (1982). *Early schooling: Cognitive and affective outcomes.* Baltimore: Johns Hopkins University Press.

Ericcson, K. A., & Simon, H. A. (1980). Verbal reports as data. *Psychological Review, 87,* 215–251.

Eron, L. (1994). Theories of aggression: From drives to cognitions. In L. R. Huesmann (Ed.), *Aggressive behavior: Current perspectives* (pp. 3–11). New York: Plenum.

Erwin, P. (1993). *Friendships and peer relations in children.* New York: Wiley.

Estes, E. (1974). *The hundred dresses.* San Diego: Harcourt Brace.

Evertson, C. (1985). Training teachers in classroom management: An experimental study in secondary classrooms. *Journal of Educational Research, 79,* 51–58.

Evertson, C., & Emmer, E. (1982). Effective management at the beginning of the school year in junior high classes. *Journal of Educational Psychology, 74,* 485–498.

Evertson, C., Emmer, E., Clements, B., & Worsham, M. (1994). *Classroom management for elementary teachers* (3rd ed.). Boston: Allyn & Bacon.

Evertson, C., & Harris, A. (1992). What we know about managing classrooms. *Educational Leadership, 49,* 74–78.

Fairchild, T. (1975). *Managing the hyperactive child in the classroom*. Austin, TX: Learning Concepts.

Fincham, F., Hokoda, A., & Sanders, R. (1989). Learned helplessness, test anxiety, and academic achievement: A longitudinal analysis. *Child Development, 60,* 138–145.

Fine, M., Overholser, J., & Berkoff, K. (1992). Diagnostic validity of the passive–aggressive personality disorder: Suggestions for reform. *American Journal of Psychotherapy, 46,* 470–484.

Fiore, T., Becker, E., & Nero, R. (1993). Educational interventions for students with Attention Deficit Disorder. *Exceptional Children, 60,* 163–173.

Forman, S. (1993). *Coping skills interventions for children and adolescents*. San Francisco: Jossey-Bass.

Fortman, J., & Feldman, M. (1994). Controlling impulsive expression of anger and aggression. In M. Furlong & D. Smith (Eds.), *Anger, hostility, and aggression: Assessment, prevention, and intervention strategies for youth* (pp. 441–472). Brandon, VT: Clinical Psychology Publishing.

Fouse, B., & Brians, S. (1993). *A primer on attention deficit disorder*. Bloomington, IN: Phi Delta Kappa Educational Foundation.

Fowler, J., & Peterson, P. (1981). Increasing reading persistence and altering style of learned helplessness children. *Journal of Educational Psychology, 73,* 251–260.

Freiberg, H. J., Stein, T., & Huang, S. (1995). The effects of a classroom management intervention on student achievement in inner-city elementary schools. *Education Research and Evaluation, 1,* 36–66.

Fremouw, W. M. (1984). Cognitive-behavioral therapies for modification of communication apprehension. In J. A. Daly, & J. C. McCroskey (Eds.), *Avoiding communication: Shyness, reticence, and communication apprehension* (pp. 209–215). Beverly Hills, CA: Sage.

Frick, P. (1994). Family dysfunction and the disruptive behavior disorders: A review of recent empirical findings. *Advances in Clinical Child Psychology, 16,* 203–226.

Frick, P., & Lahey, B. (1991). The nature and characteristics of Attention-Deficit Hyperactivity Disorder. *School Psychology Review, 20,* 163–173.

Friedman, R., & Doyal, G. (1992). *Management of children and adolescents with Attention Deficit-Hyperactivity Disorder* (3rd ed.). Austin, TX: Pro-Ed.

Friedman, R., & Karagan, N. (1973). Characteristics and management of elective mutism in children. *Psychology in the Schools, 10,* 249–252.

Furlong, M., & Smith, D. (Eds.). (1994). *Anger, hostility, and aggression: Assessment, prevention, and intervention strategies for youth*. Brandon, VT: Clinical Psychology Publishing.

Furman, W., Rahe, D. F., & Hartup, W. (1979). Rehabilitation of socially withdrawn preschool children through mixed-age and same-age socialization. *Child Development, 50,* 915–922.

Furtwengler, W. J., & Konnert, W. (1982). *Improving school discipline: An administrator's guide*. Boston: Allyn & Bacon.

Gesten, E., Weissberg, R., Amish, P., & Smith, J. (1987). Social problem-solving training: A skills-based approach to prevention and treatment. In C. Maher & J. Zins (Eds.), *Psychoeducational interventions in the schools* (pp. 26–45). New York: Pergamon.

Gettinger, M. (1988). Methods of proactive classroom management. *School Psychology Review, 17,* 227–242.

Glass, C. R., & Furlong, M. R. (1984, August). *A comparison of behavioral, cognitive, and traditional group therapy approaches for shyness.* Paper presented at the annual meeting of the American Psychological Association, Toronto.

Glasser, W. (1969). *Schools without failure.* New York: Harper & Row.

Glasser, W. (1977). Ten steps to good discipline. *Today's Education, 66*(4), 61–63.

Glasser, W. (1986). *Control theory in the classroom.* New York: Harper & Row.

Glasser, W. (1990). *The quality school: Managing students without coercion.* New York: Harper & Row.

Goetz, T., & Dweck, C. (1980). Learned helplessness in social situations. *Journal of Personality and Social Psychology, 39,* 246–255.

Goldstein, A. (1988). *The Prepare Curriculum.* Champaign, IL: Research Press.

Goldstein, A., & Glick, B. (1987). *Aggression replacement training: A comprehensive intervention for aggressive youth.* Champaign, IL: Research Press.

Goldstein, A., Harootunian, B., & Conoley, J. (1994). *Student aggression: Prevention, management, and replacement training.* New York: Guilford Press.

Goldstein, A., Sprafkin, R., Gershaw, N., & Klein, P. (1980). *Skillstreaming the adolescent: A structured learning approach in teaching prosocial skills.* Champaign, IL: Research Press.

Goldstein, S., & Goldstein, M. (1990). *Managing attention disorders in children: A guide for practitioners.* New York: Wiley.

Gomez, K., & Cole, C. (1991). *Attention Deficit Hyperactivity Disorder:* A review of treatment alternatives. *Elementary School Guidance and Counseling, 26,* 106–114.

Good, T., & Brophy, J. (1995). *Contemporary educational psychology* (5th ed.). White Plains, NY: Longman.

Good, T., & Brophy, J. (1997, in press). *Looking in classrooms* (7th ed.). New York: HarperCollins.

Goodwin, S. E., & Mahoney, M. J. (1975). Modification of aggression through modeling: An experimental probe. *Journal of Behavior Therapy and Experimental Psychology, 6,* 200–202.

Gordon, T. (1970). *Parent effectiveness training.* New York: Wyden.

Gordon, T. (1974). *Teacher effectiveness training.* New York: Wyden.

Gorrell, J., & Trentham, L. (1992). Teachers' preferred modes of helping students. *Journal of Research and Development in Education, 25,* 142–148.

Gottfredson, G., & Gottfredson, D. (1986). *Victimization in six hundred schools: An analysis of the roots of disorder.* New York: Plenum.

Grabe, M. (1985). Attributions in a mastery instructional system: Is an emphasis on effort harmful? *Contemporary Educational Psychology, 10,* 113–126.

Graham, S. (1984). Teacher feelings and student thoughts: An attributional approach to affect in the classroom. *Elementary School Journal, 85,* 91–104.

Hajzler, D., & Bernard, M. (1991). A review of rational–emotive education outcome studies. *School Psychology Quarterly, 6,* 27–49.

Hallahan, D., Marshall, K., & Lloyd, J. (1981). Self-recording during group instruction: Effects on attention to task. *Learning Disabilities Quarterly, 4,* 407–413.

Hallahan, D., & Sapona, R. (1983). Self-monitoring of attention with learning disabled children: Past research and current issues. *Journal of Learning Disabilities, 16,* 616–620.

Hamachek, D. (1978). Psychodynamics of normal and neurotic perfectionism. *Psychology: A Journal of Human Behavior, 15,* 27-33.

Hargreaves, D., Hester, S., & Mellor, F. (1975). *Deviance in classrooms.* London: Routledge & Kegan Paul.

Harris, K. (1985). Definitional, parametric, and procedural considerations in timeout interventions and research. *Exceptional Children, 51,* 279-288.

Harris, K. R., & Brown, R. D. (1982). Cognitive behavior modification and informed teacher treatments for shy children. *Journal of Experimental Education, 50,* 137-143.

Hartup, W. (1989). Social relationships and their significance. *American Psychologist, 44,* 120-126.

Hawkins, D., Doueck, H., & Lishner, D. (1988). Changing teaching practices in mainstream classrooms to improve bonding and behavior of low achievers. *American Educational Research Journal, 25,* 31-50.

Haynes, N., & Comer, J. (1993). The Yale School Development Program: Process, outcomes, and policy implications. *Urban Education, 28,* 166-199.

Heckhausen, H. (1991). *Motivation and action* (P. Leppman, Trans.). Berlin, Heidelberg, Germany: Springer-Verlag.

Henker, B., & Whalen, C. (1989). Hyperactivity and attention deficits. *American Psychologist, 44,* 216-223.

Hoffman, M. (1983). Affective and cognitive processes in moral internalization. In E. Higgins, D. Ruble, & W. Hartup (Eds.), *Social cognition and social development: A sociocultural perspective* (pp. 236-274). Cambridge: Cambridge University Press.

Hoffman, M. (1991). Empathy, social cognition, and moral action. In W. Kurtines & J. Gewirtz (Eds.), *Handbook of moral behavior and development: Vol. 1. Theory* (pp. 275-302). Hillsdale, NJ: Erlbaum.

Hoffman, S. (Ed.). (1991). Educational partnerships: Home and school community [Special Issue]. *Elementary School Journal, 91*(3).

Honig, A. (1987). The shy child. *Young children, 42,* 54-64.

Hops, H., Walker, H., & Greenwood, C. (1979). PEERS: A program for remediating social withdrawal in school. In L. Hamerlynck (Ed.), *Behavioral systems for the developmentally disabled in school and home environments* (pp. 48-88). New York: Brunner/Mazel.

Horne, A., & Sayger, T. (1990). *Treating conduct and oppositional defiant disorders in children.* New York: Pergamon.

Hudley, C. (1994). Perceptions of intentionality, feelings of anger, and reactive aggression. In M. Furlong & D. Smith (Eds.), *Anger, hostility, and aggression: Assessment, prevention, and intervention strategies for youth* (pp. 39-56). Brandon, VT: Clinical Psychology Publishing.

Hudley, C., & Graham, S. (1993). An attributional intervention to reduce peer-directed aggression among African-American boys. *Child Development, 64,* 124-138.

Huesmann, L. R. (Ed.). (1994). *Aggressive behavior: Current perspectives.* New York: Plenum.

Hughes, J. (1988). *Cognitive behavior therapy with children in schools.* Elmsford, NY: Pergamon.

Hughes, J., & Hall, R. (Eds.). (1989). *Cognitive-behavioral psychology in the schools: A comprehensive handbook.* New York: Guilford Press.

Hutton, J. (1984). Teacher ratings of problem behaviors: Which student behaviors "concern" and "disturb" teachers? *Psychology in the Schools, 21,* 482–484.

Hyde, E. (1976). A behavioral study of maturity in children of elementary-school age. *Elementary School Journal, 77,* 140–149.

Jackson, N., Jackson, D., & Monroe, C. (1983). *Getting along with others.* Champaign, IL: Research Press.

Jackson, R., Cleveland, J., & Mirenda, P. (1975). The longitudinal effects of early identification and counseling of underachievers. *Journal of School Psychology, 13,* 119–128.

Johnson, O. G. (1956). The teacher and the withdrawn child. *Mental Hygiene, 40,* 529–534.

Jones, V. (1988). *A systematic approach for responsibly managing the disruptive and irresponsible behavior of at-risk students.* Paper presented at the annual meeting of the American Educational Research Association, New Orleans.

Jones, V. (1996). Classroom management. In J. Sikula, T. Buttery, & E. Guyton (Eds.), *Handbook of research on teacher education* (2nd ed.). New York: Macmillan.

Jones, V., & Jones, L. (1995). *Comprehensive classroom management* (4th ed.). Boston: Allyn & Bacon.

Juvonen, J., & Weiner, B. (1993). An attributional analysis of students' interactions: The social consequences of perceived responsibility. *Educational Psychology Review, 5,* 325–345.

Karlin, M., & Berger, R. (1972). *Discipline and the disruptive child: A practical guide for elementary teachers.* West Nyack, NY: Parker.

Kauffman, J., Hallahan, D., Mostert, M., Trent, S., & Nuttycombe, D. (1993). *Managing classroom behavior: A reflective case approach.* Boston: Allyn & Bacon.

Kazdin, A. (1989). *Behavior modification in applied settings* (4th ed.). Pacific Grove, CA: Brooks/Cole.

Kazdin, A. (1994). *Behavior modification in applied settings* (5th ed.). Pacific Grove, CA: Brooks/Cole.

Kearney, P. (1987). Power in the classroom. *Journal of Thought, 22*(4), 45–50.

Kendall, P. (Ed.). (1991). *Child and adolescent therapy: Cognitive-behavioral procedures.* New York: Guilford Press.

Kendall, P., & Braswell, L. (1985). *Cognitive-behavioral therapy for impulsive children.* New York: Guilford Press.

Kendall, P., & Hollon, S. (1979). *Cognitive-behavioral interventions: Theory, research, and procedures.* New York: Academic Press.

Kendall, P., Ronan, K., & Epps, J. (1991). Aggression in children/adolescents: Cognitive behavioral treatment perspectives. In D. Pepler & K. Rubin (Eds.), *The development and treatment of childhood aggression* (pp. 341–360). Hillsdale, NJ: Erlbaum.

Kennedy, J. (1990). Determinants of peer social status: Contributions of physical appearance, reputation, and behavior. *Journal of Youth and Adolescence, 19,* 233–244.

Kennelly, K., Dietz, D., & Benson, P. (1985). Reinforcement schedules, effort vs. ability attributions, and persistence. *Psychology in the Schools, 22,* 459–464.

Kettlewell, P., & Kausch, D. (1983). The generalization of the effects of a cognitive-behavioral treatment program for aggressive children. *Journal of Abnormal Child Psychology, 11,* 101–114.

King, C., & Kirschenbaum, D. (1992). *Helping young children develop skills: The social growth program.* Pacific Grove, CA: Brooks/Cole.

Kirby, E., & Kirby, S. (1994). Classroom discipline with attention deficit hyperactivity disorder children. *Contemporary Education, 65,* 142–144.

Knaus, W. J. (1974). *Rational emotive education: A manual for elementary school teachers.* New York: Institute for Rational Living.

Knoff, H. (1987). School-based interventions for discipline problems. In C. Maher & J. Zins (Eds.), *Psychoeducational interventions in the schools* (pp. 118–141). New York: Pergamon.

Koestner, R., Ryan, R., Bernieri, F., & Holt, K. (1984). The effects of controlling versus informational limit-setting styles on children's intrinsic motivation and creativity. *Journal of Personality, 52,* 233–248.

Kohn, A. (1993). *Punished by rewards: The trouble with gold stars, incentive plans, A's, praise, and other bribes.* Boston: Houghton Mifflin.

Koplow, L. (1983). Feeding the "turtle": Helping the withdrawn child to emerge in the classroom. *Exceptional Child, 30,* 127–132.

Kottler, K., & Kottler, E. (1993). *Teacher as counselor: Developing the helping skills you need.* Newbury Park, CA: Corwin.

Kounin, J. (1970). *Discipline and group management in classrooms.* New York: Holt, Rinehart & Winston.

Krasilovsky, P. (1992). *The very little girl.* New York: Scholastic.

Krouse, J., & Krouse, H. (1981). Toward a multimodal theory of academic underachievement. *Educational Psychologist, 16,* 151–164.

Krumboltz, J., & Krumboltz, H. (1972). *Changing children's behavior.* Englewood Cliffs, NJ: Prentice-Hall.

L'Abate, L., & Milan, M. (1985). *Handbook of social skills training and research.* New York: Wiley.

Ladd, G., & Mize, J. (1983). A cognitive-social learning model of social skills training. *Psychological Review, 90,* 127–157.

Larrivee, B. (1992). *Strategies for effective classroom management: Creating a collaborative climate.* Boston: Allyn & Bacon.

Larson, J. (1994). Cognitive-behavioral treatment of anger-induced aggression in the school setting. In M. Furlong & D. Smith (Eds.), *Anger, hostility, and aggression: Assessment, prevention, and intervention strategies for youth* (pp. 393–440). Brandon, VT: Clinical Psychology Publishing.

Laub, L., & Braswell, L. (1991). Appendix C: Suggestions for classroom teachers of ADHD elementary school students. In L. Braswell & M. Bloomquist, *Cognitive-behavioral therapy with ADHD children: Child, family, and school interventions* (pp. 349–354). New York: Guilford Press.

Lazerson, D. B. (1980). "I must be good if I can teach!"—Peer tutoring with aggressive and withdrawn children. *Journal of Learning Disabilities, 13,* 43–48.

Lepper, M. (1983). Social-control processes and the internalization of social values: An attributional perspective. In E. Higgins, D. Ruble, & W. Hartup (Eds.), *Social cognition and social development: A sociocultural perspective* (pp. 294–330). Cambridge: Cambridge University Press.

Lepper, M., & Greene, D. (1978). *The hidden costs of reward: New perspectives on the psychology of human motivation.* Hillsdale, NJ: Erlbaum.

Lerner, J., Lowenthal, B., & Lerner, S. (1995). *Attention deficit disorders: Assessment and teaching.* Pacific Grove, CA: Brooks/Cole.

Lew, M., Mesch, D., Johnson, D. W., & Johnson, R. (1986). Positive interdependence, academic and collaborative-skills group contingencies, and isolated students. *American Educational Research Journal, 23,* 476–488.

Lewin, F., Nelson, R., & Tollefson, N. (1983). Teacher attitudes toward disruptive children. *Elementary School Guidance and Counseling, 17,* 188–193.

Lochman, J., Burch, P., Curry, J., & Lampron, L. (1984). Treatment and generalization effects of cognitive-behavioral and goal-setting interventions with aggressive boys. *Journal of Consulting and Clinical Psychology, 12,* 915–916.

Loeber, R. (1982). The stability of antisocial and delinquent child behavior: A review. *Child Development, 53,* 1431–1446.

Loney, J. (Ed.). (1987). *The young hyperactive child: Answers to questions about diagnosis, prognosis and treatment.* New York: Haworth.

Love, M., & Baer, D. (1991). Tired of tattlers? Then teach your students to stand up for themselves. *Learning, 19*(7), 74–76.

Maccoby, E. E., & Martin, J. A. (1983). Socialization in the context of the family: Parent–child interaction. In P. Mussen (Ed.), *Handbook of child psychology* (4th ed., Vol. IV, pp. 1–101). New York: Wiley.

Macmillan, A., & Kolvin, I. (1977). Behavior modification in teaching strategy: Some emergent problems and suggested solutions. *Educational Researcher, 20,* 10–21.

Mandel, H., & Marcus, S. (1988). *The psychology of underachievement: Differential diagnosis and differential treatment.* New York: Wiley.

Manning, B. (1991). *Cognitive self-instruction for classroom processes.* Albany: State University of New York Press.

Markle, A., Rinn, R., & Goodwin, B. (1980). Effects of achievement motivation training on academic performance of underachievers. *Psychological Reports, 47,* 567–574.

Maselli, M., & Altrocchi, J. (1969). Attribution of intent. *Psychological Bulletin, 71,* 445–454.

Matson, J. (Ed.). (1993). *Handbook of hyperactivity in children.* Boston: Allyn & Bacon.

Matson, J., & Ollendick, T. (1988). *Enhancing children's social skills: Assessment and training.* Oxford: Pergamon.

McCall, R., Evahn, C., & Kratzer, L. (1992). *High school underachievers.* Newbury Park, CA: Sage.

McCallum, R., & Bracken, B. (1993). Interpersonal relations between school children and their peers, parents, and teachers. *Educational Psychology Review, 5,* 155–176.

McCaslin, M., & Good, T. (1992). Compliant cognition: The misalliance of management and instructional goals in current school reform. *Educational Researcher, 21,* 4–17.

McCaslin, M., & Good, T. (1996). *Listening in classrooms.* New York: HarperCollins.

McCombs, B. (1984). Processes and skills underlying continuing intrinsic motivation to learn: Toward a definition of motivational skills training and interventions. *Educational Psychologist, 19,* 199–218.

McCormack, S. (1989). Response to Render, Padilla, and Krank: But practitioners say it works! *Educational Leadership, 47*(7), 77–79.

McCroskey, J. (1984). The communication apprehension perspective. In J. A. Daly & J. C. McCroskey (Eds.), *Avoiding communication: Shyness, reticence, and communication apprehension* (pp. 13–38). Beverly Hills, CA: Sage.

McDaniel, T. (1989). The discipline debate: A road through the thicket. *Educational Leadership, 47*(7), 81–82.

McGinnis, E., & Goldstein, A. (1984). *Skillstreaming the elementary school child.* Champaign, IL: Research Press.

McIntyre, T. (1989). *A resource book for remediating common behavior and learning problems.* Boston: Allyn & Bacon.

Medway, F. (1979). Causal attributions for school-related problems: Teacher perceptions and teacher feedback. *Journal of Educational Psychology, 71,* 809–818.

Medway, F., & Venino, G. (1982). The effects of effort feedback and performance patterns on children's attribution and task persistence. *Contemporary Educational Psychology, 7,* 26–34.

Meichenbaum, D. (1977). *Cognitive-behavior modification.* New York: Plenum.

Mergendoller, J., & Marchman, V. (1987). Friends and associates. In V. Richardson-Koehler (Ed.), *Educators' handbook: A research perspective* (pp. 297–328). White Plains, NY: Longman.

Metz, M. (1978). *Classrooms and corridors.* Berkeley: University of California Press.

Millman, H., Schaefer, C., & Cohen, J. (1980). *Therapies for school behavior problems: A handbook of practical interventions.* San Francisco: Jossey-Bass.

Millon, T. (1981). *Disorders of personality.* New York: Wiley.

Mills, R., & Rubin, K. (1990). Parental beliefs about problematic social behaviors in early childhood. *Child Development, 61,* 138–151.

Moore, W. L., & Cooper, H. (1984). Correlations between teacher and student background and teacher perceptions of discipline problems and disciplinary techniques. *Psychology in the Schools, 21,* 386–392.

Morrison, E. (1969). Underachievement among preadolescent boys considered in relationship to passive aggression. *Journal of Educational Psychology, 60,* 168–173.

Morrison, G., & Sandowicz, M. (1994). Importance of social skills in the prevention and intervention of anger and aggression. In M. Furlong & D. Smith (Eds.), *Anger, hostility, and aggression: Assessment, prevention, and intervention strategies for youth* (pp. 345–392). Brandon, VT: Clinical Psychology Publishing.

Nafpaktitis, M., Mayer, G., & Butterworth, T. (1985). Natural rates of teacher approval and disapproval and their relation to student behavior in intermediate school classrooms. *Journal of Educational Psychology, 77,* 362–367.

Natriello, G., & Dornbusch, S. (1984). *Teacher evaluative standards and student effort.* New York: Longman.

Newcomb, A., Bukowski, W., & Pattee, L. (1993). Children's peer relations: A meta-analytic review of popular, rejected, neglected, controversial, and average sociometric status. *Psychological Bulletin, 113,* 99–128.

Novaco, R. (1975). *Anger control: The development and evaluation of an experimental treatment.* Lexington, MA: Heath.

Nowicki, S., & Duke, M. (1992). *Helping the child who doesn't fit in.* Atlanta: Peachtree.

Oden, S. (1982). Peer relationship development in childhood. In L. Katz (Ed.), *Current topics in early childhood education* (Vol. 4). Norwood, NJ: Ablex.

O'Leary, K., & O'Leary, S. (Eds.). (1977). *Classroom management: The successful use of behavior modification* (2nd ed.). New York: Pergamon.

Olweus, D. (1979). Stability of aggressive reaction patterns in males. *Psychological Bulletin, 86,* 852–875.

Olweus, D. (1993). *Bullying at school: What we know and what we can do.* Oxford: Blackwell.

Olweus, D. (1994). Bullying at school. In L. R. Huesmann (Ed.), *Aggressive behavior: Current perspectives* (pp. 97–130). New York: Plenum.

Pacht, A. (1984). Reflection on perfection. *American Psychologist, 39,* 386–390.

Palincsar, A., & Brown, A. (1984). Reciprocal teaching of comprehension-fostering and comprehension-monitoring activities. *Cognition and Instruction, 1, 117–175.*

Parke, R., & Slaby, R. (1983). The development of aggression. In P. Mussen (Ed.), *Handbook of child psychology* (4th ed., Vol. IV, pp. 547–641). New York: Wiley.

Parker, J., & Asher, S. (1987). Peer relations and later personal adjustment: Are low accepted children at risk? *Psychological Bulletin, 102,* 357–389.

Parsons, R. (1983). The educational setting: A cultural milieu fostering passive–aggressiveness. In R. Parsons & R. Wicks (Eds.), *Passive–aggressiveness: Theory and practice* (pp. 174–193). New York: Brunner/Mazel.

Parsons, R., & Wicks, R. (Eds.). (1983). *Passive–aggressiveness: Theory and practice.* New York: Brunner/Mazel.

Patterson, C., Kupersmidt, J., & Griesler, P. (1990). Children's perceptions of self and of relationships with others as a function of sociometric status. *Child Development, 61,* 1335–1349.

Patterson, G. (1982). *Coercive family process. Social learning approach series* (Vol. 3). Eugene, OR: Castalia.

Patterson, G., Reid, J., & Dishion, T. (1992). *Antisocial boys.* Eugene, OR: Castalia.

Pellegrini, A., & Horvat, M. (1995). A developmental contextualist critique of Attention Deficit Hyperactivity Disorder. *Educational Researcher, 24,* 13–19.

Pepler, D., King, G., & Byrd, W. (1991). A social-cognitively based social skills training program for aggressive children. In D. Pepler & K. Rubin (Eds.), *The development and treatment of childhood aggression* (pp. 361–379). Hillsdale, NJ: Erlbaum.

Pepler, D., & Rubin, K. (Eds.). (1991). *The development and treatment of childhood aggression.* Hillsdale, NJ: Erlbaum.

Perry, D., Perry, L., & Boldizar, J. (1990). Learning of aggression. In M. Lewis & S. Miller (Eds.), *Handbook of developmental psychopathology* (pp. 135–146). New York: Plenum.

Peter, D., Allan, J., & Horvath, A. (1983). Hyperactive children's perceptions of teachers' classroom behavior. *Psychology in the Schools, 20,* 234–240.

Pfiffner, L., & Barkley, R. (1990). Educational placement and classroom management. In R. Barkley, *Attention deficit hyperactivity disorder: A handbook for diagnosis and treatment* (pp. 498–539). New York: Guilford Press.

Phillips, D. (1984). The illusion of incompetence among academically competent children. *Child Development, 55,* 2000–2016.

Piper, W. (1991). *The little engine that could.* New York: Putnam.

Pittman, S. (1985). A cognitive ethnography and quantification of a first-grade teacher's selection routines for classroom management. *Elementary School Journal, 85,* 541–558.

Plewis, I. (1991). Underachievement: A case of conceptual confusion. *British Educational Research Journal, 17,* 377–385.

Prawat, R. (1980). Teacher perceptions of student affect. *American Educational Research Journal, 17,* 61–73.

Raphael, T. (1984). Teaching learners about sources of information for answering comprehension questions. *Journal of Reading, 27,* 303–311.

Redl, F., & Wineman, D. (1951). *Children who hate.* New York: Free Press.

Reeves, J., Werry, J., Elkind, G., & Zametkin, A. (1987). Attention deficit, conduct, oppositional, and anxiety disorders in children: II. Clinical characteristics. *Journal of the American Academy of Child and Adolescent Psychiatry, 26,* 144–155.

Reid, M., & Borkowski, J. (1987). Causal attributions of hyperactive children: Implications for teaching strategies and self-control. *Journal of Educational Psychology, 79,* 296–307.

Reimers, T. M., Wacker, D. P., & Koeppl, G. (1987). Acceptability of behavioral interventions: A review of the literature. *School Psychology Review, 16, 212–227.*

Relich, J., Debus, R., & Walker, R. (1986). The mediating role of attribution and self-efficacy variables for treatment effects on achievement outcomes. *Contemporary Educational Psychology, 11,* 195–216.

Render, G., Padilla, J., & Krank, H. (1989). What research really shows about assertive discipline. *Educational Leadership, 47*(7), 72–75.

Rimm, S. (1986). *Underachievement syndrome: Causes and cures.* Watertown, WI: Apple.

Robin, A., Schneider, M., & Dolnick, M. (1976). The turtle technique: An extended case study of self-control in the classroom. *Psychology in the Schools, 13,* 449–453.

Roedell, W., Slaby, R., & Robinson, H. (1976). *Social development in young children: A report for teachers.* Washington, DC: National Institute of Education.

Rogers, C., & Freiberg, H. J. (1994). *Freedom to learn* (3rd ed.). New York: Merrill.

Rohrkemper McCaslin, M. (1989). Self-regulated learning and academic achievement: A Vygotskian view. In B. Zimmerman & D. Schunk (Eds.), *Self-regulated learning and academic achievement* (pp. 143–168). New York: Springer-Verlag.

Rohrkemper, M., & Bershon, B. (1984). The quality of student task engagement: Elementary school students' reports of the causes and effects of problem difficulty. *Elementary School Journal, 85,* 127–147.

Rohrkemper, M., & Brophy, J. (1983). Teachers' thinking about problem students. In J. Levine & M. Wang (Eds.), *Teacher and student perceptions: Implications for learning* (pp. 75–104). Hillsdale, NJ: Erlbaum.

Rohrkemper, M., & Corno, L. (1988). Success and failure on classroom tasks: Adaptive learning and classroom teaching. *Elementary School Journal, 88,* 299–312.

Rosén, L., O'Leary, S., Joyce, S., Conway, G., & Pfiffner, L. (1984). The importance of prudent negative consequences for maintaining the appropriate behavior of hyperactive students. *Journal of Abnormal Child Psychology, 12,* 581–604.

Rosenberg, M., Wilson, R., Maheady, L., & Sindelar, P. (1992). *Educating students with behavior disorders.* Boston: Allyn & Bacon.

Rosenholtz, S. (1989). *Teachers' workplace: The social organization of schools.* New York: Longman.

Ryan, B. (1979). A case against behavior modification in the "ordinary" classroom. *Journal of School Psychology, 17,* 131–136.

Sabornie, E. (1991). Measuring and teaching social skills in the mainstream. In

G. Stoner, M. Shinn, & H. Walker (Eds.), *Interventions for achievement and behavior problems* (pp. 161–177). Silver Spring, MD: National Association of School Psychologists.

Safer, D., & Allen, R. (1976). *Hyperactive children: Diagnosis and management.* Baltimore: University Park Press.

Safran, S., & Safran, J. (1984). Elementary teachers' tolerance of problem behaviors. *Elementary School Journal, 85,* 237–243.

Sandoval, J. (1982). Hyperactive children: 12 ways to help them in the classroom. *Academic Therapy, 18,* 107–113.

Sarason, I., & Sarason, B. (1981). Teaching cognitive and social skills to high school students. *Journal of Consulting and Clinical Psychology, 49,* 908–918.

Schaefer, C., & Millman, H. (1981). *How to help children with common problems.* New York: VanNostrand Reinhold.

Schloss, P., & Smith, M. (1994). *Applied behavior analysis in the classroom.* Boston: Allyn & Bacon.

Schunk, D. (1985). Self-efficacy and classroom learning. *Psychology in the Schools, 22,* 208–223.

Shavelson, R. J., & Stern, P. (1981). Research on teachers' pedagogical thoughts, judgments, decisions, and behaviors. *Review of Educational Research, 51,* 455–498.

Shaver, K. G. (1985). *The attribution of blame: Causality, responsibility, and blameworthiness.* New York: Springer-Verlag.

Shelton, T., Anastopoulos, A., & Linden, J. (1985). An attribution training program with learning disabled children. *Journal of Learning Disabilities, 18,* 261–265.

Sheridan, S., Kratochwill, T., & Elliott, S. (1990). Behavioral consultation with parents and teachers: Delivering treatment for socially withdrawn children at home and school. *School Psychology Review, 19,* 33–52.

Siegel, E., Siegel, R., & Siegel, P. (1978). *Help for the lonely child: Strengthening social perception.* New York: Dutton.

Smith, D. (1981). Classroom management and consultation: Implications for school psychology. *Psychology in the Schools, 18,* 475–481.

Soodak, L., & Bodell, D. (1994). Teachers' thinking about difficult-to-teach students. *Journal of Educational Research, 88,* 44–51.

Spaulding, R. L. (1983). A systematic approach to classroom discipline, Part I. *Phi Delta Kappan, 65*(1), 48–51.

Spaulding, R. (1978). Adapting teaching styles to learning styles. *Journal of Classroom Interaction, 14*(1), 10–18.

Spivack, G., & Shure, M. (1974). *Social adjustment of young children.* San Francisco: Jossey-Bass.

Steinberg, L., Elmen, J., & Mounts, N. (1989). Authoritative parenting, psychosocial maturity, and academic success among adolescents. *Child Development, 60,* 1424–1436.

Stewart, M., & Ashby, H. (1981). Treatment of hyperactive, aggressive, and antisocial children. In T. Kratochwill (Ed.), *Advances in social psychology* (Vol. 1, pp. 307–327). Hillsdale, NJ: Erlbaum.

Stipek, D. (1984). Developmental aspects of motivation in children. In R. Ames & C. Ames (Eds.), *Research on motivation in education* (Vol. 1, pp. 145–174). Orlando: Academic Press.

Stollak, G., Scholom, A., Kallman, J., & Saturansky, C. (1973). Insensitivity to children: Responses of undergraduates to children in problem situations. *Journal of Abnormal Child Psychology, 1,* 169–180.

Strain, P. S., Shores, R. E., & Timm, M. A. (1977). Effects of peer social initiations on the behavior of withdrawn preschool children. *Journal of Applied Behaviour Analysis, 10,* 289–298.

Strauss, C., Forehand, R., Smith, K., & Frame, C. (1986). The association between social withdrawal and internalizing problems of children. *Journal of Abnormal Child Psychology, 14,* 525–535.

Swanson, J., et al. (1993). Effect of stimulant medication on children with Attention Deficit Disorder: A "review of reviews." *Exceptional Children, 60,* 154–162.

Swap, S. (1993). *Developing home–school partnerships: From concepts to practice.* New York: Teachers College Press.

Swift, M., & Spivack, G. (1975). *Alternative teaching strategies: Helping behaviorally troubled children achieve.* Champaign, IL: Research Press.

Thomas, A., & Pashley, B. (1982). Effects of classroom training on LD students' task persistence and attributions. *Learning Disability Quarterly, 5,* 133–144.

Thompson, C., & Rudolph, L. (1992). *Counseling children* (3rd ed.). Pacific Grove, CA: Brooks/Cole.

Tollefson, N., & Chen, J. (1988). Consequences of teachers' attributions for student failure. *Teaching and Teacher Education, 4,* 259–265.

Tollefson, N., Tracy, D., Johnsen, E., Farmer, A., & Buenning, M. (1984). Goal setting and personal responsibility training for LD adolescents. *Psychology in the Schools, 21,* 224–233.

Vernon, A. (1989). *Thinking, feeling, behaving: An emotional education curriculum for children.* Champaign, IL: Research Press.

Viorst, J. (1988). *I'll fix anything.* New York: Macmillan Child Group.

Vygotsky, L. (1962). *Thought and language.* Cambridge, MA: MIT Press.

Walker, H. (1987). *The ACCESS Program (Adolescent Curriculum for Communication and Effective Social Skills).* Austin, TX: Pro-Ed.

Walker, H., Colvin, G., & Ramsey, E. (1995). *Antisocial behavior in school: Strategies and best practices.* Pacific Grove, CA: Brooks/Cole.

Walker, H., McConnell, S., Holmes, D., Todis, B., Walker, J., & Golden, H. (1983). *The Walker Social Skills Program: The ACCEPTS Program.* Austin, TX: Pro-Ed.

Watson, A., & Dodd, C. (1984). Alleviating communication apprehension through rational emotive therapy: A comparative evaluation. *Communication Education, 33,* 257–266.

Weaver, C. (Ed.). (1994). *Success at last: Helping students with attention deficit (hyperactivity) disorders achieve their potential.* Portsmouth, NH: Heinemann.

Weiner, B. (1992). *Human motivation: Metaphors, theories, and research.* Newbury Park, CA: Sage.

Weinstein, C., & Mayer, R. (1986). The teaching of learning strategies. In M. Wittrock (Ed.), *Handbook of research on teaching* (3rd ed., pp. 315–327). New York: Macmillan.

Weinstein, C., & Mignano, A., Jr. (1993). *Elementary classroom management: Lessons from research and practice.* New York: McGraw-Hill.

Weiss, G., & Hechtman, L. (1986). *Hyperactive children grown up: Empirical findings and theoretical considerations.* New York: Guilford Press.

Wentzel, K., & Erdley, C. (1993). Strategies for making friends: Relations to social behavior and peer acceptance in early adolescence. *Developmental Psychology, 29,* 819–826.

Whalen, C., & Henker, B. (1991). Therapies for hyperactive children: Comparisons, combinations, and compromises. *Journal of Consulting and Clinical Psychology, 59,* 126–137.

Whalen, C., Henker, B., & Hinshaw, S. (1985). Cognitive-behavioral therapies for hyperactive children: Premises, problems, and prospects. *Journal of Abnormal Child Psychology, 13,* 391–410.

Whitmore, J. (1980). *Giftedness, conflict, and underachievement.* Boston: Allyn & Bacon.

Wlodkowski, R. (1978). *Motivation and teaching: A practical guide.* Washington, DC: National Education Association.

Wood, M., & Long, N. (1991). *Life space intervention: Talking with children and youth in crisis.* Austin, TX: Pro-Ed.

Wragg, E. C. (1983). Training skillful teachers. *Teaching and Teacher Education, 1,* 199–208.

Wu, S., Pink, W., Crain, R., & Moles, O. (1982). Student suspension: A critical reappraisal. *Urban Review, 14,* 245–303.

Wubbels, T., & Levy, J. (1993). *Do you know what you look like? Interpersonal relationships in education.* London: Falmer.

Zahavi, S., & Asher, S. (1978). The effect of verbal instructions on preschool children's aggressive behavior. *Journal of School Psychology, 16,* 146–153.

Zaragoza, N., Vaughn, S., & McIntosh, R. (1991). Social skills interventions and children with behavior problems: A review. *Behavioral Disorders, 16,* 260–275.

Zimbardo, P. G. (1977). *Shyness: What it is, what to do about it.* Reading, MA: Addison-Wesley.

Zimmerman, B., & Schunk, D. (Eds.). (1989). *Self-regulated learning and academic achievement.* New York: Springer-Verlag.

Index